Teacher Empowerment Toward Professional Development and Practices

Ismail Hussein Amzat · Nena P. Valdez
Editors

Teacher Empowerment Toward Professional Development and Practices

Perspectives Across Borders

Editors
Ismail Hussein Amzat
School of Education and Modern Languages
University of Utara Malaysia
Kedah
Malaysia

Nena P. Valdez
Faculties of Humanities and Business
President University
Cikarang
Indonesia

ISBN 978-981-10-4150-1   ISBN 978-981-10-4151-8   (eBook)
DOI 10.1007/978-981-10-4151-8

Library of Congress Control Number: 2017934639

© Springer Nature Singapore Pte Ltd. 2017
This work is subject to copyright. All rights are reserved by the Publisher, whether the whole or part of the material is concerned, specifically the rights of translation, reprinting, reuse of illustrations, recitation, broadcasting, reproduction on microfilms or in any other physical way, and transmission or information storage and retrieval, electronic adaptation, computer software, or by similar or dissimilar methodology now known or hereafter developed.
The use of general descriptive names, registered names, trademarks, service marks, etc. in this publication does not imply, even in the absence of a specific statement, that such names are exempt from the relevant protective laws and regulations and therefore free for general use.
The publisher, the authors and the editors are safe to assume that the advice and information in this book are believed to be true and accurate at the date of publication. Neither the publisher nor the authors or the editors give a warranty, express or implied, with respect to the material contained herein or for any errors or omissions that may have been made. The publisher remains neutral with regard to jurisdictional claims in published maps and institutional affiliations.

Printed on acid-free paper

This Springer imprint is published by Springer Nature
The registered company is Springer Nature Singapore Pte Ltd.
The registered company address is: 152 Beach Road, #21-01/04 Gateway East, Singapore 189721, Singapore

Preface

In this era of accountability, schools are being made more and more answerable for the achievement and performance of students. Furthermore, in line with the needs of the global knowledge economy, schools are being pushed to raise standards and improve the quality of teaching and teachers to prepare students for the current and future workplace. Consequently, teacher education is a key issue being debated in the world of education today. This book "Teacher Empowerment Toward Professional Development and Practices: Perspectives Across Borders" is a timely response to the need for continuous teacher development around world especially in developing countries. Teacher professional development (TPD) or continuous professional development (CPD) involves the empowerment of teachers through autonomy, accountability and continuous learning. Continuous teacher development is the core concern of all educational organizations and is the means by which teacher improvement can be attained.

Effective student learning does not happen in a vacuum. First of all, schools needs to be transformed into learning communities, for both students and teachers, and this is facilitated by the school leadership which implements the policies for teacher training and teacher development. By fostering a spirit of shared leadership and collaboration, school management can create a culture of learning where teachers share their ideas and learning experiences and review their classroom practices to upgrade their teaching skills for the betterment of the school and student achievement. Such practices can be further enhanced by the integration of technology into the classroom that uses instructional tools and online activities to engage students in their learning. The integration of technology into the classroom also boosts students' creativity. However, it requires professional training and teacher competence in computer-based instruction (CBI).

From the above points, it is clear that teacher education and development is a matter of critical importance for all schools. Students require quality teachers and teachers need to continually upgrade their knowledge in order to meet the needs of the twenty-first century and the changes in student diversity and learning styles. Teachers are responsible for preparing and delivering high-quality lessons that maximize learning. Pedagogy therefore needs to keep pace with developments in education, moving from a more traditional, teacher-centred approach, such as memorization or lecturing to more learner-centred methods that engender comprehension and application of knowledge. Teachers and students both need to grow as individuals. The road to good teaching is an arduous one, requiring a wealth of experience and a variety of techniques.

As the majority of the chapters of this book relate to developing countries, it draws attention to the fact that there is a serious call for educational reform and an indication that teacher empowerment as well as professional development is needed. There is a public outcry over the state of the educational system in Africa and other developing countries. The decline in educational standards of some developing countries has adversely impacted teacher education and the quality of their teaching. Thus, it is clear that the lack of proper educational resources has taken its toll on teacher's professional development as well as their teaching practices. Its also important to note that, even in some developing countries where the educational system is well structured, there continues to be a struggle to provide quality education and to offer continuous education and professional development for teachers.

Therefore, this book addresses the problems and issues related to teacher training and teacher development in developing countries as well as the educational policies relating to them. It draws on studies written by authors from a variety of international backgrounds, mostly from developing countries and shares their research and findings. Their research therefore looks at teacher empowerment, professional development and teaching practices from different perspectives.

The combination of chapters within this book strongly affirms that teacher professional development is an art of self-empowerment. Teacher autonomy, leadership and efficacy are set to grow over the coming decades as precursors for professional development. This book believes that, as demonstrated by the empirical findings, reports and theories provided by various authors in their chapters, there is a strong relationship between teacher's empowerment and their professional development. An example to illustrate this relationship could be when teachers are autonomous in designing school curriculum. Here they select their own teaching materials for instruction and lead their classrooms, and they participate in the decision-making process. Ultimately it creates a sense of belonging, empowerment and accountability. It motivates them to engage in lifelong learning activities and paves the way for further improvement in their area of expertise whilst also becoming practitioners.

Empowering teachers is a type of mechanism to boost trust amongst teachers. It instills a sense of autonomy in teachers to pursue their personal and professional growth in order to remain relevant in their fields whilst also improving teaching and learning. It can be argued that, less empowered or motivated teachers may seek alternative careers and find refuge in other professions or careers that empower and better motivate them. To further support this argument, the authors in this book are active researchers in their respective fields related to teacher professional development.

The chapters within this book provide insights, findings, theories, concepts and methods for teachers seeking to improve their repertoire of instructional strategies or their other professional practices.

Part I of this book shows how shared leadership, autonomy and accountability are prerequisites for effective leaders and managers and their multifaceted roles. It also offers self-development approaches for empowering teachers and motivating them to improve their professional practices.

Chapter 1: 'Evolution of Teacher Leadership as a Challenging Paradigm in Rethinking and Restructuring Educational Settings' by Adnan Boyac and Yakup Oz reveals teacher leadership to be a changing concept involving transformational leadership, distributed leadership and organizational structures that guide the management of schools, as well as promoting constructivist and collaborative professional learning for teachers.

Chapter 2: 'Promoting Teachers' Leadership Through Autonomy and Accountability' by Nabi Bux Jumani and Samina Malik looks at teachers as the cornerstone of schools. Teacher quality and competency are a central issue for school improvement. Hence, developing teachers' capacity to engage in self-directed learning transforms them from being mere administrators and record keepers to become accountable, autonomous and productive leaders who engage in decision-making.

Chapter 3: 'Sharing School Leadership: Teacher Empowerment or Principal Relegation?' by Ismail Hussein Amzat looks at school power-sharing and leadership from a new angle. The author questions that power should be shared, arguing that total autonomy for teachers renders the principal redundant and powerless. However, he concurs that shared leadership and partial power-sharing help to improve school performance and student achievement due to the participation of teachers in the decision-making process and the development of school programs.

Chapter 4: 'Changing Definition of Teacher Professionalism: Autonomy and Accountability' by Joseph Wu, Hoi-Yan Cheung and Raymond M.C. Chan considers teacher professionalism and how it benefits society from the perspectives of the different stakeholders of schools (teachers, students, and parents) in Hong Kong.

Chapter 5: 'Teachers' Autonomy and Accountability in Assessing Students' Physical Education in School-Based Assessment' by Ruzlan bin Md. Ali and Arsaythamby Veloo recognizes that school-based assessment (SBA) is one methods for supporting teacher autonomy and developing their sense of accountability. The chapter discusses assessment in physical education (PE) and covers both the theoretical and practical aspects of this. It also discusses the impact of PE assessment on the teachers' orchestration and design of assessment activities as well as their responses to ensuring fairness in the eyes of stakeholders when determining the level of students' performance.

Part II sheds light upon professional training and the role of lifelong learning for the improving teaching and promoting continuous development of teachers' knowledge, skills and performance.

Chapter 6 presents 'Transforming Education through Teacher Empowerment and Development in Namibia: Possibilities and Challenges' by Cornelia Ndahambelela Shimwooshili Shaimemanya. In this chapter, the author advocates teacher empowerment as a vehicle for transforming world education, particularly in developing countries. The chapter also discusses the issue of teacher training, development and empowerment for the improvement of teacher quality in Namibia and the achievement of Vision 2030 in a knowledge-based economy.

Chapter 7: 'Mathematics Continuous Professional Development and Its Relevance to the New Era in South Africa' by Zingiswa MM Jojo addresses the perceived incompetence of mathematics teachers in South Africa. As a solution, the introduction of sustained professional development, lifelong learning and peer-learning is presented as well as teachers are encouraged to engage in critical self-reflection and innovation in the mathematics classroom.

Chapter 8: 'Professional Training and Lifelong Learning for School Heads of Departments: A Gateway for Headship Continuous Improvement' by Sharon Thabo Mampane focuses on the training of heads of department (HoDs) to promote lifelong learning through mentoring and coaching, as well as exploring innovative ways of supporting lifelong learning through school middle-management training and professional development.

Chapter 9: 'Engaging Teachers in Lifelong Learning in Oman for Knowledge Growth and Development: Government Roles and Higher Institutions' by Ismail Hussein Amzat, Salim Hamed Al-Mahruqi, Muhajir Teslikhan and Turkiya Al Omairi presents teachers' perceptions and engagement in lifelong learning (LLL) in Oman, and the role played by the government and higher education institutions in engaging and encouraging teachers in LLL activities. The authors affirm that in spite of significant efforts on the part of the government to improve the Oman education system, there are still areas of weaknesses and room for improvement.

Chapter 10: 'Counseling Ethics Education for Enhanced Professional Identity and Development: Guidance and Counseling Teachers Lifelong Learning Acquisition Empowered' by Noor Syamilah Zakaria, Jane Warren and Ab. Rahim Bakar presents an in-depth case study exploring and interpreting how guidance and counseling teachers will help them to learn, understand, experience, and apply counseling ethics to evolve their professional identity and develop a counselor education training program. The chapter calls for substantial changes in the instructional approaches used at higher educational institutions in Malaysia, for the promotion of lifelong learning of guidance and counseling teachers and the enhancement of their identity as counseling professionals.

Chapter 11: 'An Approach to Motivation and Empowerment: The Application of Positive Psychology' by Christine W.Y. Mak, Samuel M.Y. Ho, Rita Ching and Edmund T.T. Lo explains how positive psychology empowers teachers and students by giving them hope. The authors attempted to make a theoretical link between teacher motivation and student motivation using positive psychology. At the end of the chapter they formulate their 'SHINE' intervention for improving positive psychology among teachers.

Part III explores the thinking abilities required of teachers in the twenty-first century teaching, learning as well as the pedagogical shortcomings of conventional teaching practices.

Chapter 12: 'Teacher Responsive Teaching and Learning Initiatives Through Action Research' by Mary Koutselini introduces action research as a form of teacher empowerment. Teaching is presented as a cyclical process whereby teachers plan, act and respond to students' needs, evaluate their actions and then replan new actions based on students' responses and participation. The author suggests that in this way, teachers and students learn new skills, strategies and communicative attitudes.

Chapter 13: 'Teaching and Learning for Real-life: The Application of Real-life Moral Dilemma Discussion (Re-LiMDD) for Classroom Interaction' by Vishalache Balakrishnan explores the application of real-life moral-dilemma discussion (Re-LiMDD) in the teaching and learning of the social studies classroom and non-social studies classroom. The author argues that linking content to students' real lives encourages deep learning and equips them with higher order thinking skills (HOTS) as a natural and authentic process.

Chapter 14: 'Infusing Thinking-Based-Learning in the Twenty-First Century Classroom: The Role of Teacher Skillful Thinking Skills Training' by Muhammed Yusuf explores and reviews TBL related theories, applications and practices in teaching and learning. It also emphasizes the importance of professional training in TBL for boosting students' 'skillful thinking'. The author claims that promoting skillful thinking will enable teachers to infuse TBL into classroom activities and enhance students' skilful thinking across the globe.

Chapter 15: 'Theory into Practice: The Content of Pre-service Teachers' Reflections in North Cyprus' by Anas Musa Ismail and Çise Çavuşoğlu focuses on the reflections of pre-service English language teachers in Northern Cyprus. The author states that there is a need to develop and incorporate reflective dialogue between pre-service teachers and their supervisors, and between pre-service teachers themselves during teaching practicums.

Part IV contains chapters dealing with the influence of professional learning communities (PLCs) and the use of information and computer technology (ICT) in education for teacher empowerment and professional development and how technology enhances discussion and interaction between teachers and learners both inside and outside the classroom.

Chapter 16: 'Fostering Teachers' Professional Development Through Collaboration in Professional Learning Communities' by Steyn Trudie presents a case study about how a school succeeded in developing a PLC. The author asserts that PLCs play a big role in teacher empowerment and that the principal's leadership role is instrumental in driving the professional learning process.

Chapter 17: 'School-Based Professional Learning Community: Empowering Teachers as Assessment Leaders in the Change Context' by Garima Bansal presents a case study about the influence of a school-based PLC on teachers' class-based, formative assessment practices. The author suggests ways of establishing successful school-based PLCs that enhance teacher empowerment and professional development.

Chapter 18: 'Professional Learning Communities in a Web 2.0 World: Rethinking the Warrants for Professional Development' by Yvonne Liljekvist, Jorryt van Bommel and Christina Olin-Sheller explores the potential of using technology to develop PLCs for in-service mathematics teachers in Botswana. The authors believe that these emerging technologies will improve classroom experiences and professional development not only for mathematics teachers but for also teachers of other disciplines as well.

Chapter 19: 'Emerging Technologies as Tools for Enhancing Professional Learning Communities of Mathematics Teacher Development in Botswana' by M.J. Motswiri, E. Zimudzi, K.G. Garegae and A.A. Nkhwalume shows how theoretical reflections of PLCs in a Web 2.0-world enhance teachers' professional development. The authors discuss how Swedish teachers use social media to expand their PLC beyond the school environment, representing a new behaviour among teachers that changes the opportunities and framework for professional development and growth.

Chapter 20: 'Using an e-Portfolio for Teaching and Teacher Continuous Learning: A Process for Professional Development Enhancement' by Byabazaire Yusuf focuses on the experiences and written reflections of postgraduate and in-service teachers using e-portfolios to teach English language. The author maintains that the use of e-portfolios in the teaching will facilitate the sharing of content knowledge, the improvement of pedagogical skills and the promotion of collaborative activities. It will also help teachers to engage in lifelong learning and professional development.

Due to the international backgrounds of its authors, this book spans a range of areas that are of crucial importance to teacher education and professional development, such as teacher empowerment, professional training, teacher knowledge and skills development and the improvement of pedagogical practices. As such, it enables teachers to keep ahead of changes in the field of education and stay relevant in a rapidly changing world. For these reasons, this book will be of interest to teachers, researchers, practitioners and policy-makers who work in international settings. It should also be read by academic planners and educationists engaged in teacher training, teacher development, educational innovation and school improvement.

Kedah, Malaysia   Ismail Hussein Amzat, Ph.D.

Acknowledgements

As editor, I am indebted to the contributions of many individuals without whom this book would not have come to fruition. I would therefore like to extend my sincere thanks to the authors for their dedication in finding time from their busy schedules to write the chapters that make up this book. Thanks to their effort and academic expertise that this book has become a reality. I am also indebted to Springer, my co-editor, for his trust in me. Had it not been for his support, my team and I could never have accomplished the task of publishing our first book and due to his continuous support, this present book was also published. Allow me to thank my second co-editor, Prof. Nena P. Valdez for her immense contribution and spirit of teamwork. My appreciation also goes to Dr. Byabazaire Yusuf for his contribution at the proposal stage and for serving as an internal reviewer. My co-editor and I would like to thank the School of Education and Modern Languages, Universiti Utara Malaysia, for their academic support, especially our new Dean, Associate Professor Dr. Yahya Don for his kind support and acknowledging the visiting scholars' academic contributions.

Ismail Hussein Amzat (Ph.D.)

Contents

Part I Teacher Empowerment: Leadership, Autonomy and Accountability

1   Evolution of Teacher Leadership as a Challenging Paradigm in Rethinking and Restructuring Educational Settings........... 3
    Adnan Boyaci and Yakup Oz

2   Promoting Teachers' Leadership Through Autonomy and Accountability 21
    Nabi Bux Jumani and Samina Malik

3   Sharing School Leadership: Principalship Empowerment or Relegation? 43
    Ismail Hussein Amzat

4   Changing Definition of Teacher Professionalism: Autonomy and Accountability 59
    Joseph Wu, Hoi Yan Cheung and Raymond M.C. Chan

5   Teachers' Autonomy and Accountability in Assessing Students' Physical Education in School-Based Assessment........ 71
    Ruzlan Md-Ali and Arsaythamby Veloo

Part II Teacher Empowerment: Professional Development and Lifelong Learning

6   Transforming Education Through Teacher Empowerment in Namibia: Possibilities and Challenges 87
    Cornelia Ndahambelela Shimwooshili Shaimemanya

7   Mathematics Continuous Professional Development and Its Relevance to the New Era in South Africa 103
    Zingiswa M.M. Jojo

8 Professional Training and Lifelong Learning for School Heads of Departments: A Gateway for Headship Continuous Improvement 121
Sharon Thabo Mampane

9 Engaging Teachers in Lifelong Learning in Oman for Knowledge Growth and Development: Government Roles and Higher Institutions 135
Ismail Hussein Amzat, Salim Hamed Al-Mahruqi, Muhajir Teslikhan and Turkiya Al Omairi

10 Counseling Ethics Education for Enhanced Professional Identity and Development: Guidance and Counseling Teachers Lifelong Learning Acquisition Empowered 153
Noor Syamilah Zakaria, Jane Warren and Ab. Rahim Bakar

11 An Approach to Motivation and Empowerment: The Application of Positive Psychology 167
Samuel M.Y. Ho, Christine W.Y. Mak, Rita Ching and Edmund T.T. Lo

Part III Teacher Empowerment: Teacher Responsive Teaching and Learning Initiatives

12 Teacher Responsive Teaching and Learning Initiatives Through Action Research 185
Mary Koutselini

13 Teaching and Learning for Real-Life: The Application of Real-Life Moral Dilemma Discussion (Re-LiMDD) for Classroom Interaction 195
Vishalache Balakrishnan

14 Infusing Thinking-Based Learning in Twenty-First Century Classroom: The Role of Training Programme to Enhance Teachers' Skilful Thinking Skills 211
Muhammed Yusuf

15 Theory into Practice: The Content of Pre-service Teachers' Reflections in North Cyprus 221
Anas Musa Ismail and Çise Çavuşoğlu

Part IV Teacher Empowerment: Professional Learning Communities and Emerging Technologies

16 Fostering Teachers' Professional Development Through Collaboration in Professional Learning Communities 241
G.M. Steyn

17 **School-Based Professional Learning Community: Empowering Teachers as Assessment Leaders in the Change Context**.. 255
Garima Bansal

18 **Professional Learning Communities in a Web 2.0 World: Rethinking the Conditions for Professional Development**......... 269
Yvonne Liljekvist, Jorryt van Bommel and Christina Olin-Scheller

19 **Emerging Technologies as Tools for Enhancing Mathematics Professional Learning Communities in Botswana**............... 281
M.J. Motswiri, E. Zimudzi, K.G. Garegae and A.A. Nkhwalume

20 **Using an E-Portfolio for Teaching and Teacher Continuous Learning: A Process for Professional Development Enhancement**... 295
Byabazaire Yusuf

Part I
Teacher Empowerment: Leadership, Autonomy and Accountability

Chapter 1
Evolution of Teacher Leadership as a Challenging Paradigm in Rethinking and Restructuring Educational Settings

Adnan Boyaci and Yakup Oz

Abstract This chapter will examine teacher leadership as a challenging concept associated with school effectiveness and improving student success. From a historical perspective, roles and functions of teacher leadership have evolved over time depending on the system paradigm employed in school settings. The shift from the paradigm of machine bureaucracy to the redefinition of the school as a professional learning community has underlined a wide range of critical concepts explaining both formal and informal roles of teacher leadership via teacher autonomy, transformational and distributed leadership, and school improvement. Teacher leadership roles have been accepted as teachers acting as catalysts for disseminating their skills, knowledge, and the best practices to their colleagues, albeit the boundaries of formal structures of school organizations even if they do not have any administrative titles or formal responsibilities in the school processes.

1.1 Introduction

In today's world, education systems play a more vital role in the development of countries than ever before. As knowledge provides more added value than any other resource, the importance of education becomes both more prominent and salient. In this context, projects aimed at increasing schooling rates, student outcomes, and school effectiveness at each level of the education system are high on governments' political agendas.

In order to increase student outcomes, a lot of school improvement reforms all over the world have affected each other. These reforms have changed the roles of shareholders in the education system and given them new responsibilities. In particular, school managers and teachers have become the very basic agents of change

---

A. Boyaci (✉) · Y. Oz
Department of Educational Administration, Anadolu University, Eskisehir, Turkey
e-mail: adnanboyaci2100@gmail.com

Y. Oz
e-mail: yakupoz573@yahoo.com

not only in classrooms, but also in communities. Schools as social organizations have experienced a transformation from structurally administrated organizations into organizations led by all the stakeholders. School managers are no longer the only leaders in schools, but teachers are too. Hence, the aim of this chapter is to examine teacher leadership from a developmental and international perspective, respectively.

This chapter consists of two parts. The first part begins with a brief history of teacher leadership, the definition of the teacher leadership phenomenon, and the roles of teacher leaders. Later, a broad conceptual framework comprised of three teacher leadership-related sections are presented: (1) school structure, (2) transformational and distributed leadership, and (3) constructivist learning theory.

The second part, which is comprised of two sections, is related to policy implications and focuses on teacher leadership in the Turkish context. The former section is related to the history of teacher leadership and the professionalization of teaching in Turkey. The following section aims to shed light on how teacher leadership functions in the Turkish context.

1.2 A Brief History of Teacher Leadership

During the twentieth century, schools were hierarchical and bureaucratic organizations solely led by school principals, since the schools themselves were relatively small and served a limited number of people. However, over time the nature of schools has evolved, in line with social and economic changes (Sergiovanni 1996), and the distribution of roles has started to change.

Teacher leadership can be examined in three periods. In the beginning, formal administrative roles were appointed via managerial changes, when teachers obtained positions or titles as department heads or union representatives (Hart 1990). That was a top-down school leadership model (Hart 1995) and the roles of teachers were extensions of school administrations (York-Barr and Duke 2004). These formal roles maintained the existing school hierarchies in decision-making processes (Owens and Valesky 2010).

However, in the second period, based on legislation and school reform movements, teachers began to become more important for sustainable student achievement (Muijs and Harris 2007) and started to take more responsibilities in accordance with instructional goals in schools (York-Barr and Duke 2004). With the 'No Child Left Behind' and site-based management initiatives, schools were considered to be too complex for principals to lead by themselves (Leblanc and Shelton 1997). Moreover, school-site managerial strategies that give pedagogical control to teachers became popular, and teachers were freed from the consequences of other people's decisions, due to being given managerial positions within the school hierarchy (Conley and Bacharach 1990). Within this framework, teacher leadership evolved into a role of instructional leader (Hart 1990; Smylie 1996). Hence, the principal's responsibilities began to decrease and increasing student achievement by enhancing teacher's power and autonomy became inevitable (Murphy 2005; Smylie et al. 2002). In this form of teacher leadership, teachers were encouraged by career ladder programs (Little 1988) and had roles designed to utilize their expertise, such as curriculum leaders, mentors, and staff developers (Lewis 2014, p. 10) which were a blend of bureaucratic roles with human resource development functions (Owens and Valesky 2010).

Finally, the third period of teacher leadership has emerged. According to Silva et al. (2000), it is anti-hierarchical and values collegiality and professionalism that make teachers creators and reformers of school culture. In return, teachers promote change among their colleagues by encouraging examination of instructional practices, experimentation with new methods, and curriculum reform (York-Barr and Duke 2004). This brings about a new concept known as the professional development school. According to Darling-Hammond et al. (1995, p. 91), these schools are developed around a constructivist understanding of learning for both teachers and students, and with all members of the school community, they produce new knowledge and profound understandings. In professional development schools, teachers learn by teaching, redesigning schools, and collaborating (Darling-Hammond et al. 1995). Teacher leaders now need to share decisions about the missions, goals, programs, operations, assessments, and pursue a better teaching and learning for the entire school (Spillane 2006) so that they can produce the best educational practices with effective communication and dialogue (Darling-Hammod and Richardson 2009).

1.3 Conceptual Definition of Teacher Leadership

Teacher leadership is a difficult phenomenon to define (Childs-Bowen et al. 2000) and it has been delineated by different researchers in different practices across time. When the implication of the clarifications is examined, it can be seen the conceptual framework of teacher leadership lies behind different explanations. For instance, Harris and Muijs (2004) mainly highlight the contributory role of teacher leadership in the development of their colleagues. Similarly, Troen and Boles (1994) propose teacher leadership as a 'collective leadership type where teachers develop professional qualifications by working in collaboration' (p. 11). Moreover, Wasley (1991) defines teacher leadership as 'the proficiency in encouraging colleagues towards change' (p. 32). According to Swanson et al. (2011, p. 153), teacher leadership is 'knowledge, skills and dispositions demonstrated by teachers who positively impact student learning by influencing adults.' Teacher leadership also proposes that teacher leaders have more influential roles within and beyond the classroom (Barth 2001; Katzenmeyer and Moller 2001; Beachum and Dentith 2004; Rutherford 2006; Watt et al. 2010). Besides, teacher leadership also requires accountability of such influential roles from teacher leaders by making teachers responsible for achieving the outcomes of their leadership (Katzenmeyer and Moller 2009, p. 6). Consequently, teacher leaders influence and change the behaviors of colleagues in the school. When they do this, it is a collaborative action with colleagues and teacher leaders should be accountable for the results of the expected performances of their leadership.

Roles of Teacher Leaders: Lieberman and Miller (2004) point out three roles for teacher leaders as advocates, innovators, and stewards focusing on the teacher leaders' role in the process of change. Advocates stand up for the improvement of student learning, innovators come with new implementations to transform the school, and stewards serve for sustainable improvement. However, in defining teacher leadership, one of the critical points that needs to be taken into consideration is to evaluate the formal and informal roles of teacher leaders.

Crowther et al. (2002) emphasize formal teacher leadership roles to understand and explore the dynamics of successful school revitalization. These formal types of teacher leadership roles mostly include career ladder teachers, mentor teachers participating in district-level committees, or site-based management teams working with principals and other colleagues (Hart 1994). In this sense, the roles of teacher leaders have been articulated with formal titles and administrative positions (Harris 2005; Sherrill 1999, p. 57) which also make teacher leaders responsible for the formation of school improvement teams, instructional support groups, advisory councils, curriculum development, planning professional development, policy development and decision-making, budgeting, acquiring and allocating material resources, scheduling activities, assigning tasks and advising with regard to personnel matters in school organizations (Smylie 1992).

On the other hand, teacher leadership roles have also been considered to be a catalyst for disseminating skills of teachers beyond the boundaries of formal structures of school organizations. The teacher leaders are also required to disseminate their knowledge and best practices to colleagues although they do not have any titles or formal responsibilities in the school processes (Spillane 2006; Katzenmeyer and Moller 2001; Leithwood and Jantzi 2000a). Such teacher leaders emerge spontaneously and organically and take initiative to address a problem (Danielson 2007). Informal teacher leaders may have a wide range of roles in almost everything in school settings such as encouraging parent participation, working with colleagues in small groups and teams, modeling reflective practice, articulating a vision for improvement, resolving instructional problems (York-Barr and Duke 2004), choosing textbooks, hiring principals, determining the teacher in the next classroom, designing the new curriculum, hiring librarians, or buying computers for schools (White 1992).

However, sometimes these formal and informal roles may be obstructed or supported by different factors originated from the professional norms/culture, organizational structure, and resources of and interpersonal relationships, commitments and intellectual/psychosocial characteristics of individuals, incentives, recognition, and role clarity in school organizations (Katzenmeyer and Moller 2009; Murphy 2007; Johnson and Donaldson 2007; Lieberman and Miller 2004; York-Barr and Duke 2004, pp. 270–271; Doyle 2000; Zinn 1997).

1.4 Theoretical Paradigms for Reinterpretation of Teacher Leadership in Managing and Leading Schools

Teacher leadership has evolved over time based on the changing paradigms that affect the delivery of educational services in schools. These paradigm shifts are in administration, leadership styles, as well as the teaching and learning approaches applied in educational settings. During each paradigm shift teacher leadership gains new dimensions that affect the roles of teacher leaders.

School Structure and Teacher Leadership: Changes in the administration of schools are related to the distribution of authority in the formal organizational structure of them. For a long time, schools were seen as factories having hierarchical organizational structures. Within the scientific management and rational system theory, the emerging terms were efficiency, optimization, design and improved performance (Scott 1992), that were supposed to promote formalization and essentiality of specialization, standardization, hierarchy of authority, division of labor and a narrow span of control (Hoy and Miskel 2005). These approaches existed in the pyramid theory of a school having a top-down management style where the state and other distant authorities were the managers, whereas heads, teachers, and students were workers. The idea that lay beneath these approaches was that the way to control the work of others was to assign one person to take responsibility for direction, supervision, and inspection (Sergiovanni 2001). Hence, within this perspective, teacher leadership had formal roles based on title or credentials, and were extensions of the state and district boards or school administrations.

However, this theory had a narrow perspective on schools, due to perceiving them as formal organizations, and was not appropriate for the school's purposes, ways of working, relationships among families and students, content of work of teachers and the nature of effective teaching and learning environments (Sergiovanni 2001). Consequently, two popular approaches were developed regarding the structures of educational organizations: (a) schools as loosely coupled organizations put forth by Weick (1976) and (b) schools as professional bureaucracies by Mintzberg (1980, p. 239).

According to Weick (1982, p. 673), schools are not like other organizations because of their being more loosely joined. Additionally, since the sphere of the organization is fairly large, expecting a few teachers to keep track of all students seems rather unrealistic. Also, ties among people are loosened because very few people are permanently involved in everything that happens within a school. Moreover, loose ties between decisions and implementations occur often, because administrators need to catch up with procedural transactions. Schools are partially capable of fulfilling managerial activities compared with business organizations, in which an intervention to the processing is much more feasible (Weick 1982). As a result, the loosely coupled characteristics of schools reveal the significance of the professional role of teachers, their interactions among students and managers, and their positions as leaders in the classrooms.

Apart from that, Mintzberg (1980) emphasizes professional autonomy within the concept of professional bureaucracy. He defines five types of structures for organizations. Educational institutions can be categorized as professional bureaucracies among these structure types. The operating core is the most essential part of a professional bureaucracy. It is where the input is transformed to output within organizations. In educational institutions, it is the classrooms where teaching and learning processes occur.

Professional bureaucracy relies on the standardization of skills in the operating core for coordination in which jobs are highly specialized but minimally formalized (Mintzberg 1980, p. 322), so that the decentralization and standardization of skills are provided at the same time (Hoy and Miskel 2005). In other terms, teachers are given considerable autonomy in their work since they are highly trained specialists in the operating core, they work relatively freely, not only of the administrative hierarchy, but also of their own colleagues, and this coordination is achieved by standard skills and predetermined behaviors. They also tend to maintain collective control of the administration of organization, so that managers share the administrative tasks with teachers (Mintzberg 1980, p. 334). Having a professional bureaucracy structure, schools depend on professionally autonomous teachers and teacher leadership can also be considered to be a new form of the professional autonomy of a teacher. Thus, opportunities for collective inquiry, scrutiny, reflection, and decision-making processes are needed for promoting teacher professionalism and school success (Tschannen-Moran 2009).

Both the approaches of Weick and Mintzberg toward organizational structures have transformed the concept of teacher leadership from an administrational responsibility to a more professional and instructional activity where teachers come forward and take responsibilities, such as curriculum leaders, mentors, and staff developers starting with the site-based management and school improvement practices until today.

Moreover, Hoy and Sweetland (2000, 2001) base their justification on the mutual interaction between the bureaucratic structures of school organizations and teacher autonomy. They claim that centralization and formalization may not hamper the dissemination of teacher autonomy. In their framework, schools are bureaucratic organizations composed of centralization and formalization. However, bureaucracy does not always play a disabling role in the autonomy of teachers. School structure may facilitate teacher's work and allows them to make professional decisions and share them among fellow teachers. Also, enabling formalization composed of flexible sets of best practices may facilitate more effectively dealing with the inevitable problems (Hoy and Miskel 2005; Hoy and Sweetland 2000, 2001). These enabling and hindering school structures have different features and different results in educational contexts and improve with different processes experienced by teachers over time as shown in Table 1.1 (Hoy and Miskel 2005).

Table 1.1 Enabling and hindering school structure

Formalization	Enabling Structure	Hindering Structure
	Promotes flexible rules and procedures	Enforces rigid rules and procedures
	Views problems as learning opportunities	Views problems as constraints
	Values differences	Demands consensus
	Encourages initiative	Punishes mistakes
	Fosters trust	Fosters suspicion
Centralization	Facilitates problem solving	Demands compliance
	Promotes cooperation	Embraces control
	Encourages openness	Fosters mistrust
	Protects teachers	Punishes teachers
	Encourages innovation	Discourages change
	Seeks collaboration	Rules autocratically
Processes	Participative decision-making	Unilateral decision-making
	Problem solving	Enforcement
Context	Teacher trust	Teacher distrust
	Truthfulness and authenticity	Truth spinning and deception
	Cohesiveness	Conflict
	Teacher sense power	Teacher sense powerlessness

Hoy and Miskel (2005)

As seen in Table 1.1, enabling school structure promotes teacher autonomy, empowerment, and professional development. This kind of school structure may provide a more conducive environment for the development of teacher leadership. **Teacher Leadership in the Context of Transformational and Distributed Leaderships**: Changes in leadership theories related to school managers and the emergence of new leadership styles are also essential in explaining teacher leadership. Although the 'great man' theory of leadership that emphasizes the personal skills of leaders is still effective in schools (Murphy 2005); based on the behavioral and situational theories of leadership, professional teacher leaders can also be developed (Katzanmeyer and Moller 2009) and teacher leadership is a corner stone for educational change and school improvement (Katzenmeyer and Moller 2009; Harris and Muijs 2004). Especially in discussing the delegation of power in school organizations, the concept of teacher leadership has come to the forefront in connection with transformational and distributed leadership theories.

Leithwood and Jantzi (2000b) suggest that transformational leadership has three components, namely setting direction, developing people, and redesigning the organization. Transformational leaders motivate, inspire, and move people toward a goal or a vision (Bass 1985) and trust them with responsibilities and two way of communication (Bass and Avolio 1994). While doing that they use idealized influence, intellectual stimulation, inspirational motivation, and individual consideration (Boyd 2009; Bass and Bass 2009). Transformational teachers provide teacher development opportunities and solve problems together, and help staff members to develop and maintain a collaborative, professional school culture (Leithwood 1992).

In this sense, teacher leaders may have similar roles as transformational leaders regarding school improvement and increasing student achievement. Similarly, teacher leaders navigate the structure of schools, nurture relationships, model professional growth, and help others with change and have a required set of skills that include understanding the policies of the school, rallying collegial support, assisting others in the change process and challenging the status quo (Silva et al. 2000). Within that context, in the late 1990s, teacher leadership was defined through transformational leadership (Ash and Persall 2000) aspiring to enhance the standards of schools with low academic achievement.

The other leadership style related to teacher leadership is distributed leadership. Distributed leadership is a leadership practice shared by many members of an organization (Harris 2003). According to Gronn (2002), it is a collective phenomenon in which members are involved in the flow of activities and also a concrete action that combines initiatives and the expertise of members in order to create a greater outcome than their individual actions. Based on Bolman and Deal's (2008) 'overbound' and 'underbound' systems that power concentration high and low, respectively, the power in distributed or shared leadership falls somewhere in between (Topolinski 2014). Therefore, distributed leadership is basically about not only the actions of a hero based on knowledge and skills, but the interactions between members and situations (Spillane 2006). All individuals contribute to leadership practice whether they are formally designated as leaders or not (Harris and Spillane 2008, p. 31).

In the context of educational institutions, distributed leadership can promote school effectiveness by building school capacity (Leithwood et al. 2011; Pont et al. 2008) and improving school and student learning (Harris 2011; Hallinger and Heck 2009; Leithwood et al. 2006; Bennett et al. 2003). Harris (2004, p. 16) found that successful heads recognizing the limitations of a singular leadership approach see their leadership role as being primarily concerned with empowering others to lead. Besides, in terms of accountability, school principals can no longer be the only decision-makers working to improve schools and student achievement (Watt et al. 2010; Beachum and Dentith 2004). Hence, teacher leaders may support the acceptance of decisions and responsibilities to successfully achieve the goals of the school (Seashore Louis et al. 2010). Accordingly, distributed leadership theory has much in common with the dimensions of teacher leadership (Aliakbari and Sadeghi 2014).

Teacher Leadership in the Context of Constructive Learning Theory: Regarding constructivist theory, each learner individually and socially constructs meaning and knowledge which is produced by the experiences of a learner or a community of learners (Hein 1991). Teachers need to improve the quality of their teaching, expertise, the innovativeness of their teaching skills and effectiveness through continuous learning (Harris and Muijs 2004) in order to maintain student learning. According to the constructivist theory of learning, they either do this individually or collaboratively.

Starting from the 1990s, professional learning communities emerged as a way to engage teachers and staff in collaborative learning to improve student outcomes (Harris 2002). A professional community allows teachers to work collaboratively to reflect on their practice, examine evidence about the relationship between practice and student outcomes and make changes to improve both teaching and student learning (McLaughlin and Talbert 2006).

In discussions of teacher leadership, constructivist learning theory has provided a platform on which skills, knowledge, and experiences concerning teacher leadership are learned and shared in a constructive way among colleagues so as to make schools professional learning communities. In these communities teaching and learning necessitate a holistic process in which the learning of teachers accelerates the learning of students and at the core of this process is the collaboration and interaction of teacher leaders with colleagues and students (Hord 1997; McMahon et al. 2005; DuFour and Eaker 2005). Collaboration for the improvement of student learning is one of the main principals of teacher leadership, which necessitates shared vision, responsibility, and experiences of mutual trust and support.

Hence, if teachers have the chance to develop their own professional learning, they are able to provide colleagues with their expertise, skills, and information. When teachers work in schools that promote learning and collegiality, they are able to reveal their leadership skills (DuFour 2004). In such communities, teachers move from thinking individually to perceiving themselves as members of a community in which they are responsible for both their own and their colleagues' professional learning (Lieberman and Pointer-Mace 2009), which explains the roles and functions of teacher leaders.

1.5 Teacher Leadership Policy and Practices in Turkey

Theory and practice are constructed by the norms, beliefs, and the values of the social system in which education as a system and organization is built (Child 2003 cited in Shah 2010). Weber (1993), underlines the relationships between religious beliefs, sociocultural attitudes and the values of individuals, and social action formed by the interaction of institutions in society. In the Weberian framework of social systems, it is necessary to understand formal rationality and substantive rationality with a focus on the impact of cultural, religious and political systems (ideational system) on social institutions. Education is one of the major components of this system and a deeply cultural concept; thus, culture and the ethos of leadership vary in fundamental ways across nations (Fullan 2008).

The concept of teacher leadership and its practices also vary across societies and cultures. Different perspectives on and interpretations of viewing teacher leadership not only originated from the philosophical and theoretical assumptions behind it, but also from the different articulated components of culture such as religion, tradition, values, norms, and the emergence of the ethos of leadership throughout the history of societies. How a particular society perceives and conceptualizes teacher leadership, depending on the dominant cultural and belief systems prevailing in that society or community, could be helpful to understand its implementations and to compare it at different sociocultural settings.

In this part of the chapter, a brief history of the teaching profession and the leadership roles of teachers in a Turkish context are explained, focusing on their perceived social, cultural religious values in Turkish society.

A Brief History of Teacher Leadership in Turkey: Teacher training in today's Turkey can be traced to the late Ottoman period in which the first modernization movements were initiated. Education has always been regarded as one of the most important agents of change in the reform movements for the social, economic, and cultural development of the country in both the Ottoman Empire and the modern Turkish Republic (Shaw and Shaw 1977; Somel 2001). Furthermore, political education has always been accepted as the carrier of dominant ideology of the reforms shaped by the bureaucratic elites. In this process, teachers have gained new 'modern' roles as leaders in the transformation of society. Since the teaching profession has a highly valued status originating from the social, cultural, and religious values, teachers have been placed on a status of disseminating 'modern' ideology of the reforms as the social leaders (Boyaci 1998).

With the proclamation of the Turkish Republic, Mustafa Kemal Atatürk, its founder, placed education and teachers at the core of the modernization process of the Turkish Republic as in the late Ottoman period, except that he ended the dual structure of education in society, traditional-modern, by abolishing all traditional educational institutions in accordance with the Union of Teaching Law in 1924. From that date, teachers became the central members of the state bureaucracy and were engaged with distinctive state functions within which their primary mission was to educate the masses along the lines of Kemalist principles. They were aligned with the modernization and secularization process in Turkey focusing on Western-oriented social, economic, and political transformations (Boyaci 1998).

The transformative power of teachers as leaders in society continued with the opening of village institutes in 1940. Their students were mostly from the villages. The ultimate goal was not only to train teachers to teach students in rural areas but also to train students coming from rural areas as leaders of village communities to foster the socioeconomic and sociocultural development of the country. Especially with transformational leadership roles and the skills of teachers, village institutes played huge roles in the modernization of society until they were closed in 1954. Teachers were leaders not only in schools or classrooms, but also in society, and were carriers of the mission of the young republic aiming to transform the people and the country into a contemporary civilized nation (Boyaci 1998).

In 1960s, the professional qualifications of teachers were criticized and they started to lose their missionary and transformative roles. In this context, technical and institutional skills came to forefront. There were career ladder applications as master teacher and head teacher revealing formal roles before. However, this time teachers gained new roles such as program specialists and teaching coordinators (Guven 2004).

In these days, leadership role of teachers in transforming the nation is not in the first order in the political agenda of the government, but teachers still have leadership roles in society. Today, teacher leadership roles in schools have come to forefront in order to provide school improvement by increasing professional qualifications of teachers. In this sense, in accordance with the European Qualifications Framework, professional qualifications of teachers were prepared in 2005 (MoNE 2006). Besides, teacher career ladder was redesigned the same year due to the old system being dysfunctional. Same titles are still being maintained as teacher, master teacher and head teacher. By redesigning the career ladder for teachers and creating the teacher qualifications framework, Turkey has tried to improve and support teacher leadership and the professionalization of teaching.

Teacher Leadership in Turkish Context: It is hard to find a definite agreement on the definition and dimensions of teacher leadership in world literature, and it is the same for teacher leadership concept in the Turkish context.

Despite the Turkish legislative framework for education mostly arranges the function of the education system centrally as an integrated part of the public administration system, education laws, and regulations recognize the autonomy of schools and teachers, especially for issues such as the improvement of teaching and learning activities, school environment interactions, and the professional development of teachers. For example, the *Board of Education and Discipline* (Talim Terbiye Kurulu) as the highest level committee at MoNE decides curriculum structures, roles, responsibilities, competencies of teachers, recognizes and encourages teacher autonomy by taking care of sociocultural and socioeconomic environmental characteristics of the schools. In this sense, in spite of the instructional curriculum being centrally structured and implemented all over the country, teachers are allowed to make the necessary changes required by the social, cultural and economic settings of their schools.

In terms of the participation of teachers in decision-making processes in schools, MoNE has tried to reform the school management system by establishing decentralized models focusing on inclusive process management since the beginning of 1995. For example, Total Quality Management (TQM), School Improvement Teams (SIT) were put into practice. The ultimate goal has been to create an autonomous school and for professionals to be much responsive to their community out of the centrally organized bureaucratic order of command. By doing so, it is assumed that the accountability of schools could be realized at local level.

Moreover, for the empowerment of teachers in Turkey, MoNE has employed a model called School Site Professional Development (SSPD). This model assumes that the professional competencies of teachers could be improved by focusing on the indigenous conditions of the schools they work for and the individual demands of the teachers. In this sense, school principals are entitled to arrange professional development activities and encouraged to motivate teachers to attend different professional development programs including M.A., M.Ed., and Ph.D. Paralleling the employment of this model, graduating from M.A., M.Ed., Ph.D. or certificate programs and attending in-service training activities organized by public, private, or civil organizations have been credited in promotion of teachers to attainment of 'master' or 'head teacher' titles.

Despite the existence of such policies in favor of teacher leadership, as a centralized education system, most of the reforms are top-down in Turkey. Thus, teacher leaders show more formal roles. In this context, although they are not defined specifically, the Regulation of Primary Education Institutions based on Elementary Education Law, No: 222, contains some tasks and responsibilities and roles of teachers. According to Beycioglu (2009) these roles are collaborative working, producing innovative ideas, work in teams, participating in decision-making, guiding students or colleagues, acting as program specialist and educational planner, inspiring colleagues, leading in school improvement processes, budgeting, and participating in the administration of the school.

However, the practices regarding teacher leadership roles are the results of different interpretations of individuals in school settings. And these interpretations determine how degree of autonomy teachers should have and on what practices teachers should reveal leadership roles. As an example, Can (2006, 2007) emphasizes that according to both teachers and school managers, most teachers value collegial cooperation, want to join in-service or development programs, work in teams, motivate students at a high level; have problem-solving skills at middle level; are prone to change, produce projects, conduct educational researches, and produce policies at a low level. Also, teachers emphasize to take leadership roles in instructional and classroom-based activities, whereas school managers emphasize that teachers should take leadership roles in quality education, discipline, and school wide activities. Besides, Can (2015) found that according to most school managers, teacher leadership behaviors mainly focus on curriculum and content knowledge, valuing collaboration among teachers, motivating students to learn, solving conflicts, guiding new teachers or colleagues, affecting students, taking responsibilities in extracurricular activities, and completing given tasks. However according to a few school managers, teacher leadership includes leading change, having vision, identifying organizational problems and trying to solve them, joining school wide activities and taking risks, contributing to generating a powerful school culture, joining projects related to continuing learning and development, and developing independent school projects.

Additionally, there are some factors affecting teacher leadership in the Turkish case. According to Ozcetin (2013), when school managers support teacher leadership and try to improve school capacity, they experience difficulties with financial issues, passive teachers, and low family support to schools, emotional difficulties, time management and low vision. Moreover, school managers emphasize that the courage, sense of entrepreneurship, characteristics of teachers, working environment, financial capacity, and the time management skills of teachers are effective components in terms of teacher leadership behaviors. However, teachers propose that motivation and resources, attitudes of school managers toward teachers, collegial support and opportunities for professional development in school affect revealing teacher leadership behaviors (Can 2015).

Consequently, in implementing teacher leadership in school settings it is necessary for Turkey to create a positive school culture. School principals as educational leaders could create an institutional capacity for collaboration among teachers, a positive and inclusive school culture in which teachers take initiatives and roles without the mandatory formal roles of a bureaucratic system. In this sense, the educational leadership skills of principals can be developed within three main categories as leadership content knowledge, professional experience in working with teachers and data-based decision-making strategy (Bellibas 2015).

1.6 Conclusions

This chapter mainly examines teacher leadership from a developmental and international perspective. It identifies teacher leadership as a changing concept throughout transformational and distributed leadership, organizational structures determining the management of schools, and constructivist learning theory promoting the collaborative professional learning of teachers.

Teacher leadership has become a popular concept and process within school reform movements and site-based management applications that empowers teachers in school management practices. However, many roles and responsibilities of teachers make it very difficult to define the concept and identify a structured theory for it. So, teacher leadership is mostly discussed based on transformational, distributed and a bit of instructional leadership in the literature. These terms can never explain teacher leadership by themselves. Teacher leadership is like an umbrella covering those leadership styles and related with other terms for developing school capacity, teacher empowerment, and autonomy. Thus, this chapter presents a holistic approach that covers teacher leadership and terms related to it, by identifying the relationship between a set of theories on the management and organizational structures of schools and teacher leadership, which also forms the distinctive side of the chapter. Besides, teacher leadership has always been thought of as a culturally sensitive concept. In this regard, teacher leadership in the Turkish case has been explored with regard to the social, cultural, and religious values attributed to teachers as leaders in society throughout history.

In conclusion, teachers would be very basic change agents in every action taken for increasing student learning and success, and developing school capacity. A school manager seeking to reach the goals of the school could create a positive school culture in which teachers take initiatives by themselves without the imposition of formal authority. In other words, the convergence of both the formal and informal roles of teachers and the leadership skills of the school principals promote the expected outcomes of the changes. Creating conditions providing teacher leadership is an important problem to solve for school managers when they enhance collegiality among teachers against the bureaucratic and hierarchical nature of schools. Understanding the organizational nature of schools as loosely coupled organizations, professional bureaucracies and centralization and formalization in the organizational structure of schools could be useful to overcome such a dilemma.

References

Aliakbari, M., & Sadeghi, A. (2014). Iranian teachers' perceptions of teacher leadership practices in schools. *Educational Management Administration & Leadership, 42*(4), 576–592.
Ash, R. C., & Persall, J. M. (2000). The principal as chief learning officer: Developing teacher leaders. *NASSP bulletin, 84*(616), 15–22.
Barth, R. (2001). Teacher leader. *Phi Delta Kappan, 82*(6), 443–449.
Bass, B. M. (1985). *Leadership and performance beyond expectations.* Collier Macmillan: Free Press.
Bass, B. M., & Avolio, B. J. (1994). *Improving organizational effectiveness through transformational leadership.* Thousand Oaks: Sage.
Bass, B. M., & Bass, R. (2009). *The Bass handbook of leadership: Theory, research, and managerial applications.* Simon and Schuster.
Beachum, F., & Dentith, A. M. (2004). Teacher leaders creating cultures of school renewal and transformation. In *The Educational Forum* (Vol. 68, No. 3, pp. 276–286). Taylor & Francis Group.
Bellibas, M. S. (2015). Principals' and teachers' perceptions of efforts by principals to improve teaching and learning in Turkish middle schools. *Educational Sciences: Theory & Practice, 15*(6), 1471–1485.
Bennett, N., Wise, C., Woods, P., & Harvey, J. (2003). *Distributed leadership: Full report.* Nottingham, UK: National College for School Leadership.
Beycioglu, K. (2009). İlköğretim okullarında öğretmenlerin sergiledikleri liderlik rollerine ilişkin bir değerlendirme (Hatay ili örneği). *İnönü Üniversitesi Sosyal Bilimler Enstitüsü. Yayınlanmamış Doktora Tezi.*
Bolman, L. G., & Deal, T. E. (2008). *Reframing organizations: Artistry, choice, and leadership,*, 4/E.
Boyaci, A. (1998). *Shift in socioeconomic status of teaching profession: The Teachers in Eskişehir* (Master's Thesis, Middle East Technical University).
Boyd, B. L. (2009). Using a case study to develop the transformational teaching theory. *Journal of Leadership Education, 7*(3), 50–59.
Can, N. (2006). Öğretmen liderliğinin geliştirilmesinde müdürün rol ve stratejileri. *Erciyes Üniversitesi Sosyal Bilimler Enstitüsü Dergisi, 21*(2), 349–363.
Can, N. (2007). Öğretmen liderliği becerileri ve bu becerilerin gerçekleştirilme düzeyi. *Erciyes Üniversitesi Sosyal Bilimler Enstitüsü Dergisi, 22*(1), 263–288.
Can, N. (2015). Öğretmen liderliğinde müdürlerin etkisi. *Dumlupınar Üniversitesi Sosyal Bilimler Dergisi, 27*(27).
Child, J. (2003). Theorizing about organization cross-nationally: Part 2. In *Managing across cultures: Issues and perspectives.* London: Thomson.
Childs-Bowen, D., Moller, G., & Scrivner, J. (2000). Principals: Leaders of leaders. *NASSP Bulletin, 84*(616), 27–34.
Crowther, F., Kaagan, S., Ferguson, M., & Hann, L. (2002). *Developing teacher leaders. How teacher leaders enhance school success.*
Conley, S. C., & Bacharach, S. B. (1990). From school-site management to participatory school-site management. *The Phi Delta Kappan, 71*(7), 539–544.
Danielson, C. (2007). The many faces of leadership. *Educational leadership, 65*(1), 14–19.

Darling-Hammond, L., & Richardson, N. (2009). Research review/teacher learning: What matters? *Educational Leadership, 66*(5), 46–53.

Darling-Hammond, L., Bullmaster, M. L., & Cobb, V. L. (1995). Rethinking teacher leadership through professional development schools. *The Elementary School Journal, 96,* 87–106.

Doyle, M. (2000). *Making meaning of teacher leadership in the implementation of a standards-based mathematics curriculum.*

DuFour, R. (2004). What is a "professional learning community"? *Educational Leadership, 61*(8), 6–11.

DuFour, R., & Eaker, R. (2005). *Professional learning communities at work TM: Best practices for enhancing students achievement.* Solution Tree Press.

Fullan, M. (2008). *What's worth fighting for in headship?* UK: McGraw-Hill Education.

Gronn, P. (2002). Distributed leadership. In *Second international handbook of educational leadership and administration* (pp. 653–696). Springer Netherlands.

Guven, I. (2004). Etkili Bir Öğretim İçin Öğretmenden Beklenenler. *Milli Eğitim Dergisi, Sayı, 164,* 127–141.

Hallinger, P., & Heck, R. H. (2009). Distributed leadership in schools: Does system policy make a difference. *Distributed Leadership,* 101–117.

Harris, A. (2002). *School improvement: What's in it for Schools?* Psychology Press.

Harris, A. (2003). Teacher leadership as distributed leadership: Heresy, fantasy or possibility? *School leadership & management, 23*(3), 313–324.

Harris, A. (2004). Distributed leadership and school improvement leading or misleading? *Educational Management Administration & Leadership, 32*(1), 11–24.

Harris, A. (2005). Distributed leadership. In B. Davies (Ed.), *The essentials of school leadership* (pp. 160–172). London: PCPC.

Harris, A. (2011) Distributed leadership: Current evidence and future directions. *Journal of Management Development, 30*(10), 20–32.

Harris, A., & Muijs, D. (2004). *Improving schools through teacher leadership.* UK: McGraw-Hill Education.

Harris, A., & Spillane, J. (2008). Distributed leadership through the looking glass. *Management in Education, 22*(1), 31.

Hart, A. W. (1990). Impacts of the school social unit on teacher authority during work redesign. *American Educational Research Journal, 27*(3), 503–532.

Hart, A. W. (1994). Creating teacher leadership roles. *Educational Administration Quarterly, 30*(4), 472–497.

Hart, A. W. (1995). Reconceiving school leadership: Emergent views. *The Elementary School Journal, 96,* 9–28.

Hein, G. (1991). *Constructivist learning theory.* Institute for Inquiry. Available at: http://www.exploratorium.edu/ifi/resources/constructivistlearning.html

Hord, S. M. (1997). *Professional learning communities: Communities of continuous inquiry and improvement.*

Hoy, W., & Miskel, C. (2005). *Educational administration: Theory, research, and practice.* New York, NY: McGraw Hill.

Hoy, W. K., & Sweetland, S. R. (2000). School bureaucracies that work: Enabling, not coercive. *Journal of School Leadership, 10*(6), 525–541.

Hoy, W. K., & Sweetland, S. R. (2001). Designing better schools: The meaning and measure of enabling school structures. *Educational Administration Quarterly, 37*(3), 296–321.

Johnson, S. M., & Donaldson, M. L. (2007). Overcoming the obstacles to leadership. *Educational Leadership, 65*(1), 8–13.

Katzenmeyer, M., & Moller, G. (2001). *Awakening the sleeping giant: Helping teachers develop as leaders.* Corwin Press.

Katzenmeyer, M., & Moller, G. (2009). *Awakening the sleeping giant: Helping teachers develop as leaders.* Corwin Press.

Leblanc, P. R., & Shelton, M. M. (1997). Teacher leadership: The needs of teachers. *Action in teacher education, 19*(3), 32–48.

Leithwood, K. A. (1992). The move toward transformational leadership. *Educational Leadership, 49*(5), 8–12.

Leithwood, K., & Jantzi, D. (2000a). Principal and teacher leadership effects: A replication. *School Leadership & Management, 20*(4), 415–434.

Leithwood, K., & Jantzi, D. (2000b). The effects of transformational leadership on organizational conditions and student engagement with school. *Journal of Educational Administration, 38*(2), 112–129.

Leithwood, K., Day, C., Sammons, P., Harris, A., & Hopkins D. (2006). *Successful school leadership: What it is and how it influences pupil learning*. Research Report Number 800, NCSL/Department for Education and Skills, University of Nottingham, Nottingham, England.

Leithwood, K., Jacobson, S. L., & Ylimaki, R. M. (2011). Converging policy trends. In *US and cross-national policies, practices, and preparation* (pp. 17–28). Springer Netherlands.

Lewis, D. A. (2014). *Teacher leadership practices in successful elementary schools: A study of the identification, development, and utilization of teachers as leaders in consistently high performing elementary schools in eastern North Carolina*.

Lieberman, A., & Miller, I. (2004). *Teacher leadership*. San Francisco, California: Jossey-Bass.

Lieberman, A., & Pointer-Mace, D. (2009). Making practice public: Teacher learning in the 21st century. *Journal of Teacher Education*.

Little, J. W. (1988). *Assessing the prospects for teacher leadership*.

McLaughlin, M. W., & Talbert, J. E. (2006). *Building school-based teacher learning communities: Professional strategies to improve student achievement* (Vol. 45). Teachers College Press.

McMahon, A., Stoll, L., Thomas, S., Wallace, M., Greenwood, A., Hawkey, K., et al. (2005). *Creating and sustaining effective professional learning communities*. London: Department for Education and Skills.

Mintzberg, H. (1980). Structure in 5's: A synthesis of the research on organization design. *Management Science, 26*(3), 322–341.

MoNE. (2006). Öğretmenlik mesleği genel yeterlikleri. *Electronic Journal* [Online]: http://oyegm.meb.gov.tr/yet/index.htm. Adresinden.

Muijs, D., & Harris, A. (2007). Teacher leadership in (In) action three case studies of contrasting schools. *Educational Management Administration & Leadership, 35*(1), 111–134.

Murphy, J. (Ed.). (2005). *Connecting teacher leadership and school improvement*. Corwin Press.

Murphy, J. (2007). Teacher leadership: Barriers and supports. In *International handbook of school effectiveness and improvement* (pp. 681–706). Springer Netherlands.

Owens, R. G., & Valesky, T. C. (2010). *Organizational behavior in education: Instructional leadership and school reform* (10th ed.). New York: Allyn & Bacon.

Ozcetin, S. (2013). *Öğretmen liderliğinin okulun liderlik kapasitesinin gelişimine etkisi: Bir durum çalışması* (Doctoral dissertation, Master's thesis, Akdeniz University, Antalya, Turkey). Retrieved from tez.yok.gov.tr/UlusalTezMerkezi.

Pont, B., Nusche, D., & Moorman, H. (2008). *Improving school leadership, volume 1 policy and practice: Policy and practice (vol. 1)*. OECD publishing.

Rutherford, C. (2006). Teacher leadership and organizational structure. *Journal of Educational Change, 7*(1–2), 59–76.

Scott, W. R. (1992). *Organizations: Rational, natural, and open systems* (3rd ed.). Englewood Cliffs, NJ: Prentice Hall.

Seashore Louis, K., Dretzke, B., & Wahlstrom, K. (2010). How does leadership affect student achievement? Results from a national US survey. *School Effectiveness and School Improvement, 21*(3), 315–336.

Sergiovanni, T. J. (1996). *Leadership for the schoolhouse: How is it different? Why is it important?* Jossey-Bass, Inc. Publishers, 350 Sansome Street, San Francisco, CA 94104.

Sergiovanni, T. J. (2001). *Leadership: What's in it for schools?*. London: Routledge Falmer.

Shah, S. J. (2010). Re-thinking educational leadership: Exploring the impact of cultural and belief systems. *International Journal of Leadership in Education, 13*(1), 27–44.

Shaw, S. J., & Shaw, E. K. (1977). *History of the Ottoman Empire and modern Turkey: Volume 2, Reform, revolution, and republic: The rise of modern Turkey 1808–1975* (Vol. 11). Cambridge University Press.

Sherrill, J. A. (1999). Preparing teachers for leadership roles in the 21st century. *Theory into Practice, 38*(1), 56–61.

Silva, D., Gimbert, B., & Nolan, J. (2000). Sliding the doors: Locking and unlocking possibilities for teacher leadership. *The Teachers College Record, 102*(4), 779–804.

Smylie, M. A. (1992). Teachers' reports of their interactions with teacher leaders concerning classroom instruction. *The Elementary School Journal, 93*, 85–98.

Smylie, M. A. (1996). Research on teacher leadership: Assessing the state of the art. In *International handbook of teachers and teaching* (pp. 521–591). Springer Netherlands.

Smylie, M., Conley, S., & Marks, H. (2002). Exploring new approaches to teacher leadership for school improvement. In *Educational leadership challenge: Redefining leadership for the 21st century* (pp. 162–188).

Somel, S. A. (2001). *The modernization of public education in the Ottoman Empire, 1839–1908: Islamization, autocracy, and discipline* (Vol. 22). Brill.

Spillane, J. P. (2006). *Distributed leadership*. San Francisco, CA: Jossey-Bass.

Swanson, J., Elliott, K., & Harmon, J. (2011). *Teacher leader stories: The power of case methods*. Corwin Press.

Topolinski, C. C. (2014). *The influence of teacher leadership and professional learning on teachers' knowledge and change of instructional practices in low performing schools*.

Troen, V., & Boles, K. (1994). Two teachers examine the power of teacher leadership. In D. R. Walling (Ed.), *Teachers as leaders: Perspectives on the professional development of teachers* (pp. 275–286). Bloomington, IN: Phi Delta Kappan.

Tschannen-Moran, M. (2009). Fostering teacher professionalism in schools the role of leadership orientation and trust. *Educational Administration Quarterly, 45*(2), 217–247.

Wasley, P. A. (1991). *Teachers who lead: The rhetoric of reform and the realities of practice*. New York: Teachers College Press.

Watt, K. M., Huerta, J., & Mills, S. J. (2010). Advancement Via Individual Determination (AVID) professional development as a predictor of teacher leadership in the United States. *Professional Development in Education, 36*(4), 547–562.

Weber, M. (1993). *The sociology of religion*. Beacon Press.

Weick, K. E. (1976). Educational organizations as loosely coupled systems. *Administrative Science Quarterly, 21*, 1–19.

Weick, K. E. (1982). Administering education in loosely coupled schools. *The Phi Delta Kappan, 63*(10), 673–676.

White, P. A. (1992). Teacher empowerment under "ideal" school-site autonomy. *Educational Evaluation and Policy Analysis, 14*(1), 69–82.

York-Barr, J., & Duke, K. (2004). What do we know about teacher leadership? Findings from two decades of scholarship. *Review of Educational Research, 74*(3), 255–316.

Zinn, L. F. (1997). *Supports and barriers to teacher leadership: Reports of teacher leaders*.

Chapter 2
Promoting Teachers' Leadership Through Autonomy and Accountability

Nabi Bux Jumani and Samina Malik

Abstract Teachers are considered a cornerstone in a school setup. Therefore, teachers' quality and competency is the central point for the improvement of whole school. When teachers handle their classrooms alone, recognize their abilities that can influence every student's learning and select and organize their curricula by themselves, then the teacher leadership is an imperative instead of an option. Standards for the teacher leaders consist of seven domains that describe various dimensions of teacher leaderships, which could help them in finding various opportunities within the teaching profession. Certain conditions facilitate the promotion of teacher leaderships in schools such as safe environment, supportive administrator, and absence of "tall poppy syndrome." Teacher autonomy is teachers' capacity to engage in self-directed teaching, which may include general professional autonomy, collegial professional autonomy, and individual autonomy. To accomplish instructional goals and encouraging conducive learning environment, teachers need to have freedom for decision-making and providing best opportunities for students' complete development. Teacher accountability concentrates on both the procedures and results of teaching. Both the terms autonomy and accountability are interrelated as when teachers may be given autonomy to work in their own way, yet being accountable and strive for the teacher leadership on the whole.

N.B. Jumani (✉)
Faculty of Social Sciences, International Islamic University, Islamabad, Pakistan
e-mail: nbjumani@yahoo.com

S. Malik
Department of Education and Director Female Campus, International Islamic University, Islamabad, Pakistan

2.1 Introduction

Teacher is considered a linchpin in a school setup. His art heavily impacts on the students' achievement. Therefore, teachers' quality and competency is the central point for the improvement of whole school. Many countries are supplying high quality of teachers, and many are struggling to meet the new standards of quality teachers and training them as future leaders. This challenge is becoming more acute when educational systems demand more ambitious teachers, to prepare their students with skills and knowledge that increase their success rate in this growing globalized and digital world (Jackson and Stewart 2012).

When teachers handle their classrooms alone, recognize their abilities that can influence every student's learning and select and organize their curricula by themselves, then the teacher leadership is an imperative instead of an option. As with the time, one teacher and single classroom schools have been converted into multiroom buildings and multiroom buildings are moving in multibuilding schools, the status of the teacher becomes as an employee instead of as expert. With the passage of time as school grow in size is increased complexities in administrative tasks became highly demanding and structured, top-to-down hierarchies and powerful well-structured administration that have positioned the teachers at the lower side of hierarchy and quitting them from organizational tasks. Many people agree this that nowadays management of schools has become more complex and demanding and recognized as bureaucratic institutions in nature. Unluckily efforts made for educational reforms and increasing quality education emphasized the increase in teaching professionalism that in result increased the bureaucratic aspect of administration. The organizations tend to adopt standardized procedures of appointing the teachers, implementing highly structured and uniform curriculum in schools and following rigid policies. This all move the whole educational system toward centralized in nature (Wattleton 2000). The teachers' professionalism became more at risk because it is followed by strict rules and procedures. In such background achievement and accountability is considered as direction and prescription. It will definitely move students and teachers into threatening situations.

According to Jackson and Stewart (2012), the autonomy of teachers leads them toward the perfect leadership, when teachers are involved in decision-making role, taking the responsibilities, and involving in administrative and management tasks consequently move the institution toward improvement and address the continuing students' cognitive and social growth. When teacher leaders are empowered accepting the responsibilities, and finding their power in knowledge they start to accept challenging situations and positively inquire educational issues and learn new instructional methods that help them to promote self-trust in classrooms and curriculum decisions.

2.2 Definition of Teacher Leader

There is a lot of work seen that is trying to define teacher leaders, but the definition for the term "teacher leader" still vary from one to others. This is because the roles of teachers cover a wide range of activities. Leadership is one of them. Katzenmeyer and Moller (2001) maintain that teacher leaders are those teachers who lead within or beyond the classrooms, positively contribute to a teacher learner and leaders community, and finally influence others for the improvement in educational tasks. Further, they supported the concept of 'teacher leadership' as saying "there is 'sleeping giant' in every school which is a strong channel for making changes and works for school improvement." School leaders make efforts to wake this giant by realizing all teachers that they are leaders and providing them opportunities to explore their leadership skills. Wasley (1991) defined teacher leader as the ability of teachers to convince the colleagues to accept change and do things which could not be considered to be done with out the influence of a leader. McGhan (2002) described the term 'teacher leader' as collegial and less hierarchical version of school leadership which is a main person that contributes in whole school reform efforts. Further, he elaborated his point of view as saying it as 'negotiated' order that is a totally contradictory concept from the traditional one that is unidirectional or top-down style of leadership. Most of teacher leader definitions can be divided into two main categories, first is recognizing the teacher leader as someone different from rest of teachers, it is one who is considered as special being and comes in a special class. Second category of teacher leaders is such group of people who are all leaders and work collectively to optimize the whole process of teaching and learning. Here all teachers are leaders, work as professionals, and make sure that all challenges are being welcome (Wattleton 2000).

2.2.1 Roles and Responsibilities

It is observed in many researches that individual and single-person leadership is increasing throughout the world particularly in developed countries like America, Canada, and Australia. Many countries are conducting various teacher leadership programs and investing on teacher leader trainings showing that this concept of teacher leaders is widely accepted by many researchers and practitioners, throughout the world. The teacher leadership in its true essence is considered as enhancing leadership tasks and decision-making powers for teachers without taking them out of the classrooms. In contrast to traditional approach of leadership, the teacher leadership is featured by a kind of collective leadership in which teachers enhance their experiences and expertise by working collaboratively with their colleagues. By reviewing the extensive literature various tasks and roles are identified for teacher leaders that further give light upon the various natures of teacher leaders' activities and responsibilities. Katzenmeyer and Moller (2001) have identified three main components of teacher leaders' responsibilities:

  i. Leaderships of other teachers or students: work as coach, mentors, curriculum expert, trainers, facilitators, for creating new approaches and leading the study groups.
  ii. Leadership for operational tasks: make efforts to organize the school and achieve its goals through working as head of department, as member of task forces, and as action researcher.
  iii. Leadership through decision-making or partnership: work as member of committees, leader of partnership with business, higher institutions and parent teacher associations.

Similarly, Gehrke (1991) defined some more responsibilities and roles for teacher leaders such as

a. Constantly improve their classroom teachings
b. Organize and lead all of school practices
c. Provide curriculum development knowledge
d. Participate in various school decision-making
e. Giving in-service training to colleagues, and
f. Participate in the performance evaluation of teachers.

Day and Harris (2002) proposes four key dimensions of teachers leadership roles such as

  i. The way in which teachers translate the school improvement principles into the practices of individual classrooms. This is the central responsibilities of the teachers as a leader that ensures all links within schools are safe and working further maximizes the opportunities for the overall development of teachers.
  ii. The second dimension of the responsibilities of teacher leader emphasizes upon the participative leadership, where all teachers feel themselves as the part of the transition or progress and possess a sense of ownership. Here a teacher leader encourages other teachers to hold hands for a particular development that leads toward more collaborative way of working. Furthermore, he/she work with colleagues to enhance school improvement and lead all of them to accomplish a collective goal.
  iii. Teacher leader sometimes performs a mediating role in school improvement project. As teacher leaders are considered as a source of expertise and information. They have guts to draw new expertise and resources and take external assistance whenever it requires.
  iv. One of the most important dimensions of teacher leaders' role is developing close relationships with every teacher for enjoying the mutual learning.

There are some other dimensions or type of responsibilities of the teacher leaders observed in various research works such as performing action research, promoting peer classroom observation, and continuously developing a culture of professional development through establishing a collaborative environment. Many studies supported the idea that mentoring, orientation, and continual professional development of other teachers is seen crucial as through encouraging collaborative environment, new ideas emerged that contribute to the whole progress of the school.

Some other teacher roles are identified by various studies as curriculum developer, leaders of the school improvement team, mentoring of the new and less-experienced staff and sometimes as action researcher that always have a strong link to the classrooms. Teacher leaders are seen as expert teachers who remain busy within their classrooms but perform different roles at different time periods as following the principles of influential leadership. Teacher leaders are considered as important for the teachers' empowerment, by involving them in decision making within the schools and promoting the democratic environment in the schools (Gehrke1991). A teacher leader should have ability to work collaboratively with peers, observing each other's classes and discussing various possibilities for the improvement of whole teaching and learning process (Muijs and Harris 2003).

Barth (1999) explained the teacher leaders role beyond participating in decision-making and collaborating, such as for him a teacher leader has to perform certain tasks which are generally undertaken by a senior manager for example:

a. Selecting text books and instructional materials
b. Designing the curriculum
c. Determining certain codes of conduct related to the students behavior
d. Deciding on tracking
e. Planning staff development programs
f. Determining promotion and retention rules
g. Deciding school budgets
h. Evaluation of the teachers' performance
i. Appointing new administrators and teachers.

This list of teacher leaders' roles and responsibilities depicts that a teacher leader must be part of all important decision-making plans. Some other supporting writers feel that a teacher leader can work with a senior management while making important decisions related to the specific tasks of school rather replacing them.

2.3 Standards for Teacher Leaders

Standards for the teacher leaders consist of seven domains that describe various dimensions of teacher leaderships (Fig. 2.1).

According to Smylie (2010) individual teacher leaders could not equip all of or many of the dimensions instead there are many situations in which teachers have to imagine their leadership roles. These standards could help them in finding various opportunities for opting different leadership standards within the teaching profession.

Fig. 2.1 Domains of standards for teacher leaders (*source* Smylie 2010)

2.3.1 Domain 1: Fostering a Collaborative Culture

A teacher leader must be aware of the principles related to children learning and know how to develop a collaborative culture for collective tasks. This knowledge helps the teacher leaders to create an environment of respect trust and cooperation that in turn support the continuous improvement of teaching learning process. There are certain tasks related to this domain which a teacher leader is expected to perform such as:

a. Use group process to assist his colleagues, work together for solving the various problems, make decisions, manage the conflicts, and enhance significant changes.
b. Possess skills for presenting ideas, leading discussions, have knowledge of his/her and others' needs to share goals and professional development.
c. To enhance students learning a teacher leader creates trust among fellows, extends collective wisdom, and generates ownership and actions, and
d. Make efforts to welcome the challenging situations.

2.3.2 Domain 2: Accessing and Using Research

Under this domain teacher leaders must comprehend how to create new knowledge using the research and intimate rules and policies to enhance teaching learning processes. A teacher leader supports others to learn how inquiry and research can be a continuous part of their learning and professional development. Certain tasks related to this domain include:

a. Help their colleagues in use of research for learning appropriate approaches to maximize students learning.
b. Assist other teachers how to analyze students' achievement data, interpretation of the results, and use the findings for the improvement of the whole teaching and learning process.
c. Help the colleagues to join other organizations and higher institutions for the interaction to handle critical educational issues and problems.

2.3.3 Domain 3: Promote Professional Learning

A teacher leader always tries to be equipped with the new innovations related to emerging technologies school communities and use this knowledge to endorse, design, and assist professional development for his colleagues that further support in achieving the schools improvement plans. Functions and tasks related to this domain are specified as

a. Plan professional learning with the collaboration with the colleagues and school administrators that is team based, job oriented, and continue over time.
b. Identify individual differences among his/her colleagues and support them in professional learning by identifying, promoting, providing differential tasks.
c. Assist professional learning among colleagues.
d. Identify and use various technologies for the endorsement of cooperative and differentiated professional development of colleagues.
e. Provide constructive feedback related to their professional development.
f. Use emerging educational, economic, and social trends in the planning of professional learning programs.

2.3.4 Domain 4: Support Improvement in Teaching and Students Learning

The teacher leader has to have deep understanding about the all teaching learning processes and provides continuous professional development to the colleagues by modeling the reflective practices. Furthermore he/she ensures that all teaching practices are aligned with the shared vision of school. Teacher leaders' tasks related to this specific domain include:

a. Facilitate class- and school-based data for the improvement of curriculum, teaching, evaluation, and school culture.
b. Facilitate his colleagues to use research-based practices for the betterment of teaching learning process.
c. Provide assistance to the colleagues for collective professional growth by mentoring, coaching, and facilitating.

d. Lead them to combine the skills, knowledge, and expertise for the improvement of students' learning and curriculum development.
e. Support the teachers to use emerging technologies to enhance students' learning and appropriate use of the information available on the Internet, utilize social media to encourage collaborative learning, and connect various people and resources existing around the world.

2.3.5 Domain 5: Use of Assessment

Teacher leaders are generally equipped with the skills related to the effective use of formative and summative assessments methods. They utilize this information and share their skill with the colleagues to use assessments to create relevant decisions that can improve student's learning and overall school progress. Regarding this teacher leaders have to perform certain tasks such as:

a. Support the teachers how to use various assessment tools aligned to national and international standards.
b. Collaborate with the colleagues to design and implement of these assessment tools and use obtained scores and interpretation of students' data to solve various predetermined issues.
c. Support the colleagues to use assessment data for the improvement of instruction practices.

2.3.6 Domain 6: Improve Outreach and Collaboration with Families and Community

Teacher leaders are very well awarded of the fact that families, societies, cultures, and communities are really influential figures for the educational processes and student's learning. They work with their colleagues to foster cooperation and collaboration among various stakeholders such as families, community members, and leaders to improve all of educational system and maximize opportunities for students' learning. For this teacher leader has to

a. Possess knowledge about the different social backgrounds of ethnicities, cultures, and dialects to promote effective collaboration among all stakeholders.
b. Model effective communications skills and collaborative behavior with all stakeholders to maximize students' achievement who come from various social backgrounds.
c. Support colleagues for their own self-assessment related to the understanding of various ethnicities, cultural differences, and different social backgrounds. How they can create various strategies to handle different students and enrich their experiences with multicultural educational practices.

d. Create a communal understanding of different educational requirements for different families, and communities.
e. Address the diverse educational needs teacher leader has to collaborate with different families, social groups and colleagues and develop comprehensive strategies to accomplish all those needs.

2.3.7 Domain 7: Advocating Students' Learning and Profession

Teacher leaders comprehend how policies and plantings are made and what could be the role of school leaders, teachers, and other stakeholders while forming the educational policies. While using this knowledge teacher leaders advocate their students' needs and support various activities that can enhance effective teaching, promote students' learning and serve as influential being in the school and in the communities. For this teacher leaders must

a. Share information with their colleagues, related to the policies formation process and how these policies and plans can influence the teaching learning process.
b. Use research with the collaboration of the colleagues to support teaching learning processes.
c. Collaborate with teachers to utilize opportunities to advocate the rights and needs of the students.
d. Advocate for the professional resources such as financial, man power, and other material resources and help colleagues to utilize all these facilities to enhance their experiences and learning to achieve organizational objectives.

2.4 Conditions that Promote Teacher Leadership

Many studies illustrate that most of schools are not hospitable for the teacher leaders especially unofficial or informal teacher as leader. Commonly a school administrator is considered as influential being who can foster the conditions to promote teacher leaders. There are certain conditions determined by Danielson (2007) that facilitate the promotion of teacher leaderships in schools.

2.4.1 A Safe Environment for Risk Taking

To promote teacher leadership it is essential that administrators and other teachers do not criticize when a teacher leader presents ideas and plans which may seem at first unusual or strange. This confidence will encourage the teacher leader to think creatively and handle difficult issues and critical situations. A safe environment must be provided to the teacher leaders in which administrator ensure that teachers are free to express new ideas and can take professional decisions. For instance, an administrator can arrange various discussion sessions in which he/she may ask how we can foster professional environment within the school. How you would like to create classroom environment in the schools. Promoting such professional climate an administrator can facilitate teacher leaders to practically participate for sharing different ideas and bringing innovation in schools.

2.4.2 Supportive Administrator

Only a committed administrator can foster and promote teacher leadership. Administrators must be supportive and encouraging beings, who offer help to the teachers to develop such professional skills to take advantages from their leading roles, i.e., decision-making, data analysis, and interpretation of the data. Unfortunately, some administrators could not have courage to recognize others efforts and most of time take all credit for others contributions. Whereas the fact is this, that the more power an administrator will share the more authority he/she would get.

2.4.3 Absence of "Tall Poppy Syndrome"

It is not always the administrators who are the pessimistic character and against the teacher leaders, sometimes the teachers themselves are not willing to perform leadership role or sometimes other teachers create hurdles in the ways of the teacher leader. In Australia, this condition is known as "Tall Poppy Syndrome," those who stick their heads up risk being cut down to size. These are the teachers who seem mostly reluctant to declare their colleagues that they are nominated as teacher leader or recognized by the national board for professional teaching standard. To control such situation an administrator must take an initiative to promote a culture in which teachers who initiate new ideas and do something different from traditional setup.

2.4.4 Opportunities to Foster Leadership Skills

As it is discussed in many studies that to promote leadership skills among teachers does not mean to arrange a lot of training programs and workshops for them instead they only need certain skills related to curriculum planning, applying assessment techniques, strategies for instructional improvement and facilitation. These skills can be promoted through school-level professional development, various courses, and seminars. An administrator must provide sufficient opportunities to the teachers considering their convenience level.

2.5 Autonomy

Numerous researches are found discussing "what is autonomy?" Many researchers answered it in different perspectives such as Sitch (2005) stated autonomy as capacity and responsibilities to bring change and manage one's attitudes and capabilities in a productive way. Teachers possess autonomy when they are able to have control over any situation and possess freedom to handle all matters using their own approach. For Moses (2007), it is a decisional freedom that people use to make their own choices without feeling hesitation of their authorities. Moses discussed various dimensions of autonomy related to educational settings. Generally educational institutions offer autonomy to their teachers to decide their work and employment conditions, to assess students' progress, establish educational objectives and decide curriculum, decide academic standards, engage in continuous research and innovations, direct administration and finance, and provide organizational governance (Moses 2007).

To answer the question "how to create opportunities to offer autonomy to teacher professionals so that they can possess authority for curriculum development, deciding academic standards and procedures evaluation" Bowen (2006) referred to the law of autonomy given by Kant. The law of autonomy emphasizes upon the freedom for decision-makers to take appropriate decisions which are often unattained because of sway or pressure of the organizational authority. Professional autonomy is the key aspect of self-determination among the employees that relates to the self-choice of goals. Kuvaas (2009) elaborated that the supportive attitude of leaders for autonomy, competence, and skill development is essential for the intrinsic motivation that leads the individuals for self-determination. Further is emphasized by the researcher that social conditions and environment heavily impact through the individuals' perception about their autonomy upon their intrinsic motivation. The key benefit of the professional autonomy discussed by Penuel et al. (2010) is when organizations that offer freedom to its employees to construct their practices, control over the decisions, and develop self-efficacy in result improve their practices and minimize all issues.

For Rothstein (2003), the term autonomy covers a sense of overconfidence, and self-importance is hampered with emotional feelings, and that's why lack the depth of meaning related to what individuals are trying to practice, that include freedom from evaluation, decision-making ability, openness in expressing their views, or lack of boundaries. Professional autonomy employees need strict evaluation of their own practices for improving all tasks. According to Streshley and Bernd (1992) effective administrators support the professional development of the teachers by offering them to participate in decision-making that can influence the whole schools. Freedom of choice and decision-making promote creativity and enhance experiences of the employees that further lead them to social consciousness and enhance universal values (Moses 2007). To endorse high-level dedication among staff members, it is crucial for administrators to promote autonomy among their staff members for enhancement of their creativity. Providing opportunities for teachers autonomy and encouraging them to participate in goal setting will lead to accomplish the institutional agenda (Streshley and Bernd 1992).

2.5.1 The Concept of Teacher Autonomy

'Teacher autonomy' is defined in many ways. Benson (2000) defines teacher autonomy as "right to freedom from control," for Little (1995) teachers' capacity to engage in self-directed teaching. Some define teacher autonomy differently and they believe it as a process of constructing a personal identity as professionals must combine with the interests of the society. To some importance must be given to the teacher autonomy that will lead it toward the students autonomy, this concept has been evolved in the researches where learners' autonomy is considered as key factor for the teaching learning process. Some feel autonomy is the capacity for autonomous decision-making and possessing the skills for showing readiness and action that illustrate motivation and confidence to carry out their decisions (Wilches 2007). Some studies suggested as teachers' autonomy can be observed in both aspects as self-directed professional growth and independence from managed by others. This discussion can be summarized the multidimensional concept of the teachers autonomy and significant relation between the teachers' professional development and teachers' autonomy. In a nutshell, teacher autonomy can be defined as 'teachers' eagerness, aptitude, independence, and self-control to take decisions and implement them.

2.5.2 Forms of Teacher Autonomy

Figure 2.2 describes the forms of Teacher Autonomy.

2.5.2.1 General Professional Autonomy

This type of teacher autonomy refers to the surrounds of professional tasks such as organization of school tasks, rules and regulations (laws), teacher training, curriculum development, and concept of control as organizational system will be managed by the objectives or prescribed rules. At this level, professional teacher autonomy is based on the permission to organize the forms of teachers' tasks, for example, following the principles or control of the institution. Teachers have not been able to dictate working conditions for their professional development at this

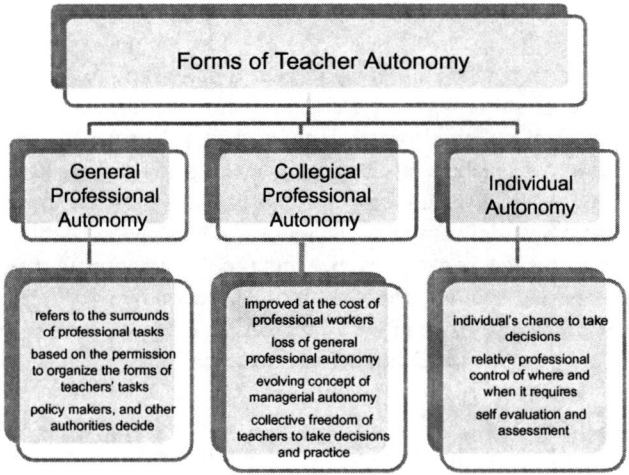

Fig. 2.2 Forms of teacher autonomy

level. For many people collective agreement on working hours and other significant practices of teaching are considered as inconvenience for teachers. Decentralization of the school administration increases the power of teachers to decide various forms of content and evaluation procedures (Wilches 2007). The striking challenge related to the general professional autonomy is that most of developments have been occurred without the practical involvement of the teachers. For example, generally capitalists as principals own the large private entrepreneurships and school organizers has less or more unexpected development that results less considerations for the teachers work and tasks as not discussed and given proper importance. Such type of development directs more de-professionalization of the teachers and teaching profession as teachers have not been given the authority to organize or decide various tasks related to the school development. Instead of teachers, politicians, policy makers, and other authorities decide the ways of development instructional practices for the schools (Wilches 2007). In short, the private companies and state organizations conditioned and form the teaching profession and teachers' practices and concept of professional autonomy in general practically can be denoted as de-professionalization.

2.5.2.2 Collegial Professional Autonomy

The concept of decentralization involve that problems related to pedagogical concepts, organizational work control are addressed by the local management and they take various decisions. One interpretation of this managerial autonomy, enjoyed by the principals of the schools, has improved at the cost of professional workers. The loss of general professional autonomy and evolving concept of managerial autonomy in the schools give a challenge to the exercising autonomy at the practice level. But when we focus on the definition of collegial autonomy, no one can be upheld at the practice level even if general professional autonomy has abolished and local management of schools poses a question who will organize the professional work. The concept of collegial professional autonomy for teachers focuses on the collective freedom of teachers to take decisions and practice at local level. Here teachers are given collective authority to take decisions related to designing their instructional strategies, develop new pedagogical ideas and concepts. This form of autonomy encourages teachers to organize and run the school authority on the bases of cooperation and collegiality. Here teachers are encouraged to make joint efforts to organize and create professional practices. This concept of autonomy merges the collegial and managerial autonomy. This must be kept in mind that collegial autonomy may be executed in an institution where teachers may have to follow strict organizational rules and principles and may face restrictive ideas. Here teachers are required to accomplish their work within team collectively according to the ideas given by others. Despite this fact, teachers have to take decisions about the content selection, pedagogical choice, and selection of the work-based professional competencies (Wilches 2007). Generally, collegial autonomy is based on two different processes, e.g., it may be observed as delegated and preferred principles for deciding the work and practices from a managerial perspective or it may be observed as collegial outcome of individual autonomy in which preferences of the individual teachers result in collegial practices and decisions.

2.5.2.3 Individual Autonomy

Individual autonomy is based on the individual's chance to take decisions related to the content selection, decide and form teaching practices such as choice of the teaching material, instructional strategies, and assessments procedures. Individual autonomy, no doubt depends upon the individual choices but it does not mean that they possess complete freedom as they have to respect the authoritative rules and instructions, for example, following the marking criteria, etc. The individual autonomy can be enjoyed only when local administration limits their control over them and shows strong trust on the individual teachers (Wilches 2007).

The professional teaching practices may be for temporary time period that is why individual autonomy offers relative professional control of where and when it requires. Some may criticize that such form of autonomy gives over freedom and flexibility to the teachers but, in fact, this freedom is constantly under challenging situations and demand from teachers for being more alert and conscious about their work. To bind the teachers for specific time period such as from morning till evening, it severely affects the individual autonomy but it is essential for the needs of students, instructional concepts and institutional priorities. Individual autonomy does not mean that there is no evaluation and control related to the teaching practices. However, they have to conduct self-evaluation and assessment to improve their own practices.

2.5.3 Benefits of Teacher Autonomy

Teacher autonomy enjoys the freedom to make decisions and professional choices related to the development of curriculum, deciding instructional strategies, etc. Professional direction and autonomy would enable teachers to make instructional decisions and judgments regarding instructional practices. With the professional, autonomy teachers possess the right to arrange learning processes according to their choices. Various studies emphasized that effective organizations mostly distributed the decision-making powers among its employees (Chaleff 2009). Traditional bureaucratic approaches of school management do not support this innovative concept of organizational structure, but evidences of many researchers illustrate the great influence of this change in organizational structures that leads to drastic change in the daily practices of the teachers who are professionally independent and autonomous beings.

Additionally, it is argued in many studies that standardized instructions supersede professional autonomy in obtaining the accountability goals. Standardized instructions and curriculum are the aspects of systematic process of creating, assessing and evaluating instructional processes. Instructions based on this concept cannot weaken the concerns for the teacher's professional freedom. Teachers require freedom from restricted curriculum, because no one can force a teacher to be sincere with program developed by other source. Teachers have a comprehensive knowledge about all of academic goals, contents, practices, and assessment procedures. Even they are equipped with the skills to organize and use this information useful and persuasive for learners. Instead of following the readymade content that overlook the teachers' experiences and skills for creating effective instructional strategies for students learning, they need opportunities to discuss freely about their expectations and practices for making personal decisions. Teachers autonomy liberate them from the traditional bureaucratic concept of teaching learning processes and prompt them to utilize their own innovative ideas and decisions making power for the enhancement of whole teaching learning processes.

2.5.4 Implications of Teachers Autonomy for Teachers Leadership

Enhancing professionalism among teachers by promoting teacher autonomy has the potential to ensure teachers as best leaders. The concept of traditional hierarchical administration and leadership is now considered as out of fashion. Teachers as leaders can play a crucial role to empower all administrator and staff members. Empowered teachers usually contribute as a force for administrators and integrated group to enhance all teaching learning process (Chaleff 2009).

Mostly teachers apply their leadership skills in classrooms to prepare, support, and direct the students' learning activities. For effective teaching and providing best opportunities for students leaning, teachers require a certain level of autonomy to implement their leadership tactic to handle immediate issues during the teaching (Blanchard 2007).

To accomplish instructional goals and encouraging conducive learning environment, teachers need to have freedom for decision-making and providing best opportunities for students' complete development. Most of time teachers' practices are determined by the local authority whereas for achieving best leadership qualities, teachers need freedom and autonomy for promoting educational goals (Wilches 2007).

2.5.5 What is Not Part of Teachers Autonomy

Researchers have illustrated certain distorted meaning of the term 'Autonomy' which is denoted while discussing the teacher autonomy. There are certain concepts or situations that are not considered as teacher autonomy.

a. Teachers' autonomy does not mean total independence or isolation. Whereas it is denoted as responsibility, mutual support, interdependence, and commitment. The concept of teacher autonomy in isolation are defend educational policies that compel collaborative practices have control over the teachers' tasks and impose homogeneity of teaching and learning depended on standardized curriculum and teaching strategies.
b. Teachers' autonomy does not mean to assign teachers additional responsibilities or duties and consider them as more accountable for their commitments and job. Furthermore, teacher autonomy must not be considered as a strategy to minimize teachers' obligations toward school communities (Wilches 2007). The teachers' autonomy must be considered as the teachers' right to take initiatives and implement their professional practices to maximize the progress of the institutions.
c. Teachers' autonomy should not be claimed as technical, political, or psychological issue or just for the sake of promotion autonomy among students as it has been suggested in many studies. Instead the teacher autonomy involves beliefs, professional competencies for successful control over school matters.
d. Teacher autonomy is not a fixed concept that only some can possess the autonomy and others cannot. Whereas this concept is flexible and changeable that can be different across various domains of teachers' power of decision-making, and it varies and used according to the situational and personal constraints.

e. Teachers' autonomy does not mean as an absolute condition of freedom. It refers to the responsible execution of decision-making within the constraints about the interest and need of the school stakeholders. Researchers who describe teacher autonomy in the resistance to their colleagues and students or see teacher professionalism in terms of their common capability to take decisions without considering other stakeholders of the school, give a wrong perception to their readers and justify the imposed standards and practices that have been criticized in many studies.

2.6 Accountability

Accountability is answerability, blameworthiness, responsibility, and the yearning of record giving (Dykstra 1939). Accountability is the certification and assumption of commitment in regard to exercises, things, decisions, and methodologies including the association, organization, and use within the degree of the part or employment position and wrapping the dedication to report, clear up, and be at risk for occurring results (Mulgan 2000). Accountability implies answering for one's activities, and especially the consequences of those activities. It is a multilayered idea which characterizes a relationship of control between various gatherings, and has an association with trust. Accountability is a social work on seeking after specific purposes, characterized by particular connections and evaluative systems (Ranson 2003).

2.6.1 The Concept of Teacher Accountability

Teachers are focused on giving quality programs and welcome accountability techniques that are successful, genuinely actualized, and that accomplish significant results. Teacher accountability concentrates on both the procedures and results of teaching (Linn and Haug 2002). Teacher accountability implies answering for teacher's activities, and especially the consequences of those academic activities. It characterizes a relationship of control between various factors. Teacher accountability is evaluation of specific teaching purposes (Saha and Dworkin 2009).

2.6.2 Benefits of Teacher Accountability

When somebody chooses to become a teacher, they take the obligation to teach our country's youth. Numerous individuals imagine that inside the educational system, teachers are the ones who are responsible for the improvement and learning advancement of students (Saha and Dworkin 2009). An essential inspiration for expanded accountability is to enhance the framework or parts of it. It is essential to have teacher accountability for (a) better arrangement between open goals and the reasons schools endeavor to accomplish and (b) improved execution with respect to schools, ordinarily characterized by conventional accomplishment criteria (Leithwood and Earl 2000).

2.6.3 Measures of Teachers Accountability

The school and educational authorities may take many measures for teacher accountability, which might include

a. Teacher accountability may be founded on expert showing norms and ought to be sufficiently complex to evaluate showing quality over the continuum of improvement from novice to expert instructor.
b. Accountability might incorporate multifaceted proof of instructor practice, students' learning, and expert commitments that are considered in a coordinated manner, in connection to each other and to the institutional setting. Any appraisals used to gain judgments about students' progress ought to be fitting for the particular curriculum and students who are being educated by that teacher.
c. Assessment ought to be joined by helpful criticism, and associated with expert advancement opportunities that are significant to instructors' objectives and necessities, including formal learning opportunities and peer collaboration, observation, and training.
d. Expert teachers may be made available for the help and review process for new educators and for educators requiring additional help. They can give the extra subject-particular assistance and individual force expected to guarantee that concentrated and successful help is offered and that choices around residency and continuation are very much grounded (Darling-Hammond et al. 2012).

2.6.4 Implications of Teachers Accountability for Teachers Leadership

The only way to make teachers as leaders through accountability demands transforming the responsibility from ruinous and discouraging bookkeeping drills into a productive choice making that enhances educating, learning, and administration in the system of accountability. Teachers may be made proactive in creating students-focused responsibility frameworks. These frameworks catch the numerous parts of showing that test scores do not uncover, they tell the stories behind the numbers. Instructors can make responsibility frameworks that upgrade educator inspiration and lead to huge enhancements in students' accomplishment and value, even in generally low-performing schools. Responsibility for learning discloses how to construct a student-centered responsibility framework by analyzing key pointers in educating, initiative, educational programs, and parent and group contribution. Concentrating on the classroom, it traces instructors to get to be pioneers in responsibility by utilizing a four-stage procedure of observation, reflection, combination, and replication of effective teaching practices (Reeves 2004).

Teachers' autonomy can be perceived as actual capacity to exert control over teaching, evaluation, curriculum development, proper functioning of the school, and professional development practices following the limits of educational goals, approved by the schools and community. This promotion and implementation of autonomy is attributed by strong relationship among personal factors such as teachers' professional awareness, skills, beliefs and dispositions that forms presentation, educational policies, administrative support, working conditions, and interests of all stakeholders of the school that leads the teachers' strong decision making capacity. Teacher accountability is being answerable for the works of a teacher. Both the terms autonomy and accountability are interrelated in the aspect that teachers may be given autonomy to work in their own way, yet being accountable and strive for the teacher leadership on the whole.

Bibliography

Barth, R. S. (1999). *The Teacher Leader*. Providence, RI: The Rhode Island Foundation.
Benson, P. (2000). Autonomy as a learners' and teachers' right. In B. Sinclair, I. McGrath, & T. Lamb (Eds.), *Learner autonomy, teacher autonomy: Future directions*. Harlow, UK: Pearson Education.
Berry, B., Daughtrey, A., & Wieder, A. (2010). Teacher leadership: Leading the way to effective teaching and learning. *Center for Teaching Quality and Teachers Network*.
Blanchard, K. (2007). *Leading at a higher level*. Upper Saddle River, NJ: Prentice Hall.
Bowen, S. A. (2006). Autonomy in communication: Inclusion in strategic management and ethical decision-making, a comparative case analysis. *Journal of Communication Management, 10*(4), 332–352.
Chaleff, I. (2009). *The courageous follower*. San Francisco: Berrett-Koehler Publishers Inc.
Charter School Patterns of Innovation. (2009). Promote Teacher Autonomy and Accountability. *A New Architecture for a New Education*. Ball State University: A Building Better Communities Project.
Danielson, C. (2007). The many faces of leadership. *ASCD, 65*(1), 14–19.
Darling-Hammond, L., Jaquith, A., & Hamilton, M. (2012). *Creating a comprehensive system for evaluating and supporting effective teaching*. Stanford, California: Stanford Center for Opportunity Policy in Education (SCOPE).
Day, C., & Harris, A. (2002). Teacher leadership, reflective practice, and school improvement. In *Second international handbook of educational leadership and administration* (pp. 957–977). Springer Netherlands.
Dykstra, C. A. (1939, February). The quest for responsibility. *American Political Science Review, 33*(1), 1–25. doi:10.2307/1949761.JSTOR1949761
Desurmont, A., Forsthuber, B., & Oberheidt, S. (2008). *Levels of autonomy and responsibilities of teachers in Europe*. Belgium: Eurydice European.

EFEE. (2015). *Professional autonomy, accountability and efficient leadership and the role of employers' organisations, trade unions and school leaders*. Netherlands: European Trade Union Committee for Education.
Frostenson, M. (2015). Autonomy in education three forms of professional autonomy: De-professionalisation of teachers in a new light. *National Journal of Studies in Educational Policy (NordSTEP)*.
Gehrke, N. (1991). *Developing teacher leadership skills* (Vol. 5). ERIC: ERIC Digest.
Harris, A., & Muijs, D. (2005). *Improving schools through teacher leadership*. Open University Press.
Jackson, A., & Stewart, V. (2012). *Teaching and leadership for the twenty-first century the 2012 international summit on the teaching profession*. New York: Pearson Foundation.
Katzenmeyer, M., & Moller, G. (2001). *Awakening the sleeping giant. Helping teachers develop as leaders*. Thousand Oaks, California: Corwin Press.
Kuvaas, B. (2009). A field test of hypotheses derived from selfdetermination determination theory among public sector employees. *Employee Relations, 31*, 39–56.
Kwan, D. (2013). *Senior librarians' perceptions on successful leadership skills: A case study*. United States: ProQuest LLC.
Little, D. (1995). Learning as dialogue: The dependence of learner autonomy on teacher autonomy. *System, 23*, 175–181.
Leithwood, K., & Earl, L. (2000). Educational accountability effects: An international perspective. *Peabody Journal of Education, 75*(4), 1–18.
Linn, R. L., & Haug, C. (2002). The stability of school building scores and gains. *Educational Evaluation and Policy Analysis, 24*(1), 27–36.
McGhan, B. (2002). A fundamental education reform: Teacher-led schools. *Phi Delta Kappan, 83*(7), 538–540.
Moses, I. (2007). Institutional autonomy revisited: Autonomy justified and accounted. *Higher Education Policy, 20*(3), 261–274.
Muijs, D., & Harris, A. (2003). *Teacher leadership: Principles and practice*. Institute of Education, University of Warwick: National College for School Leadership.
Mulgan, Richard. (2000). 'Accountability': An ever-expanding concept? *Public Administration, 78*(3), 555–573. doi:10.1111/1467-9299.00218
Penuel, W. R., Riel, M., Joshi, A., & Pearlman, K. L. (2010). The alignment of the informal and formal organizational supports for reform: Implications for improving teaching in schools. *Educational Administration Quarterly, 46*(1), 5.
Pont, B., Nusche, D., & Moorman, H. (2008). *Improving school leadership, Volume 1: Policy and practice*. France: OECD.
Printy, S. M. (2008). Leadership for teacher learning: A community of practice perspective. *Educational Administration Quarterly, 44*(2), 187–226.
Ranson, S. (2003). Public accountability in the age of neo-liberal governance. *Journal of Educational Policy, 18*(5), 459–480.
Reeves, D. B. (2004). *Accountability for learning: How teachers and school leaders can take charge* (Vol. 160). Alexandria, VA: Association for Supervision and Curriculum Development.
Rothstein, J. (2003). Autonomy or professionalism? *Physical Therapy, 83*, 206–207.
Saha, L. J., & Dworkin, A. G. (2009). *Teachers and teaching in an era of heightened school accountability: A forward look* (pp. 1177–1185). US: Springer.
Shamsi, R. U., Imtinan, K., & Ahad, A. (2010). *Teacher leadership as an approach to school improvement: The case of Pakistan*. VDM Publishing.
Sitch, G. (2005). Professionalism and autonomy: Unbalanced agents of change in the Ontario education system. *Education and Law Journal, 15*(2), 139–155.
Smylie, M. (2010). *Teacher leader model standards teacher leadership exploratory consortium*. United States: teacherleaderstandards.org.

Spence, J. M. (2013). *A phenomenological study of strategies to increase teachers' professional autonomy.* University of Phoenix: ProQuest LLC.
Stoll, L., & Temperley, J. (2009). *Improving school leadership the toolkit.* UK: OECD.
Streshley, W., & Bernd, M. (1992). School reform: Real improvement takes time. *Journal of School Leadership, 2*(3), 320–329.
Thoreau, H. D. (2009). *Teacher leadership skills framwork.* Washington: CSTP.
Wasley, P. A. (1991). *Teachers who lead: The rhetoric of reform and the realities of practice.* New York: Teachers College Press.
Wattleton, F. (2000). *Teachers as leaders.* Retrieved March 8, 2016, from http://www.corwin.com/upm-data/11324_Merideth_Chapter_1.pdf
Wilches, J. U. (2007). Teacher autonomy: A critical review of the research and concept beyond applied linguistics. *Íkala, revista de lenguaje y cultura, 12*(18).

Chapter 3
Sharing School Leadership: Principalship Empowerment or Relegation?

Ismail Hussein Amzat

Abstract In current developments concerning school leadership, the assumption of a single individual taking responsibility for and controlling every single aspect of running a school from the most crucial concern to the most trivial has been put on trial. In the modern approach to school administration, a distributed leadership model is proposed and introduced as a source of empowering teachers towards collective responsibility, creating accountability and developing a sense of encouragement for participating in the decision-making process. However, with the application of these theories in school sectors, the question remains as to whether the implications of sharing or distributing school leadership power were considered when the model was first created. In other words, at a minimum deep deliberation is required during the application due to the potential impacts or repercussions that sharing or distributing leadership and power might have on the role and position of principalship. This paper sheds light on the effectiveness of distribution and shared leadership in a school setting, examining the level of power to be shared, and the extent of trust and professional training given to teachers prior to power distribution.

3.1 Introduction

During the past few decades, leadership was believed to be an art from trait leadership perspective and to be a science from a behavioural perspective. In the present time, researchers have placed an emphasis on the critical role that school leadership plays in school improvement and student productivity. Empirically, they all have concluded that a great principal stands at the helm of every successful school. Many studies have ranked school leadership as second in importance only to teacher quality (Hechinger 2011). Hattie (2003), Leithwood et al. (2006), Tooley (2009), Day et al. (2009, 2010), New Leaders for New Schools (2009),

I.H. Amzat (✉)
School of Education and Modern, Languages, Universiti Utara Malaysia, Changlun, Malaysia
e-mail: ihussein@uum.edu.my

and Barber et al. (2010), as cited by England (2012), have all confirmed that school leadership plays a second crucial role in student learning outcomes. In a joint report of the National Association of Secondary School Principals and the National Association of Elementary School Principals in the United States called *Leadership Matters*, school leadership was considered second to classroom instruction among all school-related factors that contribute to what students learn at school.

Those findings and reports show the importance of school leadership on teaching and learning. Due to the rapid changes in our today's world, the scope of principalship has widened and new portfolios have been added, especially on issues related to instruction. Fresh demands for new instructional leadership have arisen due to the awakening of globalization as well as with respect to socioeconomic and technology advancements (Ylimaki 2014a). Hence, change is about school principals going beyond their traditional instructional leadership to create a data-driven instructional system to guide the practices of teaching and learning (Halverson et al. 2007).

Those changes require school leaders to step out from behind their managerial desks and go beyond traditional instructional leadership roles by setting new, comprehensive and coherent curriculum aligned with professional standards (Ylimaki 2014b); sustaining a culture of collaboration (O'Connor et al. 2014); and creating a motivating learning environment (Ylimaki 2014b). This change also calls for new supervision of instruction (Burke and St. Maurice 2014); developing assessment and accountability systems to monitor student progress (Ylimaki 2014b); increasing the instructional leadership capacity of staff (Hackney and Henderson 2014); promoting the most effective technology to support teaching and learning (Dikkers 2014); and monitoring the impacts of instructional programs (Brunderman and Dugan 2014). Responding promptly and actively to these new calls and demands at school will definitely put the effectiveness of school leaders on trial and will call for them to evaluate critically their leadership roles in today's modern era.

Meanwhile, many studies around the world have shown the advantage of shared leadership and encouraged the distribution of power due to the complexity of today's educational setting. To deal with complexity, several substantial theories and models have been developed and introduced including distributed leadership, collective leadership, team leadership, horizontal leadership and substitute leadership. Dispersed leadership is another newly introduced leadership theory. This theory shares the same characteristics and features with the rest by advocating the diffusion of leadership and power to all organizational members instead of depending on a single official or formal leader. Self-management of the organization is the most apt term to describe this leadership (Warner 2012). Self-management shares the same meaning with shared and distributed leadership theories because self-management exerts leadership influence at all levels in the organization and in all roles (Bolden et al. 2003).

These theories and models share almost the same meanings, objectives and functions. They have very strong links, and some are even used interchangeably. Hence, their main focus is in general is to empower self-leadership among organizational members and reduce the tasks of organizational leadership (Lunenburg 2010a). Shared leadership is linked with distributed leadership for broad leadership distribution among teams (Bolden 2011). Shared leadership is assumed to open the boundaries of leadership (Bennett et al. 2003) and duties and responsibilities are shared (Kocolowski 2010). The same is true with respect to transformational leadership, which transforms an organization and inspires people in an organization to be self-dependent.

Notwithstanding, their similarities in functions, the power and benefits that these theories and models have for organizational improvement, especially in terms of distributed and shared leadership in terms of task delegation, sharing, autonomy, collectivity and accountability, is undeniable. A distribution of power throughout the school system is recommended by many studies to improve student learning outcomes (Humphreys 2010).

Within this context, some serious questions have been posted about this distribution of power. These questions include: Whose interests are being served by particular distributions? Are all distributions intended to enhance teaching and learning? It is possible that distributed leadership could support the abuse of power? (Maxcy and Nguyen 2006; Mayrowetz 2008; Humphreys 2010). These are critical questions that need answers, and even further debates are required to warrant the application of these theories and models especially in education sectors.

But, given the scenarios of who is in control under shared and distributed leadership, this current work has mainly focused on shared and distributed leadership and sets out to ask and discuss: (1) to what extent can leadership and responsibility be shared with teachers?, (2) if sharing is inevitable, in which situations or occasions should power or leadership be shared and distributed?, (3) as shared and distributed leadership paves the way for participation, should there be various levels of teacher participation in the decision-making?, (4) as prerequisites, what are the levels of teachers' preparedness for handling external pressures, challenges, expectations and responsibilities? and (5) what is the adequacy of the professional development training that they have obtained? As monitoring teaching and instruction is the core business of every school principal, taking or sharing this role might undermine the principalship role as the sole instructional leader. This work ends with the belief that teachers should be empowered and encouraged to share leadership and responsibility, but not at the expense of school principal's position.

3.2 Shared Leadership Effectiveness and Implications

Relentless efforts have been made to develop concepts to unify shared leadership definitions but achieving this objective has tended to be elusive. One reason, according to Kocolowski (2010) in his meta-survey of leadership studies, is that, although research using shared studies is abundant in healthcare and education, studies outside these two fields are scarce. Kocolowski said (p. 24) that the most widely cited definition of shared leadership comes from Conger and Pearce (2003), who said that shared leadership is "A dynamic, interactive influence process among individuals in groups for which the objective is to lead one another to the achievement of group or organizational goals or both" (p. 1).

Shared leadership is considered to be a relative new paradigm, shifting leadership from a formal leader to followers by sharing power and involving in decision-making. Based on his review of the relevant literature, Kocolowski wrote that shared leadership generally might be defined operationally as:

> a dynamic, collaborative process (Conger and Pearce 2003) whereby influence is distributed (Carson et al. 2007) amongst a plurality of networked individuals, often referred to as teams, for the purpose of achieving beneficial outcomes for the organization. Characteristics of shared leadership teams include decentralized interaction, collective task completion, reciprocal support and skill development (Wood 2005), shared purpose, and a unified voice (Carson et al.), all enhanced via social interaction that involves mutual accountability, partnership, equity, and ownership (Jackson 2000).

According to Goldsmith (2010) in an article in the *Harvard Business Review*, shared leadership is defined as utilizing all of the human resources in an organization by giving opportunities to individuals in their areas of expertise and developing a sense of empowerment to assume leadership roles.

All these definitions indicate that the shared leadership model reduces the complexity of a single individual's position by sharing power and accountability. This model has been reported to help in developing a team with one common goal, namely, improving learning.

Shared leadership can be defined in educational setting as a collaboration of a school principal with teachers, staff, students and parents to face school challenges. It creates a sense of partnership by asking everyone to contribute to a school climate and each person to be responsible for his or her own actions (Hughes and Pickeral 2013). Traditional theorists, such as Robert Greenleaf on Servant Leadership, Victor Vroom on Expectancy Theory, Douglas McGregor on X and Y Theory, Paul Hersey and Ken Blanchard on Situational Theory, and James MacGregor Burns and Bernard Bass on Transformation Theory state that, if employees are intrinsically motivated and empowered, they will be honest and perform well for the organization while taking responsibilities rather than managers solely caring for these responsibilities. In their works and writings, they highlighted the importance of followers' involvement in the decision-making process and organizational success (Ensley et al. 2006a).

Thus, the following questions may now be asked. To what extent teachers are equipped with decision-making skills and knowledge? What is the level of their experiences in being involved in such kind of decisions? How many decision-making processes they have been involved in and what are the outcomes of the decisions they involved in? What outcomes have they generated from these decisions and what decision outcomes have they derived from these processes?

The Wallace Foundation which is a New York-based philanthropy whose charge is foster improved learning and enrichment for children sought answers to these questions. In a report, issued in 2010, entitled *Learning from Leadership: Investigating the Links to Improved Student Learning*, the Foundation recommended that the distribution of leadership include teachers, parents, and district staff in order to improve student achievement (p. 103). Among the other key findings were that:

1. An investment in the professional development of school leaders had limited effects on student achievement unless districts also developed clear goals for improvement (p. 145);
2. Planned aligned patterns of distributed leadership seemed more likely to contribute the most to school improvement efforts (p. 177);
3. Priorities included instructional and curriculum leadership, and teamwork and shared leadership focused on improvement objectives (p. 215);
4. Principals were most effective when they saw themselves as working collaboratively towards clear, common goals with district personnel, other principals and teachers; and
5. When leadership is distributed or shared between teachers and principals, teachers'working relationships with each another are stronger and student achievement is higher (p. 282).

3.3 Shared, Vertical and Transformational Leadership: Clash of Theories

In an organization in which leadership numerous theories and styles are incorporated, noticeable clashes of shared leadership can exist with respect to other models and theories in terms of functions, practices and objectives. Vertical leadership functions are said to be difficult to implement when shared leadership is present (Mielonen 2011), but some studies in the United States have reported that shared leadership predicts team effectiveness better than vertical leadership (Pearce and Sims 2002; Pearce et al. 2004; Ensley et al. 2006b; Sui-Yi 2012). However, shared leadership is much most complex and time consuming than vertical leadership (Burke 2006) and less effective when teams have low performance. With respect to maintaining organizational structure and hierarchy, shared leadership might be less effective as organizational hierarchy is crucial in sustaining organization management success and performance.

According to Routhieaux (2015), an organizational culture may pose a big threat to the application of shared leadership. Organizational culture impacts organizational decision-making and a culture of sharing leadership and power might work effectively in one organization and less effectively in another. An organization that has a culture of shared leadership will enjoy the fruits of collective efforts and collaborative process of information while sharing leadership could be very difficult to apply in an organization that has a long history and culture of executive directors making all major decisions.

If leadership must be shared, then all types of vertical leadership, including transformational, transactional, servant, moral, and instructional, among others, must also be shared. As emphasized in earlier theories and models, the question arises as to whether workers or followers who are intrinsically motivated have obtained the necessary skills and professional development training to qualify for a new post. Consequently, the issue of power sharing between leader and follower has caused confusion and unsettled feelings among some scholars. Adding to this concern is that groups may be performing well when they are motivated, experienced, knowledgeable, but do not have a formal leadership structure (Manz and Sims 1984; Ensley et al. 2006a). In reality, this sharing of leadership, power and authority could be understood or seen as a process of relegating formal leadership structure and the communizing of authority. As a result, organization members, teams and followers may lose their purposes, suffering from a less clear vision of the organization and duties.

Philosophically, the belief is often that, if there is no leader, there is no rule. No matter the success or effectiveness of shared leadership, a formal leader is still needed to empower self-leadership among members due to the functions of leadership for influencing, guiding, empowering and controlling others to find the correct path while assuring organizational goals are achieved. A harmful situation may arise in a situation in which an official leader is viewed as redundant and insignificant due to leadership-sharing among members. This state of affairs could backfire and lead to chaos as well as personal issues involved in managing the organization and decision-making.

Pintor (2013) has called for caution in using shared or team leadership, as not all teams or situations are suitable for shared leadership. She recommended that shared leadership be used in situations full of complexity and when interdependent tasks exist for which a group of workers may be dependent on other groups; in creative situations or when alternative ideas are needed; for highly committed employees; and in instances in which the task is not urgent. Other than these situations, she warned against applying shared leadership, as sharing might delay task completion and aggravate conflicts between team members.

3.4 Shared Leadership: Implications for the Group Decision-Making Process

The consolidation of significant findings on the effectiveness of shared decisions-making indicates that, although shared leadership promotes teamwork practices in an organization, at the same time, the application of team-based knowledge work has been reported to have less effect on team work performance (Ashley 1992; Verespej 1990; Bligh et al. 2006). Thus, teams are often reported to fail due to their inabilities to live up to their capabilities, the failure to coordinate the actions and behaviours of team members, and the absence of proper leadership guidelines (Burke et al. 2003; Bligh et al. 2006).

In addition, the findings on shared leadership and team effectiveness in educational settings have shown mixed results, as shared leadership sometimes only helps in terms of monitoring group works without increasing their performance (Carte et al. 2006). For example, in Tasmanian schools, school leaders prefer interacting with each other more than interacting with teachers (Boardman 2001; Hall 2001; Kocolowski 2010), while in contrast, teachers were found to be manipulated and unhappy in New Zealand primary schools when their voices were not heard after involvement in decision-making (Court 2003). These inconsistencies may lead to a call for caution in sharing leadership in educational sectors. Nonetheless, sharing responsibility for power and leadership with teachers as well as staff is often advisable and recommended for boosting their talents, allowing a sense of belonging, and permitting accountability to flourish. But this sharing must be justified, as peoples' feelings cannot be ignored, and group members should know their limits and rules and not abuse the complexity surrounding shared leadership (Hall 2001; Kocolowski 2010).

Likewise, when decisions are carried out by means of consensus, such consensus could possibly be difficult to reach and, as a result, a decision might be delayed (Miles and Watkins 2007). The participation of workers in decision-making may pose a dilemma for any organizational decision when problems of team attitudes, internal battles and individual career goals are present (Jackson 2000). In such a critical situation, according to Miles and Watkins (2007), relevance for power and leadership sharing does not exist, especially when ideas that differ among participants are irreconcilable and thus might hinder decision-making and continuous progress (Kocolowski 2010). In addition to this, dealing with daily changes in an organization, it calls for quick action of the management and plans must executed without delay. The questions that arise then are: how long will an organization's management wait to reach a consensus in decision-making? To what extent has the organization eliminated the differences between workers and internal problems that could hamper organizational decisions and performance?

Nonetheless, in cases of participative decision-making, an employee's participation in decision-making often leads to improved creativity (Zubair et al. 2015). Participation in decision-making has been reported to affect job satisfaction, employee performance, organizational productivity, employee motivation and organizational commitment (Alutto and Belasco 1972; Agwu and Olele 2014; Zubair et al. 2015) and has been reported to have a strong relationship with employee motivation (Irawanto 2015). However, in some instances in which everyone is allowed to participate in making a decision, some authors believe that consistency in making decisions is difficult to achieve. According to Gunnarsson (2010), Lunenburg (2010b), and Schoenfeld (2011), group decision-making is subject to social pressure towards conformity, individual domination, conflicts, conflicting between primary and secondary goals, unwanted compromises, ambiguous responsibility and increased time consumption.

Looking at this issue from a psychological perspective, human beings are different, and each human has different internal or personal values. As a result, each teacher also has different instincts, behaviours, attitudes, competences, personality and backgrounds that he or she bring to his or her respective schools, which potentially could influence decisions. For example, if a worker or staff member is not in good terms with the top management or principal and personal feelings, issues, hostilities and differences exist between them, a possibility exists that decision-making can become personal and that favouritism, arguments and rancorous situations may eventually jeopardize organizational productivity. Shared or distributed leadership in relationship to involvement in decision-making is reported to be successful when a group of workers has great relevant knowledge and the skills and the abilities to contribute, and this involvement should be limited to specific situations (Ensley et al. 2006b). Pearce's (1997) research supports this notion while contextualizing what should and should not be shared.

At this stage, forward and continuous research needs to be conducted on the outcomes of shared decision-making. Perhaps before sharing decision-making, research should examine how team members work and join together to formulate leadership in the team context and the development of members and leadership as time goes by. In addition, if teamwork and participation in decision-making are successful, can shared leadership and decision-making be successful when it comes to organizational policy formulation? Also, to what extent can managerial posts be shared? Moreover, when power is shared with co-workers and the team members, directly or indirectly, they tend act as leaders themselves, and apparently the assigned leader may lose momentum. This issue of moving power to co-workers and team members without referring to a particular leader must be researched and examined in terms of effectiveness when power is relinquished to team members (Crevani et al. 2007, 2010; Friedrich et al. 2009).

3.5 Distributed Leadership Effectiveness and Its Implications

The concept of distributed leadership is considered an old one (see Humphreys 2010 for a more complete discussion). In 1984, Murgatroyd and Reynolds stated that the position of leadership is not meant for a formal organizational leader and can take place at any level depending on the situation (see also, Law and Glover 2003). As years have gone by, this concept has become well established and teacher leadership has become a well-developed and promoted practice (Devaney 1987; Lieberman 1988; Wiess and Cambone 1994; Louis et al. 1996; Wheatley 1999). To date, Spillane (2006), Duignan (2006) have greatly contributed to the enlightenment of the concept of distributed leadership throughout their remarkable works, even though they have different concepts and understanding of distributed leadership. Nonetheless, both have agreed that distributed leadership plays big role in teaching and learning as well as that distributed leadership engages all members of the school community, not just the principal and deputy principal (see Humphreys 2010, for a more complete list of their contributions).

This leadership is of the type that appeals to the concept of togetherness, teamwork and cooperation among teachers to collectively assume responsibility and accountability in their works at school. Still, sometimes or practically speaking, successful interaction among teachers is difficult to accomplish and not always that easy to achieve as the concept of teamwork among teachers leads to the concept of "teacher leaders" (Humphreys 2010). Conway (1976, 1984), Conway and Calzi (1996), Smylie (1994), York-Barr and Duke (2004; cited in Mayrowetz 2008), uncertainty remains at to whether shared or democratic leadership can lead to school improvement. Correspondingly, scholars and researchers around the world also have expressed their doubts about the effectiveness of distributed leadership in educational settings. Distributed leadership has been opposed in terms of efficiency, effectiveness and being unable to add to school improvement despite its advantages (Humphreys 2010). In addition, the final report of research to the Wallace Foundation (2010) also indicated that leadership can be distributed depending on what is to be accomplished and the availability of professional expertise. The report further stated that no single pattern of distributed leadership is consistently related to student learning. Therefore, the report concluded that, "while there are many sources of leadership in schools, principals remain the central source" (p. 54).

Additionally, Leithwood and Jantzi (1998) have reported about finding less student engagement when power is shared or distributed among school principals and teachers. Timperley (2005) concluded that a risk in distributing leadership exists that could lead to incompetence when leadership is distributed. Despite Harris's (2004) great support of the distributed leadership approach, some difficulties she outlined apply to distributed leadership in the school sector. These include cultural barriers and the competition for power or position in a school that create an environment unconducive to disagreement between the young and old in terms of freedom of expression. In reality, these difficulties could pose a threat to a school entity. These are strong reasons why leadership should not be completely distributed and power totally shared, as school principals are answerable for whatever happens in the schools. School principals should be solely in control of the school and distributing or relinquishing power could leave the school weakened and uncontrollable, especially when it comes to financing, legal and human resource issues, as well school administration (OECD 2008; Humphreys 2010).

New research by Harris (2012) has evidenced the importance of the school principal in the application of distributed leadership. She highlighted that distributed leadership should take place properly and be fostered in a school when there is support of the principal. She argued further that principals play an important part in the teacher-leadership equation and in bringing distributed leadership alive in schools. However, she conceptualized distributed leadership for principals as allowing necessary change to occur in their leadership position by "letting go" or "passing on" some authority and power to teachers and staff. However, Wright (2008) advised caution despite the shift of leadership paradigm when applying distributed leadership. Hatcher (2005) reported that improper execution of distributed leadership or its implementation in a "top-down" approach could lead to misinterpretation, wrong delegation, and coercion of distributed leadership. It is also highly debated that less attention is paid to the roles, responsibilities or situations in the exercise of leadership by a formal leader in Spillane's (2006) distributed framework. With these trajectories, it is ethically and professionally unfair to hold principals accountable for their actions and school performance when legislation and policies defining their roles as school principals are ignored (Wright 2008).

3.6 Research Implication for Future Practices

This work shares some vital implications for the application of shared and distributed leadership in a school setting. Caution is required for adopting the shared leadership model in a school setting, especially when teachers are not well trained to lead, lack instructional leadership skills or are in a situation in which the organizational focus is unclear. Nevertheless, shared and distributed leadership could definitely improve teamwork and promote self-leadership among the people in an organization that is full of complexity if the application is well planned. Distributed leadership is widely acknowledged and empirically shown around the world to instil a sense of collectiveness and encourage teachers and staff to embrace leadership roles and practices. The theory has currently gained much attention in educational settings and lately its effectiveness has been reported to improve school leadership practices.

However, confronted with rapid changes and demands for new instructional leadership model, sharing school leadership without strong preparation or orientation is fragile. Distribution of power without cutting-edge professional development training for teachers makes implementing it even more of a balancing act in practice. The newness of the distributed leadership model in the educational sector perhaps could be one reason why some educational policy-makers and principals remain sceptical of relinquishing power or recommending total distribution. Additionally, some authors and researchers in the literature have debated the level of power and leadership that should be shared and distributed.

In spite of these debates and scepticism, shared and distributed leadership models have provided a new definition of leadership, meaning duties and practices. But due to the different implications given and the strong cautions of authors and researchers on this issue, some limitations to the power and leadership are present. Hence, more research is needed to specific outline areas, powers, duties, responsibilities that are potentially for sharing and levels in leadership and decision-making that are allowed for distribution and involvement without degrading the principalship position as an authorized leader or rendering him or her ineffective as a formal leader.

3.7 Conclusion

This work had several objectives. First, this work aimed to give credibility to shared and distributed leadership and the collective roles that such leadership played in achieving organizational goals, empowering workers, especially school teachers, the effectiveness of teamwork and productivity. Second, the work posed several questions on the level of leadership and power that should be shared as well as the context in which it should be shared. It discusses the need for further research in applying shared and distributed leadership successfully, especially in educational sectors. Thus, this paper argues that enhancements in shared leadership should occur without undermining a school principal's position, which at the end could render him or her redundant or powerless.

Unconditionally, the progress and success of a school should not solely rest on shared or distributed leadership. This means that we should not completely believe or conceptualize that a school cannot progress or perform better without leadership and that power sharing is the ultimate solution. On the other hand, other major factors also contribute highly and significantly to a school's success and performance. One critical element is school instructional supervision. This factor fits within the role that a school principal plays in the continuous professional development (CPD) of teachers to improve teaching and learning and is a factor, according to Leithwood et al. (2004), that is second only to classroom instruction in its impact on learning.

An effective school leader always makes a difference in terms of teaching. An effective principal does not always expect a teacher to join forces or always seek help from a teacher before he or she leads the school or perform his or her duties. Although principals do not directly influence learning, indirectly they influence learning through practicing high-quality instructional leadership, supporting teacher professional development and providing a conducive climate for teaching and learning. These are the critical values that an effective school leader must exhibit, which cannot be shared or distributed. Rarely are such values and determinations found in a situation in which leadership and responsibility are shared or distributed. This rarity could be due to the preferences and reservations of everyone brought into an organization, which, as a result, could have significant impacts on organizational practices, decisions and operations.

In light of this, it is likely impossible for all employees, whether new or old, to possess adequate skills, prior knowledge and training in leadership and strategic management. Besides, the assumption can be made that not all of them would like to take upon themselves, the challenge of becoming leaders on their own, taking accountability, or having an appetite for power. From a pragmatic perspective, leadership posts are full of temptations and self-leadership requires strong human beings possessing responsibility and accountability. In some circumstances, some might not want to be independent or want to be a self-leader, perhaps due to additional work, self-responsibility and self-accountability that come along with the duties. In some schools, however, teachers might opt to take self-leadership roles due to workload and complexity in teaching. Hence, they might opt out for autonomy for the accountability that is attached with it.

Notably, this paper has neither disputed the effectiveness of shared and distributed leadership nor denied their application. Shared and distributed leadership can be the impetus for teacher motivation and a force for empowerment. This work, as part of the requirements for successful self-leadership, seeks a teacher's physical, mental, and spiritual preparedness. Forcing teachers or staff to lead without their readiness may sometimes yield positive results and empowerment, but it also might boomerang. Some may grasp the power gracefully and develop a strong leading practice, while some may perhaps fall short in coping with challenges under shared —and distributed leadership circumstances. Surprisingly, some may take up the challenge as an opportunity for empowerment, while some may look at it in an opposite way.

This work has contributed significantly to the issue of power sharing and leadership distribution in education. It has developed new arguments that need to be tabled, a topic that needs to be debated and questions that need serious answers, especially in the school sector, concerning when power should be shared and leadership should be distributed. This paper calls for additional forward-thinking research examining at which level teachers should be involved in the school decision-making process. It calls for an extensive examination of decision effectiveness when group members of school staff are involved. It contemplates the role of a formal or appointed leader when power and leadership are distributed and shared. At the present time, this theory is still in its infancy, especially in educational settings. This conclusion agrees with researchers around the world in the field of education who have called for further empirical work on the development of theories and models of shared leadership to allow for their proper application in educational settings.

References

Agwu, M. O., & Olele, H. E. (2014). Perception survey of employees participation in decision making and organizational productivity in Julius Berger Nigeria PLC Bonny Island. *British Journal of Economics, Management & Trade, 4,* 620–637.

Alutto, J. A., & Belasco, J. A. (1972). A typology for participation in organizational decision making. *Administrative Science Quarterly, 17*(1), 117–125.

Ashley, S. (1992). US quality improves but Japan still leads (study by Ernst & Young and American Quality Foundation). *Mechanical Engineering, 24,* 114–126.

Bennett, N., Wise, C., Woods, P. A., & Harvey, J. A. (2003). Distributed leadership: A review of literature. National College for School Leadership. *Open Research Online.* Retrieved from http://oro.open.ac.uk/8534/

Bligh, M. C., Pearce, C. L., & Kohles, J. C. (2006). The importance of self-and shared leadership in team based knowledge work: A meso-level model of leadership dynamics. *Journal of Managerial Psychology, 21*(4), 296–318.

Boardman, M. (2001). The value of shared leadership: Tasmanian teachers' and leaders' differing views. *International Studies in Educational Administration, 29*(3), 2.

Bolden, R. (2011). Distributed leadership in organizations: A review of theory and research. *International Journal of Management Reviews, 13*(3), 251–269.

Bolden, R., Gosling, J., Marturano, A., & Dennison, P. (2003). *A review of leadership theory and competency frameworks.* Exeter, England. University of Exeter, Centre for Leadership Studies. Retrieved from http://www2.fcsh.unl.pt/docentes/luisrodrigues/textos/Lideran%C3%A7a.pdf

Brunderman, L., & Dugan, T. (2014). Monitor and evaluate the impact of the instructional program. In R. M. Ylimaki (Ed.), *The new instructional leadership* (pp. 168–186). New York: Routledge and University Council for Educational Administration (UCEA).

Burke, C. S., Fiore, S. M., & Salas, E. (2003). The role of shared cognition in enabling shared leadership and team adaptability. In C. L. Pearce & J. A. Conger (Eds.), *Shared leadership: Reframing the hows and whys of leadership* (pp. 103–122). Thousand Oaks, CA: Sage.

Burke, P., & St. Maurice, H. (2014). Supervise instruction. In R. M. Ylimaki (Ed.), *The new instructional leadership* (pp. 61–85). New York: Routledge and University Council for Educational Administration (UCEA).

Carson, J. B., Tesluk, P. E., & Marrone, J. A. (2007). Shared leadership in teams: An investigation of antecedent conditions and performance. *Academy of Management Journal, 50*(5), 1217–1234.

Carte, T. A., Chidambaram, L., & Becker, A. (2006). Emergent leadership in self-managed virtual teams: A longitudinal study of concentrated and shared leadership behaviors. *Group Decision and Negotiation, 15*(4), 323–343.

Conger, J. A., & Pearce, C. L. (2003). A landscape of opportunities: Future research in shared leadership. In C. L. Pearce & J. A. Conger (Eds.), *Shared leadership* (pp. 285–303). Thousand Oaks, CA: Sage.

Conway, J. A. (1976, March). Test of linearity between teachers' participation in decision making and their perceptions of their schools as organizations. *Administrative Science Quarterly, 21*(1), 130–139.

Conway, J. M. (1984). The myth, mystery, and mastery of participatory decision making in education. *Administrative Science Quarterly, 20*(3), 11–40.

Conway, J., & Calzi, C. (1996). The dark side of shared leadership. *Educational Leadership, 53*(4), 45–49.

Court, M. (2003). Towards democratic leadership: Co-principal initiatives. *International Journal of Leadership in Education, 6*(2), 161.

Crevani, L., Lindgren, M., & Packendorff, J. (2007). Shared leadership: A post-heroic perspective on leadership as a collective construction. *International Journal of Leadership Studies, 3*(1), 40–67.

Crevani, L., Lindgren, M., & Packendorff, J. (2010). Leadership, not leaders: On the study of leadership as practices and interactions. *Scandinavian Journal of Management, 26*(1), 77–86.

Devaney, K. (1987). *The lead teacher: Ways to begin.* New York: Carnegie Forum on Education and the Community.

Dikkers, S. M. (2014). Promote the use of the most effective and appropriate technologies to support teaching and learning. In R. M. Ylimaki (Ed.), *The new instructional leadership* (pp. 147–167). New York: Routledge and University Council for Educational Administration (UCEA).

Duignan, P. (2006). *Ethical leadership: Key challenges and tensions.* Melbourne: Cambridge University Press.

Ensley, M. D., Hmieleski, K. M., & Pearce, C. L. (2006a). The importance of vertical and shared leadership within new venture top management teams: Implications for the performance of startups. *Leadership Quarterly, 17*(3), 217–231.

Ensley, M. D., Hmieleski, K. M., & Pearce, C. L. (2006b). The importance of vertical and shared leadership within new venture top management teams: Implications for the performance of startups. *Leadership Quarterly, 17*(3), 217–231.

England, S. (2012). The importance of leadership in high-performing schools. *Curriculum Leadership Journal, 10*(16). Retrieved from http://www.curriculum.edu.au/leader/vol_10_no_16,35632.html?issueID=12676

Final Report of Research to the Wallace Foundation. (2010). *Learning from leadership project: Investigating the links to improved student learning*. University of Minnesota, University of Toronto & Wallace Foundation. Retrieved from http://conservancy.umn.edu/bitstream/handle/11299/140885/Learning-from-Leadership_Final-Research-Report_July-2010.pdf?sequence=1&isAllowed=y

Friedrich, T. L., Vessey, W. B., Schuelke, M. J., Ruark, G. A., & Mumford, M. D. (2009). A framework for understanding collective leadership: The selective utilization of leader and team expertise within networks. *The Leadership Quarterly, 20*(6), 933–958.

Goldsmith, M. (2010). Leadership: Sharing leadership to maximize talent. *Harvard Business Review*. Retrieved from https://hbr.org/2010/05/sharing-leadership-to-maximize

Gunnarsson, M. (2010). *Group decision making*. Frederick, MD: Verlag.

Hall, V. (2001). Management teams in education: An unequal music. *School Leadership & Management, 21*(3), 327–341.

Hackney, C., & Henderson, J. (2014). Develop the instructional and leadership capacity of staff. In R. M. Ylimaki (Ed.), *The new instructional leadership* (pp. 107–123). New York: Routledge and University Council for Educational Administration (UCEA).

Halverson, H., Grigg, J., Pritchett, R., & Thoma, C. (2007). The new instructional leadership: Creating data-driven instructional systems in school. *Journal of School Leadership, 17*(2), 59–194.

Harris, A. (2004). Distributed leadership and school Improvement: Leading or misleading? *Educational Management Administration and Leadership, 32*(1), 11–24. doi:10.1177/1741143204039297

Harris, A. (2012). Distributed leadership: Implications for the role of the principal. *Journal of Management Development, 31*(1), 7–17.

Hatcher, R. (2005). The distribution of leadership and power in schools. *British Journal of Sociology of Education, 26*(2), 253–267.

Hattie, J. (2003). *Teachers make a difference: What is the research difference?* Retrieved February 2, 2005, from http://www.acer.edu.au/workshops/documents/Teachers_Make_a_Difference_Hattie.pdf

Hechinger (2011). *School Leadership: Why school leadership matters*. Hechinger Report. Retrieved from http://hechingerreport.org/why-school-leadership-matters/

Hughes, W., & Pickeral, T. (2013). *School climate and shared leadership*. National School Climate Center (NSCC). Retrieved from https://www.schoolclimate.org/publications/documents/sc-brief-leadership.pdf

Humphreys, E. (2010). *Distributed leadership and its implication on teaching and learning*. Unpublished doctoral dissertation, NIU Maynooth University, Kildare, Ireland. Retrieved from http://eprints.maynoothuniversity.ie/2041/1/Distributed_Leadership_Ed_D_Thesis_%28EH%29_May_2010~2.doc.pdf

Irawanto, D. W. (2015). Employee participation in decision-making: Evidence from a state owned enterprise in Indonesia. *Management, 20*(1), 159–172.

Jackson, S. (2000). A qualitative evaluation of shared leadership barriers, drivers and recommendations. *Journal of Management in Medicine, 14*(3/4), 166–178.

Kocolowski, M. D. (2010). Shared Leadership: Is it time for a change? *Emerging Leadership Journeys, 3*(1), 22–32.

Law, S., & Glover, D. (2003). *Educational leadership and learning: Practice, policy and research*. Buckingham, United Kingdom: Open University Press.

Leithwood, K., & Jantzi, D. (1998). *Distributed leadership and student engagement in school*. Paper presented at the annual meeting of the American Educational Research Association, San Diego, April 13–17.

Leithwood., K., Louis, K.S., Anderson, S., & Wahlstrom, K. (2004). *How leadership influences student learning*. New York: The Wallace Foundation. Retrieved from http://www.wallacefoundation.org/knowledge-center/Documents/How-Leadership-Influences-Student-Learning.pdf

Lieberman, A. (1988). Teachers and principals: Turf, tension, and new tasks. *Phi Delta Kappa, 6* (9), 648–653.
Louis, K. S., Marks, H. M., & Kruse, S. (1996). Teachers' professional community in restructuring schools. *American Educational Research Journal, 33*(4), 757–798.
Lunenburg, F. C. (2010a). Substitutes for leadership theory: Implications for university faculty. *Focus on Colleges, Universities and Schools, 4*(1), 1–5.
Lunenburg, F. C. (2010b). Group decision making. *National Forum of Teacher Education Journal, 20*(3), 1–7.
Manz, C. C., & Sims, H. P. (1984). Searching for the "unleader": Organizational member views on leading self-managed groups. *Human Relations, 37*(5), 409–424.
Maxcy, B. D., & Nguyen, T. S. (2006). The politics of distributing leadership: Reconsidering leadership distribution in two Texas elementary schools. *Educational Policy, 20*(1), 163–196.
Mayrowetz, D. (2008). Making sense of distributed leadership: Exploring the multiple usages of the concept in the field. *Educational Administration Quarterly, 44*(3), 424–435.
Mielonen, J. (2011). *Making sense of shared leadership: A case study of leadership processes and practices without formal leadership structure in the team context*. Acta Universitatis Lappeenrantaensis (Unpublished doctoral dissertation). Lappeenranta University of Technology, Lappeenranta, Finland. Retrieved from http://www.doria.fi/bitstream/handle/10024/72459/isbn%209789522651655.pdf
Miles, S. A., & Watkins, M. D. (2007). The leadership team: Complementary strengths or conflicting agendas? *Harvard Business Review, 85*(4), 90–98.
Murgatroyd, S. J., & Reynolds, D. (1984). Leadership and the teacher. In P. Harling (Ed.), *New directions in educational leadership*. London: Falmer Press.
O'Connor, B. H., Stevens, V. A., & Gonzalez, N. (2014). Nurture and sustain a culture of collaboration, trust, learning, and high expectations. In R. M. Ylimaki (Ed.), *The new instructional leadership* (pp. 10–26). New York: Routledge and University Council for Educational Administration (UCEA).
OECD (2008) *Improving school leadership policy and practice*. Retrieved from https://www.oecd.org/edu/school/49847132.pdf
Pearce, C. L., & Sims, H. P. (2002). The relative influence of vertical cs. Shared leadership on the longitudinal effectiveness of change management teams. *Group Dynamics: Theory, Research, and Practice, 6*(2), 172–197.
Pearce, C. L., Yoo, Y., & Alavi, M. (2004). Leadership, social work and virtual teams: The relative influence of vertical vs. shared leadership in the nonprofit sector. In R. E. Riggio, & S. Smith-Orr (Eds.), *Improving leadership in nonprofit organizations* (pp. 180–203). San Francisco, CA: Jossey-Bass.
Pearce, C. L. (1997). *The determinants of change management team (CMT) effectiveness: A longitudinal investigation* (Unpublished doctoral dissertation). University of Maryland, College Park, Maryland.
Pintor, S. (2013). *When is sharing leadership in teams effective?* The Paul Merage School of Business. Retrieved from http://merage.uci.edu/ResearchAndCenters/CLTD/Resources/Documents/%5B612%5DPintor_Sandra__When%20is%20Sharing%20Leadership%20in%20Teams%20Effective_2013.pdf
Routhieaux, R. L. (2015). Shared leadership and its implications for nonprofit leadership. *Journal of Nonprofit Education and Leadership, 5*(3), 139–152.
Schoenfeld, A. H. (2011). *How we think: A theory of goal-oriented decision making and its educational applications*. New York: Routledge.
Smylie, M. A. (1994). Redesigning teachers' work: Connections to the classroom. In L. Darling-Hammond (Ed.), *Review of Research in Education, 20* (pp. 129–177). Washington DC: American Educational Research Association.
Spillane, J. P. (2006). *Distributed leadership*. San Francisco, CA: Jossey-Bass.
Sui-Yi, C. (2012). *Exploring the implications of vertical and shared leadership for team effectiveness in retail shops in Hong Kong*. A thesis submitted for the degree of Doctor of

Business Administration to the Faculty of Business & Law Newcastle Business School. The University of Newcastle, New Castle, United Kingdom.
Timperley, H. (2005). Distributed leadership: Developing theory from practice. *Journal of Curriculum Studies, 37*(4), 395–420.
Verespej, M. A. (1990). When you put the team in charge. *Industry Week, 239*(23), 30–32.
Warner, J. (2012). *What is leadership? Ready to manage.* Retrieved from http://blog.readytomanage.com/what-is-leadership/
Wheatley, M. J. (1999). *Leadership and the new science: Discovering order in a chaotic world.* San Francisco: Berrett-Koehler Publishers.
Wiess, C., & Cambone, J. (1994). Principals, shared decision-making and school reform. *Educational Leadership, 16*(3), 287–301.
Wood, M. (2005). Determinants of shared leadership in management teams. *International Journal of Leadership Studies, 1*(1), 64–85.
Wright, L. L. (2008, February 7). Merits and limitations of distributed leadership: Experiences and understandings of school principals. *Canadian Journal of Educational Administration and Policy, 69*, 1–33. Retrieved from https://www.umanitoba.ca/publications/cjeap/pdf_files/wright.pdf
Ylimaki, R. M. (2014a). *The new instructional leadership.* New York: Routledge and University Council for Educational Administration (UCEA).
Ylimaki, R. M. (2014b). Create a comprehensive, rigorous and coherent curricular program. In R. M. Ylimaki (Ed.), *The new instructional leadership* (pp. 27–44). New York: Routledge and University Council for Educational Administration (UCEA).
York-Barr, J., & Duke, K. (2004). What do we know about teacher leadership? Findings from two decades of research. *Review of Educational Research, 74*(3), 255–316.
Zubair, A., Bashir, M., Abrar, M., Baig, S. A., & Hassan, S. Y. (2015). Employee's participation in decision making and manager's encouragement of creativity: The mediating role of climate for creativity and change. *Journal of Service Science and Management, 8*(3), 306–321.

Chapter 4
Changing Definition of Teacher Professionalism: Autonomy and Accountability

Joseph Wu, Hoi Yan Cheung and Raymond M.C. Chan

Abstract Teacher professionalism has long been a topic of great interest to various stakeholders in education. A review on the extant literature suggested that there were different views on its conceptualization and operationalization. In general, skills and knowledge are two key elements central to the constitution of teacher professionalism. In fact, the definition of teacher professionalism is always changing following new expectations and requirements on teachers, particularly during education reform in a society. These changes may lead to a redistribution of power among different stakeholders in the education system. Teachers are sometimes being empowered but sometimes are being depowered during the changes. In facing challenges coming from the changes, some teachers can get further personal growth and professional development. Over the past decades, Hong Kong has undergone a series of education reforms that exert considerable impacts on teaching profession. In the road of these education reforms, teachers are being empowered through decentralization of decision-making power from central government officials to school-based management. However, this process of teacher empowerment is not monotonous. In recent years, new demands on teaching professionals tend to induce constraints on teachers in exercising their power. The process of teacher empowerment and depowerment in the road of education reform in Hong Kong is a very typical example to illustrate the changing nature of definition of teacher professionalism.

Teacher professionalism has long been a topic of great interest to various stakeholders in education. Different countries, such as England and Wales, have tried to establish greater educational accountability to stakeholders by having greater

J. Wu (✉)
Department of Applied Social Sciences, City University of Hong Kong, HKSAR, China
e-mail: joseph.wu@cityu.edu.hk

H.Y. Cheung
Faculty of Education, University of Macau, Macau, China

R.M.C. Chan
Department of Education Studies, Baptist University of Hong Kong, HKSAR, China

control and regulation by their central governments (Poulson 1998). Such a shift of accountability to stakeholders in education will impose new expectations on teaching professionals and will trigger a new definition of teacher professionalism. These redefinitions of teacher professionalism always bring in new situations of teacher empowerment and professional development. In this book chapter, we exemplify this changing nature of teacher professionalism within the context of Hong Kong's educational system, and discuss how each of these changes will impact upon teacher empowerment and may link to professional development. We begin our chapter with an explanation of how enhancing teacher professionalism can bring benefits to a society from the perspectives of different stakeholders in education (teachers, students, and parents). This is followed by an illustration of how definitions of teacher professionalism can be varied across studies and in different societies.

Teacher professionalization is never a static process. Education reforms can lead to new expectations of the teaching professionals, which may lead to changes in definitions of teacher professionalism. Along with these changes, teachers may get further professional growth and development. We use the education reforms that have taken place in Hong Kong over the past few decades as an example to illustrate this idea of the "changing" nature of teacher professionalism and its linkage with teacher empowerment and professional development. With lessons learnt from these experiences, the implications of this changing nature of teacher professionalism for teacher professional development, practice, and empowerment are discussed.

4.1 Defining Teacher Professionalism

Teacher professionalism is not a new topic to educators; it has been studied for decades (Berg 1989; Talbert and McLaughlin 1994; Day 2002; Evans 2011). A number of variables can be included in the concept of professionalism. Day's study (2002) suggested that it is related with elements such as strong technical culture, service ethic (caring for students and expectations for their success), professional commitment, and professional autonomy. Furlong et al. (2000) indicated that knowledge, autonomy, and responsibility are three important concepts of teacher professionalism. Talbert and McLaughlin (1994) suggested that technical culture, service ethic, and professional commitment are three key elements of teacher professionalism. In sum, teachers who are considered as having professionalism must have a strong knowledge base, be committed to students' needs, have high ethical awareness, and have strong individual and collective identities.

A study by Rizvi and Elliot (2005) found that teachers working in government primary schools in Karachi, Pakistan, perceived teacher professionalism as having four dimensions, namely teacher efficacy, teacher practice, teacher leadership, and teacher collaboration. Campbell (1996) indicated that some teachers think of professionalism as conformity to the perceived norms of collective associations, and that unethical behaviors are always associated with unprofessional behaviors. Professional ethics may be seen as a significant element to teacher professionalism, and when teachers demonstrate unethical behaviors, collegial loyalty can be damaged badly.

A study by Lai and Lo (2007) compared teacher professionalism in two Chinese cities—Hong Kong and Shanghai. Teachers from the two cities were found to have different perceptions and interpretations of teacher professionalism. From interviews with the Hong Kong teachers, there was evidence of a belief that professional teachers should have professional knowledge, be able to apply appropriate teaching methods to their students, and be willing to help students to develop their value systems. In China, the teachers thought that they should comply with the principles of education as recommended by the government. It seems that teacher professionalism is a changeable concept that is context dependent.

4.2 Changing Definition of Teacher Professionalism

Teacher professionalization is never a static process. Factors internal and/or external to the teaching professional (e.g., curriculum changes, advancement in technology, changes societal expectation, changes in government policy, changes in the needs of stakeholders) are continuously exerting their impacts to sharpen the constitutions of what entitles one to be a "professional teacher." Education reform is one major event that may initialize these changes, which in turn trigger new expectations of teacher professionals and lead to a redistribution of power among different stakeholders in the education system. Teachers are sometimes being empowered via these changes but sometimes are being depowered by these changes. Teachers can get professional growth and development through facing the challenges brought by the changes.

4.3 Lessons Learnt from the Hong Kong Education System

The ways in which various changes can exert impacts on the definition of teacher professionalism can be illustrated by considering various education reforms that have taken place in the Hong Kong education system over the past few decades. To set the context, this section will start with a brief review of the reforms that have been undertaken over the past few decades.

According to an analysis by Tang (2011), there were three historical periods of educational change that linked to the broader social, economic, and political histories of Hong Kong. The first period (1965–1984) was an era of quantitative expansion which led to an increased demand for teachers. The second period

(1984–1997) was an era of quality, marked by concerns that teachers should gain more power and autonomy in the core processes of education (such as curriculum design and implementation via a school-based approach). The third period is an era of excellence, competition, and accountability (post-1997) in which teacher's work in schools is under close surveillance by various stakeholders (students, parents, senior management, alumni, and the general public) (see Tang 2011, pp. 368–370 for a more elaborated discussion on this periodization of education change in Hong Kong).

4.3.1 1965–1984: An Era of Quantitative Expansion

In the first period of educational change, the government exerted quite a tight and centralized control on almost every aspect of school administration. The major duty of teachers (as prescribed in their employment contracts) was to carry out routine teaching under the centralized curricula. Teachers were more or less "technicians" of teaching in this era. Though not defined explicitly, "teacher professionalism" in this period generally pointed toward classroom skills of teaching and knowledge of the central curricula laid down by the government. Though teachers could have some freedom to decide how to teach, they often had no (or very little) power to decide what to teach. As frontline teachers were quite alienating from the process of decision-making of central policy in this period of time, they could get more time and space to develop their competency in daily classroom teaching. Through practicing autonomy within the classrooms and accountability toward their students, teachers got professional growth and development in their skills and knowledge of teaching.

4.3.2 1984–1997: An Era of Quality Concerns

After an expansion of quantity, there was a rising concern about the quality of education in the second period of educational change. The Education Commission published seven reports that provided a number of authoritative "recommendations" for school education. These recommendations eventually turned out to be sorts of government policies in various education sectors. In this period there was a shift of centralization to school-based management and curriculum development. Teachers at this period of time were no longer expected to be faithful executors of the curricula laid down by the central government. They were required to develop their own competencies to apply skills and knowledge learnt in their teacher training programs to their own classroom teaching. When teachers were being empowered in their daily work, they were being expected to be "competent" in carrying out their duties. The Education Commission (1992) adopted "The Teaching Profession" as the theme of its fifth report. This signified an official recognition of "teaching" as a "profession" by the government. Such recognition brought in further autonomy and empowerment to the teaching profession, but at the same time teachers were expected to bear more responsibility for their students' educational outcomes. In the previous time period (1965–84), a "professional teacher" could be defined as someone who had achieved an academic qualification (e.g., by completing a teacher training program accredited by the Education Department of Hong Kong government), so that s/he was eligible to carry out teaching duties in a regular classroom.

In this new time period, personal conduct beyond teacher competency and academic qualifications was another emerging criterion for teaching as a profession. Though challenging, an increasing need on entitlement of teacher professionalism could open a new horizon of teacher empowerment and leads to possibilities of further professional development. In 1982, the professional status of teachers was addressed formally for the first time in the report titled "A Perspective on Education in Hong Kong" (Visiting Panel Commissioned by the Hong Kong Government 1982). In this document, teachers' professional conduct was considered to be one very important concern for the development of teacher professionalism. As recommended by the Education Commission Report No. 1 (Education Commission 1984), a Preparatory Committee was formed in 1987 by 63 educational bodies to draft a professional code for education workers. The finalized code was proposed and renamed the "Code for the Education Profession of Hong Kong" (hereafter referred to as "the Code") in 1990 (Council on Professional Conduct in Education 1995). The Code has served as the guiding principle for teachers in their everyday teaching practices as well as their personal conduct. According to the Code, teachers are "required" to have commitments not just to the profession and the community, but also to students, colleagues, employers, and parents/guardians (Council on Professional Conduct in Education 1995). These documents could indeed heighten the awareness of teachers on issues of ethics in teaching professionals. Teachers were being empowered by the "Do" (What they can do) and depowered by the "Don't" (What they should not do) of the Code. In facing this new challenge, teacher could get professional growth and development in another domain of teacher professionalism beyond skills and knowledge of teaching (i.e., the "attitudes" domain).

4.3.3 1997 and Beyond: New Demands of Professionalism Due to Close Surveillance of Various Stakeholders

Starting from the return of Hong Kong's sovereignty from Britain to China in 1997, there has been an ongoing quest for excellence in education. This striving for excellence has been manifested as an increasing demand on teachers' competencies through certification. For language teachers, mandatory qualifications such as the Language Proficiency Requirement for Teachers (Education and Manpower Bureau 2004) have been set. Putonghua and English teachers are required to have academic degrees in relevant languages as well as demonstrated abilities in classroom teaching of the relevant languages. According to the Education Bureau (2014), in order for English and Putonghua teachers to get the Certificate of Merit, they have to attain an overall proficiency level of 4 or above. Many experienced language teachers are very dissatisfied with this requirement, particularly as they are only group of teachers subject to this type of expectation. They feel strongly that their classroom experiences in language teaching are not being honored by the government as a professional practice.

It seems that teacher professionalism in this time period has been defined as a combination of academic qualifications (such as subject knowledge in language and pedagogical content knowledge in language teaching for language teachers) and personal competency. It seems that the concept of competency has been broadened and moved beyond the boundary of subject matter (e.g., a physics teacher should be competent in the knowledge of physics itself and the pedagogical content knowledge of teaching physics) to some generic skills and knowledge of classroom teaching and learning (e.g., the use of IT in interactive classroom teaching and learning). Though teachers can get further personal growth and professional development through meeting the evolving needs on them, quite often they feel frustrated of running into expectations of the authorities. Teachers have very limited power to negotiate regarding these requirements. The ever-increasing demands on them have imposed great pressures on teachers, which can lead to deterioration in their mental health. In order to address the heightened levels of dissatisfaction in teachers, the pace of the reform appears to have been slowed down in recent years.

Due to the rapid change and demands for new knowledge and skills for effective teaching and learning, teachers' commitment to change and continuous professional development has become one very important concern for teacher professionalism. In fact, Hong Kong teachers' continuing professional development had been overlooked before the 2000s. Before 2002, teachers' professional development was encouraged but not considered as a "compulsory" requirement (Chan and Lee 2008), and was not encouraged by school leaders and administrators. The situation has been changed since the Advisory Committee on Teacher Education and Qualifications (ACTEQ) issued the document "Towards a Learning Profession: The Teacher Competencies Framework and the Continuing Professional Development of Teachers" in November 2003 (ACTEQ 2003). According to this document, a Teacher Competencies Framework and Policy Framework for Teachers' Continuing Professional Development was proposed as the reference for "establishing direction and creating momentum in continuing professional development" (ACTEQ 2003, p. 1). As proposed in this Document, all teachers, irrespective of their rank and capacity, are required to engage in Continuing Professional Development activities of not less than 150 h in a three-year cycle" (ACTEQ 2003, p. 13). This mandatory requirement on teachers states clearly and explicitly that continuous professional development is a "must" rather than an "option" in their professional lives.

Apart from skills, knowledge and competency, there has also been an emerging dimension in the definition of Hong Kong teacher professionalism after the return of sovereignty to China in 1997. As a way to maintain a stable society, Hong Kong's colonial government was quite successful in creating a fairly apolitical environment in its education sector. Issues related to teachers' "attitudes" were rarely touched upon in official documents from the Hong Kong government.

In Hong Kong, arguments concerning political issues have become serious after the return of sovereignty to the People's Republic of China. There are concerns on about the appropriateness of teachers' roles in major political and social issues. The question is whether it is appropriate for teachers to take up the ethical responsibility to defend their political mandate, and to serve as a moral sample in sensitive political and social issues. Some state that teachers should be "neutral" in discussing political and social issues. In this regard, teachers are supposed not to share their own political orientations, nor persuade students to be involved actively in political activities. For example, it has been suggested that overpersuasion, indoctrination into one's own political orientation, or persuading students to join in a voting campaign are considered as "unethical" (e.g., Ching 1995). However, on the other hand, according to Klaassen (2012), being a teacher nowadays means that one needs the courage to keep to certain professional and moral standards and to promote the development of universal moral norms and values. Besides demonstrating the bravery to do this, moral courage also indicates the perseverance to adhere to the goals that are oriented toward the well-being of the pupils who are in need of the teacher's daily help and strength to reach desired cognitive, social, and moral goals. Under this line of thinking, the Union of Education Norway (Utdanningsforbundet) stated clearly that it is teachers who have an ethical responsibility to show courage and defend their political mandates (The Union of Education Norway n.d.), thus making the teacher role into something beyond "sharing."

Other than teachers' involvement in political and social issues, there is a hot debate about the role of teachers as "moral examples." In recent years in Hong Kong, there have been reports of teachers accused of unprofessional behavior, including failing to report for duty with no reason, reporting for duty drunk, having sexual relationships with students and former students, and many other vices. The Council for Professional Conduct in Education received 40 complaints about misconduct by teachers and school administrators within 6 months in 2012, which was about 67% of the total number of cases being received from the previous 2-year period (Oriental Daily News 2012). The chairman of the Council for Professional Conduct in Education described this as "a big jump" (South China Morning Post 2012). In relation to this, there has been wide discussion about whether moral modeling, and "moral standards" should be included in teachers professional codes of conduct. In many Chinese societies, as influenced by traditional Chinese culture, the teacher is not just expected to teach subject-related matter, but is also involved in educating young people to have appropriate value systems. Therefore, the teacher is generally accepted as a moral educator who takes the responsibility for cultivating students' moral values (Watkins and Biggs 1996). The Character Development Foundation also stated that it is one very important component in teacher professionalism that "the educator serves as an exemplary moral leader, following ethical practices toward students, families, colleagues, administrators, and the profession. The educator upholds high ethical standards of personal integrity, civility, compassion, responsibility, truthfulness, honesty, and courage, knowing that these are needed to inspire public confidence and trust" (Character Development Foundation n.d.). The International Institute for Educational Planning has also stated that "the articulation of good habits that members should acquire, the duties that they should follow, and the attending consequence of such behaviors, makes it clear that ethics in a profession must be viewed from both professional and business viewpoints in order to assure the highest possible standards" (Nuland 2009; p. 21).

However, to a certain extent, increased regulations or codes not only limit professional autonomy, but also take away teachers' powers. It seems that "external regulation does more harm than good" (Dresscher 2007, p.13). According to Ozga (1988), teacher professionalism was a form of "direct" or "indirect" control of political, economic, social, and cultural circumstances. He noted a marked shift in the mode of state regulation of teacher professionalism from a "licensed" form of autonomy to a more tightly controlled 'regulated' one. To a certain extent, more guidelines, rules, or any forms of control over teachers' work would lead to de-professionalized or even proletarianized teachers (Hextall et al. 2007). Findings from different studies have also reflected that some teachers have reservations in considering themselves as "moral models." Teachers, in general, tend to keep their own autonomy and expect to have their own choices of lifestyle undisturbed by their professional identity. A study in Hong Kong reflected that more than 40% of teachers disagreed with the idea having guidelines in the professional code of conduct to "control" teachers' personal activities such as "gambling", "alcohol", or "open relationships" (Chan et al. 2013). In a study by Klaassen (2012), only around half of the teachers (44.6%) were of the opinion that a certain degree of moral courage was necessary to fulfill an exemplary function. The other half (52.2%) thought that it was not necessary to demonstrate courage in order to be an example.

In facing new demands and new perspectives from different stakeholders, moral requirement for teachers seems to have been listed by some educators as an important element for a new professionalism in education (e.g., Klaassen and Maslovaty 2010). Teachers do not live just within the framework of professionalism, they are also members of society and other contexts (Dresscher 2007). How to prepare them to be aware of their professional obligations will be a very critical agenda, which may eventually affect the whole teacher training system as well as the philosophy of teacher training program in future.

4.4 Conclusion and Looking Forward

Education reforms in Hong Kong over the past few decades can serve as exemplars for this changing nature in defining teacher professionalism and its impact on teacher empowerment and professional development. It can be anticipated that this dynamic nature of defining teacher professionalism will be continued into the future. Teachers need to be well prepared for changes rather than resisting them. "Lifelong learning" will be an integral part of teachers' lives in the journey of teacher professionalism.

Owing to different new demands and expectations placed on the teaching, some teachers may not be able to adapt well to these new challenges and demands. It is not just about workload issue, but also related to teachers' self-efficacy and professional identity. Starting from the 2000s, there was emerging evidence of negative impacts on teachers' physical and mental health, such as mood disorders, suicide tendencies, over high pressure, high resignation rates, super high workload (Cheng 2009), and unacceptable long working hours (Chan et al. 2013). In this regard, how to create a better working environment and rebuild the image and confidence of the teaching profession is of paramount importance (Cheng 2009). In Hong Kong, the topic of stress management has been included in many teacher training programs (some in preservice and some in in-service training courses) and teachers seem to have benefitted from them. These successful experiences in Hong Kong to promote teachers' well-being can be borrowed across borders (probably with some adaptations) for teachers to cope with the changing needs and demands on them in other societies.

Another lesson that can be learnt from the Hong Kong experience is that the pace of education reform should not be too fast. There was estimation from the Hong Kong Professional Teachers' Union that more than ten new educational initiatives were launched in a 10-year period (2000–2010) of education reform in Hong Kong. These initiatives introduced both specific (e.g., requirements for more sophisticated subject and pedagogical content knowledge for English teachers) and general (e.g., requirements for IT skills for all teachers) changes to the definition of teacher professionalism. Though teachers can be benefited from getting personal growth and professional development in meeting these new demands, too frequent changes can bring in undesirable interruptions to the routine of teaching life. Most teachers (including both new and experienced ones) found it difficult to adapt themselves successfully to their rapid changing roles in society and became tired of having to reestablish new professional identities again and again. Some teachers even regarded the increasing demands and needs imposed on them as a sign of diminishing autonomy in the profession and a way of taking away the power from them. For smooth implementation of an educational initiative triggered by an education reform, bureaucracies in any society should consider establishing the right balance between accountability (toward various stakeholders of education) and autonomy (of the teaching professional). For any change, if teachers can get an experience of being empowered in their practice, they will be more likely to endorse the change.

Are teachers in Hong Kong being further empowered in the road of education reform? Upon recognition of the diversity of school cultures and acknowledgement of individual differences in the learning process, Hong Kong has adopted a school-based approach in recent education reform. Such an approach tends to decentralize the power of decision-making from the government officials to school management. As a consequence, teachers can gain more and more power from the central government through active participation in the decision-making process. This process of teacher empowerment is not monotonous. In recent years, new demands on teaching professionals tend to impose more and more invisible constraints on teachers in exercising their power. Along with the changing definition of teacher professionalism, teachers in Hong Kong are in the turbulence of empowerment and depowerment. Nevertheless, teachers are getting more opportunities to get personal growth and professional development by engaging themselves in the changes. In recent years, debate on the political positioning of teachers in Hong Kong has posed a question to the teaching professional across the borders. In a collectivistic society, teachers as members of the society are supposed to be able to sacrifice their own interests for the benefit of society. In contrast, teachers from individualistic societies are supported to voice their needs and opinions openly. How to build up teachers' courage to work against unreasonable demands from society and to uphold their professional identity will be a challenge not only to teachers in Hong Kong but also to those across borders. In facing this challenge, teachers in Hong Kong need to be empowered further to uphold their professional beliefs and practices.

References

Advisory Committee on Teacher Education and Qualifications. (2003). *Towards a learning profession: The teacher competencies framework and the continuing professional development of teachers*. Hong Kong: Government Logistics Department.
Berg, G. (1989). Education reform and teacher professionalism. *Journal of Curriculum Studies, 21*(1), 53–60.
Campbell, E. (1996). Ethical implications of collegial loyalty as one view of teacher professionalism. *Teachers and Teaching, 2*(2), 191–208.
Chan, R. M. C., & Lee, J. C. (2008). Teachers' continuing professional development: Are we on the right track? In J. C. Lee & L. P. Shiu (Eds.), *Developing teachers and developing schools in changing context* (pp. 71–99). Hong Kong: Hong Kong Institute of Education Research.
Chan, R. M. C., Lau, K. M., Wu, S. W., Wu, J. K. F., Lee, S. H., Fung, M. C., et al. (2013). *Education research report series: A Research Study on Hong Kong Teachers' Professional Ethics and Moral Conduct: Preliminary Analysis [教育研究報告系列:香港教師教學專業與道德操守的檢視:初步資料分析]*. Hong Kong: Education Convergence and Hong Kong Primary Education Research Association.
Character Development Foundation. (n.d.). *A code of ethics for educators*. Retrieved August 22, 2014, from: http://www.charactered.org/ethicstext.htm
Cheng, Y. C. (2009). Hong Kong educational reform in the last decade: Reform syndrome and new developments. *International Journal of Educational Management, 23*(1), 65–86.
Ching, K. M. (1995). *Hong Kong education in the era of political change. (In Chinese: 政治變動中的香港教育)*. Hong Kong: Oxford University Press.
Council on Professional Conduct in Education (1995). *Code for the education profession of Hong Kong*. Hong Kong: Council on Professional Conduct in Education. Retrieved January 19, 2016, from: http://cpc.edb.org.hk/en/download/code.pdf
Conley, S., & Muncey, E. M. (1999). Organizational climate and teacher professionalism: Identifying teacher work environment dimensions. In H. J. Freiberg (Ed.), *School climate* (pp. 107–128). NY: Taylor and Francis.

Darling-Hammond, L. (1990). Teacher professionalism: Why and how? In A. Lieberman (Ed.), *Schools as collaborative cultures: Creating the future now* (pp. 25–50). London: Falmer.

Day, C. (2002). School reforms and transitions in teacher professionalism and identity. *International Journal of Educational Research, 37*(8), 677–692.

Dresscher, E. (2007). *Professional ethics in teaching and professional teachers organisations: An inquiry into the background of Education International's declaration on professional ethics.* Retrieved August 21, 2014, from: http://old.ei-ie.org/ethics/file/(2007)%20Professional%20Ethics%20in%20Teaching%20and%20Professional%20Teachers%20Organisations%20by%20Eduard%20Dresscher.pdf

Education Commission. (1984). *Education Commission Report No. 1.* Hong Kong: Government Printer, Hong Kong.

Education and Manpower Bureau. (2004). Implementation of recommendations of Standing Committee on Language Education and Research on Language Teacher Education and Qualifications. Education and Manpower Bureau circular Memorandum 54/2004.

Education Bureau. (2014). *Language proficiency assessment for teachers.* Retrieved from: http://www.edb.gov.hk/en/teacher/qualification-training-development/qualification/language-proficiency-requirement/lpat.html

Education Commission. (1992). Education Commission Report No.5. Hong Kong: Government Printer.

Evans, L. (2011). The 'shape' of teacher professionalism in England: professional standards, performance management, professional development and the changes proposed in the 2010 White Paper. *British Educational Research Journal, 37*(5), 851–870.

Furlong, J., Barton, L., Miles, S., & Whitty, G. (2000). *Teacher education in transition.* Buckingham: Open University Press.

Hextall, I., Gribb, A., Gewirtz, S., Mahony, P., & Troman, G. (2007). *Changing teacher roles, identities and professionalism: An annotated bibliography.* England, London: King's Colleage, Roehampton University, & T.L.R.P. Teaching & Learning Research Programme. Extracted August 21, 2014, from: http://www.tlrp.org/themes/seminar/gewirtz/papers/bibliography.pdf

Klaassen, C. (2012). Just a teacher or also a moral example? In D. Alt, & R. Reingold (Eds.), *Changes in Teachers' moral role. From passive observers to moral and democratic leaders,* (pp. 1–11). Rotterdam: Sense Publishers.

Klaassen, C., & Maslovaty, N. (2010). Teachers and normative perspectives in education: An introduction. In C. Klaassen & N. Maslovaty (Eds.), *Moral courage and the normative professionalism of teachers* (pp. 1–12). Rotterdam: Sense Publishers.

Lai, M., & Lo, L. N. K. (2007). Teacher professionalism in educational reform: The experiences of Hong Kong and Shanghai. *Compare, 37*(1), 53–68.

Nuland, S. (2009). *Teacher codes: Learning from experiences.* France: International Insititue for Educational Planning.

Oriental Daily News (December 20, 2012). *Complaint cases related to teachers' behaviors increase.* (In Chinese: 教職員涉不當行為 投訴趨升). Hong Kong: Oriental Daily News. Retrieved August 21, extracted from: http://orientaldaily.on.cc/cnt/news/20121220/00176_051.html

Ozga, J. (Ed.). (1988). *Schoolwork: Approaches to the labour process of teaching, Milton Keynes.* UK: Open University Press.

Poulson, L. (1998). Accountability, teacher professionalism and education reform in England. *Teacher Development, 2*(3), 419–432.

Rizvi, M. (2008). The role of school principals in enhancing teacher professionalism. Lesson from Pakistan. *Educational Management Administration Leadership, 36*(1), 85–100.

Rizvi, M., & Elliot, B. (2005). Teachers' perceptions of their professionalism in government primary schools in Karachi, Pakistan. *Asia Pacific Journal of Teacher Education, 33*(1), 35–52.

Robertson, S. L. (1996). Teachers' work, restructuring and postfordism: Constructing the new professionalism'. In I. Goodson & A. Hargreaves (Eds.), *Teachers' professional lives.* London: Falmer Press.

South China Morning Post (December 20, 2012). *Officials accused of blocking creation of teachers' professional group*. Hong Kong: South China Morning Post. Retrieved August 21, extracted from: http://orientaldaily.on.cc/cnt/news/20121220/00176_051.html

Talbert, J. E., & McLaughlin, M. W. (1994). Teacher professionalism in local school contexts. *American Journal of Education, 102*(2), 123–153.

Tang, S. Y. F. (2011). Teachers' professional identity, educational change and neo-liberal pressures on education in Hong Kong. *Teacher Development: An International Journal of Teachers' Professional Development, 15*(3), 363–380.

Union of Education Norway. (Utdanningsforbundet) (n.d.). *Professional ethics for the teaching profession*. Norway: Union of Education Norway. Retrieved Aug 21, 2014, from: https://www.utdanningsforbundet.no/upload/1/L%C3%A6rerprof_etiske_plattform_a4_engelsk_31.10.12.pdf

Visiting Panel commissioned by the Hong Kong Government. (1982). *A Perspective on education in Hong Kong*. Hong Kong: Government Printer, Hong Kong.

Watkins, D. A., & Biggs, J. B. (1996). *The Chinese learner: Cultural, psychological and contextual influences*. Hong Kong & Australia: CERC & ACER.

Whitty, G. (2000). Teacher professionalism in new times. *Journal of In-service Education, 26*(2), 281–295.

Chapter 5
Teachers' Autonomy and Accountability in Assessing Students' Physical Education in School-Based Assessment

Ruzlan Md-Ali and Arsaythamby Veloo

Abstract School-Based Assessment (SBA) became the educational policy for Malaysian secondary schools since 2011. SBA recognizes the need for school teachers to be given the autonomy and accountability in assessing their students' performance. Hence, they are given the freedom to design quality assessment activities aligned with their instructional strategies and students' learning outcomes. This chapter discusses the case of a physical activity assessment in Physical Education (PE) that focuses on the implementation of the National Test Standard for Students' Physical Activities. The test comprises the National Physical Fitness Standard (NPFS) and Body-Mass Index (BMI). The NPFS assessment program assesses physical fitness through four activities, namely up-and-down the bench, pumping, star jump, and sit-ups. On the other hand, BMI is determined by dividing the body weight by the height. A total of 30 PE teachers, consisting of 16 non-PE optionists and 14 PE optionists from 15 secondary schools were interviewed. The chapter discusses the impact of empowerment on the orchestration and design of assessment activities and responsive practices in determining students' performance. The chapter also highlights the challenges faced by PE teachers in implementing SBA and in assessing students' ability and how they overcame these challenges. The empowerment had inspired the PE teachers to reconsider their role and the status of PE education in secondary schools. PE teachers began to accept the fact that they are now becoming significant in SBA, and they need to function effectively as assessors within SBA.

R. Md-Ali (✉) · A. Veloo
School of Education and Modern Languages, College of Arts and Sciences,
Universiti Utara Malaysia, Sintok UUM 06010, Malaysia
e-mail: ruzlan@uum.edu.my

A. Veloo
e-mail: arsay@uum.edu.my

© Springer Nature Singapore Pte Ltd. 2017
I.H. Amzat and N.P. Valdez (eds.), *Teacher Empowerment Toward Professional Development and Practices*, DOI 10.1007/978-981-10-4151-8_5

5.1 Introduction

In supporting qualified and successful educational processes and practices, teachers are expected to be highly professional and possess substantial expertise. The pressing demands of today's world and the concern of the educational community require prompt and appropriate responses from teachers. In most instances, teachers are empowered by their superiors to execute certain educational directives, which may include matters about students' learning and assessment. Teacher empowerment can be viewed as the confidence to make and the power to enact situational appropriate instructional decisions that improve the quality of education for students (Harpell and Andrews 2010). Being empowered, teachers would have a greater say in the learners' learning and affairs. Nevertheless, to ensure that teachers play their role effectively, they need to be continually well prepared and competent.

The education system in Malaysia, which is exam-oriented and over recognizing the academic achievement of students, has resulted in students becoming less active in the co-curriculum activities while at the same time giving pressure to teachers, parents, and especially, the students themselves. For instance, teachers are being pressured to complete the syllabus within the stipulated time frame, making them focused more on the end products than the process of learning.

Assessment plays a very important role in the process of learning and teaching (van de Watering et al. 2008). The winds of change have made an assessment to be even more important and significant in determining a student's real ability (Omar Mohd Hashim 2003). The type and method of assessment practiced by teachers have effects on students' learning. The Malaysian Teacher Education Division (TED) is entrusted by the Ministry of Education to formulate policies and guidelines to prepare teachers for the new implementation of assessment (Faizah 2011). Continuous SBA is implemented in all grades and all levels. Then, students take common public examinations at the end of each level.

SBA is optimized to assess the academic and non-academic aspects, giving acknowledgments and autonomy to teachers to implement formative and summative assessments in their school. SBA was implemented in 2011 for Year One pupils in primary schools, and starting from 2012 for Grade 7 students in secondary schools. SBA could produce holistic human capital that is stable physically, emotionally, spiritually, and intellectually as envisioned in the National Philosophy of Education. SBA is said to be holistic in nature as it assesses the cognitive, affective, and psychomotor aspects of students. It also assesses students' academic and non-academic performance (MOE 2012).

In non-academic areas, PE teachers are empowered to implement all the PE assessment activities. Empowerment entails teachers' autonomy and accountability towards students' PE performance. To exercise autonomy and accountability, teachers are expected to be committed toward fulfilling stakeholders' trust and demand. However, issues related to PE teachers' knowledge and skills to implement the PE assessment effectively in line with SBA need fair attention.

According to the Malaysian Ministry of Education, SBA in the Malaysian education system involves a combination of centralized and SBA. Academic assessment is school-based as well as centralized, whereas non-academic assessment, such as Psychometric Assessment and Physical, Sports and Co-curriculum Activities Assessment (PAJSK), is school-based. PAJSK is administered to obtain information about students' capacity and the potential for physical, sports, and co-curriculum activities. The assumption is that because students control their individual capacity and mental processes, their physical and health development can be monitored and improved.

5.2 Physical Education in School-Based Assessment

Maintaining physical fitness and the level of one's health is irrefutably imperative (Dugan 2008). Fitness regarding performance refers to an individual's ability to compete in sports activities. To do this, one has to have sufficient energy, endurance, and skills. One has to, therefore, start at an early age so that the culture of exercise can be sustained (Birch 2008), and it becomes an everyday habit. When students are physiologically and psychologically fit, they can protect themselves from the dangers of hypokinetic illness (lacking in movements) such as heart disease, obesity, and other ailments that involve the muscles and bones. Having an optimum fitness level would help students to do their daily activities more efficiently and effectively without feeling tired or exhausted. Students who are fit contribute to filling the country's needs for people who are healthy and active.

According to Jamil (2008), to obtain complete information about the development and potential increase of one's fitness, one needs to be assessed. Therefore, PE teachers have a role to develop and increase the level of their students' performance and fitness to achieve the objectives of PE curriculum in Malaysia.

Choosing a suitable type of exercise and maintaining the frequency of exercise play a very important role in the physical fitness training program because assessment can be done continuously. The implementation of a standardized assessment will motivate students to take care of their health to a better level (Pate et al. 2010). A standardized or fitness guideline is needed to ease the process of physical fitness test (Welk and Morrow 2008) which is used to assess the result of the physical activities for physical fitness (Cooper Institute for Aerobics Research 2004).

No systematic evaluation by PE teachers before the implementation of SBA existed. The absence of such assessment was unfortunate because the contents of

PE could not be effectively disseminated by the PE teachers to students at all levels. As a result, the PE teachers were not serious to deliver the contents because the subject was not centrally assessed. In other words, schools and students found the subject to be not as important in comparison to other academic subjects.

Before SBA was implemented, the PE evaluation was individually conducted by schools, and it was known as School-Operated Evaluation (PKS). PKS measured students' achievement level on practical, theoretical, affective, social, and moral values. When SBA was introduced, PE assessment was transformed; it no longer depended on summative examinations alone. With this transformation, the role of PE teachers began to change, so too the status of PE which had been long due. SBA entails empowerment of PE teachers and the change in the status of PE in schools. PE teachers began to accept the idea that they are a significant stakeholder in SBA, and they need to function effectively as assessors. Payne (2003) suggested that teachers need to reevaluate intensely the assessment processes in PE to enhance its implementation in schools. The assessment process of this subject has to be done holistically. However, at present, there is no standard test that can be used to assess PE continuously (Idris 2005).

5.3 National Test Standard for Students' Physical Activities

The National Test Standard for Students' Physical Activities comprises the NPFS and the BMI. NPFS and BMI evaluate and report students' physical activities and are carried out during the learning and teaching of the Physical and Health Education subject. PE teachers have to keep a record of their students' NPFS and BMI.

5.4 The National Physical Fitness Standard (NPFS) Assessment

The NPFS assessment was introduced by the Ministry of Education in 2005 and implemented fully on Form Five students in the year 2008. All NPFS reports are part of the fitness component in SBA. The NPFS assessment program assesses physical fitness through four activities, namely up-and-down the bench, pumping, star jump, and sit-ups.

5.5 Body-Mass Index (BMI) Assessment

BMI measures body mass against one's height, an indirect measurement of the body composition because it is closely related to the fat infused in the body weight and height of an individual (Reilly 2006). BMI is determined by dividing the body weight (in kilogram) with the height (in meters) that is squared. BMI is also a measure of obesity (Ikeda et al. 2006) and is also used by schools to check students' physical activities (Harris et al. 2009). Physical activities play a very important role in maintaining healthy body weight (Hill and Wyatt 2005). In fact, systematic physical activities should be practiced at the children's stage (Birch 2008).

5.6 Autonomy and Accountability Towards Physical Assessment

The implementation of SBA has not only given school teachers in Malaysia the autonomy to assess their students' performance, but also the accountability for reporting their students' real performance. In this regard, PE teachers are no exception in the NPFS and BMI assessments. This means that PE teachers need to know what assessment is and why it needs to be implemented. In SBA, PE teachers are fully empowered to prepare the assessment activities. Using a given guideline, PE teachers can seek students' help and ideas in selecting and preparing the activities because students should know about the activities they will be assessed on. In designing the activities, PE teachers should understand that they are accountable for determining their students' competence in PE. Figure 5.1 shows the relationship between autonomy and accountability towards PE assessment in the Malaysian PE education, especially in relation to the NPFS and BMI.

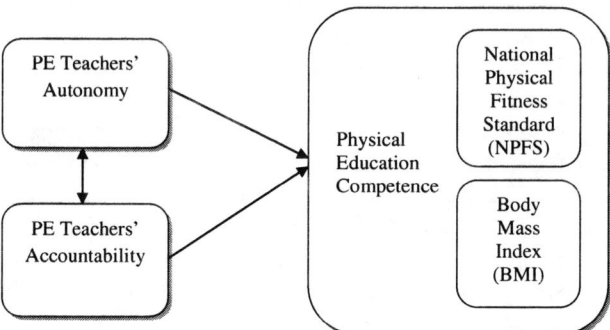

Fig. 5.1 Framework of PE teachers' autonomy and accountability towards PE competence based on NPFS and BMI

5.7 Results

Based on the framework of PE Teachers' Autonomy and Accountability towards PE Competence on NPFS and BMI, the researcher conducted face-to-face semi-structured interviews to elicit information on their perception of the implementation of PE assessment in SBA in Malaysian secondary schools. The interviews focused on teacher autonomy in the implementation of PE assessment, their accountability in the implementation of PE assessment, their understanding of assessment in PE, the NPFS test, the BMI test, accountability in implementing PE assessment, autonomy versus knowledge and skills, accountability towards parents (stakeholders), and accountability and autonomy on the availability of infrastructure for assessment. The responses of 30 PE teachers, comprising 16 non-PE optionists and 14 PE optionists from 15 secondary schools, are discussed below.

5.8 Teacher Autonomy in the Implementation of PE Assessment

In SBA, teachers are empowered to carry out the PE assessment. Empowerment signifies autonomy, which means having the ability to act. Also, autonomy implies that teachers have the freedom to assess their students without constraints or time limits. PE teachers who carry out an assessment in schools agree that the NPFS test is best administered by the teachers themselves. Some PE teachers admitted they lack the skills (expertise) in PE because they are not PE optionists. In contrast, teachers who are PE optionists reported that they encountered no major issues in implementing the test because they had received appropriate training. Hence, teachers who are not PE optionists need to be appropriately trained before they are empowered to assess PE in schools.

Lack of equipment for PE assessment is a major issue in some schools. Some PE teachers raised a concern about the lack of equipment in their schools which they felt could hinder the smooth implementation of the NPFS test. The lack of PE equipment was attributed to the financial constraint faced by their schools due to a large number of students.

Even though PE teachers are given full responsibility for preparing the assessment activities and ask students to contribute their ideas for the activities based on a given guideline, they claimed that the assessment activities were rather limited because of a large number of students to be assessed. As a result, the content of the assessment is more or less standardized every year. While the teachers agreed that they should be given full responsibility for administering the test, they encountered some constraints in implementing the assessment.

5.9 Teacher Accountability in the Implementation of PE Assessment

Teacher accountability means teaching responsibilities that must be understood and implemented. This implies that a teacher needs to cover the PE curriculum and its implementation. PE teachers are also in the position to identify who among their students have problems in the PE activities and determine the appropriate assessment activities for them. PE teachers agreed they need to be honest and transparent when measuring and recording their students' performance. That is, in assessing the student's performance, PE teachers should not be biased.

5.10 Teachers' Understanding of Assessment in Physical Education

When asked about their understanding of the assessment in PE subject, the PE teachers who were interviewed indicated that SBA comprises formative tests where assessment is done on a learning unit after or during the learning of PE. To the PE teachers, apart from the fitness assessment, PE also has its formative assessment, which is the evidence test. The formative assessment is needed to gather evidence that demonstrates students' mastery. In the old assessment system, PE teachers only provided exercises to students after a chapter was completed, but now PE teachers have extra work to do. They have to record what students have done and can do as one of the components of the formative assessment.

As a form of evidence test, formative assessment can act as a learning tool to enable PE teachers to know how much students understand the PE lessons. PE teachers need to guide their students until they can achieve the competent levels as prescribed by the ministry's guidelines. In short, the formative assessment indirectly enhances the sense of responsibility of the PE teachers for developing the students' competence in PE. The PE teachers also noted that the evidence system would provide the opportunity for students to address their weaknesses before their final achievements are entered into the SPPBS system since the actual report on the student's achievement in PE will only be made available at the end of the year.

As the formative assessment in PE helps teachers to determine their students' mastery level in a particular skill or unit taught, students are assumed to have enough time to acquire the appropriate skills in the learning unit before proceeding to learn new skills. PE teachers also understood that formative assessment does not necessarily take the form of test papers or assignments in the form of documentations, for example, portfolios. However, some PE teachers failed to understand the concept of formative evidence tests as a developmental assessment tool where teachers have the opportunity to assist students in PE in the best way possible so that the students could reach their maximum potential.

Some PE teachers understood formative assessment as an assessment of students' learning, which could be made more effective to help students if feedback is given to the students in a timely and proper manner. When giving feedback, PE teachers should not compare the student's performance with other students, but instead, should refer to each student's achievement as a set of prescribed performance standards. The PE teachers should also understand that these assessments provide information to bridge the gap between the current and the desired levels of learning.

5.11 The National Physical Fitness Standard (NPFS) Test

To PE teachers, NPFS covers activities that must be systematically carried out to nurture students' physical fitness. NPFS covers assessment of the physical aspects of the body abilities and the muscles' response to a stimulus resulting from a fitness activity. NPFS covers physical activities and is expected to produce students who are healthy and active. PE teachers can monitor their students' physical capabilities.

Test techniques and procedures in physical fitness assessment should be carried out according to age, gender, student's capability, appropriateness of equipment used, and the environment of the test. Fitness assessments should be done on a continuous basis. However, efficient implementation of NPFS depends on the time as well as the equipment available. The PE teachers interviewed reported that among the constraints they faced when implementing an assessment on a continuous basis are a lack of time, a large number of students, and availability of appropriate equipment. Because of these constraints, the assessments were carried out twice a year, that is, in March and August. As a result, the NPFS could not be substantially met. The PE teachers also reported most students were not aware of the concept of NPFS and the significance of its four components (up-and-down the bench, pumping, star jump, and sit-ups) if they exercise on their own. However, some PE teachers felt that students should continuously do the exercises by themselves to avoid getting the hypokinetic disease and possibly even heart disease. The PE teachers felt that NPFS can motivate students to adopt a healthy lifestyle. They also hoped that the students would become more responsible and capable of handling their well-being toward the prosperity of the nation, which is in line with the country's philosophy of education.

5.12 The Body-Mass Index (BMI) Test

The BMI test is one of the components in the assessment of PE activities. PE teachers faced no difficulty in running the test because students can do the BMI test themselves. The procedure to determine the height and weight is easy to understand, and the calculation of the BMI index can be done easily. Moreover, the students can record the level of physical fitness, do the analysis and interpretation, keep records of their fitness, and make the necessary follow-ups.

PE teachers are more likely to use the BMI assessments as a medium for nurturing students to take care of their personal health by maintaining a lifestyle of doing exercises and sports and healthy eating habits.

5.13 Accountability in Implementing PE Assessment

PE teachers faced challenges in interpreting the given assessment guidelines, especially when it comes to identifying and deciding the students' levels of performance according to on the stated criteria. Students who did not achieve or acquire the desired skills have to be guided further until they could achieve the skills. Some PE teachers resorted to carrying out alternative activities to be administered to students when assessing their skills. Such action is indicative of being accountable for developing the students within the stipulated time frame.

5.14 Autonomy Versus Knowledge and Skills

Although PE teachers are given the autonomy to carry out PE assessment, most did not receive proper training. Hence, they do not have the appropriate knowledge and skills. This issue needs to be addressed well because some PE teachers are PE optionists and others are not. Lacking the appropriate knowledge and skills could result in biased and unfair PE assessment. As PE teachers do not explain the purposes of BMI and fitness tests, students tend not to be aware of them. Also, some PE teachers do not monitor whether or not their students continuously do the fitness tests themselves.

One of the issues related to the ineffective execution of PE assessment is the cascading of knowledge of PE assessment by the authorities. The PE teachers reported that the training courses given by the authorities to disseminate knowledge of SBA were not only insufficient to ensure effective continuous assessment of PE but were short and not continuously provided. The courses on SBA generally and on PE specifically should be conducted on an ongoing basis to ensure teachers can understand the PE assessment better and assess PE continuously. The PE teachers realized that they did not have the knowledge and skills when conducting the assessments. Second, the head of departments, who were the ones who tended to attend the courses, often failed to disseminate clear information to the teachers. As a result, the PE teachers carried out the assessment according to their understanding.

At times, the PE teachers were not informed about the training workshops or the persons who should be attending them. In some cases, those who had already attended the PE training workshops did not give in-house training but simply distributed the handouts given during the workshops with the expectation that other

PE teachers read and understand the content themselves. As a result, the PE teachers did not comprehend the content and thus could not carry out the tests effectively.

5.15 Accountability Towards Parents (Stakeholders)

Parents' knowledge about SBA constitutes another constraint faced by PE teachers. The PE teachers reported that parents were still unclear of the concepts embedded within the SBA system and were interested in the number of 'As' their children obtained when the parents came to the school to collect their children's report cards. When parents do not understand the change in the approaches to learning and assessment, the PE teachers felt that the parents could ignore their role in the implementation of SBA even though the parents could contribute to their children's performance in the PE assessment.

The PE teachers concurred that students could perform the tasks assigned to them at home. However, since their parents were not well informed about SBA, they were unable to provide adequate settings and facilities for their children. These facilities might be in the form of supporting reading materials, computers, the Internet, etc. The unavailability of these resources at the students' home made it difficult for the PE teachers to provide follow-up activities. Also, parents with little knowledge about the importance of these resources would have trouble guiding their children to complete their assignments given by the teachers.

5.16 Accountability and Autonomy on Availability of Infrastructure for Assessment Issues

The PE teachers faced problems with physical facilities and tools when doing activities for the PE assessment. Some activities had to be conducted in poor conditions. Not only was the equipment in poor condition, but it was also inadequate. So, the PE teachers sometimes had to use alternative equipment although they were aware that the alternative equipment could produce different results.

Besides equipment issues, the availability of spaces for sport and assessment activities are another constraint. Open spaces such as game courts, football fields, and spaces sufficiently large could make the PE assessment effective and fair. For urban schools, space availability is quite a burden since securing playing fields that are fairly large would be expensive. The built-up area of urban schools could also be the reason these schools provide relatively narrow or small spaces for recreational facilities related to PE.

Despite the constraints faced, the accountability and autonomy given to PE teachers in Malaysian secondary schools have made them motivated, creative, and confident to take alternative actions in implementing the PE assessment within the guideline. It can be said that the empowerment given to the PE teachers to manage the PE assessment in SBA has enabled them to use their creative thinking to perform the assessment the best way possible. As pointed out by Kimwarey et al. (2014), empowered individuals are said to have the skills and knowledge to act on a situation or even improve it in a positive way.

5.17 Implications

Generally speaking, the SBA has developed a positive attitude towards PE assessment among PE teachers. They are now more serious in doing the assessment and perceive PE as a subject that is on par with other academic subjects. They too feel that they are now in a position to teach and train their students in a more structured manner. Consequently, students also develop an appropriate perspective towards PE.

PE teachers should be properly trained to assess using the standard guideline to ensure a valid and reliable assessment of PE. Proper training can assist the teachers to confront assessment issues appropriately, for instance, those related to the well-being of their students which include obesity, gender, ethnicity, interests, body size, health conditions, etc. PE teachers can also gain valuable knowledge and skills in assessing the physical aspects of students' body capabilities and their muscles' responses to a stimulus resulting from fitness activities carried out. Hence, PE teachers can monitor their students' fitness levels.

With PE teachers and students reevaluating the role of PE in SBA, PE is now seen as a subject with the potential of producing students who are healthy and active during and outside school hours. For example, students can be empowered to conduct the BMI test because the procedure is easy to understand and operate. Moreover, they can record their levels of physical fitness, do the analysis and interpret the result, keep records of their fitness, and consequently do follow-up activities. These records may serve as indicators for them to consistently take appropriate actions to monitor the development of their health and physical fitness.

Schools need to increase the number of times they conduct an assessment in a year to ensure their students are in their best condition when being assessed. Increasing the frequency of assessment can increase the validity of their actual performance and would contribute to the overall fairness of the PE assessment.

Since PE teachers indicate that they still lack appropriate skills and knowledge in PE assessment, relevant stakeholders may feel apprehensive with the teachers who feel that no one could challenge their decision over students' performance because the teachers have been given the autonomy to do so. That is, the PE teachers may not use the standards to assess their students, resulting in unfair and biased PE assessment. When such situation occurs, the stakeholders might challenge the decisions made. In other words, even though the PE teachers are empowered to perform the PE assessment, abuse or misuse of autonomy by the teachers is a serious concern among the stakeholders.

5.18 Conclusion

In general, Malaysia PE teachers have an appropriate understanding of PE assessment in line with SBA. However, differences in knowledge and understanding of SBA generally and PE assessment specifically still exist. PE teachers also have constraints in identifying the appropriate and relevant methods or approaches in implementing this assessment. Nevertheless, PE teachers in this study indicated their willingness and readiness to enhance their knowledge of PE assessment within SBA and were receptive to using the methods of assessment and in particular the implementation of PE assessment. In Malaysia, PE was made a core subject since 1989. It is believed that the implementation of SBA can support PE contributions towards the development of students' cognitive, affective, and psychomotor learning experience. That is, teachers' effectiveness in implementing PE assessment will contribute to the healthy, active, and productive future generations. The knowledge, skills, and experience obtained by the students through PE will enable them to practice a healthy culture and lifestyle. Any attempt to improve the PE assessment in schools must pay attention to the PE teachers' role in decision-making and to increasing opportunities for meaningful and collective participation in PE assessment. Also, it is crucial to empower administrators, teachers, and students so that students can benefit from the PE assessment.

References

Adimin, J. (2008). Pengetua dan guru besar sebagai pemimpin pentaksiran di sekolah. *Ehwal Pendidikan, 17.*
Birch, L. L. (2008). Development of food acceptance patterns in the first years of life. In *Proceedings of the Nutrition Society, 57* (pp. 617–624). Boston, Pearson Education.
Cooper Institute for Aerobics Research. (2004). *The FITNESSGRAM test administration manual* (4th ed.). Champaign, IL: Human Kinetics.
Dugan, S. A. (2008). Exercise for preventing childhood obesity. *Physical Medicine & Rehabilitation Clinics of North America, 19,* 205–216.
Harpell, J. V., & Andrews, J. J. W. (2010). Administrative leadership in the age of inclusion: Promoting best practices and teacher empowerment. *Journal of Educational Thought, 44,* 189–210.
Harris, K. C., Kuramoto, L. K., Schulzer, M., & Retallack, J. E. (2009). Effect of school-based physical activity interventions on Body Mass Index in children: A meta-analysis. *Canadian Medical Association Journal, 180*(7), 719–726.
Hashim, O. M. (2003). *Pentaksiran pendidikan alaf baru satu lambang keunggulan.* Kuala Lumpur: Paper presented at Seminar Pentaksiran Pendidikan Kebangsaan.
Hill, J. O., & Wyatt, H. R. (2005). Role of physical activity in preventing and treating obesity. *Journal of Applied Physiology, 99,* 765–770.
Idris, N. (2005). *Pedagogi dalam Pendidikan Matematik.* Kuala Lumpur: Utusan Publication & Distributor Sdn. Bhd.
Ikeda, J. P., Crawford, P. B., & Woodward-Lopez, G. (2006). BMI screening in schools: Helpful or harmful. *Health Education Research, 21,* 761–769.

Kimwarey, M. C., Chirure, H. N., & Omondi, M. (2014). Teacher empowerment in education practice: Strategies, constraints and suggestions. *Journal of Research & Method in Education*, 4(2), 51–56.

Majid, F. A. (2011). School-based assessment in Malaysian schools: The concerns of the English teachers. *Journal of US-China Education Review*, 8(10). Accessed from http://education.uitm.edu.my/v1/images/stories/publication/faizah/article7.pdf

Ministry of Education (MOE). (2012). *Preliminary report Malaysia education blueprint 2013–2025*. Retrieved from http://www.moe.gov.my/userfiles/file/PPP/Preliminary-Blueprint-Eng.pdf

Pate, R. R., O'Neill, J. R., & Mitchell, J. (2010). Measurement of physical activity in preschool children. *Medicine and Science in Sports and Exercise, 42,* 508–512.

Payne, P. G. (2003). The technics of environmental education. *Environmental Education Research, 9*(4), 525–541.

Reilly, J. (2006). *Evaluation of a cross-community preschool arts initiative in Northern*. In the European Educational Research Association Annual Conference, Geneva. European Educational Research Association.

van de Watering, G., Gijbels, D., Dochy, F., & van der Rijt, J. (2008). Students' assessment preferences, perceptions of assessment and their relationships to study results. *High Education, 56,* 645–658.

Welk, G. J., & Morrow, J. R. (2008). *FITNESSGRAM reference guide*. Dallas, TX: The Cooper Institute.

Part II
Teacher Empowerment: Professional Development and Lifelong Learning

Chapter 6
Transforming Education Through Teacher Empowerment in Namibia: Possibilities and Challenges

Cornelia Ndahambelela Shimwooshili Shaimemanya

Abstract Considering that teacher empowerment takes many forms (teacher autonomy, decision-making, collaborative leadership, etc.), I take the position that teacher empowerment is excellent in transforming education in developing countries. My objective is to demonstrate this through a review of literature, legislative, and policies in Namibia. I complete the review with an in-depth analysis of key informant interviews on teacher empowerment in Namibia. I argue that although the Cabinet of the Republic of Namibia directed the Ministry of Education to implement several resolutions that emanated from the 2011 National Education Conference (e.g., upgrade teachers—at both national and foreign institutions, strengthen teacher training and development, provide more in-service teacher education and more teaching and learning materials for mathematics, science, technology, lower primary and languages, reduce the administrative work load of teachers to afford more time for teaching and learning activities; improve pre-service and in-service training of teachers in national languages), there is unfortunately a paucity of research data in the country pertaining to concerns and challenges regarding teacher quality and quality education as well as teacher empowerment. I conclude that for Namibia to achieve Vision 2030 and become a knowledge-based economy, we need to invest in research on teacher empowerment.

6.1 Introduction

The Republic of Namibia regards education as the main driver for national development and as such invests highly in the quality of its education system; well above 20% of the total government expenditure goes to the education sector. In an

---

C.N. Shimwooshili Shaimemanya (✉)
Educational Research and Education for Sustainable Development, University of Namibia, Windhoek, Namibia
e-mail: cshaimemanya@unam.na

effort to realize Vision 2030, the Namibian Fourth National Development Plan (NDP4) prioritizes improvement of the quality of the Namibian education by improving early childhood development and care services, expansion of secondary education and vocational training and improved quality of teacher education and training (Office of the President 2004). Namibia has thus made great progress in enhancing the quality of education but a lot more still needs to be done. However, despite significant investment and numerous efforts to strengthen education and skills, our education system is still perceived as performing below its potential and, therefore, remains a strategic area under the NDP4. Education is acknowledged to be the single most important aspect of human development, and a critical success factor for economic advancement and increased equality.

Like all other nations, Namibia subscribes to the post-2015 sustainable development agenda. This new international education agenda as set out in Goal 4 (Quality Education) is holistic, ambitious and aspirational and is inspired by a vision of education that transforms the lives of individuals, communities, and societies. It aims to ensure inclusive and equitable quality education and to promote life-long learning opportunities for all. This agenda helps Namibians to renew their commitment towards enhancing the quality of education in Namibia. The new education agenda attends to the unfinished business of the Education for All (EFA) goals and the education related Millennium Development Goals (MDGs) while effectively addressing current and future global and national education challenges.

In the Namibian Education Act of 2001, teacher education and quality of teachers have been given special recognition since no education system can thrive without planning and developing the teachers who are to mend the minds of the young ones, children, and youth. Teachers at all levels are very important in the overall development of any nation and therefore the quality of any educational system depends to a great extent on the quality of teachers. This is in terms of academic, professional qualification, and experience as well as their level of competency. Unfortunately qualified teachers are grossly inadequate in Namibia especially at the primary level.

The 2001 Education Act was reviewed from July 2015 to bring it into line with the latest developments and current needs of the country's education system through a consultative process including parents and concerned members of the public, government agencies, teachers' unions and wider civil society, among other development partners. The planned amendments aim to meet the challenges facing the education sector in order to ensure inclusive and equal access to teaching and learning in Namibia. The Steering Committee (for the Education Act Review), with the support of the United Nations Children's Fund (UNICEF), facilitated a series of consultations through the Regional Directorates of Education and Law Reform in an effort to provide quality education to the Namibian child. The newly amended Education Act will align educational programmes to relevant policies and legislation, as well as national objectives such as Vision 2030, NDP4 and Sustainable Development Goals, in order to equip learners with the necessary skills that will drive the future economy. It should be noted that the new Education Act is not yet out but there is an issue paper which cannot be quoted at the moment. The country has also a Draft Educator Policy which still needs to be finalized.

6.2 Defining the Teacher

A teacher is generally referred to as the educationist/educator or instructor. Although the term *teacher* is interpreted and understood in different ways, in the context of this study, a teacher is defined as someone who is entrusted with the education and molding of the young minds be it at primary or secondary school level.

6.3 Literature Review on Teacher Empowerment

Literature indicates that "teacher empowerment is a complex construct" (Short 1994, p. 488). Michele and Browne (2000: 89) agree that empowerment "is the foundation stone upon which radical reform can be built".

According to Palmleaders (2004) although many new projects in schools include a hive of activities, the change is at a superficial level and only when people are empowered does deep fundamental change takes place at the core of the school system. Short and Greer (1997) and HighBeam Research (2004) identified the dimensions of empowerment in education as given in Table 6.1.

Although teacher empowerment is said to be a complex construct, it can be identified and recognized if these dimensions are present. Smith and Greyling (2006) posit that these dimensions could be grouped into two broad categories: enabling experiences and allowing the individual to display existing competencies and learn new ones.

Table 6.1 Dimensions of empowerment in education

Dimension	Description
1. Decision-making	Participation of educators in critical decisions that directly affect their work
2. Professional growth	Perceptions that the working environment provides opportunities to grow and develop professionally
3. Status	Perceptions that one has professional respect and admiration from colleagues and the community
4. Self-efficacy	Perceptions that one has the skills and ability to facilitate learning by developing effective programmes
5. Autonomy	Perceptions that one can control certain aspects of one's work life freedom to make certain decisions
6. Impact	Perceptions that one has an effect and influence on learners and the school environment doing something worthwhile

6.4 Dimensions of Teacher Empowerment

Squire-Kelly (2012) argues that as from 2002, the center for Teaching Quality began conducting research on teacher working conditions; surveys with questions on five domains (time, professional development, leadership, empowerment, and facilities and resources) were administered to approximately 256, 949 educators in five states in the United States of America; one of the domains was teacher empowerment (Berry et al. 2007). Researchers analyzed the results to determine if there was a correlation between each respective domain and student achievement. The findings show a positive correlation between teacher empowerment and student achievement.

6.5 Decision-Making

Another dimension of empowerment is decision-making (Short and Johnson 1994; Martin et al. 2001). Teachers would feel empowered if they are allowed to have a role in making decisions about their work environment (Hirsch et al. 2006). Hirsch et al. (2006) suggest teachers are the best equipped individuals to make decisions about what happens in their classrooms.

6.6 Professional Growth

Professional growth concerns the teacher's perception of whether or not they are allowed to develop their skills (Rinehart and Short 1994; Short and Johnson 1994). Teachers should be allowed to collaborate with their peers and participate in professional learning concerning various teaching strategies (Hirsch et al. 2006). Professional learning is imperative for teachers to meet the needs of the diverse learners of today (Hirsch et al. 2006). According to Martin et al. (2001), teachers should model life-long learning.

6.7 Status

Status is another dimension of empowerment (Klecker and Loadman 1998; Short and Johnson 1994). Status refers to the amount of attention a teacher receives from parents, students, community members, peers, and superiors (Klecker and Loadman 1998; Short and Johnson 1994). Status also refers to a teacher's belief that their work is valued by their colleagues (Klecker and Loadman 1998).

6.8 Self-efficacy

Another dimension of empowerment is self-efficacy (Short and Johnson 1994; Klecker and Loadman 1998). Self-efficacy is the belief that one possesses the ability to perform their job effectively (Janssen 2004; Short and Johnson 1994). According to Martin et al. (2001) teacher empowerment is important to self-efficacy.

6.9 Autonomy

Teacher empowerment involves autonomy (Short and Rinehart 1992). Klecker and Loadman (1998) define autonomy as the sense of freedom to make decisions. It is important to regard teachers as professionals and allow them to make decisions concerning their job (Hirsch et al. 2006).

6.10 Impact

The final dimension of empowerment is impact. Martin et al. (2001); Short and Johnson (1994) concur that impact is the perception that one influences the school environment. Having a positive impact on the school environment can have a positive effect on a teacher's self-esteem (Martin et al. 2001; Short and Johnson 1994).

6.11 Empowerment of Teachers and Staff

It is essential to empower teachers to influence more school-based decisions. Emerick et al. (2007) argue that "the strengths of many redesigned and early college high schools rests with the empowerment of teachers to influence and take ownership of many critical decisions influencing instruction, not only in their own classrooms, but also in the broader schools where they work", p. 15. It is unfortunate that classroom teachers continue to be institutionally controlled by all other players such as administrators, curriculum specialists, parents, and learners (Scott 2004). As Steyn (2001) argued, staff empowerment has become a managerial buzzword, evoking images of positive commitment and participation in the work place or school. Steyn believes that staff empowerment is based on the fact that people feel good about and proud of what they are doing. However, staff is often confused with task allocation.

Figure 6.1 (Smith and Greyling 2006) depicts two dimensions to create four different strategies: importance of the activity and completeness of authority and

Authority/responsibility   Four basic strategies to assign activities:

You take care for it

Empowerment	Dumping
Development	Double-dumping

Look into it and report back

                    Important   Unimportant

                         Importance of activity

Fig. 6.1 Staff empowerment matrix (Steyn 2001:154)

responsibility. From this empowerment quadrant, the ideal situation means entrusting staff with the necessary power to decide and act upon a task considered to be important. As illustrated in Fig. 6.1, dumping implies giving staff meaningless tasks to do and not allowing them to make decisions (managers still retain meaningful activities). The double dumping strategy includes the allocation of non-essential tasks while still requiring staff to report back for final approval. Managers assign important tasks to staff members in the development quadrant, but require them to bring the information and decision back for review or approval.

Squire-Kelly (2012) believes that empowerment is allowing the teacher to be an active participant in the instructional decisions of the school/recognizing teachers as the experts about teaching and learning issues. She further argues that to empower teachers is to encourage them to be involved in quality professional learning and providing it. Teacher empowerment is acknowledging teachers' major contributions to improving student achievement. School leaders play an integral role in creating an atmosphere where teacher empowerment can occur (Leech and Fulton 2008; Hulpia et al. 2009).

The literature has inconclusive evidence as to whether teacher empowerment directly affects student achievement. Findings from some large studies indicate a correlation between teacher empowerment and student achievement. However, other findings indicate no correlation. Squire-Kelly (2012) therefore concludes that it appears that if teachers feel empowered because they have control over integral parts of their job; or due to the fact that they are actively involved in decision-making; or they believe that they are able to differentiate for all students; are well respected by their peers and the community they serve; are allowed to grow professionally; and they believe that they have influence over the work environment, they will be more effective and this should have an impact on student achievement.

In this age of accountability, teachers are being held accountable for student achievement in Namibia particularly as more and more students do not make to the next grade each year. However, it is not understood how empowered teachers are in schools and the extent to which their empowerment is related to student achievement. Nor do we really have an understanding of the challenges teachers face in the schools that prevent them from "being empowered".

The purpose of this research was to establish the teachers understanding of teacher empowerment, determine what should be done to empower Namibian teachers, establish quality education challenges in Namibia, establish the teacher quality challenges in Namibia, determine to what extent our educational policies (institutional/national) support teacher empowerment. The research further aims to explore the possibilities for teacher empowerment in Namibia, establish whether teacher empowerment can transform education in developing countries such as Namibia, find out whether for Namibia to achieve Vision 2030 and become a knowledge-based economy, we need to invest in research on teacher empowerment to transform our education system.

6.12 Methods

In the process of examining the individual and collective factors and processes of teacher empowerment so as to transform our education to enable us to achieve Vision 2030, it was necessary to content with the "what" of teacher empowerment—what should be done to empower teachers and the "how" of teacher empowerment—how can we empower teachers/mechanisms for empowering teachers. To achieve the study goals, the researcher did a comprehensive literature review and complimented it with 20 key informant interviews from the National Institute for Educational Development (NIED), University of Namibia teacher educators, teachers in the schools and Teachers Union. The unit of analysis/the major entity that is being analyzed in this study are the teachers since the study focused on teacher empowerment as a means to transform education in Namibia. The fieldwork for this study was carried out over a period of 2 months at different intervals. It was important to interview these key players because the education system is only as strong as its teachers.

Similarly, I wanted to establish the concerns and challenges regarding teacher quality and quality education as well as teacher empowerment in an effort to help Namibia achieve Vision 2030 and become a knowledge-based economy.

6.13 Research Findings

One of the interview questions was posed to determine teachers' understanding of the term *Teacher Empowerment*. The following are some of the responses from teachers/teacher educators/teacher unionists:

Providing teachers with requisite skills that will make them perform better or discharge their duties efficiently and effectively wherever they are posted. Teacher empowerment has to do with the enhancement of teacher competencies and ability to effectively deliver teaching, facilitate learning and prepare students/learners for the future endeavours. This is in line with giving teachers opportunities to grow professionally, providing them opportunities to gain knowledge and skills every now and then, so that they feel confident, valued, knowledgeable and skilled about what they do every day. Is to provide more support to the teacher in order to excel in his/her career as a teacher. It is being equipped with the necessary information and resources. Accessing all the necessary resources to teachers. Being intellectual (sic) fit. It means acknowledging teacher in-service training. Giving the teachers the right to participate in the determination of goals and policies. Teacher empowerment has to do with giving teachers chances to grow professionally and to be active participants in matters that affect their work. It means to make teacher more confident. It is the support and assistance granted to teachers in order to empower them.

Asked what in their opinion do teachers need to be empowered on teachers said, *"yes, teachers need to be empowered." "They need professional knowledge on dealing with educational issues and challenges which they confront on a daily basis; being able to take decisions without waiting for the bureaucratic processes they normal take time to complete before teachers can act.* In addition, they believe that other factors to be considered include (see Table 6.2).

Furthermore, participants identified a host of factors as quality education challenges in Namibia as given in Table 6.3.

There are several teacher quality challenges in addition to quality education challenges in Namibia (see Table 6.4).

Asked to indicate to what extent our educational policies (institutional/national) support teacher empowerment, teachers argue that *although there seems to be favourable policies for continuous professional improvement of teacher competence, implementation procedures appear to be too complicated to the extent that some teachers may give up on embracing opportunities for further studies. The teachers [are] not involved when (sic) in the formulation of such policies and they need to be interpreted to teachers very well. Some policies such as those related to postgraduate studies seem to be misinterpreted, especially when undergraduates intent to take up studies at postgraduate level but do not meet the admission requirements. Not at all; they are just reversing the system instead of forwarding it* [remarked one teacher]. *To a medium extend [sic], [educational policies support teacher empowerment]. Not at all because they are only implemented without guidance. Postgraduate Courses in the Faculty of Education require certain qualifications, which were (are) not offered at undergraduate level in the Faculty; that allow articulation to a Masters level (for instance the admission criteria of Masters of Educational Psychology (Guidance and Counselling) that requires a Major in Psychology. Our educational policies (institutional/national) support teacher empowerment through continuous professional development (trainings and workshops), in-service training (e.g. the English Language Proficiency Programme) and Scholarships for undergraduate and postgraduate studies. Most policies only demoralize and intimidate teachers and requires (sic) the teacher to*

Table 6.2 What teachers need to be empowered on

Number	Empowerment Need
1.	Sound knowledge of the subject matter
2.	Strong ability and competency in applying the teaching methodologies and approaches
3.	Strong knowledge of the theories of teaching and learning
4.	Strong ability to apply various assessment strategies
5.	Outstanding ability to stimulate learning among students/learners
6.	Ability to facilitate learning—creating an environment suitable for learning
7.	Notable competencies in using ICT for teaching and learning
8.	Ability to use textbooks as a means to facilitate intellectual development
9.	Strong interpersonal relations (ability to distinguish between personal and professional relations)
10.	Teachers need to get the chance and liberty to work as professionals and not have someone behind them all the time
11.	Willingness to learn from students/learners
12.	Discipline over the learners
13.	Updated curriculum instead of uniformal (sic) curriculum/there is a need in (sic) curriculum update
14.	Use of advanced multimedia
15.	More workshops in subjects they are teaching
16.	Interpretation of Education Act
17.	Interpretation of new educational policies
18.	Be given a chance to share experience with other members
19.	They need regular trainings and workshops
20.	They need opportunities for study
21.	They need a constant support system in terms of expertise and resources

adhere to rules and regulations but do not really help when it comes to classroom level. To a less extent, our educational policies support teacher empowerment.

Teacher opinions were also sought about the possibilities for teacher empowerment in Namibia. Although some teachers stated that there are no possibilities for teacher empowerment in Namibia, others emphasized that "*definitely, teachers with more knowledge will be able to operate in this knowledge-based economy more effectively and efficiently. Yes, teachers need to excel in their subjects they are teaching. Yes, [teacher empowerment can transform education in developing countries] provided it is practical then [sic] theoretically [sic]*".

Possibilities for teacher empowerment include

– *Training especially in curriculum development*
– *Teacher be given a chance to gain new experience daily*
– *Consult teachers before amending or creating policies that affect them*
– *Teacher encouragement by promoting them as well as salaries increment*

Table 6.3 Quality education challenges in Namibia

Number	Quality education challenge
1.	Untrained teachers
2.	Low English proficiency/English language
3.	Teachers' and students' laissez faire attitude to education
4.	Shortage of teaching and learning materials/lack of facilities/appropriate teaching materials and competent staff
5.	Teacher/learner ratio
6.	No empowerment
7.	Flooding (in some areas)
8.	Team work [lack of it]
9.	Inadequate information
10.	Teaching/learning aids
11.	Teachers lack knowledgeable (sic) ICT usage especially in remote areas
12.	Lack of support from the subject advisers
13.	Workshops by Senior Education officers
14.	There is a large gap between policy implementation and rhetoric
15.	Officers are too politically oriented and thus are bias in their judgment
16.	Bureaucracy is killing the system
17.	Leadership at schools
18.	Textbooks do not correspond with the syllabus
19.	Lack of discipline among both teachers and learners
20.	Lack of motivation (to excel) among learners
21.	A perception that teaching is just any other job, rather than being a 'calling'
22.	Inadequate parental support of children in school
23.	Rural–urban migration—leading to overcrowded classrooms
24.	Lack of basic amenities and incentives in rural areas
25.	A not-yet—strong early childhood education
26.	Not all children learning in their mother tongue in their early years
27.	Unmotivated/unpassionate teachers
28.	Low status of education in the country
29.	Overloaded curricula

- *Supporting continuous [Continuous Professional Development] through trainings and workshops/in-service training*
- *Participating in workshops*
- *Creating forums/platforms for exchange of ideas and strategies among teachers in the country and outside*
- *Promoting teacher mobility internationally as well as retention*
- *Providing professional incentives and conducive working environments*
- *Respecting teachers and teaching as a profession.*

Table 6.4 Teacher quality challenges in Namibia

Number	Teacher quality challenge
1.	Negative attitude
2.	Poor training
3.	Alcoholism
4.	Low salaries
5.	Quality of training offered to teachers
6.	Lack of support from regional advisories/poor support from advisory services
7.	Mismatch between teacher specialization and subject matter being taught at school (history specialist teaching mathematics)
8.	Inadequate trained teachers at some regions
9.	Lack of personal commitment/motivation among some teachers
10.	Pedagogical incompetence (teaching methodologies, techniques and strategies)
11.	Poor subject matter knowledge
12.	Poor preparations (by some teachers)
13.	Incompetence in using teaching/learning materials including ICT
14.	Lack of teacher training in ICT usage
15.	Lack of passion for teaching (a teacher being an agent for transformation)
16.	Few teachers of the highest caliber (most who take on teaching as a career are those in the mediocre academic lane—) perception
17.	Still some unqualified teachers esp. at early childhood level
18.	Not given a chance to make decisions
19.	Lack of motivation/passion/extra mile in the teachers
20.	Poor teaching practices from the institutions
21.	Lack of in-service training
22.	Lack of support from the school management
23.	Teaching/learning aids/insufficient teaching aid/materials
24.	Poor working conditions
25.	Advanced resources/lack of resources
26.	Discipline of learners in schools
27.	Lack of support from the parents
28.	ICT training
29.	Use of advanced multimedia

Teachers think that teacher empowerment can transform education in Namibia in the following manner:

> Once teachers' challenges have been documented, appropriate and targeted interventions could be developed and implemented. Teachers' competence will be increased in specific areas as documented. Once teachers competence have been increased, these teachers will be able to deliver high quality teaching and learning services and the learners will have better opportunities to learn in a more favourable environment. Learners learning in a favourable environment will be able to perform better in their subjects. School management will improve and it is likely to lead to overall improvement and transformation of education in

the country. By promoting more support for professional development, forums for exchange of ideas, mobility, etc., you allow growth, knowledge gain, versatility, confidence, ownership, trust and all ingredients of empowerment. Teacher empowerment can very much [transform education in developing countries]. This will enable learners to receive quality education. Yes, because high performing schools have administrators who articulate vision, help teachers grow professionally and play a leading role in determining the school's climate. Yes, if teachers are empowered, quality education will be delivered to improve the general working (sic). Yes, in so many ways, [teacher empowerment can transform education in developing countries such as Namibia]. Teachers will work if they are treated as professionals, and they will work with joy as a result. Officers at the regional offices should just stop coming to schools asking for files, they need to advise on the subject content.

Asked whether they believe that for Namibia to achieve Vision 2030 and become a knowledge-based economy, we need to invest in research on teacher empowerment, teachers argued that certainly *"by researching on teacher empowerment we will unravel the new techniques that we can use to transform our education system for the better."* They strongly believe that investment in teacher empowerment will add value to the process of attaining the goals of Vision 2030, in that: *Teachers are regarded as the agents of transformation, transforming young people who are the leaders in waiting through education as the strategy and vehicle for improving the standard of living among ordinary people. Through investment in research on teacher empowerment, sufficient evidence will be gathered which can be used to inform decisions. Evidence on teachers' opportunities and challenges would be helpful in promoting results-based management and accountability, planning and development of tailor-made and targeted interventions, monitoring and evaluation of national educational interventions to promote good governance. We need to invest [in research] yes. We need to understand what makes teachers empowered and what can be done to help them. If teachers are not empowered, then learners are not motivated, their minds are not stimulated enough, they won't find education fun, they don't perform well and don't have good opportunities to develop the country further.*

Yes, for Namibia to achieve Vision 2030 and become a knowledge-based economy, we need to invest in research on teacher empowerment. Yes, because teacher empowerment will improve the quality of education and training and improve the competencies of workers. Yes, the reason why many schools are not excelling in Namibia it is because of poor teacher empowerment. Teachers need to be empowered; it is all about a Namibian child for us to have a well-educated nation by 2030. "Education is the most powerful weapon which you can use to change the world" (Nelson Mandela). Investing in research on teacher education will help us to ensure that *"teachers will be delivering quality education." In order to attain Vision 2030, all people should be literacy [sic] to eliminate unemployment and poverty.* But not everyone is optimistic. One teacher firmly remarked: *No, we must be realistic, instead of fooling people up to now nothing show a step toward 2030. No, waste of resources, since government is experiencing critically [sic] debt.*

6.14 Improving Teaching Practices Through Action Research and Reflecting Teaching

Hines (2013) argues that there is a need for teachers, administrators, and school systems to become involved in professional development activities in the increasingly complex and challenging profession of teaching. He believes that it is important for professionals to undertake a unit in action research methodology because it provides those professionals working in the education system with a systematic, reflective approach to address areas of need within their respective domains. In her study that investigated teachers' perceptions of the influences of action research on their thinking about instructional practices and the impact of this thinking on teaching practices focusing on teachers' perceptions about the overall teacher role, teachers' knowledge about teaching, teaching practices, and reflective practices, Brown (2002) found that teachers perceived changes in the four areas of investigation. Data in her study revealed that as change occurred in any of the three areas of teaching practices, contents within reflective practices, and knowledge about teaching, a motion of growth began and dispersed into all areas which ultimately influenced the underlying role of the teacher. She further argued that engaging in the stages of action research provided teachers with a methodical structure for implementing and analyzing the teaching and learning process (Brown 2002). There is thus a need to change our schools learning environment to promote staff development opportunities such as action research and reflective teaching. It is important to hear from teachers themselves issues around the teaching/learning process. "If teacher research is concerned with the practical wisdom of professional teachers, their voices and their articulation of the reality of understating students and schools, then those voices have to be heard across the academy" (Hollingsworth and Sockett 1994, p. 17). Action research is a means by which teachers are enabled to actively engage in combining the practice of teaching and the practice of research. The intricate weave of these two components embodies the art and science of teaching.

Reflective practice on the other hand is viewed as "a means by which practitioners can develop a greater level of self-awareness about the nature and impact of their performance, an awareness that creates opportunities for professional growth and development" (Osterman and Kottkamp 1993, p. 2). Awareness is important for behavioral change. To gain a new level of insight into personal behavior, the reflective practitioner assumes a dual stance, being, on one hand, the actor in a drama and on the other hand, the critic who sits in the audience watching and analyzing the entire performance. To achieve this perspective, individuals must come to an understanding of their own behavior, they must develop a conscious awareness of their own actions and effects and the ideas or theories-in-use that shape their action strategies.

Reflective practice is experiential learning. Experiential learning theorists, including Dewey, Lewin, and Piaget maintain that learning is most effective and most likely to lead to behavioral change, when it begins with experience. Research indicates that learning is most effective when people become personally engaged in the learning process, and engagement is most likely to take place when there is a need to learn.

6.15 Conclusions and Recommendations

Although teachers have an understanding of teacher empowerment and can articulate what they need to be empowered as well as what they perceive as challenges to offering quality education and teacher quality challenges, it appears that not much is being done in our education system to empower teachers who are the most important change agents in our education system. Most of the teachers interviewed (25–53 years old) have not received any in-service training in the last 2 years; some not even in the last 8 years even though some have been teaching for 25 years. Teachers are clearly unhappy with the current status quo.

The following conclusions and recommendations could be drawn based on the analysis of the research data:

- Without teacher empowerment in our schools there can be no transformation of education. Teacher empowerment should be an integral part of our education agenda.
- Teachers differed in how they perceived teacher empowerment. For empowerment to be successfully implemented, those entrusted with managing the schools should be empowered first so that the process can filter down to teachers and learners.
- Action research must be an integral part of every teacher education program in Namibia because it helps as Hines (2013) posited to develop knowledge and skills that are critically essential within teacher education and the teaching profession.
- Our educational policies and practices should recognize and reflect the importance of empowerment at the lower levels in our schools.
- In-service training and other measures should be put in place to overcome the quality education and teacher quality challenges as highlighted in this research paper.
- Teachers with different levels of education are different in their perceptions regarding teacher empowerment. It is therefore suggested that the values and principles of empowerment be built into the curricula of educational courses offered at higher education institutions.
- Schools should be well resourced and continuous professional development training opportunities, especially in the areas of ICT, curriculum development, subject content and assessment strategies, should be provided to our teachers.
- Teachers seem to have difficulty understanding and interpreting the Education Act. There is a need to involve teachers in the formulation of the education policies as they are the implementing agents.
- There is a need to improve the salaries and working conditions of teachers to motivate them and help "boost" their teaching morale.

- Teachers should only teach what they have been trained to teach.
- Alcoholism has been identified as one of the quality teacher challenges. The issue of alcoholism should be looked into seriously. There are just too many shebeens in the vicinity of schools that even learners are tempted to drink.
- Subject advisors should provide the much needed support to teachers to enhance their subject knowledge and give them confidence to teach as they will be feeling empowered. This will in turn improve student achievement and translate into economic development of the country.
- Parents should be involved in the school activities of their children and most importantly in disciplining the children to ensure that learning takes place in schools.
- It appears that not much is done to empower teachers. There is a great need to invest in teacher empowerment research if we are to achieve Vision 2030 and become a knowledge-based economy.

References

Berry, B., Fuller, E., & Williams, A. (2007). *Stemming the tide of teacher attrition: How work conditions influence teacher career intentions and other key outcomes in Arizona*. Retrieved from Center for Teaching Quality: http://www.teachingquality.org

Brown, B. L. (2002). *Improving teaching practices through action research* (Unpublished Doctoral Dissertation). Virginia Polytechnic Institute and State University. Blacksburg, Virginia

Emerick, S., Montgomery, D., Reeves, C., Church, K., & Hirsch, E. (2007). *Teaching and learning conditions improve high school reform efforts*. Center for Teaching Quality. Available at https://dschool.stanford.edu/groups/k12/wiki/f329e/.../Team1%20hsconditions-1.pdf

HighBeam Research. (2004). *Defining teacher empowerment*. Available at http://www.highbeam.com

Hines, G. (2013). The importance of action research in teacher education programs. *Issues in Educational Research, 23*(2), 151–163.

Hirsch, E., Emerick, S., Church, K., & Fuller, E. (2006). *Teaching and learning conditions are critical to the success of students and the retention of teachers: Final report on the 2006 teaching and learning conditions survey to the Clark County school District and Clark County Education Association*. Retrieved from Center for Teaching Quality website: http://www.teachingquality.org

Hollingsworth, S., & Sockett, H. (1994). Positioning teacher research in educational reform: An introduction. In S. Hollingsworth & H. Sockett (Eds.), *Teacher research and educational reform* (pp. 1–20). Chicago: The University of Chicago Press.

Hulpia, H., Devos, G., & Rosseel, Y. (2009). The relationship between the perception of distributed leadership in secondary schools and teachers' and teacher leaders' job satisfaction and organizational commitment. *School Effectiveness and School Improvement, 20*(3), 291–317. doi:10.1080/09243450902909840

Janssen, O. (2004). The barrier effect of conflict with superiors in the relationship between employee empowerment and organizational commitment. *Work & Stress, 18*(1), 56–65.

Klecker, B. J., & Loadman, W. E. (1998). Defining and measuring the dimensions of teacher empowerment in restructuring public schools. *Education, 118*(3), 358–405.

Leech, D., & Fulton, C. R. (2008). Faculty perceptions of shared decision making and the principal's leadership behaviors in secondary schools in a large urban district. *Education, 128* (4), 630–644.

Martin, B. N., Crossland, B., & Johnson, J. A. (2001, November). *Is there a connection: Teacher empowerment, teachers' sense of responsibility, and student success*. Paper presented at the Mid-South Educational Research Association Annual Meeting, Little Rock, AK.

Michele, F., & Browne, M. (2000). The progressive outlook: Empowerment through partnership in education. *Progressive Politics, 1*, 86–89.

Office of the President. (2004). *Namibia Vision 2030: Policy framework for long-term national development*. Namibia: Windhoek.

Osterman, K. F., & Kottkamp, R. B. (1993). *Reflective practice for educators: Improving schooling through professional development*. Newbury Park: Corwin Press INC.

Palmleaders. (2004). *Establishing empowerment*. Available at http://www.palmleaders.net

Rinehart, J. S., & Short, P. M. (1994). Job satisfaction and empowerment among teacher leaders, reading recovery teachers and regular classroom teachers. *Education, 114*(4), 570–580.

Scott, J. L. (2004). *Ultimate teacher empowerment*. Available at http://www.makesmart.com

Short, P. M. (1994). Defining teacher empowerment. *Education, 114*(4), 488–492.

Short, P. M., & Greer, J. T. (1997). *Leadership in empowered schools*. New Jersey: Merrill.

Short, P. M., & Johnson, P. E. (1994). Exploring the links among teacher empowerment, leader power, and conflict. *Education, 114*(4), 534–581.

Short, P. M., & Rinehart, J. S. (1992). School participant empowerment scale: Assessment of level of empowerment within the school environment. *Educational and Psychological Measurement, 52*(4), 951–960.

Smith, E., & Greyling, A. (2006). Empowerment perceptions of educational managers from previously disadvantaged primary and high schools: An explorative study. *South African Journal of Education*, EASA 26(4), 595–607.

Squire-Kelly, V. D. (2012). The relationship between teacher empowerment and student achievement. *Electronic Theses & Dissertations*. Paper 406. http://digitalcommons.georgiasouthern.edu/etd/406

Steyn, G. M. (2001). Staff empowerment: Creating an empowered work environment in schools. *Acta Academica, 33*, 146–167.

Author Biography

Dr. Cornelia Shimwooshili Shaimemanya is the former University of Namibia Director of Postgraduate Studies and UNESCO Education Specialist. She is currently a Senior Lecturer of Educational Research and Education for Sustainable Development at the University of Namibia. Her areas of interest include environmental science, science education, educational research, environmental education, education for sustainable development, teacher education, and curriculum\instruction. She has been the Editor-in-Chief of Namibia Educational Research Association (NERA) Journal since 2007 and serves on the Editorial Boards of Namibia Continuous Professional Development (CPD) Journal and Journal for Studies in Humanities and Social Sciences at the University of Namibia.

Chapter 7
Mathematics Continuous Professional Development and Its Relevance to the New Era in South Africa

Zingiswa M.M. Jojo

Abstract For South Africa, the unsatisfactory teaching competencies of the majority of mathematics teachers is attributed to their weak content knowledge, instructional leadership in mathematics, and several curriculum changes since 1994 in basic education. The chapter resumes by introducing professionalism in mathematics, role players in mathematics teachers' professional development, mathematics teacher professional development in the current era, instructional leadership in mathematics teaching, mathematics teacher preparation and together with the teachers' journey in mathematics teaching. This chapter also exposes teachers to effective professional mathematics teaching ensuring impact of continuing professional development: Teacher empowerment as a tool for professional development and how teachers can continue in their self-learning to empower each other as peers is discussed together with support on how teachers can engage in critical self-reflection and innovation within the mathematics classroom. The closing remarks suggest teachers' personal transformation and growth in mathematics continuous professional development with reflection are of relevance to the new era in South Africa.

7.1 Introduction

The trust and focus of this chapter is to unpack continuous professional development of mathematics teachers in the post-apartheid era South Africa. The author draws and builds an envisaged result bearing continuous professional development for mathematics teachers from various scholars in the subject. In this chapter, role players in mathematics teachers' professional development, how teachers undergo preparation and professional development in South Africa is discussed. The meaning of professionalism in mathematics, who mathematics teachers are,

---

Z.M.M. Jojo (✉)
Department of Mathematics Education, College of Education,
University of South Africa, Pretoria, South Africa
e-mail: jojozmm@unisa.ac.za

© Springer Nature Singapore Pte Ltd. 2017
I.H. Amzat and N.P. Valdez (eds.), *Teacher Empowerment Toward Professional Development and Practices*, DOI 10.1007/978-981-10-4151-8_7

professional development as a process of change, together with teachers' reflective practices and self-study are explored. The chapter also exposes teachers to effective professional mathematics teaching ensuring impact of continuing professional development. The chapter then concludes with suggestions of what makes a description of a mathematics teacher in the twenty-first century.

South Africa experiences a shortage of qualified mathematics teachers which challenges the promotion of mathematics as a subject necessary for growth of the country's economy. Bernstein et al. (2013) assert that the teaching of mathematics in South African schools is amongst the worst in the world. Current mathematics teachers in the field today are a combination of a set of teachers with non-matching school subject knowledge and contrasting models of classroom practices (Kaino et al. 2015) together with proactive, reactive and over-reactive teachers (Lindeque et al. 2016). The former teachers require continuous professional development to address and adjust to the consequences of an environment characterized by enormous infrastructural backlogs, resource limitations, an inadequate supply of quality learning support materials, and the absence of common national standards for learning and assessment (Kaino et al. 2015).

In South Africa many changes took place and the biggest change by necessity has been in the area of education since the 1994 democratic elections and post elections. The government first unveiled Curriculum 2005 (C2005) which was driven by the Outcomes Based Education (OBE). This system failed because it was highly overloaded, used vague and complex terminology and fell short of its expectations, and inadequate training of teachers and officials. This was later reviewed in 2012 and replaced by the Curriculum and Assessment Policy Statement (CAPS) in January 2012 which was rolled out in all phases. OBE though, is still the underlying philosophy which underpins CAPS (Chigonga 2013: 2; Botha 2011: 26). It is the current curriculum practiced in the country as a measure that redresses the inequalities and imbalances of the past. Mathematics Continuous Professional Development programmes, are therefore systematic efforts to change the practice, attitudes and beliefs of mathematics teachers in the classroom so as to effect the learning outcomes of students and familiarize teachers with the change in curriculum. As the South African government began to accept the existence of crisis in education, priority intervention was geared towards addressing the quality of mathematics education, improvement of quality of mathematics teachers, numeracy and mathematics teaching in lower grade levels. Professional development in this chapter has been delimited to in-service mathematics teachers.

7.2 Professionalism in Mathematics

In mathematics education, teacher professional development is an indispensable aspect in human resource management and development. Although the current government is making efforts to produce highly qualified mathematics teachers, the challenge is that there still exists a knowledge gap in terms of professional development of teachers. Teacher education is a form of professional education that has a purpose to improve the professional classroom practice of teachers (DOE 2005). Mathematics education in particular in South Africa has suffered a multitude of well-publicized problems namely:

- Shortage of mathematics teachers
- Under qualified teachers
- Teachers struggling with subject content
- Little or absence of pedagogical content knowledge and
- Poor teacher performance in mathematics in general.

Also, mathematics is taught in English, a second language for the majority of both teachers and learners. There are 11 official languages used to teach all subjects from grade R to grade 3. From grade 4 to upper levels, instruction is given in English, a language that is foreign to both teachers and learners, used in school classrooms only, and both parties switch back to their home languages outside the classroom.

In addition the frequent changes in both mathematics curricula and syllabi (OBE, curriculum 2005, NCS, and CAPS) have resulted in challenges at classroom and governmental level.
Pertaining to the classroom, there is:

- Poor learner performance standards and results,
- A lack of classroom discipline
- Insufficient resources (modern technology not an option in most rural situated schools) and
- Inadequate infrastructure.

On a governmental level, there is prevailing

- Failure of appropriate teachers' work support, inspection, and monitoring,
- Lack of continuous training of teachers in service
- Change in mathematics curricula without proper teacher training and communication
- Absence of continuity for teachers as well as learners
- Demoralization and disillusionment among teachers and
- Negative and worsening perceptions of the teaching profession as a whole.

Factors such as: (i) overcrowded classrooms, (ii) high dropout rate, (iii) low literacy and numeracy, (iv) snail's pace of teachers progress through curriculum, (v) lack of resources, (vi) ineffective leadership management, (vii) poor teacher training, (viii) unskilled teachers, (x) lack of commitment to teach by teachers and (x) a shortage of resources in education contribute to poor mathematics performance. All this points to the fact, that South Africa faces a dilemma with regards to mathematics education. The recent ANA results suggest that more than 90% of South African youth fall into this dilemma. This chapter endeavors to make recommendations for the implementation of professional development programmes that will help teachers to be exposed to good classroom practices to enhance the teaching and learning of mathematics in schools.

7.3 Role Players in Mathematics Teachers' Professional Development

There are several suggestions on who should play the vital role in continuous professional development of teachers in South Africa. Several studies (Bansilal et al. 2014; Carnoy et al. 2012; Taylor and Taylor 2012) conducted with mathematics teachers at different levels indicate that teachers don't know well enough the mathematics their learners need to learn. Who is responsible to ensure that teachers have adequate knowledge in mathematics? Various role players including the DoBE, the tertiary institution project interventions, short courses and nongovernmental organizations such as unions are the main mathematics continuous teacher professional development providers in South Africa. Distinction of this provision is made with regards to (i) structure, (ii) style and (iii) content covered by each role player.

Each provincial department, members of the Sub-Division of the Professional Development and Research Division are responsible for the implementation of the Continuous Professional Teacher Development Management system in all provinces in South Africa. This provision is facilitated through the South African Council of Education (SACE) who liaises with other stakeholders like teacher unions, School Governing Body associations and others to approve service providers in different provinces in South Africa. For example, VVOB in South Africa supports its partners, the Department of Basic Education (DoBE), the South African Council for Educators (SACE) and the Free State Department of Education (FSDOE) in improving learning outcomes of primary learners in mathematics (Vermunt 2014). Those providers investigated the relationships between learning outcomes, learners' study behavior, learners' perceptions of their learning environment and their demographic background. A number of issues that dominated in their research were whether:

- learners were encouraged to apply what they have learnt,
- learners were stimulated to connect and engage with ideas,
- learners were encouraged to ask questions that go beyond what is written in the curriculum,
- assessment evaluated deep learning or rather reinforces surface learning
- learning was limited to memorizing in the textbook, and
- How learners perceived the learning and teaching environment of mathematics.

How learners perceive the environment can be directly linked to their performance in the classroom. It is suggested in this chapter that all the stakeholders entrusted with continuous professional development of mathematics teachers, meet, reflect and agree on a model that works to improve learners' performance in mathematics.

7.4 Mathematics Teacher Preparation

The preparation of effective mathematics teachers relies on a comprehensive partnership between institutions of higher education (including faculty members focused on mathematics, mathematics education, and teacher preparation), schools and districts (including mathematics teachers and administrators), and other stakeholders such as the DoBE focusing on student success in mathematics and mathematics teacher preparation as described in the SACE policy of 2014. All the stakeholders are guided by:

- A shared vision and goals on successful mathematics teacher preparation,
- Mutual learning committed to learning from and with each other in continuing to achieve their respective missions better,
- A shared engagement and responsibility in designing suitable programmes for teachers,
- Supporting and recruiting of mentor teachers, and
- Promotion of effective educational practices that promote mathematical excellence amongst students.

The teacher knowledge, skills, and dispositions are then guided by

- Mathematical habits of the mind and construction of mathematical concepts,
- Understanding and appreciation of mathematics as a discipline,
- Specialized knowledge for mathematics teaching, and
- Knowledge of the nature of mathematics.

Mathematics teachers should then undergo intensive preparation on

- Instructional design which includes design of mathematics lesson units, selection of relevant and deep learning tasks and activities, and engagement of all students in mathematics construction practices and procedures,
- Using instructional methods differentiated to create effective mathematical learning environment that promotes motivation, engagement and understanding for all students,
- Assessment and reflection where ongoing learning is assessed using data to promote their professional growth,
- Using instructional technology especially tools used in mathematics, and
- Engaging and dealing with diversity of learners in their classrooms.

Lastly the mathematics teacher preparation should equip teachers with a sense of integrity, intellectual spirit, sense of justice and stewardship while bearing leadership qualities in their classrooms. These qualities help teachers to be honest about what they know, what they want to know and what they believe in. Teachers must demonstrate a sense of responsibility to construct mathematical knowledge, while they generate and share their knowledge on the subject. Mathematics teachers must also collaborate, advocate and ensure professional responsibility always while they emerge as leaders in their classrooms identifying and addressing needs based on thoughtful reflection and professional care.

7.5 Mathematics Teacher Professional Development in the Current Era

In recent years education reformers have focused a great deal of attention on strategies for enhancing teacher quality to promote student achievement. Mathematics provides a powerful, concise and unambiguous means of communication to explain and predict real life situations. It develops logical thinking, and it has an aesthetic appeal to attain its power through its symbols, which have their own 'grammar' and syntax. For this reason in South Africa all learners are expected to have some form of mathematics to apply in real life and in the working world. Those learners who are not competent in the subject enroll for mathematical literacy when they reach grade ten. This is to strengthen the belief that all learners can learn mathematics and must be given the opportunity to do so (Owusu-Mensa 2013: 2).

Currently, teacher education programs are geared to provide platforms where teachers participate, form partners with each other, and research their own practice while they build new knowledge, learn from one another to develop new theoretical models and insights (Bednarz et al. 2011). Some successful forms of professional development include teacher and researcher participation, teacher reflection and mathematical preparation of in-service and pre-service teachers. In teacher and researcher participation, a collaborative group model allows the teacher and researcher to engage on shared experiences where the teacher first plays a student role as they strive to make sense of various ways to teach some units in mathematics. Teachers' roles later change from students to teachers in the classroom where they implement the different strategies learnt and experienced in the collaborative groups. Ferreira and Miorim's (2011) analysis reveales that the teachers' reflection on the experiences on collaborative work showed a better understanding of the subject and growth in their professional lives. The evidence of growth in experience and change that is brought about by diverse approaches indicates the significance of reflection in teachers' development (Bednarz et al. 2011). These include written reflection, oral and written narratives, and self-regulated learning as examples of reflections that are edifying and promote teachers' professional learning (Saylor and Johnson 2014) assert that effective professional development initiatives for teachers in this era, should allow (i) collaboration amongst teachers, (ii) learning with and from other teachers, (iii) shared inquiry, and (iv) incorporate opportunities for reflection which help to transform their teaching practice.

7.6 Instructional Leadership in Mathematics Teaching

Central to the success of a teacher's mathematical professional development is instructional leadership. This is usually underpinned by the teacher's awareness and knowledge of: (i) his/her role in understanding mathematics content, (ii) changes in mathematics education, (iii) different types of approaches to mathematics teaching, and (iv) manipulatives, professional books, and professional development on mathematics initiatives. Swan (2009) defines instructional leadership as the dynamic delivery of the curriculum in the classroom through strategies based on reflection, assessment and evaluation to ensure optimum learning. Dawson et al. (2005) assert that effective mathematics professional development develops teacher's knowledge of mathematics content and how students learn mathematics, together with effective teacher's instructional and assessment practice. Instructional leadership therefore affords each mathematics teacher to learn all about the nature of mathematics teaching and learning while creating and instructional environment for teacher and student growth in mathematics. It is during instructional leadership that teacher-learning communities can be created. Those learning communities afford teachers time to collaborate and share ideas, mentor new teachers, use appropriate resources relevant to selected topics, receive guidance from and form partners with experts in school mathematics, and make connections to a broad vision of mathematics teaching. It is also in such communities that teacher and student prior knowledge in mathematics teaching and learning can be recognized with support and development of new knowledge, providing meaningful resources for the development of new mathematical understanding. Most importantly, the teacher is the instructional leader in his/her classroom. How the classroom environment is organized, the manipulatives used for teaching what, when and how, the approach to the curriculum and the strategies used all depend on how the teacher makes sense of the content. Cautiously he/she must drive each lesson for maximum student understanding such that they can connect newly acquired mathematics knowledge to existing representations and networks for better performance in the subject. Thus professional development provides and develops teachers to be instructional leaders in their mathematics classrooms.

For example, as an instructional leader a lesson on fractions the teacher could use more of the 'how' explanation for the effective application of a procedure in mathematics and the 'why' explanations to promote meaningful learning and flexible application of the concept. The learner would then develop an understanding of the meaning, relationships, properties, roles, and representations of numbers applying this understanding to new situations and problems. For example, a fraction is defined as part of a whole. Which whole? What if the unit under question is a fraction itself? For example a half of a unit is a division into two equal parts irrespective of the value of the given unit. It could be another fraction, like a fifth for example. In such scenarios, a mathematics instructional leader uses skills like problem solving, reasoning, communicating, making connections, representations, mental mathematics, estimations, comparison and technology enhance the teaching of mathematics as a leader.

7.7 Teacher's Journey in Mathematics Teaching

According to Paulsen (2014), teachers' views of mathematics influence the way in which they teach. Continuous reflection by the teacher on his/her day to day practice can be the foundation for commitment to change which must come from within the teacher him/herself. In professional development, the teacher is developed as an educational professional. Through development the teacher has a connotation related to evolution and continuity which goes beyond the traditional overlapping of basic and continued teacher education. Rather effective professional development occurs in a community of learning where the teachers learn through formulating, sharing, and challenging what they and their colleagues think they know.

Edwards (1994) is of the opinion that teacher change in a professional development process is driven by:

- perturbation experience where teachers become aware that something has to change,
- teacher's commitment to change,
- teacher's construction of a vision of what the changes might look like in the classroom,
- projection the teacher self into a set vision,
- decision to make changes within the given context, and
- being a reflective practitioner,
- construction of a goal for change that provides teachers with something tangible towards which they can work (Shaw and Jakubowski 1991),
- personalizing the goal and projecting themselves into a vision on how they will change,
- reflection on continuous growth or development which bolsters teachers' commitment and encourages them to pursue the goals that were set for particular lessons.

The secrets of how the teacher can professionally handle his/her classroom lies in a journey of adjustments of lived experiences practically put into context for a better learning outcome for both the teacher and students. Some guidelines on how the teacher can improve on experiences in his/her classroom as suggested by Kuper (2013) are:

- Teaching with such enjoyment that you don't notice that the time passes,
- Confidence in making sure that the lesson delivery of information is clear and you maintain a presence by moving around the classroom,
- Plan your lesson with an end in mind (objective) and be clear to yourself what the students will be learning,
- Using key words or ideas that you want students to remember to enhance learning,

- Organize information for students to grasp concepts, compare and contrast with existing knowledge using visuals, mind maps and linking information together,
- Stop time and again using questions to check students' understanding in the lesson,
- Maximize your teaching time by clarifying and including a timed agenda of how many minutes you are going to be spending on each part of the lesson,
- Have clear procedure for classroom behavior, and
- Indicate a void in the students' knowledge and always be ahead of them.

7.8 Effective Professional Mathematics Teaching

The findings of a research conducted by National Centre for Excellence in the Teaching of Mathematics (NCETM) in the UK revealed that the following strategies can result in effective mathematics teaching that can be achieved through:

- Teachers' change of practice to application of new ideas in their classrooms where they work with students' mathematics instead of worksheets and textbook approach,
- Embedding change by developing sharable teaching resources and trying new methods,
- Using ICT in their whole class teaching,
- Sharing knowledge and collaborate with their peers,
- Engaging in discussions and communication about mathematics,
- Persevering while discussing difficult tasks,
- Improving classroom atmosphere such that the learners become more confident, motivated and encouraged to do mathematics, and
- Reflecting on their own practice, their own learning and their students' learning.

Effective professional mathematics teaching always results in teachers' learning of mathematics through an increased awareness, improved knowledge of ways of teaching and learning mathematics and improved attitudes and motivation to do more mathematics.

In addition, Garet et al. (2001) suggest the following six features for an effective professional development programme;

- The activity to be organized as a reform type such as study group, teacher network, mentoring relationship, internship, individual research project or teacher research centre
- The duration of the activity to be enough to cover considerable work with the teachers
- Collective participation of groups of teachers from the same school or cluster
- Opportunities for active learning

- Incorporation of experiences that are consistent with teachers' goals, aligned with policy standards and encouraging continuing professional communication among teachers
- An activity with content focus in improving and deepening teachers' content knowledge in mathematics.

Recently, Middleton et al. (2015) suggest that teachers be trained on strategies for building mathematical determination where their interests and proclivities, will and skill are developed. These authors proposed a model for development of perseverance in mathematics as a self-regulatory strategy that consciously redefines the obstacle in terms of conceptual and motivational characteristics (Ibid., 2015). The model consists of (i) interests and identity, (ii) goal specificity (iii) resources, and (iv) consequences.

7.9 Professional Development as a Tool for Teacher Empowerment

In this section the chapter highlights some of the reasons why teachers should pursue professional development in mathematics teaching. One of those reasons is to be empowered. Sparrow and Frid (2001) assert that key within an empowerment model of professional development is that teachers' professional learning needs should be driven by their concerns, interests, and the realities of their daily classroom and school experiences. Murray (2010) defines empowerment as the process through which teachers become capable of engaging in, sharing control of, and influencing events and institutions that affect their lives. Teachers are then empowered to develop a professional identity, and be analytical and attentive to context. Although teachers can also be able to empower themselves, it takes a mindset that is positive, believing in one's self and what one is doing, being assertive and proactive to be self-empowered. Professional development is an ongoing process, one that evolves as you assess and reexamine your teaching beliefs and practices. An empowered teacher can:

- Develop instructional leadership skills that manifest in improved student performance and attitude,
- Be an effective teacher through a combination of professional knowledge, specialized skills and personal experiences and qualities,
- Be a reflective teacher,
- Use a collaborative teaching, share mathematical ideas and join a support group and or network,
- Critically reflect and evaluate what happens in the classroom,
- Actively engages in professional development communities and collaborative inquiry groups,
- Be active member of a subject association and

- Attend courses that develop subject knowledge or focus on classroom practice,
- Consider new knowledge and implications for his/her practice
- Engage with new knowledge, compare it with existing practice and consider how it can be implemented,
- Transform practice and is equipped to take control of his/her own learning, both in an immediate and on-going way.

Cordingley et al. (2012) assert that the mathematical needs of teachers vary from individual to individual and include:

- developing subject knowledge,
- increasing pedagogical content knowledge,
- becoming fluent with, and understanding the application of key tools that can support the learning of mathematics such as digital technologies,
- understanding the implications of relevant policy changes for classroom practice,
- developing reflective practice, and
- becoming fluent in engaging with research and understanding its implications for classroom practice.

According to Zeichner and Liston (1996), such empowered teachers who engage in reflective practice, are:

- able to identify, analyze, and attempt to solve problems that occur in the classroom;
- conscious of and questions beliefs about language teaching;
- cognizant of the institutional and cultural contexts in which they teach; and
- responsible for their own professional development.

7.10 Mathematics Teachers' Reflective Practices and Self-study

Reflective practice according to Smith (2003) describes the nexus between reflection and practice where practice encompasses both practice of teaching and practice of learning such that the experience becomes a site of learning. In study sought to examine the status of existing professional development practices and the challenges practitioners experience in the implementation of mathematics continuous professional development (MCPD) programs in various countries, Jojo (2015) notes that in Singapore mathematics teachers are subjected to a number of professional training forms. Singapore ranked first in mathematics performance in a 49-country TIMSS for the past decade. Three major roles have been played by professional development in this country: (i) changing teachers' mindset for implementing new initiatives, (ii) helping teachers to construct knowledge instead of receiving it and (iii) enhancing learning capacity for teachers to be life-long learners. Jojo (2015) further asserts that this practice is not only different from other countries but may be difficult to emulate. Ban Har (2013) lists the facts that favor Singapore as (i) Singapore is a small country with only 300 schools, (ii) All Singaporean pre-service teachers attend Singapore's one and only teacher training institution, the National Institute of Education (NIE), (iii) Almost all teachers in Singapore are trained in NIE with all budget funding provided directly from the Ministry of Education (iv) Teachers are provided with pre-service training, professional development, school leadership preparation and educational research in the institute, (v) Teacher trainees are employed by the ministry of education and are fully sponsored in a model that involves work and training together at the same time. However, in this chapter, the author argues that lesson study model and reflective practice modelled in Singapore can produce better results in mathematics teaching in South Africa.

Back from the twentieth century, researchers (Dewey 1933; Ottesen 2007; Rodgers 2002; York-Barr and Duke 2006; Zeichner and Liston 1996) consider that true reflective practice takes place only when an individual is faced with a real problem that they need to resolve and seek to resolve in a rational manner. Based on the interactional theory which examines the ways in which people make sense about prevailing situations and how they execute their activities (Prus 1996), the meanings teachers construct whilst reflecting collaboratively on planning and teaching mathematics lessons are based on the four propositions:

- Individual mathematics teachers can act and interact within larger networks of mathematics community of practice
- Mathematics teachers can add values to each other in discussions as part of a mathematics community of practice
- Mathematics teachers can engage in thought and change their behavior as they interact with others
- Mathematics teachers must focus their attention inwardly at their own practice and outwardly at the social conditions wherein they practice mathematics (Carr and Kemmis 1986).

Reflection in the mathematics classroom must be in the form of action, for the action, in action, on action and after the action of teaching (Schon 1983). This is accomplished when teachers reflect on:

- learners prior knowledge (Ward and McCotter 2004),
- the teaching strategies to be used in class per lesson (Lee 2005; Ward and McCotter 2004),
- the discipline and the teacher-learner relationship in the mathematics classroom (Lee 2005),
- whether the mathematical content is suitable for the level of learners, and
- the disturbing aspects of teaching experiences (Ottesen 2007) in mathematics classrooms.

In critical reflection Van Manen (1977) suggests that the mathematics teacher has to question moral, ethics and other criteria that affect his/her classroom practice directly or indirectly. Saleh and Hussin (2011) emphasize that once a teacher has engaged in the active process of teaching, he or she must consistently and regularly reflect on what is happening and what has happened in his or her classroom. A reflecting mathematics teacher:

- gets self-feedback that helps him/her to improve and enhance how he/she teaches
- articulates his/her own learning by critically examining it such that he/she is able to replace what doesn't work in his/her classroom practice
- learn from his/her own practice
- continually changes his/her own currently existing behavior and teaching techniques challenged and developed
- continuously enhances his/her knowledge and skills as a practitioner
- keeps a reflective diary about his/her own experience where he/she reflects on and learns from the experience
- is creative and open to innovations in order to make his/her teaching methods in classroom mathematics teaching
- participates in peer discussions to improve his/her mathematics teaching practice
- recognizes his/her individual progress, value on-going learners achievements
- increases learners' motivation for learning
- enhances and develops collaborative learning
- promotes learner independence, and enhance confidence
- has deeper understanding of his/her learners and
- evaluates his/her own teaching styles to suit mathematics content handled at a particular instance.

All these attributes are necessary to prepare mathematics teachers to be professionally developed and effective in their classrooms. This is one of the strategies that mathematics teachers can use to connect personal theories used as pedagogical tools to classroom practice through reflective writing (Smith 2003). The exercise of reflective practice connected to mathematics theory can help teachers to develop a reflective disposition that elicits, organizes and analyzes personal beliefs and application of theory. Cavanagh and Prescott (2010) posit that reflective practice is an essential part of any teachers' professional growth and encompasses planning and classroom management. Reflection is also necessary for personal and intellectual growth of mathematics teachers where open-mindedness, a shift in focus from self-absorption to self-awareness is nurtured. In this era, mathematics teachers need to progress from simple descriptions of technical aspects of teaching in their classrooms such as content delivery to the considering of the problems of teaching where alternative viewpoints are examined thoughtfully, raising new questions that may be resolved.

Mathematics teachers who engage in self-study improve their personal practice. For self-study to be a fruitful activity, Schuck (2002) suggests that teachers can use action research, reflection, narratives and autobiographies as appropriate methods to improve their practice. Self-study is strengthened when teachers interact with others. Thus self-study cannot be detached from reflective practices. They work hand in hand. But self-study goes an extra mile in helping the teacher to evaluate his/her belief of the role he/she plays in the classroom. Through self-study the belief of teaching as telling where the teacher is an expert in the subject is changed to learners' evaluation on learning. This strategy allows teachers to be accommodative of their students' thinking, modify their teaching approaches such that they research their own practices.

7.11 Conclusion

Policy makers in South Africa depend on continuous mathematics teacher professional development to equip teachers with the instructional capacity to actualize the standards to implement their preferred changes in the curriculum. High-quality professional development in mathematics focuses on specific content, and seeks to improve instruction on the construction of mathematical concepts, procedures, and problem solving. Thus teachers who seek to improve their own practice must be guided by common sense, intuition, word of mouth, personal experience, the guidance of mentors, and folk wisdom. They cannot rely on a body of knowledge and practice that has been rigorously tested for its efficacy in the country. Through professional development teachers can be flexible to choose teaching styles and adapt them to their classroom contexts. Consequently, such styles will vary from one topic to another to address effective learning of mathematics content. In an ever changing curriculum, professional development must adjust to the needs of the continuously changing and demands placed on teachers in the teaching of mathematics. What teachers believe about mathematics, the curriculum, how students learn are influenced by how they experience professional development. Professional development should provide an environment that caters for teachers to become aware of their classroom practices, to reflect on their teaching and make decisions within a group and feel nurtured and safe to change their own beliefs about teaching so that learning can be a powerful process in the teaching of mathematics. Teachers must therefore have freedom to critically examine their teaching practices while they collectively explore ways to improve their teaching and support each other as they work to transform their practice.

In conclusion, NCTM (2016) defines a mathematics teacher as someone who inspires his/her students to look beyond the textbook pages but become problem-solvers and critical thinkers. Thus continuous professional development of mathematics teachers should empower the teachers with skills that invoke not only passion for the subject but life-long learners who care and are concerned with content being taught than the learners being taught. Through professional development mathematics teachers with good technological and organizational skills, brilliance and knowledge skills of their subject area, positive attitude and respect for their learners, valuing their inquiring minds will produce productive citizens. Thus activities in professional development that support and enable mathematics teachers to be skilled in producing learners who are problem-solvers, communicate with each other and the teacher, connect mathematical concepts and represent them in a network using reasoning and proof is relevant to the twenty-first century era. Such teachers can demonstrate readiness to change, persistence, have knowledge of mathematics and have time to be self-aware and reflective.

References

Ban Har, Y. (2013). Mathematics teacher preparation and professional development in Singapore. Country Presentation on Professional Development of Mathematics Teachers, Pretoria, South Africa.

Bansilal, S., Brijlall, D., & Mkhwanazi, T. (2014). An exploration of the common content knowledge of high school mathematics teachers. *Perspectives in Education, 32*(1), 34–50.

Bednarz, N., Fiorentini, D., & Huang, R. (2011). *International approaches to professional development for mathematics teachers*. Canada: Ottawa University Press.

Bernstein, A. McCarthy, J., & Oliphant, R. (2013). *Mathematics teaching in SA adds up to multiplying class divisions*. Mail & Guardian, October 24, 2013, Johannesburg: M&G Media.

Botha, J. (2011). E*xploring mathematical literacy: The relationship between teacher's knowledge and beliefs and their instructional practices*. Ph.D. Thesis. University of Pretoria.

Cavanagh, M., & Prescott, A. (2010). The growth of reflective practice among three beginning secondary mathematics teachers. *Asia-Pacific Journal of Teacher Education, 38*(2), 147–159. doi:10.1080/13598661003678968

Carr, W., & Kemmis, S. (1986). *Becoming critical: Education, knowledge and action research*. Lewes: Falmer/Deakin University Press.

Dewey, J. (1933). *Experience and education*. New York: Collier Books.

Carnoy, M., Chisholm, L., & Chilisa, B. (2012). *The low achievement trap: Comparing schools in Botswana and South Africa*. Pretoria: HSRC Press.

Chigonga, B. (2013). *Implementing the national curriculum statement: How is instructional capacity in the teaching and learning of mathematics constructed, organized and replenished in secondary schools?* Ph.D. Thesis. University if South Africa.

Cordingley, P., Buckler, N., & Isham., C. (2012). *Evaluation of professional development providers in England 2010-2011: Evaluation report for school leaders*. http://www.curee.co.uk/files/publication/[site-timestamp]/professionaldevelopment%20providers%20report%20-school%20leaders%20final.professionaldevelopment

Dawson, S., Burnett, B., & O'Donohue, M. (2005). Learning Communities—an untapped sustainable competitive advantage for Higher education. *International Journal of Educational Management*.

Department of Basic Education, (2005). *Curriculum and Policy Statement*. Pretoria, South Africa.

Edwards, T. G. (1994). *Using a model to understand the process of change in a middle school mathematics teacher*. Paper presented at the Annual Meeting of the National Council of Teachers of Mathematics, Indianapolis, April 12, 1994.

Ferreira, A. C., & Miorim (2011). Collaborative work and the professional development of mathematics teachers: Analysis of a Brazilian experience. In N. Bednarz, D. Fiorentini, & R. Huang (Eds.), *International approaches to professional development for mathematics teachers* (pp. 137–149). Ottawa, ON: University of Ottawa Press.

Frid, S. (2001). Constuctivism and reflective practice in practice: Challenges and dilemmas of a mathematics teacher educator. *Mathematics Teacher Education and Development, 2*, 17–33.

Garet, M., Porter, A., Desimone, L., Birman, B., & Yoon, K. (2001). What makes professional development effective? Analysis of a national sample of teachers. *American Education Research Journal, 38*(4), 915–945.

Jojo, Z. M. M. (2015). Comparative study on structural organization of Mathematics Continuous Professional Development (MCPD) in selected developing and developed countries. *International Journal of Educational Sciences,* 8(1–ii), 229–240 (ISSN 0975 1122).

Kaino, M., Dhlamini, J. J., Phoshoko, M. M., Jojo, Z. M. M., Paulsen, R., & Ngoepe, M. G. (2015). Trends in mathematics professional development programmes in post-apartheid South Africa. *International Journal of Educational Sciences,* 8(1–ii), 153–163.

Kuper, L. (2013). *10 Commandments for new teachers.* Teacher Network for Teacher's Blog

Lee, I. (2005). Preparing pre-service English teachers for reflective practice. *ELT Journal, 61*(4), 321–329.

Lindeque, B., Gawe, N., & Vandeyer, S. (2016). *Context analysis. Teaching-learning dynamics.* Pearson Education South Africa (Pty) Ltd.

Middleton, J. A., Tallman, M. A., Hatfield, N., & Davis, O. (2015). *Taking the severe out of perseverance: Strategies for building mathematical determination (White paper).* Chicago, IL: Spencer Foundation.

Murray, J. (2010). Towards a new language of schorlarship in teacher educator's professional learning? *Professional Development in Education, 36*(1/2), 197–210.

National Council of Teachers of Mathematics (NCTM). (2016). *Enhance your professional development with NCTM membership.* Washington, DC: National Academy Press.

Paulsen, R. (2014). Professional development as a process of change: Some reflections on mathematics teacher development. *International Journal of Educational Sciences,* 8(1–ii), 215–221.

Prus, R. (1996). *Symbolic interaction and ethnographic research: Inter-subjectivity and the study of human lived experience.* Albany, NY: State University of New York Press.

Ottesen, E. (2007). Reflection in teacher education. *Teachers and Teaching: Theory and Practice,* (1), 31–46.

Owusu-Mensa, J. (2013). *Mentoring as a professional development for mathematical literacy teachers in the greater Taung area.* Ph.D. Thesis. University of South Africa.

Rodgers, C. (2002). Defining reflection: Another look at John Dewey and reflective thinking. *Teachers College Record, 104*(4), 842–866.

Saleh, F., & Hussin, Z. (2011). Reflective practices among mathematics teachers. *Asia Pacific Journal of Educators and Education, 26*(1), 145–157.

Saylor, L., & Johnson, C. C. (2014). The role of reflection in elementary mathematics and science teachers' training and development: A meta-synthesis. *School Science & Mathematics, 114*(1), 30–39.

Schon, D. A. (1983). *The reflective practitioner: How professionals think in action.* New York: Basic Books.

Schuck, S. (2002). Using self-study to challenge my teaching practice in mathematics education. *Reflective Practice, 3*(3), 327–337.

Shaw, K. L., & Jakubowski, E. H. (1991). Teachers changing for changing times. *Focus on Learning Problems in Mathematics, 13*(4), 13–20.

Smith, T. J. (2003). *Connecting theory and reflective practice through the use of personal theories.* Australia: Charles Sturt University

Swan, M. (2009). *Improving learning in mathematics: Challenges and strategies, department for education and skills standards unit.* University of Nottingham. ISBN: 1-84478-537-X

Taylor, N., & Taylor, S. (2012). Teacher knowledge and professional habitus. In N. Taylor, S. Van der Berg, & T. Mabogoane (Eds.), *What makes schools effective? Report of South Africa's national school effectiveness study.* Pearson: Cape Town.

Van Manen, M. (1977). Linking ways of knowing with ways of being practical. *Curriculum Inquiry, 6,* 205–228.

Vermunt, J. D. (2014). *Patterns in student learning: the past, present and a future.* Paper presented at the European Association for Learning and Instruction, SIG 4 Conference, Leuven.

Ward, J. R., & McCotter, S. (2004). Reflection as a visible outcome for preservice teachers. *Teaching and Teacher Education, 20*(3), 243–257.

York-Barr, J., & Duke, K. (2006). What do we know about teacher leadership? Findings from two decades of scholarship. *Review of Educational Research, 74,* 255–316.
Zeichner, K., & Liston, D. (1996). *Reflective teaching: An introduction.* Mahwah, New Jersey: Lawrence Erlbaum Associates.

Chapter 8
Professional Training and Lifelong Learning for School Heads of Departments: A Gateway for Headship Continuous Improvement

Sharon Thabo Mampane

Abstract This chapter focuses on the training of teachers in middle management, called Heads of Department (HoDs), for lifelong learning through mentoring and coaching. HoDs are former class teachers promoted to the role of supervising other teachers (Bush in Theories of educational leadership and management. Sage Publication, London 2011). Professional training of HoDs aims at equipping HoDs with updated abilities, interests and knowledge for teacher leadership. During mentoring, guidance, advice and information are provided to the HoDs by more experienced persons (mentors) for career development. The mentors pass down their knowledge, skills and expertise to HoDs who may not possess such skills through formal training. Coaching helps HoDs build self-confidence to improve performance during teacher leadership. During training, problem-solving hands-on activities are carried out and a relationship of trust and collaboration develops. The starting point is the identification of the learning goal and training that focuses on support, achievement of set goals and becoming more accountable for actions. The aim is to equip HoDs with the monitoring of teaching and learning skills and the identification of teacher development and support needs. Training is part of lifelong learning and essential for the facilitation of learning excellence. This chapter will therefore explore conceptual frameworks and innovative ways of supporting lifelong learning through HoD training in mentoring and coaching.

8.1 Introduction

With the onset of the democratic era, devolution of responsibility to schools and the growth of school-based management have impacted upon the role and workload of the team of school leaders (Swanepoel 2008; Rosenfeld et al. 2009). Schools in

---

S.T. Mampane (✉)
Department of Educational Leadership and Management, College of Education,
University of South Africa, Pretoria, Gauteng Province, South Africa
e-mail: mampast@unisa.ac.za

© Springer Nature Singapore Pte Ltd. 2017
I.H. Amzat and N.P. Valdez (eds.), *Teacher Empowerment Toward Professional Development and Practices*, DOI 10.1007/978-981-10-4151-8_8

South Africa operate within a legislative framework set down by national, provincial or state parliaments. One of the key aspects of such a framework is the degree of decentralisation and changes in the educational system (Bush et al. 2010). These changes have resulted in HoDs being given significant powers such as the responsibility to supervise teachers in schools (Rosenfeld et al. 2009). The term 'HoD' is used to describe individuals who are in *formal roles of responsibility* and who form the *middle leadership level* in schools (Hannay and Ross 1999). In recognition of the increasingly important role they play in schools, recent literature has been referring to them as middle leaders (Gurr and Drysdale 2013; Koh et al. 2011); however, in this chapter, the term 'Head of Departmental or HoD' is used. HoDs' roles are more demanding; however, most HoDs from former disadvantaged schools in South Africa, lack experience and training, making their tasks difficult to perform. The changing context and challenges within which HoDs operate, necessitates professional teacher empowerment in mentoring and coaching for lifelong learning (Clutterbuck 2011). Their pivotal role entails managing teachers and the constant changes in school curricula. As Heads of Department (HoDs), they are phase and subject leaders with knowledge of a specific subject area managing and supervising teachers within their specialised subject in the grades and across the phases (DoE 2000; DBE 2011; Sharitha 2013). They have to coordinate intervention strategies as well as approaches within the subject department to ensure that teachers teach accordingly (Louis et al. 2010a, b).

As teacher leaders, HoDs are accountable for empowering teachers in teaching and learning whereas previously their accountability was for input into learning processes only (Louis et al. 2010b). The recognition and importance of HoDs has led to increased attention to preparing them, not only as individual leaders, but also in the context in which they work, to enhance their leadership competencies (Hernez-Broome and Hughes 2012) for mentoring and coaching teachers to improve learner performance (McCauley and Brutus 2011). Acquisition of mentoring and coaching skills is a powerful source for improving leadership skills and for equipping HoDs with more knowledge than they already do. This chapter aims to inform, challenge and motivate HoDs to match their experiences and skills, especially in former disadvantaged schools. The aim is to enhance their strengths in areas of teacher empowerment (Scottish Executive Education Department (SEED) 2005). Key to HoD leadership competency is teacher empowerment for organisational success and improvement (Gurr and Drysdale 2013). For HoDs to acquire leadership competency, they require support and guidance in their particular learning area, to enhance teacher empowerment. Therefore, HoDs need to be "hands-on" leaders, who engage with curriculum and instructional issues; are not afraid to work directly with teachers; and are involved in teaching themselves (Horng and Loeb 2010). School principals have to ensure that HoDs receive support through professional development in mentoring and coaching.

8.2 Meta-Analysis of Mentoring and Coaching

Entering a new role of leadership in any profession may be a major challenge to the HoD who is not adequately trained or prepared. HoD leadership, a formative period where the knowledge, skills and attitudes should have been provided before practice, is crucial. Most HoDs are not prepared or trained in mentoring and coaching, what is available as Professional Teacher Development to HoDs in the South African context is inadequate (Borko 2012). Each year, schools, districts and the governments worldwide spend millions, if not billions, of Rands on in-service training workshops, but neglect the training of HoDs (Johnson 2006). This realisation has led to educational scholars and policy makers worldwide emphasising the need for professional development and support opportunities for HoDs to improve teacher knowledge, instructional practices (Timperley and Alton-Lee 2008) and improved teaching and learning in schools. This transition period can be stressful as well as challenging as new demands requiring the consolidation of acquired skills are made on HoDs. Guidance and support are important for developing confidence and competence. Support through mentoring and coaching skills is crucial for HoD professional development and for empowering HoDs for teacher supervision. Mentoring and coaching is an innovative strategy for Professional Teacher Development (PTD) and for teacher empowerment (Clutterbuck 2011).

Although PTD is crucial for nearly every educational effort to improve teaching and learning, many models developed for teacher empowerment do not address the learning goals envisaged (Supovitz and Turner 2010). The current trend in teacher empowerment, for example, does not address mentoring and coaching skills, an important part of leadership development linked to, and embedded in the HoD's on-going work. Teacher empowerment should be an integrated set of experiences (Hernez-Broome and Hughes 2012) with training standards to ensure teachers achieve teaching excellence in schools (DoE 2000). Well-developed teacher development and empowerment programs should entail a process embracing all activities (formal or informal), to enhance professional career growth (Rogan and Grayson 2003; Tecle 2006). The formal training process can take place during seminars, workshops and through collaborative learning among peers in institutions, to share good practices. Informally, training can occur through conversations, reading, learning from peers or observing a colleague (Mizwell 2010). Mentoring and coaching as part of PTD can also be made available through external expertise in the form of courses, workshops or formal qualification programmes, and through collaboration between schools or teachers across schools (e.g. observational visits to other schools or teacher networks), or within the schools in which teachers work (OECD 2009).

8.3 Importance of Mentoring and Coaching HoDs Within the S.A Context

The role and functioning of schools are changing and so is what is expected of HoDs in South Africa. HoD roles include teacher and learner supervision in increasingly multicultural settings. These types of settings require: more effective use of information and communication technologies for teaching, commitment for planning within evaluative and accountability frameworks, and parental involvement (OECD 2009). The increasing outcry about the ineffectiveness and lack of mentoring and coaching skills from HoDs to improve the quality of teaching and learning required in schools, led to the Department of Education in the Mpumalanga Province of South Africa seeking funding from the Education and Training Development Programme (ETDP) Sector in Education and Training Authority (SETA), to improve service delivery in the Mpumalanga Province schools. ETDP SETA provided sponsorship for HoD training in mentoring and coaching skills in order to address the challenges in the workplace (DBE 2011). The training programme in Mentoring and Coaching for School Leadership aimed at improving the ability and preparedness of the HoDs in performing their teacher leadership and supervision role for teacher empowerment in South African schools. Individual HoDs' career knowledge needs updating in light of recent advances in education. For example, HoDs require curriculum changes that require teacher empowerment in the development of new teaching techniques and objectives (Clutterbuck 2011).

Training HoDs in mentoring and coaching may improve the standards of teaching and learning as well as enhance monitoring and evaluation of teacher performance. Some of the benefits include future learner success, and continuous improved performance. School leaders should play a key role in ensuring team planning and collaborative learning for HoDs to master new forms of pedagogy that enable the monitoring and evaluation of teacher practice (OECD 2009). Where support is provided through HoD capacity building, results are a sound teaching and learning environment with improved school outcomes. HoDs trained in mentoring and coaching expand in leadership roles and processes; and have the capacity to produce direction, alignment and commitment. HoD leadership and supervision of teachers require effective interpersonal skills, social awareness and social skills (Day et al. 2001).

8.4 Professional Teacher Development

Professional teacher development is a priority that should be well managed for school performance to improve. The acquired knowledge would help improve schools, and most importantly, learner performance; as well as maintain a high standard of teacher leadership and supervision workforce (OECD 2009). Furthermore, personal development and growth may create employment opportunities and help create and maintain positive attitudes to learning, to keep the brain active and to prevent boredom (Louis et al. 2010b). The challenge, however, is always the issue of finances, hence the need for sponsorship from Non-Governmental Organisations (NGOs). Where funding is sourced and HoDs are trained, attitudinal development and functional development should be included (Evans 2002). *Attitudinal development* encourages willingness for change of attitudes and emotions in the work, while *functional development* leads to the acquisition of new knowledge and skills for improved and meaningful professional development and performance. The mentoring and coaching programme should include a more holistic view of HoD development and support and should be developed by a team of experts in the specific topics related to mentoring and coaching.

Mentoring and coaching if well developed, is an interesting, informative and thought-provoking area of teacher empowerment about educational issues that enable HoDs to critically engage with fellow HoDs and the lecturer during training sessions. HoDs are encouraged to work through each unit daily before attending the lecture, in preparation for class discussions, activities, group discussions, feedback and reflections for portfolio development. HoDs gain insight in the structure, content and training approach of the entire course program and learn to apply changes in curricula or other aspects of teaching practice after attending various developmental training opportunities. Acquired competences, skills and expertise in teacher supervision may be exchanged among HoDs to help improve effectiveness in teaching and learning (Clutterbuck 2011). HoDs should be equipped in skills of teacher empowerment for lifelong learning through on-going professional development. HoDs become motivated to learn and learning becomes a deliberate and voluntary act, as lifelong learning occurs. Understanding of the world and being provided with more and better opportunities to improve their quality of life, enhances knowledge (McCauley and Brutus 2011). HoDs who do not get the opportunity to get on-going professional development may not improve their skills, and teachers they supervise may be affected negatively.

8.5 Implications of the Mentoring and Coaching for Heads of Department

A cross-country comparison of the educational attainment level in South African schools reveals that improvement and attainment rate of education is up only up to Grade 11, though, generally of low quality. The Grade 11 performance is better, when compared to the performance in Grade 12, which mostly results in substantial learner drop-outs and failure to achieve a university endorsement, in comparison with other middle-income countries in Africa (Fleisch 2008; Van der Berg 2008; Taylor and Yu 2009). Although access to education has greatly improved in South Africa, the school system still caters for HoDs functioning in two different sub-systems. The first sub-system is the historically disadvantaged system where the majority of children and their teachers are located. The second sub-system consists mostly of schools that historically served white children and produces educational achievement closer to the norms of developed countries. A number of learners from the historically disadvantaged system are increasingly migrating to these schools (Van der Berg et al. 2011). This chapter discusses mentoring and coaching of HoDs from a historically disadvantaged system.

The mentoring and coaching programme for HoDs is aimed at guiding HoDs through the prescribed content of the module and to give a more comprehensive or holistic overview of specific topics for HoDs' empowerment with leadership and management skills for mentoring and coaching teachers. If HoDs are provided with guidance for career self-management, their communication and decision-making skills in the supervision of teachers, may improve. This is in line with the education policy and law for employee retention and teaching and learning (Clutterbuck 2011). All trained HoDs end up with updated abilities, interests and knowledge for effective teacher empowerment and for monitoring teaching and learning. Identification of teacher empowerment and support needs become enhanced through HoDs' interactions, critical and logical arguments, and constructive criticisms or inputs. When interacting with most HoDs during class presentations the Facilitators can observe if there is improved self-confidence and performance or an indication of comprehension or non-comprehension of teacher leadership and support, for effective teaching and learning. All HoDs should acquire expertise and knowledge to ensure effective teacher empowerment occurs in schools (Sackdanouvong 2013).

During training, problem-solving and hands-on activities are carried out to help develop relationships of trust and collaboration and to set goals in the learning activities. HoDs' training enhances accountability of mentoring and coaching and excellence in performance, and forms part of teacher empowerment for lifelong learning (CIMA 2012). Discussions on practical educational case studies and innovative ways of supporting lifelong learning through school leaders make lessons more interesting, informative and thought provoking, during engagement with fellow HoDs and lecturers. The interrelatedness of all themes and their influence on effective teaching and learning in schools are highlighted. The training and preparation for class activities allow for self-directed, individual, reflective study and much of what is achieved depends on the training, efforts and commitment of HoDs (CIMA 2012).

8.6 Implications of Mentoring and Coaching for Leadership Skills in South Africa

Mentoring and coaching is based on good rapport, and this creates powerful relationships. The relationships built on agreed upon, clear rules and boundaries before the process begins and the same parameters, are stuck to throughout. Mentoring and coaching can only succeed where there is total trust, openness and commitment to confidentiality (Clutterbuck 2011). Ideally, mentoring and coaching should be a voluntary process with no coercion, but the lack of leadership capacity in some HoDs (Fielden 2005) forces institutions to formalise these types of HoD leadership development for empowerment. Mentoring and coaching should develop into a long-term relationship between a knowledgeable person and the inexperienced person, for personal and professional growth (Clutterbuck 2011). Mentorship expertise develops with age or experience and thus experienced and expert members of staff or newly appointed staff from Teacher Training College, may become mentors to senior and experienced teachers on the use of technology in teaching and learning.

The mentors conducting the training have various core skills and are able to create rapport, paying attention to content and process, keeping an open mind, and reflecting on developmental issues through probing questions. While mentoring HoDs, the following are identified: limiting assumptions, beliefs and inability to give and receive feedback (Clutterbuck 2011). Relationships built through mentorship develop into friendship that lasts longer and HoDs later become expert mentors to newly appointed teachers starting out their teaching career. During mentoring and coaching, current constraints are challenged while new possibilities are explored to ensure accountability and support for the achievement of goals and for sustaining teacher empowerment (Ting and Hart 2004).

During training, coaching involves practical, goal-focused forms of one on-one learning ideal for behavioural change (Hall 1999). There is internal or external support, a short-term intervention intended to develop specific leadership skills, and a more extensive process involving a series of meetings over time (Hernez-Broome and Hughes 2012). Coaching should be a directive approach which involves teaching and the provision of feedback and advice or it can also be a non-directive approach that provides guidance to enable the HoD to find solutions to problems (Clutterbuck 2011). The aim of coaching is to improve performance and skills for teacher development. The coaching process entails identification of the learning goal, support for the achievement of set goals, and accountability for actions. According to Fielden (2005), effective coaching should unlock potential and maximise performance of developed skills. Coaching should result in collaboration through discussions and the assessment of developmental tasks. The advantage of coaching is that the advice and the assistance provided is tailor-made for the HoDs' individual needs and this is done within their schedule unlike development training sessions where a general programme is used within a set time (Jarvis 2004).

In South African schools, subject specialists from the Department of Education play the role of an external coach, while the HoD is the internal coach in the school. Coaching offers objective perspectives and supports the HoD's efforts of trying out new tasks for teacher empowerment. During coaching attributes such as patience, detachment, support, interest, perceptions, awareness, self-awareness and attention are strengthened (Fielden 2005). The coach, who is also a mentor, has to develop the HoD by building self-confidence, identifying suitable topics and developing tasks to be done (Fielden 2005). Knowledge, credibility, experience and authority are of paramount importance. Mentoring and coaching is now becoming a high degree of compulsory teacher empowerment, a highly managed professional development system, though with less discretion for teachers to choose the development they feel they need (Caena 2011).

There are different theories of how mentoring and coaching can be organised. Model of peer mentoring and coaching, although from 1980s, is still relevant for this chapter. According to, the training session for HoDs should aim at enabling HoDs to practice and implement the content learnt and should focus on implementation of learnt skills for teacher empowerment and student improvement in the school. The results of implementation, irrespective of whether experts or HoDs conducted the sessions, should reveal that the shared learning process leads to staff development and should directly affect student learning. The aim of mentoring and coaching sessions is for student benefit. HoDs learn, grow and change; the success is evidenced by developed skills and joy in the collaborative experience that continue after they accomplish their initial goals. Permanent on-going professional development for teacher empowerment operates in a context of training, implementation and general school improvement.

There is, however, no evidence that mentoring and coaching affect students' learning because of lack of research on how trained HoDs disseminate learnt teaching strategies and innovations for teacher empowerment in schools. The assumption is that new strategies learnt may be implemented smoothly and appropriately only after returning to school. It is therefore important that school leaders support the intensive training efforts that occurred in teacher empowerment workshops. Problems identified during implementation may require continued technical assistance at the classroom level. Mentoring and coaching skills may be practiced through new teacher empowerment strategies at school level until they become a part of the teaching practice. HoDs who have established good team relationships with their teachers, and apply mentoring and coaching skills appropriately, usually exhibit greater long-term retention of new strategies and their appropriate use over time. Thus the recommendation for schools to organise mentoring and coaching programmes that empower HoDs to lead and supervise teachers in schools (Garmston 1987). Learning to provide technical feedback requires extensive training and time, and becomes easy only after team members have mastered new behaviours. Verbal feedback and support are essential after ideas are shared. It is critical that the impact of the mentoring and coaching training be measured to determine school improvement effort. Therefore a skilful teacher empowerment programme should result in a self-perpetuating process for change, increased new knowledge and skills for teachers and students.

8.7 The Mentoring and Coaching Training Process

The mentoring and coaching training programme for HoD empowerment targeted a period of ten days, for 8 h a day. The focus was on mentoring and coaching which had implications for teacher supervision and leadership for effective teaching and learning in schools. Training followed a learner (adult) centred teaching approach/philosophy where HoDs were responsible for their own learning and facilitators facilitated the learning process. HoDs were encouraged to think using the community of inquiry skills (that involved instructional learning or teaching) and peer-assisted learning (where HoDs were engaged in collaborative activities for collective gain). The HoDs' profile consisted of 150 HoDs who were selected by the Mpumalanga Education Department to undergo training. The selected HoDs were new and experienced and had never received training before. The resources used were study guide, readers, articles and web links to articles. Training facilitation was carried out through the use of data projectors, laptops, flip charts, markers and worksheets. The professional training of HoDs was performed by University lecturers with mentorship/coaching expertise and experience. During training, individual and group work activities were used to develop HoDs for teacher empowerment. A lot of collaborative activities, presentations and interactive discussions were conducted (Clutterbuck 2011).

Groups consisted of five to six people, with role swapping between team members so that each can observe or be a presenter (Caena 2011). Other group members listened and learned from presentations made and developed skills of mentoring and coaching from the presentations. Facilitators gave constructive feedback about skills acquisition and the development progress made regarding challenges of teacher supervision and problem solving in particular phases and subjects, and how this may be incorporated into the teaching practice (Jensen 2011). In the S.A context, case studies were used to identify the training needs or gaps in teaching and learning and instruction of teachers. The collective participation of HoDs was coherent with their experiences and afforded opportunities for active learning. This participation contributed to a shared professional culture and the development of a common understanding of instructional goals, methods, problems and solutions (Caena 2011). HoDs in the development programmes showed improvement in knowledge and skills of teacher supervision and gained collective ownership of their own professional development and responsibility for improving learner performance. In the end HoDs wrote a reflective learning journal which included experiential learning that occurred during their direct participation in the daily trainings (Smith 2001). The reflective learning journals were part of a development process in teacher empowerment.

The mentoring and coaching training process was conducted mainly through facilitation, instructions, teamwork, discussions, problem solving and feedback. A two-part model for developing mentoring and coaching skills of HoDs was utilised. First, the mentoring and coaching training focused on the three elements of teacher empowerment, for developmental experiences, namely: assessment, challenges and support. *Assessment* was carried out by the facilitator and the HoD peers during class discussions, for individual and group tasks. Through assessment lecturers/facilitators identified the HoD's areas of strengths, current performance level, and developmental needs. *Challenging experiences* were addressed from practical teaching and learning case studies within the HoDs' allocated groups. HoDs worked outside their comfort zones and thereby developed new skills and abilities that provided opportunities for learning further. *Support* was provided in the form of lecturers/facilitators facilitating mentoring and coaching training to enable HoDs to handle the struggle of developing as mentors and coaches.

Second, HoD development involved a variety of *developmental experiences* and the ability to learn from them. HoDs with a high ability to learn were encouraged to reflect and share with group members and peers challenges and successes within their particular leadership context, to enhance learning. The development process included elements such as age, culture, economic conditions, gender, organisational purpose and mission, and, teaching and learning strategies. These aspects played an important role in moulding the group members and HoDs' developmental process for teacher empowerment. Along with assessment, challenge and support, HoD leadership context was an important aspects of the HoDs training process for mentoring and coaching.

8.8 Implications for Practice Within the South African Context

Different HoDs have different needs based on their *leadership experience, knowledge, skills* and *expertise*. In some cases formal leadership training may prove to be of necessity, while in other cases HoDs may possess adequate knowledge of mentoring or coaching that facilitators could learn from. Some newly appointed HoDs indicated leadership challenges regarding issues related to teacher supervision, and such HoDs appreciated empowerment through mentoring and coaching for effective teacher and learner supervision. This meant school leaders had to explore the full potential of the staff before organising the mentoring and coaching programmes to help support HoDs for the real leadership situations (Fielden 2005).

All HoDs, in the training programme, experienced and inexperienced, faced different teacher leadership and supervision challenges because of the constant changes in: the curriculum, the new instructional methods, the advances in technology, the changed laws and procedures, and learners' learning needs. HoD empowerment enabled them to find new ways out of a potentially stressful work situation. Relationships and communication encouraged team work, positive staff morale and the maintenance of high levels of achievement (Borko 2012). Feedback given during training sessions regarding monitoring and coaching skills brought in new knowledge while different experiences of addressing challenges gave the HoDs the opportunity to talk about their professional development (Fielden 2005) and shared how they have improved in expertise and work abilities (Mizwell 2010).

During mentoring and coaching, HoDs shared experiences, points of views about perceptions, and, examined understandings of how the subjects were examined with other group members (Clutterbuck 2011). Reflections about their own learning, and how and why they learned, included how they felt about a particular topic or situation, before and after being empowered, learning from mistakes and they shared their successes. Most importantly, HoDs remained positive and the application of what was learnt was enhanced. The implication about the training process is that not all HoDs have the required skills and expertise for teacher leadership. Every new position requires keenness to learn and develop. Therefore it is important that HoDs take advantage of training related to mentoring and coaching for continuous teacher empowerment to become better at what they do as well as become indispensable to the employer (Clutterbuck 2011). HoDs, who have acquired leadership expertise, are likely to experience better and more rewarding working days. Thus mentoring and coaching should be an on-going professional development for teacher empowerment because it does not only help improve performance, but may increases job satisfaction.

8.9 Conclusion

South African HoDs lack professional development skills in mentoring and coaching. Many of the problems faced in schools are linked to insufficient teacher empowerment. Capacitating HoDs is essential in mentoring and coaching for promoting teacher empowerment and for improving school effectiveness. A supportive mentoring and coaching environment is invaluable for creating a successful teaching and learning school system. School leaders who focus on improving the quality of instruction in classrooms should identify specific teaching and learning weaknesses in their schools. Schools should empower staff in acquiring best practices by motivating individual teachers through on-going professional development for continuous improvement. Successful schools have the right teachers in the school and ensure effective teaching and learning for every child. Questions such as: 'What have I learned in this training and what has this experience taught me about myself?' are key. Although mentoring and coaching is an appealing picture of the ideal, it may actually not be successful in many South African schools from previously disadvantaged settings. Challenges that prevail are: lack of access to quality training opportunities for prospective and practising teachers; a mismatch between the provision of and demand for teachers of particular types; the failure of the system to achieve dramatic improvement in the quality of teaching and learning in schools; a fragmented and uncoordinated approach to training approaches; and inefficient and poorly monitored funding mechanisms. Furthermore, HoDs in large schools may not find the time to regularly observe 250 teachers or provide extensive hands-on mentoring and coaching on curriculum and instruction. Departments of education should help improve headship practice and empower teachers by funding a sustained and developmental programme that caters for continuous teacher empowerment comprising of different sets of professional developments reflective of teachers' needs. Pre-packaged models of teacher empowerment should be replaced with a more collaborative teacher participation and decision making model of empowerment. Such challenges are likely to be overcome if teachers are supported. Empowered HoDs are independent thinkers who conceptualise professional training as a collective agreement on the importance of sustained HoD support.

References

Borko, H. (2012). Professional development and teacher learning: Mapping the terrain. *Educational Researcher, 33*(8), 3–15.
Bush, T. (2011). *Theories of educational leadership and management* (4th ed.). London: Sage Publication.
Bush, T., Joubert, R., Kiggundu, E., & Van Rooyen, J. (2010). Managing teaching and learning in South African schools. *International Journal of Educational Development, 30*, 62–68.
Caena, F. (2011). *Literature review quality in teachers' continuing professional development. European commission, education and training 2020*. Thematic Working Group: Professional Development of Teachers.
CIMA. (2012). *Mentoring and coaching—An overview*. CIMA Technical Briefing Developing and Promoting Strategy. January 2012. London: CIMA.
Clutterbuck, D. (2011). *Creating a coaching and mentoring culture*. A division of General Physics UK LTD. Available at: www.clutterbuckassociates.com
Day, C., Harris, A., & Hadfield, M. (2001). Challenging the orthodoxy of effective school. *Educational Leadership, 4*(1), 39–56.
Department of Basic Education. (2011). *Integrated strategic planning framework for teacher education and development in South Africa*. South Africa: The Departments of Basic Education and Higher Education and Training.
Department of Education. (2000). *Lead and manage a subject, learning area or phase. Advanced certificate: Education (school management and leadership)*. South Africa: Department of Education.
Evans, L. (2002). What is teacher development? *Oxford Review of Education, 28*(1), 123–137.
Fielden, S. (2005). *Literature review: Coaching effectiveness—A summary*. Modernisation NHS. Agency Leadership Centre.
Fleisch, B. (2008). *Primary education in crisis: Why South African schoolchildren underachieve in reading and mathematics*. Johannesburg: Juta Publishers.
Garmston, R. (1987). How administrators support peer coaching. *Educational Leadership, 44*(5), 18–26.
Gurr, D., & Drysdale, L. (2013). Middle-level secondary school leaders. Potential constraints and implications for leadership preparation and development. *Journal of Education Administration, 5*(1), 55–71.
Hall, E. (1999). Demand for professional skills on the increase. In *The graduate*. Pretoria: HSRC.
Hannay, L. M., & Ross, J. A. (1999). Departmental heads as middle managers. Questioning the black box. *School Leadership and Management, 19*(3), 331–344.
Hernez-Broome, G., & Hughes, R. L. (2012). Leadership development: Past, present, and future. Centre for creative leadership. *Human Resource Planning, 27*(1), 24–32.

Horng, E., & Loeb, S. (2010). *New thinking about instructional leadership.* November 2010. Kappanmagazine.org

Jarvis, P. (2004). *Adult education and lifelong learning: Theory and practice* (3rd ed.). London: Routledge Falmer.

Jensen, B. (2011). *Better teacher appraisal and feedback: Improving performance.* Grattan Institute, April 2011.

Johnson, S. S. (2006). *The workplace matters teacher quality, retention, and effectiveness.* Harvard National Education Association: Harvard Graduate School of Education.

Koh, H. H., Gurr, D., Drysdale, L., & Ang, L. L. (2011). How school leaders perceive the leadership role of middle leaders in Singapore primary schools? *Asia Pacific Education Review, 12*(4), 609–620.

Louis, K. S., Dretzke, B., & Wahlstrom, K. (2010a). How does leadership affect student achievement? Results from a national US survey. *School Effectiveness and School Improvement: An International Journal of Research, Policy and Practice, 21*(3), 315–336.

Louis, K. S., Leithwood, K., Wahlstrom, K., Anderson, S. E. (2010b). *Investigating the links to improved student learning. Final report of research findings.* The Wallace Foundation: Centre for Applied Research and Educational Improvement (CAREI).

McCauley, C. D., & Brutus, S. (2011). *Management development through job experiences. An annotated bibliography. Centre for creative leadership.* North Carolina, Greensboro: Jossey-Bass.

Mizwell, H. (2010). *Why professional development matters. Learning forward.* www.learningforward.org/advancing/whypdmatters.cfm

OECD (Organisation for Economic Co-operation and Development). (2009). *Improving school leadership. The toolkit.* UK: OECD.

Rogan, J., & Grayson, D. (2003). Towards a theory of curriculum implementation with particular reference to science education in developing countries. *International Journal of Science Education, 25*(10), 1171–1204.

Rosenfeld, P., Ehrich, L., & Cranston, N. (2009). Changing roles of heads of department: A Queensland case. In *Australian Association for Research in Education Conference, 30 November–4 December 2008.* Brisbane: Queensland University of Technology.

Sackdanouvong, K. (2013). *Middle managers: Managing change in a Lao higher education institution.* Submitted in partial fulfilment for the requirements for the Unitec degree of Master of Education Leadership and Management.

Scottish Executive Education Department (SEED). (2005). *Ambitious, excellent schools: Standard for headship.* Edingburg: Astron.

Sharitha, L. (2013). *Women middle managers in schools: Narratives about capabilities and transformational leadership* (A thesis submitted in the fulfilment of the Academic requirements for the Degree of Doctor of Philosophy). South Africa, Durban: University of Kwazulu-Natal, Faculty of Education.

Smith, P. J. (2001). *Workplace learning and flexible delivery* (Unpublished paper). Victoria: Deaken.

Supovitz, J. A., & Turner, H. M. (2010). The effects of professional development on science. *Journal of Research in Science Teaching, 37,* 963–980.

Swanepoel, C. (2008). The perceptions of teachers and school principals of each other's disposition towards teacher involvement in school reform. *South African, Journal of education., 28*(1), 39–51.

Taylor, S., & Yu, D. (2009). *The importance of socio-economic status in determining educational achievement in South Africa.* Stellenbosch Economic Working Papers No. 01/09.

Tecle, T. (2006). *The potential of professional development scenario for supporting biology teachers in Eritrea.* Enschede: Print Partiners IPS Kamp.

Timperley, H., & Alton-Lee, A. (2008). Reframing teacher professional learning: An alternative policy approach to strengthening valued outcomes for diverse learners. In G. Kelly, A. Luke, & J. Green (Eds.), *Disciplines, knowledge and pedagogy. Review of research in education* (Vol. 32). Washington DC: Sage Publications.

Ting, S., & Hart, E. W. (2004). Formal coaching. In C. D. McCauley & E. Van Velsor (Eds.), *The center for creative leadership handbook of leadership development* (pp. 116–150). San Francisco: Wiley.

Van der Berg, S. (2008). How effective are poor schools? Poverty and educational outcomes in South Africa. *Studies in Educational Evaluation, 34,* 145–154.

Van der Berg, S., Taylor, S., Gustafsson, M., Spaull, N., & Armstrong, P. (2011). *Improving education quality in South Africa.* Report for the National Planning Commission. Available from http://resep.sun.ac.za/wp-content/uploads/2012/10/2011-Report-for-NPC.pdf. Retrieved January 2016.

Chapter 9
Engaging Teachers in Lifelong Learning in Oman for Knowledge Growth and Development: Government Roles and Higher Institutions

Ismail Hussein Amzat, Salim Hamed Al-Mahruqi, Muhajir Teslikhan and Turkiya Al Omairi

Abstract Lifelong learning (LLL) remains widely discussed in today literature as a mechanism to keep updated with the latest information and knowledge. Engaging in LLL is a necessity for teachers to stay current, alerted with the changes in education, and remain on the cutting edge in the field of teaching. To keep up with new developments, it takes courage and self-determination to continue learning. Through teacher professional development (TPD), continuous learning and improvement can take place via professional training, workshops, conferences and personal reading to upgrade teaching skills, content knowledge and classroom teaching practices. Teachers are believed and empirically proven to influence student achievement. As far as student achievement is concerned, teachers' continuous learning and constant improvement are inevitable. Again, studies have evidenced that teacher engagement in continuous learning benefits both teaching and learning. Inasmuch as TPD is considered as a vehicle for teacher improvement, teacher engagement in lifelong learning (LLL) can be perceived as a driver that drives that particular vehicle where new knowledge and skills are obtained. Besides, when teachers involve in LLL, this helps them to develop continuous learning mind-set and habit which as a result will facilitate innovation and creativity among teachers. It prepares teachers with the assistance of continuous training to face the challenges,

---

I.H. Amzat (✉)
School of Education and Modern Languages, Universiti Utara Malaysia, Sintok, Malaysia
e-mail: ihussein@uum.edu.my

S.H. Al-Mahruqi
Institute of Lifelong Learning, University of Nizwa, Nizwa, Oman
e-mail: salimm8@yahoo.com

M. Teslikhan
Universitas Dr. Soetomo (UNITOMO), Surabaya, Indonesia
e-mail: muhajir98@gmail.com

T.A. Omairi
Oman Tourism College, Muscat, Oman
e-mail: Edu.english33@gmail.com

© Springer Nature Singapore Pte Ltd. 2017
I.H. Amzat and N.P. Valdez (eds.), *Teacher Empowerment Toward Professional Development and Practices*, DOI 10.1007/978-981-10-4151-8_9

and keeps teachers up to date on new research and methods of teaching twenty-first-century learners using new technology to enrich teaching as well as facilitate learning in the classroom. With this scenario, this research sets out to explore the level of teacher engagement in lifelong learning activities in Sultanate of Oman. Besides, it aims of identifying government and educational institutions roles in Oman in empowering teachers towards lifelong learning for continuous professional development (CPD) for best practices. Some empirical data were collected from teachers' lived-experiences about LLL for TPD in Oman. The findings are expected to play a pivotal role in urging Omani government and educational institutions to create a learning environment in which teachers and students becoming lifelong learners as well as where developing cultural learning mind-sets can be nurtured. It is envisaged that the findings will emphasize the need of government and education institutions' roles in fostering lifelong learning among teachers throughout their lives.

9.1 Introduction: What Do We Know About Lifelong Learning?

Lifelong learning (LLL) is the process of acquiring and expanding knowledge, skills and dispositions throughout one's life to foster well-being. It is essential for the development of our societies in the future, as learning is considered as a necessity for every individual to acquire and it goes beyond adult education or training. Lifelong learning is a mind-set and habit or attitude that everyone has to have or develop, such as range of learning (formal and informal learning), the skills, knowledge and behaviour (Laal and Salamati 2012). Lifelong learning serves multiple purposes, as it is believed to increase individual creativity and innovation as well as organization and countries (Dohmen 1999; Fischer 1999). Inasmuch as knowledge is concerned, learning is inevitable as it improves performances and therefore, learning new knowledge and skills should not be confined to formal education as people learn within the context of their work and where they live.

Moreover, in the search for the further meaning of lifelong learning, some researchers have managed to define lifelong learning as self-directed learning, autonomous learning; motivation to learn and perceived competence (Kirby et al. 2010; Chen et al. 2012). Lifelong learning may be further seen as a continuous formal education of one's youth and the sense of continuity in self-directed formal or informal education. In that sense, lifelong learner is a learner that has passion for continuous learning for his her own sake. Lifelong learners tend to participate voluntarily in learning activities and actively engage in self-education regardless of hardship and circumstances (Barth 2005). In addition, a lifelong learner is a learner that knows the value of lifelong learning in human lives. Hence, he or she recognizes the importance of lifelong learning and well motivated in involving in lifelong learning as well as eager to learn new skills.

Furthermore, lifelong learning takes place with the help or existence of formal education. As mentioned before, it happens when people themselves, take a plan and monitor their own learning as well as engaging into self-evaluation and reflection. Moreover, lifelong learning could be considered as a self-assessment tool to know if changes and improvement occur in human lives (Knapper 2006). In the context of education, however, despite the wide range of lifelong learning usage currently in education, the concept of lifelong learning is considered new in higher education and its definition remains vague and ambiguous (Kirby et al. 2010). With this ambiguity, the future of lifelong learning according to some researchers is still unknown and questionable (Jarvis 2010) as well as what will become (Preece 2011; UNESCO 2010; Barros et al. 2013).

In the context of Middle East, the effort of improving the quality of primary and second education has topped the government agenda across Middle East. Over last decade, the region has witnessed a high growth in students' enrolment into primary and secondary education. As a gateway, to improve the quality of teaching and learning in Middle East, huge emphasis has been placed on teacher quality and it is believed that teachers are an impetus to achieve this aim. Therefore, attractive incentives are provided to maintain teachers that are good academically and improve teachers' conditions of service (Chapman et al. 2012). In Oman, since the implementation of Omanisation, there are now 38,000 Omani teachers, and the number of teachers or graduate teachers has been increasing while student enrolment decreases. Furthermore, the formal training for teachers has become an issue as "formal training for teachers is still quit new in Oman" (Mammert 2010, p. 1). Besides, with the issue related to teachers in Oman, Muscat Daily online (2013) has reported teachers continuously demanding for better improvement in their working conditions such as reducing classroom teaching load, better provision and trainings. Although training on professional development is provided for new teachers at the Ministry and school level, further knowledge, skills and training on professional development, and adult learning are still needed to cope with the changes in curriculum and teaching methods in Oman, from teacher-centred approach to a student-centred one, as well as to improve practices. Potentially, these are reasons that strive this chapter to know the existence of lifelong learning among Omani teachers, teachers' interest in lifelong learning in Oman and the government and educational institutions' roles in inspiring teachers towards lifelong learning in Oman.

9.2 Education System and Teacher Training in Oman

The limelight of education and its development can be traced back to 1970 when his majesty Sultan Qaboos Bin Saeed took over the country leadership. His leadership brought modernization to education and deemed as Omani renaissance with help of oil discovery. Prior to that time, there were only three formal schools in the whole Sultanate and only 900 students. As taking over the power, he prioritized education and believed that, learning is enlightenment and light is the opposite of darkness

(Al-Jadidi 2009). From then, education in Oman has tended to develop rapidly and tremendously with the concept of making education accessible to everyone. As years go by, developing teacher's skills has come into picture for school development and Omani government has put into measurement and consideration by providing programs as well as training for teacher development (Amzat and Al-Neimi 2014). But the question is, what types of programs and training are provided? Do the programs and training include all teachers in the Sultanate? Many reports are mainly on training English and Science teachers. Any report on the effectiveness of the trainings and programs?

With the sense of preparing Omani teachers for the future, Oman Online Teacher Training (OOTT) project was introduced to provide continuing professional development opportunities for teachers and to make some changes to the content and methods. A pilot test was carried out to observe the effectiveness and implementation of this e-learning training. The outcomes of this platform are expected to assist Omani MOE in providing skills for teachers and possibility of using it for further teacher training. However, there are some difficulties in terms of implementation, as was revealed by the pilot test, such as time constraints and staff unavailability during summer holidays. Besides, the test was conducted during school time with 15 secondary school teachers. Unfortunately, only six teachers remained to complete the training online due to connectivity problems, computer illiteracy and others (Sales et al. 2008).

Nevertheless, as for recent, Omani Ministry of education has a great achievement in producing more teachers with qualifications, however, the process must continue in order to continuously improve the practices and teaching quality. Besides, it has also been reported that, MOE has expended their professional development programmes for teachers and huge budget was allocated. The programmes consist of selected courses based on teachers' professional needs. Some teachers were given opportunity to attend conferences abroad with the sense of sharing their knowledge with their colleagues to improve school performance while some funds were given to school to implement school professional development plan (MuscatDaily 2013). If this is the case, there should be a great deal of research and studies on the effectiveness of these programs. Thus, there should be findings and reports whether the plan and process of training teachers to improve the quality teaching in Oman have achieved the target and met the expectation. So far, based on researchers' knowledge and reading, there is a scarcity of studies and reports revealing the outcomes of these plans.

Again, if these investments and commitments are really putting in places and well executed and implemented, the education system in Oman, school, teachers and students performances by far should be advanced or at least by now on the to the peak. These incredible investments into teaching and learning should help in reducing student's dropout rate that reaches 6% out of student's enrolment 2013–2014, as reported by Mohammadi (2016) in the Times of Oman.

Relatively, the findings of Baporikar and Shah (2012) on quality of higher education in twenty-first century, a case study of Oman concluded that, the problem of low skills and knowledge of Omani graduates came from external factors which means that, students are coming out of schools with weak performances before entering higher institutions. Therefore, it is recommended for MOE in Oman to focus on students' performance at school level by first equipping teachers with the latest teaching skills, methods and professional knowledge needed to help the process. Since good learning relies on quality teaching, if teachers are well trained, furnished with necessary professional development skills and exposed to self-learning, there is a tendency of teacher passing these skills and knowledge to their students. Again, from their recommendations, the Omani government should look at socio-culture factor as students joining higher institutions with low motivation mind-set. They tend to memorize lesson and lectures without knowing the meaning. Objectively, modern teaching should help students to move from spoon-feeding to self-feeding and exposing them to self-learning. As a matter of fact, this self-feeding and learning can only take place when teachers themselves are first self-learners.

Corresponding to the claim of MOE providing trainings and reformation of curriculum to improve teaching and learning according to Al-Jardani (2012) should be further investigated for effectiveness purposes. Besides, it is also reported by Al-Jardani in the conclusion that, the English teachers that participated in the training on the effectiveness of the Primary Teacher's Course (PRIT) in preparing English teachers to implement the new curriculum complained that, they have difficulty in applying the concept in a real life despite their understanding of learning by doing and learner-centred learning. It is also suggested that by applying this concept to meet the expectations and interest of various participants, there should be regular revision, flexibility in implementation and training for teachers prior to this approach, especially in instructional technology. Besides, teachers should be exposed to classroom research and continuous reading and learning to improve their practices.

9.3 Lifelong Learning in Oman and What About GCC Countries?

Since it is agreed that, innovation plays a big role in catching up with the twenty-first-century challenges, Middle Eastern countries are called to response innovatively to their population growth. It is considered as an awakening call for lifelong learning engagement among teachers which in return could facilitate or help in transferring knowledge from older to younger and produce more skilled personnel. It is expected from Arab nations to design strategies of dealing with workplace-related learning needs and systems as developed countries have just done. In responding to these calls, Arab nations have responded impressively by taking a positive step by spending a high percentage of their GDPs on education compared to non-Arab nations. But the question is, to what extent this spending and investment has created culture of learning and continuous education among teachers and learners in Oman or the whole Arab region to benefit? (Andersson and Djeflat 2013).

Not to mention, GCC countries have made a great investment on education and improving their education as well as upgrading their curriculum but still, their education systems are reported to focus on the number of teachers rather than quality of teaching. GCC policy-makers have eventually realized the importance of having quality teachers and have called for reformation of education system that will constantly focus on quality rather than quantity (Barber et al. 2007). Coupled with the invasion of technology, with nation-states worldwide moving towards building knowledge societies and formation-based economies, educational policy-makers especially in GCC countries are considering revising their system on what types of knowledge necessary for teachers and students.

This movement has influenced curriculum development, teacher preparation, and education culture in GCC countries (Wiseman and Anderson 2012, 2013 cited in Wiseman and Anderson 2015). The application of ICT solely for TPD in GCC countries without looking at the impact of social and cultural context according to (Dore 2005) and borrowing East Asian policy on ICT and models has created some problems as it is hard to apply this model in other context (Mansour and Al-Shamrani 2015).

In the effort of popularizing the significance of lifelong learning in Oman, the global meeting on education held in Muscat, Oman 2014 called for global and international supports of researching goal to ensure equitable, inclusive quality education and lifelong learning for teachers all by 2030. In this meeting, the Director-general of UNESCO, Irina Bokava appealed to all educational community to unite on ensuring lifelong learning and quality education take place as it is included in UN's post-development agenda. She went on to emphasize the importance of education as she believed that "education is not a charity but a public good and a gamechanger that has an impact on all the development goals" (Kassemi 2014, p. 1).

In a symposium on Education and the twenty-first century (2013) in Oman, Al-Busaidi, Al-Harthy and Al-Riyamia mentioned that developing twenty-first century skills in Oman and other countries around the world, it is very important for all educational systems around the world to upgrade their school curriculum that will pave ways for knowledge seekers and independent lifelong learners rather than learners that seek for grade, pass or fail (Beere 2005, cited by Oman Observer 2013). As an example, in the United Emirates, people and teachers have complained about the standard of teaching dropping, students not getting quality education they deserve, and boys and girls dropping out of schools due to poor teachers' salaries, training and curriculum not involving real-life examples. After then, many questions are asked on how would education and learning take place when the environment is not encouraging to learn? Meanwhile, some solutions were rendered saying that, there should be some cooperation of online modules as part of solutions, blended-learning, and technology usage for lifelong learning (King 2012) cited by (Ahmad 2012).

9.4 Teacher's Professional Development and Lifelong Learning in Oman

In looking for relationship between lifelong learning and TPD, research of Fenwick (2001) on fostering teachers' lifelong learning through professional growth plan in Canada shows that, when lifelong learning is well implemented, it helps teachers' profession to grow and fosters learning communities in schools. When teachers take responsibility for professional growth, through a continual learning approach, it does not only help old teachers, but those who are new as well, in taking responsibility for their own professional growth and in helping their schools as well as communities to expand professional learning (Helterbran 2005).

The influence of learning community on lifelong learning of teachers has been reported lately. Research conducted by Curriculum Innovation Project (CIP) on learning communities and teacher lifelong learning in New Zealand shows that, learning communities could absolutely help teachers to develop further interest towards lifelong learning and for their students. Furthermore, in promoting professional learning, school leaders are expected to play larger roles in promoting professional learning to upskill teachers' new pedagogies and curriculum as well as reflective staff culture that support lifelong learning for teachers (Boyd 2005).

With the aim to improve teacher knowledge and professional development in Oman, there have been some initiatives, and teacher performance evaluation (TPE) is one of them to promote TPD plus accountability (Al-Yahmadi 2012). According to Al-Yahmadi, despite the reformation of the entire education system, the evaluation of the teacher performance that is initiated to improve TPD faces many and different challenges which one of them is the implementation. The implementation of the TPE is expected to boost TPD but falls short in terms of time lacking, standard ambiguity and lack of incentives (Al-Yahmadi 2012). Consequently, lack of proper implementation of TPE in Oman which is considered as a driving force for TPD could lead to teacher lacking training on professional development.

Similarly, research conducted by Al-Busaidi and Tuzlukove (2014) on local perspectives on TPD in Oman shows that most teachers participating in the research still need to attend further seminars on leadership, management, workshops, inviting syllabus design specialists, more courses on educational technology and high-quality professional development for teachers. Their findings also emphasized that, the problem and challenges facing these requests are time, budget, resources for professional development events including cultural background and access to training and development to all faculties as well as making teacher and faculties' professional development high priority. Besides, motivating teachers increases engagement in lifelong learning programs and events.

Another scenario is on TPD in Oman through reflection. Al-Lamki (2009) stated that, teachers in Oman did not make proper use of reflection to improve their teaching and development; rather, they only use it simply as required by the system by the government. Besides, in the conclusion, Al-Lamki added that, teachers did not consider reflection as a tool for professional development and good teaching practices. This may be due to lack of awareness about the importance of reflection. In contrast, Al-Riyami (2015), rejected Al-Lamki claims and conclusion about teachers' lack of awareness about the importance of reflection in improving teaching practices. Al-Riyami strongly argued that teachers in Oman are quite aware of reflection as a means for CPD and lifelong learning but the problems are, teachers are confronted with large class sizes; an unreasonable curriculum; lack of resources; and supports and external factors as these factors could make reflective practices impossible.

The infeasibility of teacher professional development in Oman and problem of its implementation were not only affecting teachers but also affecting school principals. A study on principal professional development by Hussin and Al-Abri (2015) recommended further training on professional development for school principals in Muscat to improve especially instructional and transformational leadership practices. One wonders, if there is lack of trainings on principal instructional leadership capacity, which instructional leadership is the core duty and activity for every school principals, what will happen to teacher training and professional development to improve teaching and practices? Quality teaching is globally confirmed to be the first factor position to influence student's learning, while school leadership is second.

9.5 Lifelong Learning Policy in Oman

As new era demanding for changes and twenty-first century posing its challenges on education shoulder, paradigm shift is required in traditional teaching and changes is must in the way students are learning. This shifting of paradigm is believed to help in adopting of lifelong policy. Besides, a lifelong learning policy is required due to the fast changing of society, globalization, increasing economic growth, human capital, technology, labour and knowledge. These elements call for expanding of knowledge, training, acquiring more skills, re-learning for the career development and promotion across a life cycle (Coolahan 2002).

In European countries, the policy seems to take place since December 1996 by issuing the first education white paper in 1995 entitled *"Teaching and Learning: Towards the Learning Society"*. Besides, 1996 has witnessed Europeans Union education ministers adopting the document *"Strategies for Lifelong Learning"* as a framework and policy. In 2001, a so-called *"Memorandum on Lifelong Learning"* was introduced stating "lifelong learning must become the guiding principle for provision and participation across the full continuum of learning context. The coming decade must see the implementation of this vision" (p. 3, Coolahan, p. 7). In addition, EU's lifelong learning programme as reported by Reuter and Patecka (2011) is part of education and training policy and expected to sustain human capital development, endow European people with skills, knowledge and competences. It is also expected to prepare them in order to face the changes and challenges of the market with an innovative mind-set.

Since lifelong learning is penetrating into educational sectors for continuous learning and its advocacy by UNESCO, it is expected for a proper policy to be established. Around the world, especially in South Asia countries, there is a lack of policy implementation and it remains to define the importance of lifelong learning. For example India, as the second most populous nation, we can say that there is an existence of lifelong learning as a culture but a lack of a policy and framework (Shah 2014). In Omani context, the policy on lifelong learning tends to focus solely on students engaging into lifelong learning rather than teachers. Although measures have been put into place to train teachers on how to upgrade their methods of teaching from teacher-centred to student-centred which it is believed to pave ways for LLL among students (MOE 2008; UNESCO 2010–2011). As it can be seen, this policy supports the notion of student lifelong learning rather the policy to engage teacher for continuous learning to improve their knowledge and teaching standard. With the sense of focusing on student lifelong learning, a basic education curriculum in Oman was reformed and under this reformation, it is expected from this new curriculum to equip Omani students with knowledge and skills to face global economic challenges and encourage them to engage in lifelong learning (Al-Balushi and Griffiths 2013). But the question is, to what extent this reformation has helped in engaging Omani students in lifelong learning activities. What is the employment rate and how will involvement in LLL help to improve government and private sectors?

Comparatively, a study of Al-Harthy et al. (2014) on improving interactive teaching strategies and action research with Life Skills teacher in Oman concluded that, for teachers to apply learner-centred approaches in Oman, they must first be equipped with IT skills as a modern tool for better practices. Thus, there should be continuous training for teachers in applying IT in their classrooms. Moreover, they recommended that the MOE in Oman should create learning environment that can accommodate learner-centred which as a result, will encourage self-learning among students and teachers. In a long run, this self-learning will allow teachers to reflect in their teaching for better improvement and advanced training should be provided to facilitate this process and activities. Last but not least, action research should always be in place in all-service training to check and balance teachers' performance as well as determine the effectiveness of the methods.

9.6 Methods

This study uses qualitative methods and the population of this study consists of teachers from different governorates and regions in Oman. Oman has four governorates (Muscat, Musandam, Dhofar and Al Buraymi) and five regions [Ad Dahiliyah, Al-Batinah, Al-Wusta, Al-Sharqiyah and Az Zahira (Ad Dhahirah)]. Phenomenological approach is used while semi-structured interview was conducted with the application of purposeful sampling. Choosing semi-structured interviews is the best type of interview, as it helps to have an in-depth understanding the concept of lifelong learning among teachers in Oman and the government and educational institutions' roles. As the qualitative method is concerned with saturation according to Creswell (2005) rather than generalizing sample sizes to the population, 11 teachers were selected from different regions in Oman using face-to-face interviews and protocol. The interview questions consist of three dimensions, which are

1. Understanding the concept of lifelong learning
2. Interest towards lifelong learning
3. Government and educational institutions' roles in assisting teachers in Oman to engage into lifelong learning.

Basic Knowledge and Awareness: Exploring awareness of LLL among participants, all the participants were asked about whether they understand the concept of lifelong learning and they were asked to describe or explain what is LLL is all about if they have understood the concept. Surprisingly, majority of the participants defined LLL as follows:

> P1: Lifelong learning is a personal effort of seeking for knowledge through modern network. He further explained life that: Through lifelong learning, a person can continue learning at any age. P2: Lifelong learning is a system of providing education for non-registered students for literacy and adult education. P3: Lifelong learning is a way of human continuing to study and training for rest of his or her life as long as he or she enables to study. P4: Lifelong learning is a continuous way of learning from the cradle or childhood till an old age. P5: Learning forever. P6: It is the continuous learning for the whole life. P7: Keep learning. P8: There is no stop for learning process. P9: The learning process is not controlled by time or place. P10: It is a process of studying everything until the last day of our life. P11: It is being in a state of learning driven by the intrinsic desire to attain proficiency in a desired field.

Source of Knowledge and Involvement: Participants were asked about the source of their knowledge about LLL. Some said that their awareness of LLL came from media, the Internet, college, Ministry programs, university (SQU), teaching experience, and parents, while only one participant (P7) tend lacked of knowledge about LLL

> P1: Yes, I heard about lifelong learning when I was in University as a student and when I was in secondary school although, I didn't involve in it. P2: No, I didn't heard or involve in lifelong learning before. P3: Yes, I have heard about lifelong learning before and didn't involve in it. I heard about it in through Media and friends. P4: I didn't involve in lifelong learning as I only knew about it from the Center for Lifelong Learning at Nizwa University, Oman. P5: Yes, I knew about it in my last year at the college. P6: Yes I know it from my school and from the ministry programs.

In relation to LLL involvement, the participants were asked about their involvement in lifelong learning and how they got know LLL in the past.

> P 1: I know about lifelong learning as I mentioned before at secondary school level by attending lectures on lifelong learning, listen to audio learning and the Youtube. P2: I just lately heard about lifelong learning from friends, Media and the latest technology.

P4: Although, I didn't involve or practice lifelong learning but I have attended some courses for languages and different lectures organized by experts. P8: Yes, since I Joined SQU. P9: Yes, in my teaching experience. P11: since long time by taking diploma in education and IELTS trainer and CELTA.

Interest: In terms of interest in LLL, all participants were asked about their interest in engaging in lifelong learning activity or program as well as whether they are willing to become lifelong learners. Below are some of their answers and replies

P1: Yes, I have heard about it and of cause, love to engage in lifelong learning because seeking for knowledge never ends. P2: Yes, I would like to know about lifelong learning because it is about increment in science and knowledge which leads to life improvement. P3: No, I don't have further interest to study or continue learning. P4: Yes, I have interest and I would like to involve in lifelong learning for life's exposure. P5: Yes, I want. P7: Yes, I would like to. P8: Yes. P10: Sure, I have interest.

In terms of involvement and application in their daily lives, some responded that

P5: I just known it recently and I haven't applied it yet. P6: I'm trying hard to do so since I heard about it. P8: Eight years.

Participant 6 and 7 did not respond whether they would like to involve in LLL program or activity. However, some responses and answers from the participants are contradicting as some of them have confirmed their interest to involve in LLL while at the same time they claimed of practicing and involving in LLL since long time ago. With these results, it seems that participants are still vague about the application of LLL and what is meant by involving in lifelong learning.

Government Role and Support: Referring to the role that the Omani government play in the creation of platform, system and programs that support LLL among teachers, some participants stated that there is no significant support from the government due to some government officers lacking awareness of LLL.

P1: No, there are not helps or supports from the government because the government or people in charge did not know much about lifelong learning. She continued by saying that: Also, the people in the society are not aware or familiar with lifelong learning. I believed that, if there is a demand from individuals or people in the Omani society about lifelong learning, the government might pay attention or encourage people to involve and provide the service. P2: Yes, there are some plans from the Omani government to improve work in schools through lifelong learning. P3: No, there is no effort or plan from the Omani government for lifelong learning due to the government poor planning and lack of our leaders' awareness about lifelong learning and its implementation.

He further gave an example as follows:

The Omani government has paid much attention on ICT at the beginning and they have invested a lot on it but later, the usage of ICT was ignored by people in the society. P4: No, there is no support of the government to implement lifelong learning due to the lack of public corporation and attention as well as their interest. P5: I have no idea if there is any. P6: each major has its own workshops and program. For example the new teachers have a program for two weeks, and if there is anything new in the curriculum the ministry is applying new programs as they are needed. P7: I think it's they are some but I'm not sure. P9: When I joined the workplace, ministry of education gave me a training for two weeks which is considered lifelong learning course. P10: I have no Idea about any governmental program. P11: I have no information on this.

Participants 8 and 10 seemed unaware about the roles that the government plays in facilitating and encouraging teachers to engage in LLL. Besides, from these responses received from the participants, it seemed that participants could not distinguish between lifelong learning and professional development training. Some attended some programs conducted by the government and perceived them as lifelong learning program or training. Although professional development could assist in becoming lifelong learner, both activities should be distinguished for teachers by the Omani MOE for better understanding.

Educational Institutions' Role and Support: With the reference to the role that educational institutions play in supporting lifelong learning and implementation, the participants said that

P1: No, educational institutions are not aware about lifelong learning in Oman. If there is an awareness of the government or Ministry of Education in Oman about lifelong learning, the government will equip schools with materials needed and provide training for teachers. P2: There is no plan when it comes to schools supporting lifelong learning engagement among teachers due to the schools themselves lacking the understanding of lifelong learning and its importance. P3: No, there is no attention and support from the schools in Oman on lifelong learning due to their lack of awareness about lifelong learning. P4: No, there is no support from the Omani educational institutions due to their lack of awareness of the importance of lifelong learning because the schools in Oman only focus on tradition teaching and learning. P5: We have just small workshop. P6: The headmaster reports our names to the ministry to have such courses in order to improve ourselves. P7: The schools have some workshops to improve our skills as teachers but don't know if they considered as lifelong learning. P8: In my school, it's obligatory to get higher salary to enrol in such programs and courses. P9: Yes, when a teacher is going to the ministry programs, she represents what she has learned for all the teachers in my school. P10: In our institute, we have continuous learning for all employees and it is a must to get a promotion. P11: Sometimes, Yes.

From these responses, it is clear that teachers in Oman or the participants did not understand or have comprehension of lifelong learning (LLL) and CPD. Perhaps they understand the meaning but its involvement, application and practicality seemed to be undistinguishable.

9.7 Discussion and Conclusion

From this interview report and themes generated, the lesson learnt was that Omani teachers seemed to know lifelong learning and its importance as well as the definition of lifelong learning. This is considered a good news for the Omani government as it is an indication of MOE hard working, dedication and commitment since 1970 to improve teachers' performance. But at the same time, there are rooms to improve especially when it comes to involvement in lifelong learning, the result shows that, there are significant numbers of participants not involved in lifelong learning despite their understanding and basic knowledge of lifelong learning. Besides, from the results, media, friends and the latest technology played big roles towards teachers' awareness in Oman on lifelong learning as some of the participants tend to know lifelong learning through their friends and media such as YouTube, as well as technology and awareness during their college days. This also includes attending some courses which they perceived as lifelong learning. This is somehow considered as professional development or teaching training for new teachers.

In relation to personal interest towards lifelong learning, and involvement, the results indicate that, majority of the participants or interviewees were interested and eagerly to involve in lifelong long learning while few declined perhaps, due to the age or lack of motivation. For the government and educational institutions' role in assisting teachers in Oman to involve in lifelong learning and its implementation, the results show disappointing or mixed results. There are four to five participants that unanimously agreed there is no significant support or motivation from the government and educational institutions towards teachers participating or involving in lifelong learning while the rest confirmed government roles in the implementation of LLL through schools. Each school according to them has its own programs provided for teachers but the questions are, what types of program or training? What is the content of the training or program? To what extent the training and programs are up to date? Background or the qualification of the trainers? Any report on the effectiveness of the trainings and programs?

Besides, the participants also concurred that there is an initial plan from the Omani government and educational institutions in implementing lifelong learning, but the problem of the problem is that many government and educational institutions in Omani lack awareness and planning about lifelong learning. They eventually believed that if the Omani government has great awareness about lifelong learning and highly conscious of its importance, there might be some effort, help and support from the government on lifelong learning perhaps by building a system as well as providing materials for schools and higher institutions to extensively facilitate lifelong learning among teachers as well as students in Oman.

As a conclusion, this study explored the concept of lifelong learning among teachers in Oman and their understandings. It looked at the teachers' interest towards lifelong learning and their involvement. In addition, this study also examined the role of Omani government and educational institutions in Oman on engaging teachers into LLL program, supporting activities, motivating and creating a culture for lifelong learning as well as its implementation. This study looked into three areas as just mentioned and from the three areas, five themes emerged (1—basic knowledge and awareness; 2—source of knowledge and involvement; 3—interest; 4—government role and support; and 5—educational role and support).

From the result of the interview findings, this study concludes that, some credits go to Omani government and its higher institutions at least for familiarizing teachers with LLL through university program and schools. But yet again, there remains much work for Omani MOE and schools in Oman in terms of facilitating lifelong learning and motivating teachers and students in Oman in engaging into

LLL. Since the results have shown less involvement of teachers in lifelong learning and its practicality. Thus, it is now an obligation for Omani government and educational institutions to provide more training not only for students and teachers about LLL and acquaint teachers on how to become adult learners in order to improve their teaching and practices.

Moreover, they should create a learning environment and culture in which teachers will have a deep understanding of the importance of LLL and the roles that LLL play in their professional development. Teachers should understand that LLL is a self-empowerment towards self-learning and autonomy. They should be aware of LLL and its long run advantages plus benefits in improving educational system in Oman, human capital and socio-economics growth. Indeed, it helps in keeping teachers on trick with the latest development in their areas of teaching and instructional materials. It assists further to improve the methods of teaching for better learning such as applying students-centred approach that has been reported widely in GCC countries as a major problem among teachers and students. Socially, personalizing learning helps people generally in society to know the value of knowledge through continuous learning.

9.8 Implication

This chapter drew some critical implications which should be considered by Omani MOE, universities lecturers, teachers and policy-makers. The first implication lies on the lack of empirical studies on the outcomes of government policy in Oman on teacher training and development. Thus, implication on lack of report on the government claims of providing teacher skills and school development programs. His report should be in form of evaluation whether these measures taken by the MOE achieved the purpose and objective. Examples of Omani Online Teacher Training (OOTT) that is initiated for online teaching training and development and (TPD) for teacher continuous professional development. These programs and trainings are good ones; therefore, there should be an evaluation whether they contribute significantly to the educational system in Oman and whether they constitute highly to TPD.

Additionally, the Omani government has hugely invested in education, building schools and producing more teachers to feel the gaps and some training for better improvement. In the same fashion, there should be scientific contribution from researchers and academicians in Oman on giving feedbacks on the effectiveness of this investment to advance the system without condemnation and destructive criticism of the Omani government works and efforts. With this in mind, research findings, report, evaluation and assessment could be mechanisms to know the functionality of the system, to upgrade the system, improve and instil quality services as well as practices. Lamentably, if there is scarcity of empirical studies and research on teacher lifelong learning (LLL) and teacher CPD in Oman, one wonders, how would the government know the outcomes of trainings and programs that they initiated? How would people know where things stand for teachers and what should be the next agenda for further improvement? Again, if all the literature on teacher development and lifelong learning in Oman are only concentrating on English teachers' professional training and development, what will be the performances of students under non-English teachers?

The second implication is drawn on the problem of proper planning and implementation of government programs. This requests MOE in Oman to follow up the application and implementation of their programs at the school level. Planning and policy might fail if there is no follow-up and assessment of the outcomes. There should be a clear agenda and framework on how to involve teachers in Oman in lifelong learning activities for the sake of professional development. Clear understanding and definitions of LLL and CPD are needed from the government and institutions to teachers. Perhaps, there should be a policy to help LLL to grow at schools such as using LLL as an assessment for teacher promotion in Oman and allocating incentives for teachers that engaged in LLL.

As a result, the proper implementation and agenda of teacher's lifelong learning will not only improve teaching but improve learning as well. This will bridge a gap between MOE in Oman and teachers as well as students. Teacher professional development and self-learning could help to improve low levels of student performance and dropping out in Oman. If teachers are well trained and their learning environment is conducive for continuous learning, they will be empowered and autonomous to seek for greater knowledge and eventually, they will pass their knowledge and skills to their respective students. Idiomatically, teachers are like 'breastfeeding' mothers, passing foods and nutrition they have consumed to their beloved babies. Hence, the more healthy the mother is, the healthier the baby. When teachers are self-learners, the chances of students becoming self-learners as well are very high. The more training given or provided to teachers, the more productive students they will produce.

References

Ahmad, A. (2012). Thousand in adult education in UAE let down by teaching standards. *The National*, UAE. Retrieved from http://www.thenational.ae/news/uae-news/education/thousands-in-adult-education-in-uae-let-down-by-teaching-standards

Al-Balushi, S., & Griffiths, D. (2013). The school education system in the Sultanate of Oman. In G. Donn & Y. Al-Manthri (Eds.), *Education in the broader middle east: Borrowing a baroque arsenal*. UK: Symposium Books Ltd.

Al-Busaidi, M. S., Al Harthy, Z., & Al-Riyamia, S. (2013). School curricula in Oman: Developing the 21st century skills. Education and 21st century Competencies Symposium, September 23. *Omani Daily Observer*. Retrieved from http://omanobserver.om/education-and-21st-century-competencies-symposium-delves-on-learning/

Al-Busaidi, S., & Tuzlukova, V. (2014). Local perspectives on teacher professional development: Targeting policy and practice. *Asian Journal of Management Sciences & Education, 3*(4), 74–84.

Al-Harthy, Z. S., Hussien, S., & Al Harth, H. K. (2014). Improving interactive teaching strategies: Action research with a life skills teacher in Oman. *IIUM Journal of Educational Studies, 2*(1), 12–32.

Al-Jadidi, S. A. (2009). Teaching english as a foreign language in Oman: An exploration of english language teaching pedagogy in tertiary Education. Submitted in fulfillment of the requirements of the degree of Doctor of Philosophy. School of Education. Faculty of Arts. Victoria University Melbourne, Australia. http://vuir.vu.edu.au/15216/1/Husna_Sept09.pdf

Al-Jardani, K. S. S. (2012). A study of educational reform & teacher training in Oman. *International Journal of Applied Linguistics and English Literature, 1*(1), 64–69.

Al-Lamki, N. (2009). *The beliefs and practices related to continuous professional development of teachers of English in Oman.* Unpublished Ph.D. Thesis, Leeds University, UK.

Al Riyami, T. (2015). Reflection: Is it a promising or spurious tool for teachers' professional development? *International Journal of Bilingual & Multilingual Teachers of English, 3*(1), 48–58.

Al-Yahmadi, H. H. (2012). Teacher performance evaluation in Oman as perceived by evaluators. *International Journal of Education, 1*(11), 741–747.

Amzat, I. H., & Al-Neimi, R. K. R. (2014). Teachers' turnover and their job satisfaction at basic education school in some regions in Oman: Structural equation modelling approach. *International Journal of Management in Education., 8*(1), 78–100.

Andersson, T., & Djeflat, A. (2013). *The real issues of the Middle East and the Arab Spring: Addressing research.* Innovation and Entrepreneurship: Springer.

Baporikar, N., & Shah, I. A. (2012). Quality of higher education in 21st century a case study of Oman. *Journal of Educational and Instructional Studies, 2*(2), 9–18.

Barber, M., Mourshed, M., & Whelan, F. (2007). Improving education in the Gulf. *The McKinsey Quarterly.* Retrieved from https://abujoori.files.wordpress.com/2007/04/improve-gulf-education.pdf

Barth, R. (2005). Turning book burners into lifelong learners. In R. DuFour, R. Eaker, & R. DuFour (Eds.), *On common ground: The power of professional learning communities* (pp. 115–133). Bloomington, IN: National Educational Service.

Barros, R., Moneiro, A., Nejmediie, F., & Moreira, A. J. (2013). The relationship between students' approach to learning and lifelong learning. *Psychology, 4*(11), 792–797.

Boyd, S. (2005). Teachers as lifelong learners. *A paper presented NZARE, Dunedin.* Retrieved from http://www.nzcer.org.nz/system/files/14717.pdf

Chapman, D. W., Al-Barwani, T., Al Mawali, F., & Green, G. (2012). Ambivalent journey: Teacher career paths in Oman. *International Review of Education, 58*(3), 387–403.

Chen, J. C., McGaughey, K., & Lord, S. M. (2012). *"Measuring Students' Propensity for Lifelong Learning", Australasian Association for Engineering Education (AAEE) Annual Conference, December 2012.* Victoria, Australia: Melbourn.

Coolahan, J. (2002). *Teacher education and the teaching career in an era of lifelong learning.* Paris: OECD.

Creswell, J. W. (2005). *Educational research: Planning, conducting and evaluating quantitative and qualitative research* (2nd ed.). Upper Saddle River, N.J.: Pearson Merrill Prentice Hall.

Dohmen, G. (1999). *The future of continuing education in Europe.* Bonn, Germany: German Federal Ministry of Education and Research.

Dore, L. (2005). *A nation of smart is becoming a reality in the GCC[Electronic Version] Khaleej Times Online.* Retrieved from: http://www.khaleejtimes.com/DisplayArticle.asp?xfile=data/business/2005October/business_October151.xml&section=business&col

Fenwick, T. J. (2001, May). *Foster teacher's lifelong learning through professional growth plans: A cautious recommendation for policy.* Teacher Education/Education Training: Current Trends and Future Directions. Symposium conducted at the Pan-Canadian Education Research Agenda Symposium, Laval University, Quebec City.

Fischer, G. (1999). Lifelong Learning: Changing Mindsets. 7th International Conference on Computers in Education on *"New Human Abilities for the Networked Society" (ICCE'99, Chiba, Japan).* G. Cumming, T. Okamoto and L. Gomez. Omaha, IOS Press: 21–30.

Helterbran, R. V. (2005). Lifelong learning: A stratagem for new teachers. *Academic Exchange Quarterly, 9*(4). Retrieved from http://rapidintellect.com/AEQweb/6jan3151z5.htm

Hussin, S., & Al Abri, S. (2015). Professional development needs of school principals in the context of educational reform. *International Journal of Educational Administration and Policy Studies., 7*(4), 90–97.

Jarvis, P. (2010). Inquiry journal of lifelong education. *International Journal of Lifelong Education, 29,* 397–400. doi:10.1080/02601370.2010.488802.

Kassemi, I. (2014). Muscat global meeting calls for a strong education goal in the development agenda for post-2015. *UNESCO.* Retrieved from http://www.unesco.org/new/en/media-services/in-focus-articles/muscat-global-meeting-calls-for-a-strong-education-goal-in-the-development-agenda-for-post-2015/

Kirby, J., Knapper, C., Lamon, P., & Egnatoff, W. (2010). Development of a scale to measure lifelong education. *International Journal of Lifelong Education, 29*(3), 291–302.

Knapper, C. (2006). Lifelong learning means effective and sustainable learning; reasons, ideas, concrete measures. CIEA. *A paper presented in the 25th International Course on Vocational Training and Education in Agriculture.* Retrieved from http://www.ciea.ch/documents/s06_ref_knapper_e.pdf

Laal, M., & Salamati, P. (2012). Lifelong learning; Why do we need it? *Procedia Social and Behavioral Sciences, 31*(2012), 399–403.

Mammert, L. (2010). *Learning is the future of Oman.* Middle East Online. Published, 2010-10-26. Retrieved from http://www.middle-east-online.com/english/?id=42200

Ministry of Education. (2008). *Minister of Education Congratulates Teachers on Teachers Day.* Retrieved from http://home.moe.gov.om/english/show-1-1335.moe

Ministry of Education. (2008). Inclusive education in the Sultanate of Oman. National Report Presented at the 48th Session of the International Conference of Education, Geneva

Mohammadi, E. P. (2016). Call to stem high student dropout rate in Oman. *Times of Oman.* January 8, 2016. Retrieved http://timesofoman.com/article/75093/Oman/Education/Joint-efforts-needed-to-address-student-dropout-problem-in-Oman-says-Minister-of-Higher-Education

MuscatDaily Online. (2013). *Teachers matter: Teaching in the sultanate's schools.* November 18. Retrieved from http://www.muscatdaily.com/Archive/Oman/Teachers-matter-Teaching-in-the-sultanate-s-schools-2prh

Oman Observer. (2013). Education and 21st century Competencies Symposium delves on learning. *Oman daily Observer.* Monday 23rd, September. Retrieved from http://main.omanobserver.om/education-and-21st-century-competencies-symposium-delves-on-learning/

Preece, J. (2011). Research in adult education and lifelong learning in the era of CONFINTEA VI. *International Journal of Lifelong Education, 30*(1), 99–117.

Reuter, C., & Patecka, A. (2011). EU Lifelong Learning Policy Framework. *Solidar.* http://www.solidar.org/IMG/pdf/29_lllpolicyframe.pdf

Sales, G., Al-Barwani, T., & Miske, S. (2008). Prospects and challenges of an online teacher training project in Oman. *International Journal of Education and Development using Information and Communication Technology., 4*(1), 120–130.

Shah, Y. S. (2014). Lifelong Learning in India: A Policy Perspective. *ASEM Education and Research Hub for Lifelong Learning.* Retrieved from http://asemlllhub.org/policy-briefs/lifelong-learning-in-india-a-policy-perspective/

UNESCO. (2010). *Relatório global sobre aprendizagem e educação de adultos.* Brasília: Instituto da UNESCO para a Aprendizagem ao Lon- go da Vida (UIL).

UNESCO. (2010–2011). World Data on Education. International Bureau of Education. Retreived from http://www.ibe.unesco.org/sities/default/Oman.pdf

Wiseman, A. W., & Anderson, E. (2015). A cross-nation comparison of ICT resources and science teacher's professional development in and use of ICT in the Gulf Cooperation Council countries. In N. Mansour & S. Al-Shamrani (Eds.), *Science education in the Arab Gulf States.* Springer.

Chapter 10
Counseling Ethics Education for Enhanced Professional Identity and Development: Guidance and Counseling Teachers Lifelong Learning Acquisition Empowered

Noor Syamilah Zakaria, Jane Warren and Ab. Rahim Bakar

Abstract Counseling ethics competency is an essential part of counselor identity development as required by the counseling profession, and counseling ethics education is one major component of knowledge acquisition in counseling profession training standards. The purpose of this qualitative research was to conduct an interpretive case study to explore, understand, describe, and interpret how guidance and counseling teachers learn, understand, experience, and apply counseling ethics education to their evolving professional identity and development in the counselor education training program. The main author was the primary instrument for data collection and analysis. Coding categories were developed and tentative themes emerged, were refined, and became the five emergent master themes for this research: education foundation, education integration, education application, education assimilation, and education appreciation. The discussion and interpretation are grounded in the principles of effective adult learning in counseling ethics education; to empower lifelong learning acquisition among guidance and counseling teachers toward enhanced professional identity and development.

N.S. Zakaria (✉)
Department of Counselor Education and Counseling Psychology,
Faculty of Educational Studies, Universiti Putra Malaysia, Selangor, Malaysia
e-mail: syamilah@upm.edu.my; noorsyamilah@gmail.com

J. Warren
College of Social Sciences-Counseling, Saybrook University, San Francisco, CA, USA

Ab.R. Bakar
Department of Science and Technical Education, Faculty of Educational Studies,
Universiti Putra Malaysia, Selangor, Malaysia

© Springer Nature Singapore Pte Ltd. 2017
I.H. Amzat and N.P. Valdez (eds.), *Teacher Empowerment Toward Professional Development and Practices*, DOI 10.1007/978-981-10-4151-8_10

10.1 Introduction

Jane Vella, a prominent adult educator, reminds educators to teach well with the realization that more teaching may result less learning (Vella 1994, 2002). This means adult education is not intended to only review a set of course materials; but instead, to engage students in effective and significant learning. Significant learning can be translated into many contexts. It lies in each student's ability to effectively use judgment, and consider commendable actions in executing tasks to lead a more meaningful life. Various educational experts encouraged educators to consider students' engagement in experiences to serve as foundation for significant learning (Blenkinsop and Beeman 2012). Educators must be mindful to provide students the opportunities for reflection inside and outside the classroom settings. In addition, educators are reminded to engage students' personal interests to create conditions for active thinking, as well as experiencing and fostering deep learning.

Deep learning refers to engaging meanings, not memorizing mere facts. It involves making critical analysis of new ideas, linking the new ideas to the known concepts and principles, and leading toward long-term retention for future use in an unfamiliar context of problem-solving process. Essentially, deep learning is making connection between the concepts taught and personal experiences. In addition, deep learning focuses on how concrete specifics might indicate abstract patterns, applies ideas taught in classroom to real-world situations, connects what one is learning to what one has learned previously, and discusses ideas while keeping open to enlarging one's idea based on encountering the other's idea (McAuliffe and Eriksen 2011).

In counseling profession, counseling professionals make many decisions within situations in which valid choices equally exist. Professional work in counseling is characterized with unclear problems, multiple dimensions, and commonly fraught with values and ethical implications (McAuliffe and Eriksen 2011). Therefore, counseling students need to be prepared for complexities in their counseling work, which is illustrated in many challenges such as ethnicities, gender expectations, multiple society values, moral centers, and ethical judgments (Warren and Douglas 2012; Zakaria 2007, 2013; Zakaria and Warren 2014, 2016). Consequently, counselor education training programs must offer a corresponding complexity in their training programs. Two common forms of embracing corresponding complexity in counseling profession are: (1) the way of knowing that is reflexive and includes a tolerance of ambiguity, which means counseling professionals must embrace the uncertainty as an expected condition of the work, and prepare to admit their mistakes constructively; and (2) the ability to be culturally relativistic, which means counseling professionals must be able to decenter from their cultural assumptions (Gnilka et al. 2012).

Although counseling students may engage in diverse experiential learning activities on their own, many will benefit from additional educational challenges and support. Counselor educators can provide such encouragement through experience-rich teaching strategies, within the constructivist-developmental context.

This context is comprised of pivotal teaching and learning relationship-bound elements which include safety, connection, respect, engagement, accountability, reinforcement, application, personalization, and teamwork (Vella 1994, 2002). This chapter discusses teaching and learning elements which are all necessary for effective learning in counseling ethics education for guidance and counseling teachers.

10.2 Principles for Effective Adult Learning

The nine principles for effective adult learning include: securing a feeling of safety, ensuring the existence of sound relationships, showing respect for students as agents, getting students engaged in learning, doing regular needs assessment and practicing accountability, providing sequence and reinforcement, providing opportunities for immediate application, practicing equity, and encouraging teamwork. These principles identify what educators can do to foster effective adult learning.

Securing a feeling of safety. Most adult students indicate that they need safety and affirmation of their potential and achievements in learning. They need to believe that learning experiences work for them and learning conditions are set up to achieve success. The feeling of safety can be secured in any learning environment, and educators are the most important navigators to create such an atmosphere for learning. Parallel with the counseling relationship, a deep connection creates a safe place for processing pain, which can clear the emotional blockage to foster cognitive work (Dollarhide et al. 2012). Guidance and counseling teachers can gain confidence and safety in their classroom when the counselor educator clearly creates the course design and requirements; shares background and passion in the course and profession; asks them about their expectations for the course; and acknowledges each person's contribution, both in verbal and in written work. Essentially, affirmations can empower guidance and counseling teachers to increase their contributions to the classroom community.

This first principle, securing a feeling of safety, is evidenced in two emergent master themes: education foundation and education appreciation. The education foundation master theme reflects this feeling of safety in how counseling ethics education is presented as a core and foundational introductory class. According to the guidance and counseling teachers, this foundation provided a "groundedness" and safety for them in learning a challenging course such as counseling ethics education. They viewed learning counseling ethics education at the very beginning of counseling program provided them a head start on becoming ethical guidance and counseling teachers and set a solid ethical foundation (Jungers and Gregoire 2013). The counseling ethics education class was also regarded as a safe learning venue due to the counseling ethics educator's ability to share background, passion, and experience in the course and in the profession.

The education appreciation master theme reflects this feeling of safety through the guidance and counseling teachers' gratitude toward their counseling ethics educator. The educator was described as being consistently available as a consultant, to further clarify relevant information needed in helping them understand the vague perspectives of counseling ethics dilemmas. This safety perspective also occurred in their triadic supervision sessions when there were times they faced ethical dilemmas. The triadic supervision sessions were perceived as a safe place to go and receive the supervisors' opinions on what they could do to assist the clients during the training clinic counseling sessions. The guidance and counseling teachers also expressed their appreciation for the triadic supervisors, who provided the safe space for them to share their feelings about any ethical trauma situations as well as personal life challenges (Bernard and Goodyear 2009).

Ensuring the existence of sound relationships. A positive, sound relationship between educators and adult students can impact students' learning outcomes. Guidance and counseling teachers can benefit from a strong professional connection, evidenced when counselor educator practices seemingly simple gestures in the classroom. These gestures can include addressing students by their first names; being accessible by an open physical presence, telephone, or e-mail; explaining students' roles and functions for class activities and assignments; challenging own prejudices about students; and respecting each student.

This second principle is supported in two emergent master themes: education application and education appreciation. The education application master theme reflects this sound relationship lens through the guidance and counseling teachers' ability to apply counseling ethics education knowledge and skills in real-life relationship settings. For example, they shared the opportunities to apply counseling ethics education information into their practice in training clinic counseling sessions, triadic supervision, and block supervision. These venues provided incredible learning experiences for them, given they were working with real clients in a real clinical setting. In addition, the sound relationships with their supervisors provided them a solid relational education foundation in which they could learn deeper and broader about becoming ethical counselors (Mohamed 2009).

The education appreciation master theme reflects this sound relationship lens through the guidance and counseling teachers' sense of appreciation expressed toward counselor educators at the department. Their welfare, needs, and wellness throughout the semester were cared and valued by all counseling faculty. The sense of appreciation has kept their mode of learning enthusiasm at a high level throughout the semester (Lenz and Smith 2010).

Showing respect for students as agents. Adult students need to become active participants with the educators, not the passive recipients of the authority figures. Counselor educators can show respect for guidance and counseling teachers by making the course content and learning process as an open system, and empowering them to make decisions during teaching and learning activities occurrence. This third principle, showing respect for students as agents, is evidenced in two emergent master themes: education integration and education assimilation.

The education integration master theme reflects the respect for students as agents through an open conversation and expressive environment existed in the counseling ethics education classroom. In this setting, each guidance and counseling teacher's viewpoint was validated and used to resolve any counseling ethical issues. They perceived that they were respected as important agents in the ethical decision-making process through experiential activities and assignments formulated in the counseling ethics education class. They were challenged by many simulated ethical situations, in which they were to think thoroughly about the situations given and consult with their peers on the best possible solutions in facing these ethical quandaries (Sias 2009).

The education assimilation master theme reflects the respect for students as agents through the challenging experiences given to the guidance and counseling teachers and collaborative exercises while learning counseling ethics education. They reported that they were perceived by the counseling ethics educator as a group of empowered guidance and counseling teachers who could effectively collaborate and utilize their own unique counseling ethics capacities and credibility. In many collaborative situations, the guidance and counseling teachers shared their power in the decision-making process; and all decisions were made by the entire group members, which allowed for multiple views to be put forward (Dougherty 2005).

Getting the students engaged in learning. Educators can engage adult students by setting up the tasks and inviting them to deeply embrace the course content. Engaged learning occurs when concepts and ideas from classroom are applied to out-of-class cognitions and actions (Jones 2011). Guidance and counseling teachers can benefit from this engaged learning strategy when counselor educator forms small group discussions; creates thought processing activities such as role-plays, simulations, and self-reflection; creates challenging classroom activities; and fosters conversation on any problem situations that can be generalized into other situations outside the classroom.

This fourth principle, getting the students engaged in learning is supported in two emergent master themes: education foundation and education integration. The education foundation master theme reflects the engaged learning lens through counseling ethics education discussions and activities in the classroom. The guidance and counseling teachers opined that to learn counseling ethics education, they have to be engaged in numerous activities including reading, participating in small group discussions, and thinking about different ethical situations together with their peers. Reportedly, the most beneficial learning experience for them was their engagement in group discussions about real-life scenarios which were happening to some of their peers and most counseling professionals. In addition, the journal writing activity about their beliefs, code of ethics, and laws and regulations was another engagement activity in counseling ethics education class perceived helpful by the guidance and counseling teachers (Warren et al. 2010a).

The education integration master theme reflects the engaged learning lens through experiential activities assigned in the counseling ethics education class which reportedly helped the guidance and counseling teachers to understand and experience counseling ethics education. These activities included the journaling, the professional helper interview reflection paper, the ethics bookmark, the wellness collage, and the ethics dilemma decision-making group discussion (Warren et al. 2010b, 2012). The small group discussions, role-plays, simulations, self-reflection, creative classroom activities, and classroom conversations on the importance of wellness were also seemed to engage them in learning, understanding, experiencing, and applying counseling ethics education (Zakaria 2013).

Doing regular needs assessment and practicing accountability. Educators are encouraged to do ongoing needs assessment and thus enhance their accountability to teaching. The needs assessment allows adult students to participate regularly in deciding what has been learned throughout a particular classroom activity and can contribute to the classroom dynamic. This fifth principle, doing regular needs assessment and practicing accountability, is reflected in the education application emergent master theme.

The education application master theme reflects doing regular needs assessment and practicing accountability lens through guidance and counseling teachers' utilization of counseling ethics education knowledge and skills into their practice, in both counselor education training clinic and in other courses within that particular semester. They were able to express their personal and professional needs to counseling ethics educator in counseling ethics education class, to counseling faculty at the department, and to supervisors at the training clinic. This open opportunity for expressing their essentials and necessities while being in the training program served as a needs assessment; for the counseling ethics educator, the counseling faculty at the department, and the supervisors to enhance their teaching and supervising activities, which helped these guidance and counseling teachers to learn counseling ethics education more effectively (Bernard and Goodyear 2009).

Providing sequence and reinforcement. Educators can start with simple ideas and then layer to create complexity. Adult students benefit from learning one idea, one theory, and one method before they can be asked to compare, contrast, and integrate several ideas. A counselor educator can provide sequence and reinforcement in teaching and learning process by starting with a simple, safe task; taking small steps toward building to the next tasks; returning to the previously taught facts, skills, and attitudes in a more innovative ways during a course or throughout the curriculum; and encouraging counseling students to experience the practical results of trying out ideas. This sixth principle, providing sequence and reinforcement, is supported by the education application emergent master theme.

The education application master theme reflects the sequence and reinforcement lens through the guidance and counseling teachers' experiences in sequentially learned the code of ethics in counseling ethics education class. They integrated the code of ethics into all experiential class assignments and into other counseling courses within the same semester. Interestingly, a significant challenge was reported by them when applying the code of ethics in training clinic counseling sessions. These real-life experiences in the training clinic setting provided the practicality of being and becoming ethical counseling professionals. However, research by Sias et al. (2006) has shown that the readiness for sequencing is not necessarily universal and applicable for all counseling students. Their study on conceptual and moral development revealed significant relationships between counselors' level of conceptual complexity and moral reasoning in counseling ethics education. Their findings also concluded counseling students would face difficulty extending ethical principles to the situations, when they were more complex than their mental abilities. Their study suggested to counselor educators about the importance of starting lessons with simple tasks, taking small steps toward building to the next level of difficulty, and returning to the previously taught facts, skills, and attitudes to ensure counseling students' knowledge applicability.

Providing opportunities for immediate application. Effective education requires application. In current research context, application can be achieved through extending counseling ethics education knowledge and skills into other counseling courses within that particular semester as well as in training clinic counseling sessions. Immediate application enabled guidance and counseling teachers to apply specific ethical knowledge and skills across the curriculum. This seventh principle, providing opportunities for immediate application, is reflected by the education application emergent master theme.

The education application master theme reflects providing opportunities for immediate application lens notably through triadic and block supervision sessions. As the guidance and counseling teachers began their first semester of training program, they were introduced to a plethora of new vocabularies and skills important for the counseling profession. The immediate opportunities for counseling ethics education application can reduce overload and increase confidence to their professional identity and development in the program. For the past 25 years, immediate application concept has been widely used in academic settings. The concept is evidenced in a comprehensive model that creatively integrates four powerful teaching methods: collaborative learning, experiential learning, problem-based learning, and standards-driven learning. These methods provide immediate application opportunities for students to learn in a more effective and meaningful way.

Practicing equity. Adult students often remember their educators as masters and sages on the stage. For guidance and counseling teachers, the time spent with a counselor educator in different roles throughout their learning endeavor can make a considerable difference to their evolving professional identity and development in the program. A counselor educator can practice equity by encouraging students to use first names; sitting by students as co-learners; attending workshops or presenting at conferences with students; and showing the uncertainties, vulnerabilities, and humbleness by truthfully revealing own process of thinking with students. This eighth principle, practicing equity, is supported by the education appreciation emergent master theme.

The education appreciation master theme reflects the practicing equity lens through the appreciation expressed by guidance and counseling teachers to their counseling ethics educator, counselor educators at the department, and training clinic supervisors who were willing to have dialogue with them on many ethical and developmental issues (Remley and Herlihy 2010). They expressed that whenever they felt uncomfortable as if something were not ethically right, they would seek supervision just to get feedback from others. Some of them were very hopeful their supervisors would be open to dialogue and be comfortable to have in-depth conversations about common struggles faced by many counseling students across the training programs. Practicing equity can also be seen when a counselor educator shows the uncertainties, vulnerabilities, and humbleness revealing his or her own process of thinking and experiences. A counselor educator can also certainly demonstrate equity with guidance and counseling teachers by sharing and revealing his or her own mistakes throughout career span (Warren and Douglas 2012). As a result, guidance and counseling teachers may acknowledge errors happened within the counseling profession as meaningful learning examples (Gladding 2009).

Encouraging teamwork. Working in teams can be a healthy norm for most professionals in daily professional work and life. When educators assign adult students to group discussions and classroom projects, they are preparing these students for professional teamwork in future organizations. Members of the group need to negotiate, listen, agree, disagree, compromise, and foster high tolerance to create meaningful discussions and fruitful decisions. A counselor educator can encourage teamwork among guidance and counseling teachers in various ways: having them to work in small groups, directing the groups toward a learning task, having them pay their attentions to the interpersonal and intrapersonal process of working within the groups, asking them to assess the counselor educator, and requesting them to evaluate the course formatively and summatively. This ninth principle, encouraging teamwork, is supported by the education integration emergent master theme.

The education integration master theme reflects the encouraging teamwork lens through integrating counseling ethics education knowledge and skills into classroom practices and activities. The guidance and counseling teachers identified that the group activities assigned in the counseling ethics education class provided them opportunities to collaborate, learn from others, and respect the opinions conveyed by others. They also acknowledged that they did not feel alone in the process of following through the counseling ethics education course content and application. They perceived the differences found among them offered interesting ethical perspectives that can enhance their evolving professional identity and development in the program. Occasionally, the teamwork made them realize that there is not really one right ethical decision in any situation.

10.3 Implications for Counselor Educators

Guidance and counseling teachers, together with counselor educators put forth the effort necessary to develop counseling ethics education knowledge and skills. Teaching institutions and counselor education training programs need to provide appropriate environments to facilitate students' learning and educators' teaching.

This effort is significant because training standards of the counseling profession require competence in counseling ethics (Council for the Accreditation of Counseling and Related Educational Programs [CACREP] 2016). From this chapter, implications for counselor educators emerged to enhance counseling ethics education instruction in counselor education training programs, specifically for guidance and counseling teachers.

The first suggestion for counselor educators is to create an effective and engaging classroom environment for teaching and learning counseling ethics education. According to Handelsman et al. (2005), there are three reasons ethics training is not simple: the rules taught surrounding code of ethics are vague and conflicting; learning about ethics of a profession by watching models is incomplete at best; and ethics is a study of right or wrong, but often taught as the study of wrong. Consequently, counseling ethics education is often perceived as cut-and-dry and dull course content. Jones (2011) suggested that counselor educators create a kind and fun classroom environment. Provine (2000) explained that laughter is typically not just a response to jokes created, but actually pulls people together. Therefore, making learning counseling ethics education fun may improve creativity, reduce stress, and help guidance and counseling teachers master difficult information because it can promote higher order thinking skills and de-escalates tense situations.

The second suggestion for counselor educators is to improve classroom environment for teaching and learning counseling ethics education by applying a persuasive pedagogy (Livingston 2010). In persuasive pedagogical classroom environment, there is a clear connection made between rational explanation, critical dialogue, and teaching. Counselor educators are able to provide honest reasons for any ethical situation discussions, and able to welcome any radical questions inquired by guidance and counseling teachers. To enhance counseling ethics education teaching and learning experiences, there are three questions that usually used in persuasive pedagogy: "What do I believe about the particular ethical situation?" "How do I balance my perspectives with my intentions to help clients with appropriate ethics understandings?" and "How do I make sense of the grey areas where knowledge is rarely considered absolute truth?" To implement persuasive pedagogy into teaching and learning counseling ethics education, counselor educators must be prepared to respond to tough questions from guidance and counseling teachers in the classroom, which requires further ethical considerations and explanations to produce justifiable answers.

The third suggestion for counselor educators to improve counseling ethics education is to know more about self. Counselor educators can empower guidance and counseling teachers to develop more self-awareness and do more self-evaluation. In addition, counselor educators also can encourage them to seek their own counseling services to ultimately improve knowledge about themselves, both their strengths and limitations. By participating in personal counseling, guidance and counseling teachers can better understand themselves and foster understanding about others as well. Self-awareness enables counselors to not impose their values onto clients, which is an ethical responsibility of counseling professionals (American Counseling Association [ACA] 2014).

The final suggestion for counselor educators is to infuse experiential activities into counseling ethics education teaching and learning endeavors. This chapter revealed that guidance and counseling teachers gained considerable counseling ethics education knowledge and confidence from the experiential assignments in the counseling ethics education class. The two most preferred activities revealed were the ethics bookmark and the wellness collage. At some point, guidance and counseling teachers may have gained content knowledge and skills in counseling ethics education; however, these tangible assignments make learning more real and fun. Creative-experiential assignments such as the ethics bookmark can foster consciousness on the importance of an ethical reminder. On the other hand, the wellness collage can foster awareness of self-care and the importance of wellness to the personal and professional life of a counseling professional. Due to the impact of wellness and self-care on counseling professionals' career spans, perhaps these experiential classroom activities can be assigned not just for counseling ethics education class. Instead, these activities can become longitudinally creative-experiential activities for any educational training programs.

10.4 Conclusion

This chapter sought to explore, understand, describe, and interpret how guidance and counseling teachers learn, understand, experience, and apply counseling ethics education to their evolving professional identity and development in the program. Five emergent master themes discussed were education foundation, education integration, education application, education assimilation, and education appreciation. The discussion was based on nine principles of effective adult learning by Vella (1994, 2002), which offers only one way to organize, discuss, interpret, and connect the emergent master themes. Remarkably, counseling ethics education is found to be more than just code of ethics acquisition from textbooks; it extends beyond the cut-and-dry content, which includes safety, connection, respect, engagement, accountability, reinforcement, application, personalization, and teamwork.

Counseling ethics education empowers guidance and counseling teachers as well as improves professional identity and development. The training standards of the counseling profession require counseling ethics competencies among counselors: "to ensure counseling students develop a professional counselor identity and master the knowledge and skills to practice effectively" (CACREP 2016, p. 2). The CACREP overarching mission is to promote professional competence of the counseling profession through the development of preparation standards, encouragement of excellence in program development, and accreditation of professional preparation programs. Hence, counseling students at any counselor education training programs must demonstrate competencies in their professional orientation and ethical practices, which ultimately are related to their overall professional functioning. In addition to the CACREP standards, the ACA also emphasizes that ethical competency is paramount for the counseling profession and counseling professionals (ACA 2014).

Ethics education is an important competency in the counseling profession. Lifelong knowledge acquisition and continuous professional development are crucial to improve counseling professionals' ethical awareness. The CACREP standards mandated all counselor educators to have professional responsibility to educate counseling students with many aspects of professional counseling ethics (CACREP 2016). It is notable that teaching ethics is complex; and teaching counseling ethics is challenging since there is a broad range of topics, there is not unification about its goals, and subsequently there is no specific method to teach (Zakaria 2013). On the other hand, the goals for counseling ethics education are diverse and include such areas as knowledge of the ethics codes, aptitude to practice ethically, knowledge of at least one decision-making model, awareness of ethical issues, tolerance for ambiguity, willingness to consult, ego strength, and self-care. Accordingly, a counseling ethics education course includes mandatory learning outcome components such as personal development and insights into therapeutic change; and is not a substitute for personal counseling services (Zakaria 2013; Zakaria and Warren 2014, 2016).

Counseling ethics education is anticipated to instill counseling ethics awareness and integrate professional ethics knowledge in guidance and counseling teachers; and equally encourage wellness and self-care appreciation among counseling practitioners (Zakaria 2013). Even with the complexities of counseling ethics education, counselor educators must be able to work with guidance and counseling teachers who have diverse social, cognitive, and ego developmental levels. At the heart of a sound ethical counseling practice, there lies a framework of respect, care, and sensitivity toward others in ensuring the highest professional standard of services within the counseling profession realm. This framework guarantees the care of self, care of clients, and care of colleagues; which are all based upon counseling professionals' personal and professional morals, values, principles, and personhood quality, that eventually may empower guidance and counseling teachers as well as improve their professional identity and development.

The importance of counseling ethics education to improve guidance and counseling teachers' services delivery at school setting. The significance of counseling ethics education for guidance and counseling teachers is evident. One essential aspect of leadership in the counseling profession is to know and learn about "self" and "ism." As counseling professionals, guidance and counseling teachers are able to see their role as being one who inspires to help the children, and to practice counseling competently and ethically. Their self-awareness, competency, and identity development may have a significant impact on the educational process in conveying the knowledge, managing the classroom, enhancing children's well-being, and creating a therapeutic learning ambiance. In addition, guidance and counseling teachers are expected to serve numerous roles and job requirements at school such as educating, advising, and mentoring the children. They also have to participate in research for evidence-based practices and scholarly activities, provide consultation, and serve the school and community with various accountabilities. These diverse roles and expectations certainly can provide them a broad foundation for the development of their professional identity as counseling professionals, precisely as guidance and counseling teachers.

Although there are many sources and resources can be found along the learning acquisition journey to assist guidance and counseling teachers to learn ethics education, they need to learn formal ethics education content through a direct instructional medium. This could be attending an ethics education class established in any counselor education training programs, as well as participating in ethics education workshops, conferences, or conventions. It is assumed that these direct instructional mediums embed and infuse ethics education content through good classroom ethics pedagogy. Good ethics pedagogy is a process which involves changes and enlightenments in teaching and learning ethics education.

It is always a good reminder for an ethics educator that, while intentionally teaching counseling ethics education, the counselor educator could potentially alter the guidance and counseling teachers' existing knowledge, belief system, and world view regarding certain challenging issues. Therefore, effective ethics pedagogy involves in-depth discussions on ethical challenges that may relate to their integrity. The integrity assists guidance and counseling teachers to grasp the ethics education meaning from its content. The type of teaching that derived from good ethics pedagogy is known as "persuasive pedagogy," which means to discuss various ethical perspectives while maintaining balance in the classroom practice between the ethics educator and the students. In the setting of a persuasive pedagogical classroom, there exists a special connection between three elements: rational explanations, critical dialogue, and content teaching. These connections are also relevant in teaching and learning counseling ethics education, in which the connections might enable the counselor educator to provide honest reasons for classroom discussion on any ethical conundrum, as well as to welcome any radical questions inquired by the guidance and counseling teachers (Jungers and Gregoire 2013).

Guidance and counseling teachers can grasp and comprehend much of the information about ethics education through knowing the self. To know the self means to learn more in-depth about the self; to be familiar with belief systems, values, and morals; and to discover how these interconnected constructs can affect ethical decision-making process throughout the lifespan. Another important element in assisting guidance and counseling teachers to grasp ethics understandings could be through the life experiences gained from the interactions with family, friends, community, and spirituality affiliations. Guidance and counseling teachers with ethics enthusiasm and curiosity could also learn a great deal about ethics education from a direct instructional learning environment. This can be attained by enrolling in a formal ethics education class, dialoguing with ethics educators, exchanging information with ethics experts, and even making one's own ethical mistakes throughout a career lifespan.

Currently in Malaysia, the practice of instructional approach for most primary, secondary, and tertiary teaching and learning endeavors is mostly still utilizing traditional education; which focusing more on content-based, memorization-based, examination-based, and teacher-centered learning. From this chapter, the discussion on how guidance and counseling teachers learn, understand, apply, experience, and apply counseling ethics is found to be not just knowing and learning about code of ethics from textbooks. The discussion and conclusion drawn from this chapter may contribute toward a very substantial change in instructional approach for higher educational system in Malaysia, particularly in providing a new set of methodology in teaching and learning counseling ethics education; to empower lifelong learning acquisition among guidance and counseling teachers toward enhanced professional identity and development as counseling professionals.

References

American Counseling Association. (2014). *ACA code of ethics and standards of practice*. Alexandria, VA: Author.
Bernard, J. M., & Goodyear, R. K. (2009). *Fundamentals of clinical supervision* (4th ed.). Upper Saddle River, NJ: Pearson.
Blenkinsop, S., & Beeman, C. (2012). Experiencing philosophy: Engaging students in advanced theory. *Journal of Experiential Education, 35*(1), 207–221. doi:10.5193/JEE35.1.207
Council for the Accreditation of Counseling and Related Educational Programs. (2016). *Council for the accreditation of counseling and related educational programs*. Alexandria, VA: Author.
Dollarhide, C. T., Shavers, M. C., Baker, C. A., Dagg, D. R., & Taylor, D. T. (2012). Conditions that create therapeutic connection: A phenomenological study. *Counseling and Values, 57*, 147–161.
Dougherty, A. M. (2005). *Psychological consultation and collaboration in school community settings* (4th ed.). Belmont, CA: Thomson Brooks/Cole.
Gladding, S. T. (2009). *Counseling: A comprehensive profession* (6th ed.). Upper Saddle River, NJ: Pearson.
Gnilka, P. B., Chang, C. Y., & Dew, B. J. (2012). The relationship between supervisee stress, coping resources, the working alliance, and the supervisory working alliance. *Journal of Counseling & Development, 90*, 63–70.
Handelsman, M., Gottlieb, M., & Knapp, S. (2005). Training ethical psychologists: An acculturation model. *Professional Psychology: Research and Practice, 36*(1), 54–65.
Jones, P. M. (2011). Teaching for change in social work: A discipline-based argument for the use of transformative approaches to teaching and learning. *Journal of Transformative Education, 7*(1), 8–25.
Jungers, C. M., & Gregoire, J. (2013). *Counseling ethics: Philosophical and professional foundation*. New York, NY: Springer.
Lenz, A. S., & Smith, R. L. (2010). Integrating wellness concepts within a clinical supervision model. *The Clinical Supervisor, 29*(2), 228–245.
Livingston, L. (2010). Teaching creativity in higher education. *Arts Education Policy Review, 111*, 59–62.
McAuliffe, G. J., & Eriksen, K. (2011). *Handbook of counselor preparation: Constructivist, developmental, and experiential approaches*. Thousand Oaks, CA: SAGE Publications.

Mohamed, O. (2009). *Prinsip psikoterapi dan pengurusan dalam kaunseling (Edisi kedua) Psychotherapy principles and management in counseling* (2nd ed.). Serdang, Malaysia: Penerbitan Universiti Putra Malaysia.

Provine, R. (2000). *Laughter: A scientific investigation*. New York, NY: Penguin.

Remley, T., & Herlihy, B. (2010). *Ethical, legal, and professional issues in counseling* (3rd ed.). Upper Saddle River, NJ: Prentice-Hall.

Sias, S. M. (2009). Substance abuse counselors and moral reasoning: Hypothetical and authentic dilemmas. *Counseling and Values, 53*, 195–201.

Sias, S. M., Lambie, G. W., & Foster, V. A. (2006). Conceptual and moral development of substance abuse counselors: Implications for training. *Journal of Addictions & Offender Counseling, 26*, 99–110.

Vella, J. (1994). *Learning to listen, learning to teach*. San Francisco, CA: Jossey-Bass.

Vella, J. (2002). *Learning to listen, learning to teach: The power of dialogue in educating adults* (Rev ed.). San Francisco, CA: Jossey-Bass.

Warren, J., & Douglas, K. (2012). Falling from grace: Understanding on ethical sanctioning experience. *Counseling and Value, 57*, 131–145.

Warren, J., Morgan, M. M., Morris, L. B., & Morris, T. M. (2010a). Breathing words slowly: Creative writing and counselor self-care. The writing workout. *Journal of Creativity in Mental Health, 5*, 1–16. doi:10.1080/15401383.2010.485074

Warren, J., Stech, M., Douglas, K., & Lambert, S. (2010b). Enhancing case conceptualization through film: The addiction web. *Journal of Creativity in Mental Health, 3*, 228–242. doi:10.1080/15401383.2010.507663

Warren, J., Zavaschi, G., Covello, C., & Zakaria, N. S. (2012). The use of bookmarks in teaching counseling ethics. *Journal of Creativity in Mental Health, 7*(2), 187–201.

Zakaria, N. S. (2007). Peer counselling empowerment and ethical considerations. *Educational Resources Information Center* (ED 499793). Greensboro: University of North Carolina/ERIC.

Zakaria, N. S. (2013). Counseling ethics education experience: An interpretive case study of the first year master's level counseling students (Doctoral dissertation). *ProQuest Dissertations and Theses* (UMI 3562075).

Zakaria, N. S., & Warren, J. (2014). Inquiry-based teaching and learning in counseling ethics education. In P. Blessinger, & J. M. Carfora (Eds.), *Inquiry-based learning for the arts, humanities, and social sciences: A conceptual and practical resource for educators* (*innovations in higher education teaching and learning, 2*,147–167). Bingley, UK: Emerald Group Publishing. doi.org/10.1108/S2055-364120140000002018

Zakaria, N. S., & Warren, J. (2016). Counseling ethics education: Teaching and learning development reformation. In I. Hussein Amzat & B. Yusuf (Eds.), *Fast forwarding higher education institutions for global challenges: Perspectives and approaches* (pp. 83–96). Singapore: Springer. doi:10.1007/978-981-287-603-4

Chapter 11
An Approach to Motivation and Empowerment: The Application of Positive Psychology

Samuel M.Y. Ho, Christine W.Y. Mak, Rita Ching and Edmund T.T. Lo

Abstract Research suggests that positive emotions can prevent burnout as well as lead to greater motivation and work satisfaction. In the past decades, there has been increasing interest to apply positive psychology constructs like strengths and hope in school settings to empower teachers and students. Motivation in teachers and students are related and interactive. By observing motivational thought patterns include attitudes, attributions, and goal attainments of teachers, students develop their motivation to learn. Based on the literature review as well as our own research and practical experience, this chapter will first explore the theoretical supports from perspectives of positive psychology on character strength, hope as a cognitive motivational system, interpersonal relationships and notice of positive events as the four pillars in teachers' motivation and empowerment. These altogether formulate the SHINE intervention approach. It will then discuss specific intervention examples in SHINE in school settings. By internalizing the positive psychology knowledge and skills at a personal level, teachers can promote the building of positive psychological resources at an institutional level and hence be able to generate sustainable benefits among themselves and students.

11.1 Introduction

Teachers in Hong Kong face tremendous stress, particularly in recent years with changing education policy, heightening expectations from stakeholders, accreditation culture, and significantly, increasing attitude, emotional, and behavioral problems among students (Chan 2010; Leung and Lee 2006; Ho et al. 2003; Pang 2012). Under these stressors, burnout could be a consequence, as investigated in various

---

S.M.Y. Ho (✉)
Psychology Laboratories, Department of Applied Social Sciences,
City University of Hong Kong, Kowloon Tong, Hong Kong
e-mail: munyinho@cityu.edu.hk

C.W.Y. Mak · R. Ching · E.T.T. Lo
The Women's Foundation, Sheung Wan, Hong Kong

© Springer Nature Singapore Pte Ltd. 2017
I.H. Amzat and N.P. Valdez (eds.), *Teacher Empowerment Toward Professional Development and Practices*, DOI 10.1007/978-981-10-4151-8_11

local (Chan 2010; Leung and Lee 2006; Lo 2014) and overseas studies (Kokkinos 2007; Santavirta and Solovieva 2007)—teacher burnout is a syndrome of emotional exhaustion, depersonalization, and reduced personal accomplishment (Maslach et al. 1996), which can negatively affect motivation, cognition, and work performance (Dai and Sternberg 2004).

A new set of strategies to promote teachers' motivation, inner strengths, and resilience to manage the increasing work demands and challenges should be developed. In this regards, we have conducted a number of professional development workshops in positive psychology in 19 secondary schools in Hong Kong from 2011 to 2015, under the Life Skills Program of the Women's Foundation with the support from the City University of Hong Kong, benefitting around 1000 teachers. We began the journey of positive psychology to serve two purposes. First, we want to educate school leaders and teachers with the positive psychology constructs and science. Second, we aim at building strengths, hope, positive attention, and interpersonal resources to promote the antithesis of burnout and will in turn leading to greater motivation and empowerment among teachers.

In this book chapter, we will detail a new model (Fig. 11.1) to enhance motivation and resilience for use in educational settings. The model provides us an empirically proven framework with structured directions for implementing positive psychological interventions in school settings. We will cover practical strategies by which teachers can maintain their motivation, through the integration and application of positive psychological constructs in both personal and professional lives. In particular, we will highlight hope as a cognitive system in affecting teachers' motivation and the benefits for teachers to identify and apply their unique character strengths inside and outside classroom. The use of active constructive responding style to affect interpersonal bonding, social resources, attention, and memory will also be addressed.

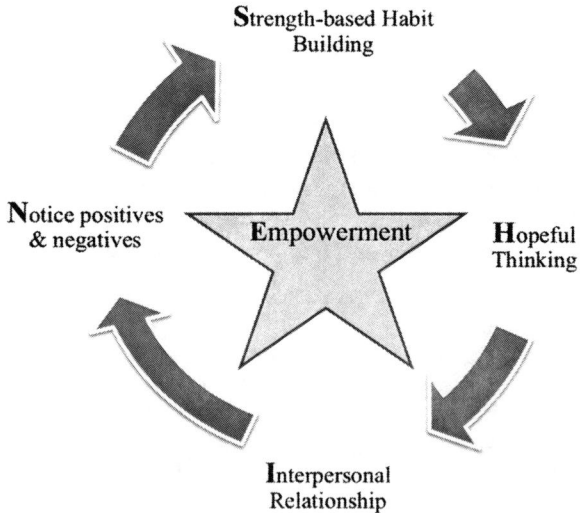

Fig. 11.1 SHINE intervention model

11.2 Shine Model Overview

Positive psychological interventions center on boosting people's psychological resources, resilience against life's stressors and motivation to achieve meaningful life as well as helping people to alleviate psychological symptoms.

We developed the SHINE model based on well-researched positive psychology constructs and a series of studies by our research team and overseas researchers.

SHINE stands for four psychological constructs, pathways, and outcome within the model

Strength-based habit building pathway guides teachers to recognize and develop their unique character strengths to increase life satisfaction and well-being to counter depersonalization.
Hopeful thinking pathway boosts a sense of control, personal efficacy, and accomplishment by building up a future-oriented hopeful thinking style.
Interpersonal relationship pathway encourages teachers to build more positive and nourishing interactions through offering capitalization and active constructive responses to others' positive sharing.
Notice both positives and negatives pathway helps teachers to gradually develop an awareness and increased sensitivity to see positive things in life to counter emotional exhaustion.
Empowerment is the outcome of interventions.

The model is a novel endeavor to organize our well-researched positive psychological constructs into a structured framework with clearly operationalized pathways to bring empowerment among teachers and students. We believe that, by internalizing the positive psychology knowledge and skills in a personal level, the well-being, motivation, and resilience of teachers are promoted and hence be able to generate sustainable benefits among themselves, students, schools, and the community.

11.3 Strength to Motivation

Teachers are encouraged to develop their unique character strengths and virtues as use of character strengths positively affects job satisfaction (Littman-Ovadia and Davidovitch 2010). Character strengths are observable positive traits manifested in an individual's thoughts, emotions, and behaviors (Peterson and Seligman 2004) and virtue is a common set of positive psychological traits recognized by the society and are beneficial to all people.

Ho and colleagues (Duan et al. 2012a, 2013; Ho et al. 2015, June 1) confirmed there are three key virtues among Chinese people, including *Cautiousness (Strength of Temperance), Interpersonal (Strength of Interpersonal)* and *Vitality (Strength of Intellectual)*.

Cautiousness consists intrapersonal traits of judgment, prudence, regulation, perseverance, learning, and modesty, reflecting a person's persistence in achieving goals and exhibit self-control.

Interpersonal consists kindness, teamwork, fairness, love, authenticity, leadership, forgiveness and gratitude, reflecting a person's love, concern and gratitude toward others.

Vitality consists curiosity, zest, creativity, hope, perspective, bravery, beliefs, social intelligence, beauty and humor, reflecting a person's positive qualities to the society.

A study of the three virtues found a significant positive relationship between the virtues and life satisfaction among subjects from Hong Kong and the Mainland (Duan et al. 2012a, b). The results support the notion of character strength promotes the individual's life satisfaction and well-being in Western theories (Park et al. 2004; Peterson et al. 2007; Shimai et al. 2006) which can be applied to Chinese contexts (Fig. 11.2).

Character strengths (e.g., hope, a character strength under the virtue of vitality) could play an important adaptive role in coping with life stresses (Ho et al. 2014). Consistent with another study conducted among Chinese teachers, those teachers with strengths of hope, zest, and higher level of emotional strengths tended to report more life satisfaction and positive experiences but less negative emotions (Chan 2009). As such, the outcome of positive emotions and psychological well-being by applying personal strengths and virtues in career life may in turn serve as an important role in preventing burnout while promoting motivation and empowerment.

Based on the above research findings and our practical experience, we recommend the implementation of strength-based intervention and activities in educational settings. The intervention can facilitate teachers' paths to sustain positive affect and

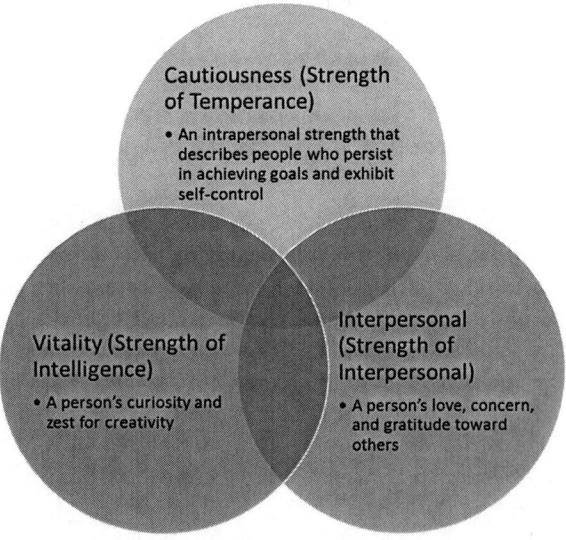

Fig. 11.2 The three key strengths (Ho et al. 2015)

enhance emotional regulation, which in turn promote both resource building and involvement with approaching goals (Elliot and Thrash 2002; Lyubomirsky 2001).

Our strength-based interventions emphasize and encourage teachers to "Change your lens, spot the strengths". Csikszentmihalyi et al. (1997) recognized teachers with the ability to spot students' strengths that the students may not be aware of or notice. This recognition may potentially promote new areas of interests and passion. The ability of shifting attention from negatives to positives and changing from focusing on weaknesses to spotting strengths, may (a) help teachers to maintain and nurture their passions in teaching; (b) value more on the intrinsic rewards of teaching than external rewards; (c) encourage mastery instead of performance orientation.

Our strength-based intervention encourage the strengthening of all three virtues as our findings show that individuals exhibiting more of the three virtues tend to report better subjective well-being (Duan et al. 2012a, b). In our programme, the development of the virtue of vitality is emphasized. This is because the virtue of vitality is most significantly related to individual's life satisfaction (Duan et al. 2012a, b). Further details of our strength-based intervention will be discussed in later sections of this chapter.

11.4 Hope as a Cognitive Motivational System

"Hope" is becoming more difficult to sustain in face of various social and economic challenges. This is no exception to teachers who faced climate of lowered morale and increased demand in the education field. In fact, teachers may be more vulnerable for losing hope or burning out (Snyder et al. 1997). The increased workload, anxiety, expectation of stakeholders and perceived little control over outcomes among teachers may further diminish their hope. We need a feasible understanding and conceptual definition of hope so that teachers can build and sustain hope practically. Here, we will operationalize hope and discuss its importance as a cognitive strategy.

In cognitive psychology, hope is defined as a cognitive motivational system (Snyder et al. 1991a, b), involving the process of thinking about one's goal, the ability to perceive viable pathways to pursue goals set and to sustain one's will in goal pursuit. In this way, emotions follow cognitions in the process of goal-directed thinking (Snyder 1994). Based on our practical experience, we recognize that cognitions play an important role in determining the power of will and motivation among teachers in pursuing their educational goals. In our model, we emphasize the construct of hopeful thinking style to boost personal efficacy, motivation and accomplishment by the application of cognitive strategies that are trainable and attainable. Under the Hopeful thinking pathway in SHINE, hope is essential in the awareness of roles and capability as teachers, setting goals, and making plans for the goals (Fig. 11.3).

First, teachers need to view themselves as capable agents of initiating wills and implementing ways to pursue meaningful educational goals. Teachers are encouraged to exercise their professional judgment to develop pathways with associated

Fig. 11.3 Components of hope

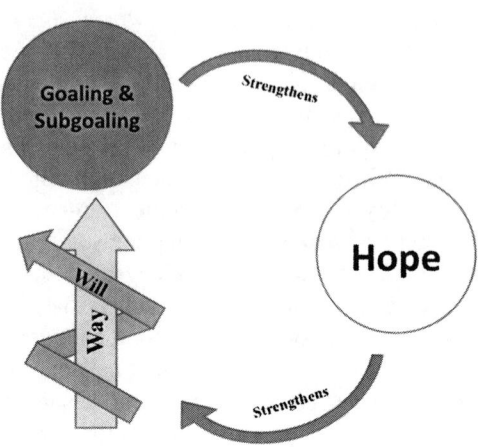

agency-inducing cognitions. Their awareness should also extend to the realization that their motivation affects students' motivation. Motivation in teachers and students are related and interactive. Teachers tend to believe that students have low levels of motivation if their own motivation is low (Gorham and Millette 1997), affecting students' learning and achievement (Gorham and Millette 1997). High agency teachers, instead, influence their students with a sense of motivation, enthusiasm, and the belief that goals can be attained.

Second, high-hope teachers develop the capacity and future-oriented cognitive style to set long-range goals (Snyder 1994). Nowadays, it is challenging for teachers to set and adhere to long-range learning goals as more stakeholders emphasize performance as an ultimate goal of education, tilting the orientations of school and teachers. However, research indicated that performance goals set up maladaptive achievement pattern and increase helpless responses when confronted with challenges (Dweck 1999). In our training, we recommend schools to create an atmosphere where teachers and students are more concerned with long-range learning goals rather than short-term performance goals.

Third, high-hope teachers can work through practical steps to achieve long-range goals. They desire to learn new skills to tackle difficulties and explore alternative means to achieve goals.

Through teaching and experiential exercises during workshop, we discussed with teachers the cognitive model of hope and practical strategies to instill and promote hopeful thinking style and explore the relationship between hope and motivation in teachers and students. We will elaborate the details of our hope-based intervention in later sections of this chapter.

In summary, Snyder et al. (1991a, b, 2002) posited a cognitive motivational system to highlight the ways how people appraise and pursue their goals would produce helpless or mastery responses. Rather than focusing and seeking ways around obstacles, high-hope teachers are clear about their educational goals. Instead of focusing on short-term goals, teachers are encouraged to establish long-range educational goals (Snyder and Feldman 2000), as meaningful long-term goals on mastery orientation are crucial for motivated, productive, and satisfying lives.

11.5 Interpersonal Relationship Building by Active Constructive Response

Interpersonal communication is another pathway for teachers' empowerment, as simple as having one to express his/her positive experiences and having responders to provide active constructive responses (ACR). Gable et al. (2004) proposed a two-dimension model on communication styles (Table 11.1). The model comprised of the active-passive dimension and constructive-destructive dimension. Active constructive responding (ACR) is defined as recognizing and elaborating the positive news, and giving enthusiastic support when positive experiences are shared. They demonstrated that engaging with others in ACR style can enhance personal well-being, facilitate social bonds, and build stronger relationships. A process of capitalization occurs when one inform another person about the occurrence of a personal positive event, generating more positive affect. The sharing of a positive event with others facilitates the discloser to selectively attend to the positive stimuli, retell, relive, and savor the event. ACR fosters capitalization and savoring of positive life experiences, prolongs and enhances the experience by increasing its salience and accessibility in memory (Gable et al. 2004). In short, we teach and encourage the practice of ACR in the school settings as it can become an effective means to enhance teachers' sensitivity to positive stimuli, increase their positive memories and emotions, so that teachers can extract more satisfaction from work lives, promote and maintain their motivation.

Teachers, like other helping professionals, have significant mental and physical demands in dealing with daily routines. Besides, independent teaching in classrooms limits teachers' opportunities to share and reflect their experiences. As a result, it is difficult for teachers to receive regular supervision and positive feedback. Teachers may feel isolated and helpless, affecting their job satisfaction, morale, and motivation.

Table 11.1 Gable et al. (2004)'s matrix on communication styles

	Constructive	Destructive
Active	Enthusiastic support Responds as happy as the sharer Ask for elaboration Receiver is validated and understood	Identify problem and point out potential down sides Bring conversation to a halt Receiver feels ashamed, embarrassed, guilty or angry
Passive	Quiet and unanimated response Conversation fizzles out Receiver feels unimportant, misunderstood or embarrassed	Ignore the event Conversation does not start Little interest is paid Receiver feels confused, guilty or disappointed

We recommend the promotion of ACR in the school settings. Whether a more formal teacher support group that encourages teachers to appreciate each others' work in an ACR, or adoption of ACR in daily conversation between school management, teachers and other supporting staff in the school, will energize teachers and promote their well-being, which can in turn motivate and empower teachers (Table 11.1).

11.6 Notice Both Positives and Negatives

'*Correct mistakes if you have made any and guard against them if you have not.* (有則改之,無則加勉)' is an old teaching from Analects of Confucius on the attitude of learning. Teaching and learning inevitably focus a lot on mistakes and negativities. Focusing only on mistakes, though, will make teachers lose the chances of appreciating the students' improvements and progresses. Under the mistake-oriented atmosphere, coupled with the Chinese characteristic of being humble in general (Furnham et al. 2001; Gibbons 1983) that does not encourage discussion of one's strengths, teachers might miss some chances of appreciating the positive sides in teaching. Our model emphasizes a balance in perception whereby teachers are guided to aware the presence of both positive and negative stimuli in most of our daily life events. Further, teachers are coached to shift their attention from negative bias towards more neutral stimuli and gear their attention towards positive events. Under the SHINE framework, we aim to enable teachers to acquire a balanced perception of the environment, either to see both positive and negative stimuli/events in the environment (Fig. 11.4). There are two areas that teachers can pay more attention to, namely strengths and growth, as described below.

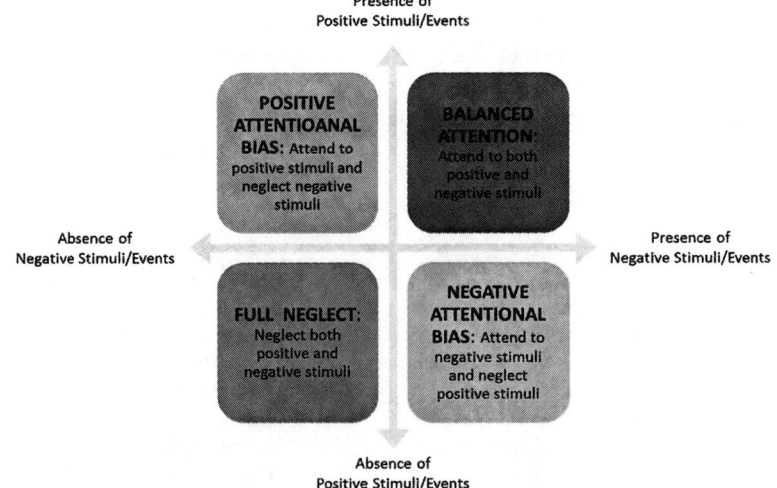

Fig. 11.4 Notice both positives and negatives

Noticing strengths is a part of the Strength-based habit building pathway in SHINE. Conscious attempts on attention are needed because teachers will need to spot out not only the conspicuous strengths in themselves and in students, but also the strengths that have potential to be developed. In the above sections, we have discussed the importance of hope and virtues as positive psychological constructs. Apart from having better subjective well-being as discussed in Strengths section, our research indicated that hope and virtues affect psychosocial well-being directly and indirectly through attention to positive information, revealing the importance of positive attention in information processing (Chan et al. 2011, 2013).

Increasing teachers' sensitivity to aware positive changes is related to recent research that identified two distinct ways in which one understands intelligence and learning. Believing intelligence being an inborn trait is said to be a *fixed mindset* thinking. In contrast, a *growth mindset* assumes intelligence can be developed over time (Blackwell et al. 2007; Dweck 2000, 2007). By definition, adopting the growth mindset on learning and intelligence will mean seeing more possibilities in teaching. Seeing these possibilities concur with the cognitive motivation system of hope and would thus motivate teachers. In the course of teaching, teachers can pay attention to students' efforts and improvements, then attribute them to the framework of growth mindset. Attention to students' effort is also a more immediate recognition of teaching accomplishment that makes teachers feel more motivated (Tardy and Snyder 2004),

Apart from motivating teachers, attention to growth also encourages students to challenge themselves more and helps students' resilience in learning. This would likely align with long-range goals that hopeful teachers have set. We will introduce the strategies in our intervention programme on increasing the attention to growth and strengths in later sections.

11.7 Pathways to Motivation and Empowerment

Guided by the SHINE model, the interventions have been developed and delivered through three structured pathways, namely *Explore, Apply and Rehearse*. The exploration pathway helps teachers to understand key concepts, engaged meaningfully in exploration and reflection through assessments and team activities. The application pathway encourages teachers to put the new skills and mindsets in action. Teachers are encouraged to rehearse the skills for growing them into habits. This section will shed light on the interventions developed to teach and implement each positive psychological constructs of our model.

We deliver interventions by interactive workshops and 4-week self-help programme. Either way, the goal is to provide teachers with the knowledge, tools, and resources to enhance their motivation, personal resilience, and hopeful thinking mindset, so they would be better enabled to provide support to their students and bring impact to the school and community (Table 11.2).

Table 11.2 Themes and exercises of 4-week self-help programme

	Week one	Week two	Week three	Week four
Target	Build strengths	Get focused	Improve communication	Enhance relationships
Day	1 = Your strengths portfolio—part 1 2 = Your strengths portfolio—part 2 3 = My unique self 4 = Use strength in new way 5 = Finding my flow 6 = Dating my flow 7 = Consolidation and directions	1 = Be presence 2 = Mindful breathing 3 = Mindful listening 4 = Mindful bell 5 = Savoring a good experience 6 = The five-finger gratitude exercise 7 = Consolidation and directions	1 = Share 2 = Active listening 3 = Listen to other's strengths 4 = Positive communication smiley 5 = Smile 6 = Tell me more 7 = Consolidation and directions	1 = Make time 2 = Express thankfulness 3 = Loving-kindness meditation 4 = Be a secret angel 5 = Give compliment 6 = Capitalize on good fortune 7 = Consolidation and directions

11.7.1 Interactive Workshop

11.7.1.1 Strength-Based Habit Building

The Brief Strengths Scale-12 (BSS-12) (Ho et al. 2015) is administered to evaluate strengths in the aspects of "Attitude" (Strength of Temperance), "Relationship" (Strength of Interpersonal), and "Energy" (Strength of Intellectual). Teachers are guided to explore their unique character strength profile. As previously discussed, research indicates that knowing and applying our strengths increases life satisfaction and well-being as well as promoting work motivation and engagement. Such scientific evidences would be introduced to the teachers.

For cultivating teacher engagement, we provide experiential exercises on "Change your lens, spot the strengths" to help teachers explore, apply, and build their character strengths with the team and their students. Teachers would also engage in other interactive games, self-reflection, and case discussions. The workshop also taps into the possibility of developing a school-wide strengths-themed programme that offers teachers and students a shared language to recognize and communicate the positive attributes and values of one another (Park and Peterson 2009). With a common language to describe strengths, it is easier to encourage the use of strengths among their students and colleagues, also for teachers' identification and debriefing in their course of teaching. To give teachers a taste of such environment, we invite teachers to explore their own strengths through structured activities, for example, describing your best possible self (Sheldon and Lyubomirsky 2006). We invite them to observe others' by teamwork games such as chair-stacking challenge or group 3D puzzle solving exercises.

We would also discuss with teachers the possibility to adopt these exercises into school curriculum design. For example, in school retreat camp or in the beginning of new academic year, teachers are guided to focus on the best possible self as a teacher, aligning their unique constellation of character strengths, personal, and professional goals to gain a comprehensive and meaningful picture of one's significant role as a teacher and caring professional. The reflection and recognition are important to fuel teachers' motivation and empowerment. We close the section by reminding teachers the habit of strength spotting and sensitivity to positive attributes can be strengthened along with practices.

11.7.1.2 Hopeful Thinking

Hopeful thinking represents the ability to perceive viable pathways to pursue the goals set, sustain one's motivation in goal pursuit, and stay in hopeful thinking style. In the workshop, teachers are presented the basic concepts of hope model. They are shown how to acquire and strengthen the cognitive strategies of hope in a step-by-step manner, followed by structured exercises that guide them to identify and prioritize their goals in personal and professional lives.

To better relate teachers to apply all these, stories and videos of high hope protagonists are used to facilitate teachers to learn identifying and analyzing the element of hope as defined in Snyder's cognitive model. From these examples, they also broaden the understanding on how hope components of goal, re-goaling, waypower, and willpower have generated adaptive and positive functioning and achievements. As hopeful cognition can be acquired through systematic training (Cheavens et al. 2006; Pedrotti et al. 2008; Snyder et al. 2002), we believe it is important for teachers to equip these skills so that they are better prepared to offer guidance and coaching to promote hope among students, along their personal empowerment and strengthening of hopeful mindset.

Student cases are also discussed to provide new perspectives for teachers to reframe the concerns presented in the cases. They are encouraged to integrate their learning in this section, to use the hopeful thinking framework to notice strengths within the students, then help them set goals, derive alternative routes for goal attainment, with a high agency cognition.

11.7.1.3 Interpersonal Relationship

Creating supportive and positive relationships are vital to motivate members in the school. Research-based practice of giving an active constructive response when someone shared positive news facilitates positive emotional exchanges, nurtures close connections and builds relationship resources.

ACR is introduced to teachers through video demonstrations (The Women's Foundation 2014) of four different responding styles in Gable's communication matrix. An example line of ACR response demonstrated in the video is "I am happy to hear your great news. Thanks for sharing with me. I know that you practice hard and now it's paying off. I can't wait listening to your new song. Tell me more about it!" Research supporting the importance and benefits of ACR is then being covered.

Teachers are guided to practice active listening and responding to good news respectfully through role-plays that depict each of the four ways of responding and discuss in small groups what kind of reactions and responses are considered as "active", "passive", "constructive", and "destructive". Practice of ACR facilitates positive connections with others and attends to others' inherent value. We recommend the following five steps SMILE skills in practicing ACR in daily communication:

1. Start with observing and listening
2. Mind your non-verbal responses
3. Intend to ask questions about details
4. Let us relive the experience and savor the positives
5. Express your appreciation and encourage strengths use.

Communication by means of ACR allows the discloser and responder duet to benefit through reliving the experience and positive emotions. Fredrickson (1998) opined that positive emotions contribute to the broadening of the thought–action repertoire, widening of attention as well as building more trust and personal resources. The section is wrapped up with these research findings.

11.7.1.4 Notice Both Positives and Negatives

Videos to demonstrate cognitive bias from "Surprising Studies of Visual Awareness" Vol. 1 & 3 are shown to develop awareness of teachers' positive and negative attentions and selective attention. Teachers are given exercises to learn to direct their attention to the positive experiences—for instance, the exercise of "savoring a good experience". They are encouraged to intentionally explore an experience by noting the experience in detail and reflecting on the good aspects of the experience. In addition, teachers would engage in the "gratitude exercise" (Emmons and McCullough 2003) to count and write down their blessings over the week, which guide them to turn the appreciation of simple things in life into a habit of perceiving positive stimuli. Teachers are then encouraged to share a positive experience and engage in the capitalization process by following the five-step SHARE strategies:

1. Slow down and direct attention to the positive experience
2. Have the experiences shared in details including different senses
3. Amplify or prolong the duration of positive feeling
4. Remember current or anticipate future positive events
5. Express thankfulness.

During the capitalization processes, teachers shift their attention to the positive stimuli, relive, and savor the experience, and consequently enrich the memory with better sense of fulfillment and more positive meanings. We further direct teachers to pay more attention to strengths and growth, as outlined in the SHINE model. In the workshop, teachers engage in video analyses, story telling and peer sharing, so they have opportunities to practise mindful listening and pay attention to the identification of strengths and growth.

11.7.2 Self-help Programme

The self-help programme (Mak et al. 2014) in length of 28 exercises, aims to provide research-based tools and resources for students and teachers to learn and practice the pathways of SHINE at their own pace and preferences, with a suggested course timeline of 4 weeks. The programme is accessible online or at hardcopies, with research-based tools and teacher resource kit available as well.

Based on SHINE, the self-help journey starts from enhancement of self-awareness in positive perspectives, to cultivation of positive attention, followed by savoring of positive emotional experiences exchange and conclude by ACR positive communication. Each topic has approximately 7 days of exercises in varied forms. After each exercise, there are different "to-do" items for the participants to complete, varying from invitation of friends' input on character strength to self-administered mindfulness exercise.

To facilitate participants' understanding of the programme framework and core psychological constructs, three group meetings will be arranged. The first meeting is held before the start of the programme. It serves the purpose of familiarizing with the population of self-help programme user and identification of those that might need extra help. The second meeting, in the middle of the programme, spends more time in exploring challenges participants face while using the programme. A sharing session is also included for them to share tips and experiences among themselves. The third meeting is set after the completion of the programme, with a purpose to consolidate the participants' learning. These meetings, especially the last one, also serve to motivate them to adhere to the daily exercises suggested by the programme.

11.8 Summary and Conclusion

This book chapter reviews the theoretical ground of the integrated approach to empowering teachers' motivation in their job. An empirically based SHINE model to guide intervention for teachers' empowerment is proposed. The SHINE model is a novel model being developed by the authors of this chapter and we believe that this model is unique in the world. The SHINE model can be incorporated into curriculums for teachers' training or conducted as separated on-the-job training programmes.

While the education system, its stakeholders and the environment are intertwined, the situation that teachers are overloaded and occasionally burned-out would not have any immediate solutions, our approach attempts to bring valid positive psychology applications to teachers and their school settings. We believe that successful interventions on teachers at a personal level would facilitate adoption of bigger changes and improvements on institution level.

We acknowledge the limitation that our integrated intervention protocol is not yet independently supported by research. However, with the theoretical basis behind each exercise, and the initial positive feedback from the 19 schools and 1000 teachers involved, we are confident this package is addressing teachers' need in self-development and in better recognizing their students' achievements, which in turn empowers them. Workshops and the self-help programme were fine-tuned along the implementation at the 19 schools to better fit in the context of teachers and schooling. After all these amendments, the next step would naturally be the systematic and statistical study and evaluation of the efficacy of the programmes.

Further extension of our approach could be on the integration of SHINE into the themes or curriculum of schools. By bringing these concepts to an institutional level, there could be more possibilities on the scale and efficacy of the approach. As our intervention involves a lot of interactions between teachers, another possible next step could be an integration with technical solutions such as mobile apps or websites to facilitate participants forming peer groups for their personal and professional growth.

Acknowledgements We would like to warmly acknowledge the Women's foundation involvement in the design and development of the research studies and their successful integration of the model into TWF's exceptional Life Skills Programme. We thank all staff and research assistants who have contributed their effort to the project.

References

Blackwell, L. S., Trzesniewski, K. H., & Dweck, C. S. (2007). Implicit theories of intelligence predict achievement across an adolescent transition: A longitudinal study and an intervention. *Child Development, 78*(1), 246–263.

Chan, D. W. (2009). The hierarchy of strengths: Their relationships with subjective well-being among Chinese teachers in Hong Kong. *Teaching and Teacher Education, 25*(6), 867–875.

Chan, D. W. (2010). Teacher burnout revisited: Introducing positive intervention approaches based on gratitude and forgiveness. *Educational Research Journal, 25*(2), 165.

Chan, M. W., Ho, S. M., Law, L. S., & Pau, B. K. (2013). *A visual dot-probe task as a measurement of attentional bias and its relationship with the symptoms of posttraumatic stress disorder among women with breast cancer* (p. 2013). Advances in Cancer: Research & Treatment.

Chan, M. W., Ho, S. M., Tedeschi, R. G., & Leung, C. W. (2011). The valence of attentional bias and cancer-related rumination in posttraumatic stress and posttraumatic growth among women with breast cancer. *Psycho-Oncology, 20*(5), 544–552.

Cheavens, J. S., Feldman, D. B., Gum, A., Michael, S. T., & Snyder, C. R. (2006). Hope therapy in a community sample: A pilot investigation. *Social Indicators Research, 77*(1), 61–78.

Csikszentmihalyi, M., Rathunde, K., & Whalen, S. (1997). Schools, teachers and talent development. In M. Csikszentmihalyi, K. Rathunde, & S. Whalen (Eds.), *Talented teachers: The roots of success and failure* (pp. 177–196). New York: Cambridge University Press.

Dai, D. Y., & Sternberg, R. J. (Eds.). (2004). *Motivation, emotion, and cognition: Integrative perspectives on intellectual functioning and development*. Abingdon-on-Thames: Routledge.

Duan, W. J., Bai, Y., Tang, X. Q., Siu, P. Y., KH, R., & Ho, S. M. (2012a). Virtues and positive mental health. *Mental Health, 38*(2), 1–8.

Duan, W., Ho, S. M. Y., Bai, Y., & Tang, X. (2013). Psychometric evaluation of the Chinese virtues questionnaire. *Research on Social Work Practice, 23*(3), 36–345.

Duan, W., Ho, S. M. Y., Yu, B., Tang, X., Zhang, Y., Li, T., et al. (2012b). Factor structure of the Chinese virtues questionnaire. *Research on Social Work Practice, 22*(6), 680–688.

Dweck, C. S. (1999). Caution-praise can be dangerous. *American Educator, 23*(1), 4–9.

Dweck, C. S. (2000). *Self-theories: Their role in motivation, personality, and development*. UK: Psychology Press.

Dweck, C. S. (2007). The secret to raising smart kids. *Scientific American Mind, 18*(6), 36–43.

Elliot, A. J., & Thrash, T. M. (2002). Approach-avoidance motivation in personality: Approach and avoidance temperaments and goals. *Journal of Personality and Social Psychology, 82*(5), 804.

Emmons, R. A., & McCullough, M. E. (2003). Counting blessings versus burdens: Experimental studies of gratitude and subjective well-being in daily life. *Journal of Personality and Social Psychology, 84*(2), 377–389.

Fredrickson, B. L. (1998). What good are positive emotions? *Review of General Psychology, 2*, 300–319.

Furnham, A., Hosoe, T., & Tang, T. L. P. (2001). Male hubris and female humility? Across-cultural study of ratings of self, parental, and sibling multiple intelligence in America, Britain, and Japan. *Intelligence, 30*, 101–115.

Gable, S. L., Reis, H. T., Impett, E. A., & Asher, E. R. (2004). What do you do when things go right? The intrapersonal and interpersonal benefits of sharing positive events. *Journal of Personality and Social Psychology, 87*(2), 228.

Gibbons, J. P. (1983). Attitudes towards languages and code-mixing in Hong Kong. *Journal of Multilingual & Multicultural Development, 4*(2–3), 129–147.

Gorham, J., & Millette, D. M. (1997). A comparative analysis of teacher and student perceptions of sources of motivation and demotivation in college classes. *Communication Education, 46*(4), 245–261.

Ho, C. L., Leung, J. P., & Fung, H. H. (2003). Teacher expectation of higher disciplinary problems and stress among Hong Kong secondary school teachers. *Educ Res J, 18*(1), 41–55.

Ho, S. M. Y., Li, W. L., Duan, W., Siu, B. P. Y., Yau, S., Yeung, G., & Wong, K. (2015, June 1). A brief strengths scale for individuals with mental health issues. *Psychological assessment, advance online publication*. http://dx.doi.org/10.1037/pas0000164

Ho, S. M., Rochelle, T. L., Law, L. S., Duan, W., Bai, Y., & Shih, S. M. (2014). Methodological issues in positive psychology research with diverse populations: Exploring strengths among Chinese adults. In *Perspectives on the Intersection of Multiculturalism and Positive Psychology* (pp. 45–57). Netherlands: Springer.

Kokkinos, C. M. (2007). Job stressors, personality and burnout in primary school teachers. *British Journal of Educational Psychology, 77*(1), 229–243.

Leung, D. Y., & Lee, W. W. (2006). Predicting intention to quit among Chinese teachers: Differential predictability of the components of burnout. *Anxiety, Stress, and Coping, 19*(2), 129–141.

Littman-Ovadia, H., & Davidovitch, N. (2010). Effects of congruence and character-strength deployment on work adjustment and well-being. *International Journal of Business and Social Science, 1*(3), 138–146.

Lo, B. L. K. (2014). Stress, burnout and resilience of teachers of students with emotional behavioural challenges. *SpringerPlus, 3*(1), 1–2.

Lyubomirsky, S. (2001). Why are some people happier than others? The role of cognitive and motivational processes in well-being. *American Psychologist, 56*(3), 239.

Mak C. W. Y., Ching, R., & Ho, S. M. Y. (2014, September). Building resilience in the school setting. In *Symposium on Youth Work and Youth Support in a Changing Society: Challenges, Opportunities and Innovations*. Hong Kong: The Women's Foundation and Department of Social Work, Chinese University of Hong Kong.

Maslach, C., Jackson, S. E., & Leiter, M. P. (1996). *Maslach burnout inventory manual* (3rd ed.). Palo Alto, CA: Consulting Psychologist Press.

Pang, I. W. (2012). Teacher stress in working with challenging students in Hong Kong. *Educational Research for Policy and Practice, 11*(2), 119–139.

Park, N., & Peterson, C. (2009). Character strengths: Research and practice. *Journal of College & Character, 10*, 4–13.

Park, N., Peterson, C., & Seligman, M. E. (2004). Strengths of character and well-being. *Journal of Social and Clinical Psychology, 23*(5), 603–619.

Pedrotti, J. T., Edwards, L. M., & Lopez, S. J. (2008). Promoting hope: Suggestions for school counselors. *Professional School Counseling, 12*(2), 100–107. doi:10.5330/PSC.n.2010-12.100

Peterson, C., & Seligman, M. E. (2004). *Character strengths and virtues: A handbook and classification*. Oxford University Press.

Peterson, C., Ruch, W., Beermann, U., Park, N., & Seligman, M. E. (2007). Strengths of character, orientations to happiness, and life satisfaction. *The Journal of Positive Psychology, 2*(3), 149–156.

Santavirta, N., & Solovieva, S. (2007). The association between job strain and emotional exhaustion in a cohort of 1,028 Finnish teachers. *British Journal of Educational Psychology, 77*(1), 213–228.

Sheldon, K. M., & Lyubomirsky, S. (2006). How to increase and sustain positive emotion: The effects of expressing gratitude and visualizing best possible selves. *The Journal of Positive Psychology, 1*(2), 73–82.

Shimai, S., Otake, K., Park, N., Peterson, C., & Seligman, M. E. (2006). Convergence of character strengths in American and Japanese young adults. *Journal of Happiness Studies, 7*(3), 311–322.

Snyder, C. R. (1994). *The psychology of hope: You can get there from here*. New York City: Simon and Schuster.

Snyder, C. R., Cheavens, J., & Sympson, S. C. (1997). Hope: An individual motive for social commerce. *Group Dynamics: Theory, Research, and Practice, 1*, 107–118.

Snyder, C. R., & Feldman, D. B. (2000). *Hope for the many: An empowering social Agendcf. Handbook of hope: Theory, measures, and applications* (pp. 402–415). San Diego, CA: Academic Press.

Snyder, C. R., Feldman, D. B., Shorey, H. S., & Rand, K. L. (2002a). Hopeful choices: A school counselor's guide to hopetheory. *Professional School Counseling, 5*, 298–307.

Snyder, C. R., Harris, C., Anderson, J. R., Holleran, S. A., Irving, L. M., Sigmon, S. T., et al. (1991a). The will and the ways: Development and validation of an individual-differences measure of hope. *Journal of Personality and Social Psychology, 60*(4), 570–585.

Snyder, C. R., Irving, L. M., & Anderson, J. R. (1991b). Hope and health. In C. R. Snyder & D. R. Forsyth (Eds.), *Handbook of social and clinical psychology: The health perspective* (pp. 285–305). Elmsford, NY: Pergamon.

Snyder, C. R., Shorey, H. S., Cheavens, J., Pulvers, K. M., Adams, V. H., III, & Wiklund, C. (2002b). Hope and academic success in college. *Journal of Educational Psychology, 94*(4), 820–826.

Tardy, C. M., & Snyder, B. (2004). 'That's why I do it': Flow and EFL teachers practices. *ELT Journal, 58*, 118–128.

The Women's Foundation. (2014). *Active constructive responding styles in school setting, DVD publication*. Hong Kong: The Women's Foundation.

Part III
Teacher Empowerment: Teacher Responsive Teaching and Learning Initiatives

Chapter 12
Teacher Responsive Teaching and Learning Initiatives Through Action Research

Mary Koutselini

Abstract Action research facilitates the participatory adaptation of professional development to the learners' needs in communities of reflective learning in the work environment. Research on professional development through action research (e.g. Reason and Bradbury in Handbook of action research. Sage, London, 2001a) provides strong evidence of teachers' and students' conceptual and actual shifts from distance to collaboration, participation and responsiveness, and a movement from teaching as content covering to teaching as reciprocal action and justified alternative decisions. The RELEASE project is presented as a good practice for teachers' empowerment, responsive teaching and learning initiatives through action research. The project indicated that students and teachers enhanced their learning, which resulted in new skills, strategies and communicative attitudes. Moreover, teachers enhanced their awareness towards the students' needs and students were encouraged to ask questions and reflect on teaching and their own learning.

12.1 Introduction

Results-based educational and curriculum theory does not considerably deal with the different biographies and world views of teachers and students, although it is well documented that curriculum change and reform cannot be realized without changes in teachers', students' and researchers' way of thinking and practices. Another stream of research points out that a very important variable affecting teachers' change is the theory–practice divide in teachers' teaching; teachers know the theories but they do not implement them during their teaching. Thus, educational change and teaching reform cannot be achieved without concomitant changes in teachers' and researchers' thoughts and practices.

M. Koutselini (✉)
Department of Education, University of Cyprus, Nicosia, Cyprus
e-mail: edmaryk@ucy.ac.cy

Nevertheless, it is an incontestable fact that teacher development is a powerful precursor in the teaching practice, which can advance students' learning results and teachers' self-confidence and independence. A number of questions arise from the fact that despite the frequent in-service training, school and teaching routines do not change. How can we transform schools into learning communities and theory into praxis? What can empower teachers to understand their own needs and the needs of their students? What can change the school ethos and culture from societies of students and teachers to communities of learning? How can we help teachers gain awareness of their strengths and limitations in respect to pedagogy? And finally, the crucial question concerns the best procedure for teachers' responsive learning and teaching and how we can transform the imposed effective 'methods' to tools of teachers' self-understanding and conceptual and attitudinal change.

To answer the above questions we engaged school teachers and school principals in an action research study in a number of schools in Cyprus. The programme RELEASE (Project ID: EACEA-521386: Towards achieving Self-Regulated Learning as a core in teachers' In-Service training in Cyprus) is presented as including useful and effective processes for developing teacher self-awareness and responsive learning. The project was funded by the European Committee, lasted one school year and was aimed at supporting participatory teacher professional development and changing teaching routines. It is important to note that because of the project, its participatory procedures at schools have been adopted by the Pedagogical Institute of Cyprus for teachers' in-service development.

12.2 Epistemological and Research Foundation

Action research was chosen as the appropriate procedure for teachers' change, development and understanding of their own and students' deficiencies. Action research, as a cyclical, non-linear process, facilitates participatory development, the sharing of responsibility for new action and experience-based knowledge (Reason and Bradbury 2001b). Collaboration, reflection on actions, evaluation and decisions for new actions and practical solutions in the classroom call for understanding theories in the context of their implementation.

The underlying assumption is that responsive teaching, which implies reciprocal responsiveness between the teacher and the student, as well as the exchange of needs and ideas, cannot be realized without teachers' liberation from the textbooks—in other words, from centred teaching. From this point of view, the cyclical incidents of action research allow teachers to decide, try out and re-evaluate their actions in the classroom based on students' responses and the expression of new needs. Thus, during action research, teachers place students' learning and their positive and negative response to teachers' action at its centre.

Research on curriculum suggests that contextual variables in the school and its environment, along with what teachers think and do, are so important that general recommendations sacrifice individual reality for the sake of prescribed routines (e.g. Doll 1993; Pinar and Reynolds 1992). These routines prevent responsiveness and the learning of both students and teachers.

From that point of view, action research promotes reflective learning and participatory professional development through adaptation of the procedures and content of development to the learners' needs in communities of reflective learning in the work environment. Research on professional development through action research (e.g. Reason and Bradbury 2001a; Koutselini 2010, 2015) indicates a conceptual and actual shift of participants from distance and individuality to collaboration, openness and exchange, and a movement from low trust in their own and colleagues' choices to self-confidence, responsive teaching and learning.

Empowerment of the participants is the result of gaining awareness of all the elements of the context's impediments and the personal constraints that prevent real change and responsiveness. The reflective paradigm of teachers' development (Carr 2004) is founded on the principle that teaching and learning must be constructed in a personal and meaningful way which must be constantly developed and adjusted in order to facilitate justified alternative actions.

The shift from positivistic approaches that promote theories and good practices that have been implemented in different contexts through ready-made procedures to professional development as a heuristic, cyclic and responsive endeavour of all participants in their own school indicates the shift from imposed knowledge to reflective and participatory learning processes. From that point of view, action research at schools aims at the personalization of learning and the work culture in communities of learning, as well as at teachers' empowerment for professional development through cyclic introspection and participatory communication.

A meta-modern perspective of education (Koutselini 1997) moves beyond the borders of the modern and post-modern processes in education and promotes an emancipatory interest which is opposed to all imposed and instrumental knowledge provided by 'experts', who rarely face challenges within the classroom. Whereas modern approaches to education result in teachers' training on theories and decontextualized trials of implementation without a real connection to classrooms, meta-modern approaches advocate engagement, reflectivity and communicative interaction in authentic environments.

From that point of view, action research is a rewarding process in the meta-modern approach, which supports the reflective paradigm of teacher development (Carr 2004; Elliott 1991). It gives meaning to human experiences during learning without fragmenting the experiences to useful or imposed tasks. Thus, it is considered appropriate for changing the school culture and developing teachers' self-regulated skills that respond to students' real needs. Action research gives teachers the opportunity to act and judge their actions whilst teaching and not only *post facto*, as the modern approaches suggest. Its theoretical foundation has its roots in the value of emancipation (Freire 1972; Habermas 1972) and the necessity to understand teaching as a contextual and continually changing endeavour that takes into account individuals' interaction in a social environment (Vygotsky 1978).

From a theoretical point of view, it is useful to point out the importance of reflection for self-understanding. As Gadamer put it (1977: 38): "Reflection on a given pre-understanding brings before me something that otherwise happens behind my back". Habermas (1972: 208) also elaborated on the concept and process of self-reflection: "Self-reflection is at once intuition and emancipation, comprehension and liberation from dogmatic dependence". Thus, teacher empowerment for professional development cannot succeed without reflective practices that set teachers free from the technical implementation of the curriculum and allow them to test new ideas in their own context (classrooms).

12.2.1 The Study

Twenty-six primary schools voluntarily participated in the RELEASE project, which aimed at promoting teachers' development at schools through action research. The construction of a reflective and responsive situated learning environment was considered as one of the most important presuppositions for teachers' and students' participatory development.

Researchers and teachers shared the challenge of the action research procedure as a means to improve communication between teachers and students in order to empower teachers to respond to the needs of students with 'problems' in mixed ability classrooms. The aim of the study was defined by the teachers who voluntarily participated in the project. Each school decided the specific problem which was to be anticipated. The most popular topics identified were: (a) the implementation of differentiation of teaching and learning; (b) language teaching to meet differentiated needs; (c) conflict resolution at schools; (d) co-operative learning for enhancement of cognitive results; and (e) students' misbehaviour.

Researchers from the University of Cyprus and trainers from the Pedagogical Institute periodically visited schools and discussed various issues with the participants, thus encouraging the continuation of the procedure and providing support for teachers' decision-making and action. From the very beginning it was explained to the principals of the schools that their role was to support teachers' meetings, encourage participation and value their efforts and actions.

Teachers met weekly for three months in order to encourage reflection on action. All participants kept a diary of events and thoughts recording their daily interaction with students, as well as their feelings about group meetings and the procedure of decision-making.

Observations in the classrooms at the beginning of the project indicated that teachers' roles had been reduced to covering the textbook content without any action to respond to real and differentiated students' needs. In these cases, textbooks function as mechanisms of teachers' pedagogical alienation that prevent empathy and responsiveness. Moreover, the practice–theory divide was evidenced in every classroom. Teachers were knowledgeable of theories concerning teaching and learning, and differentiated instruction but they implemented a textbook-centred approach during teaching: teachers and students followed the text and the activities in a linear and ordered way, with students sitting in groups without authentic, constructive collaboration. Responsiveness among teachers to students and among students was totally absent from all the teaching settings.

Researchers and principals participated in all cycles of the action research, learning from teachers' reactions, thoughts and hesitations. Although they facilitated the processes of action research, their reactions were always reflective and aimed at experience-sharing and reciprocal learning. It was clear to researchers that their role was to facilitate the process, avoiding instructions that would limit teachers' and students' engagement and responsive decisions. Also, the reflective and supporting role of principals provided space and time for teachers to have common meetings at schools. Moreover, principals participated in some of the meetings and encouraged authentic reflection. The initial feeling of mistrust of self and others, the reservations about speaking and proposing ideas, began to fade away.

In the beginning of the project teachers urged for ready-made solutions, indicating a very limited trust in discussions and proposals of alternative actions. Gradually their self-confidence and motivation increased, especially when during group discussions the mentors encouraged them to elaborate on some of their ideas through appropriate readings and action planning.

After identifying obstacles to teacher–student communication, discussions in groups helped teachers to acquire a voice, to speak out and express their feelings and hesitations. During these meetings researchers focused on issues that prevented teachers from 'seeing' the classroom, the students and responding to the different needs of different students.

Moreover, the discourse analysis of their initial written reflections evidenced their attitudes and implicit theories towards learning and teaching. From this point of view, students were to blame for their low achievement. Gradually teachers admitted that their lack of self-confidence for decision-making resulted in routine teaching, which was considered safe and acceptable since it was broadly implemented. The fact that teachers and schools in Cyprus are not accountable for their results due to the absence of any accountability system favours routine teaching which covers the content of the textbooks.

12.3 Responsiveness as a Result of Empowerment

Teachers cannot become responsive unless they are given the power to make responsible decisions based on students' needs and to dare to try out new approaches. To implement an action research project is neither simple nor easy, since reflection must be genuine and the interplay between action and reflection must be based on the pedagogical autonomy of teachers that enhances their awareness. Teaching is seen as 'praxis' and experience that gain meaning from the way participants understand the experience and their attitudes towards it. From this point of view, teachers and students 'live' the experience of teaching and learning as a unique and ongoing process within which they understand themselves and others and gradually become able to communicate, to share and to care.

Participation of the researchers and mentors in the reflection groups in school contexts encouraged the exchange of ideas, knowledge and positive attitudes towards new approaches. Constructive feedback through reflection in groups cultivated positive attitudes and improved the classroom learning environment, reflective lesson planning and student–teacher communication. Gradually teachers and the principal of each school developed a commitment to their task: the improvement of teacher–student communication that results in learning.

Teachers' motivation and willingness to participate, as well as the results obtained, were greater in schools where the school principals supported and valued teachers' initiatives, participated in the meetings of reflection and new action, acknowledged the project's importance and contributed in the pedagogical discussions. The research suggests that trust building, teamwork and collaboration between teachers and school principals cultivate professional culture and improve quality (e.g. Snoek and Moens 2011). Hargreaves (1998) also underlined the importance of a trusting environment that enables teachers to take responsibility for their actions.

Action research proved to be a rewarding developmental procedure for teachers, principals and mentors; since only in authentic collaboration and reflective meetings can they develop their pedagogical ability and succeed in transforming knowledge into practice. Participation in action research can transform teachers into pedagogues-learners who gradually gain self-confidence and reject ready-made and undifferentiated solutions to classroom 'problems'. It is important to consider that the empowerment of different teachers with different attitudes, experiences and knowledge demands the differentiation of teachers' development.

Action research proved to be a rewarding developmental procedure for students too, as the improvement of their performance in terms of participation and achievement was evidenced in their daily communication and assignments, and in teachers' diaries and reports. The most important thing was for teachers and principals to deliberate on (liberate themselves from) the teaching of textbooks, and for students to express their difficulties, personal constraints and informal evaluation of the classrooms' communication and learning climate.

During group reflections teachers decided what they should change and what activities to try out in order to become responsive to the students' real needs; they were interested in the results of their interventions and they cared about students' attitudes towards their teaching, learning and the classroom environment.

Teachers' responsiveness and discussions inspired colleagues at schools. Whereas at the beginning of the project only one group of three teachers from each school participated, during the action research the majority of teachers in 20 out of the 26 schools joined the initial group and participated in the actions and reflections. Consciousness and the valuing of teachers' pedagogical autonomy are the cornerstones of teachers' empowerment. Teachers discover their power to empower each other and to plan and enact effective teaching in mixed ability classrooms and to deal with the school's and students' problems.

Action and reflection through action research transformed teaching into a decision-making process and empowered teachers to take responsible decisions with the criterion being their students' learning and well-being.

Communication in 'communities of learning and practice' suggests a non-isolated individual development. It is well documented (i.e. Brown and DuGuid 1995; Cochran–Smith and Lytle 1999; Cochran–Smith 2003) that inquiry learning communities facilitate professional development and a re-examination of teachers' and principals' role and actions. The interplay between action and reflection becomes an empowering developmental procedure, which gives teachers the opportunity to evaluate their decisions and re-construct previous meaning.

Eraut (2000) argued that knowledge in education is situated in and grows out of a context. If knowledge and learning are indeed situated, then the most effective in-service education will be contextualized and situated in authentic classroom practice. Today, it is widely accepted that some of the most powerful professional learning occurs when there is the opportunity to be part of a learning community, an inquiry community.

Teachers enter education programmes and schools with explicit and implicit conceptions about their role as teachers and they can be very persistent in holding certain beliefs and misconceptions. Reflection in communities of learning provides teachers with the unique opportunity to negotiate their beliefs and change misconceptions through discussion, decisions and actions, reflections and new actions. In the final analysis they try out their ideas in the classroom and either abandon wrong conceptions and approaches or enhance processes and ideas. Empowerment is the result of teachers' participation in learning communities.

Engaging school teachers in an action research in-service development in communities of learning is a means of pedagogical self-awareness and responsive decision-making. Teachers are more likely to be anxious when they are left alone to change their routines; action research as a collaborative procedure should be regarded as an effective tool for empowering teachers to feel safe to share fears, hesitations and ideas. The cyclical, reflective developmental process proved to be effective for the emancipation of both researchers and teachers, who changed their attitudes towards and their concepts of teaching and learning.

It is also necessary to focus on the role of principals for the construction of the communities of learning and the implementation of action research at schools. Theories that argue for the profiles of effective principals without considering their pedagogical roles for developing their own and teacher leadership seem too simplistic to provide solutions to the complex problems encountered in contemporary schools and teacher education. It can be argued that school principals should receive better training to be able to encourage participation in action research at schools. School principals, if properly informed and developed, can dramatically help towards the upgrade of professional participatory development at the school level, because they can motivate teachers and facilitate discussion, co-teaching, co-planning and peer observation. The role of principals is evidenced in the teachers' discourse at the end of the school year: "without the principal's support it would have been very difficult to become involved in time-consuming activities and meetings"; "the principal's involvement facilitated collaboration and reflection"; "principals valued the project and supported the duration of the endeavour"; "the principal ensured that reflection, collaboration for action, and peer classroom observation will not stop"; "it was important that the principal participated as an equal member of the group and participated in the mutual learning and sharing of ideas".

The RELEASE project had multi-level positive implications. Teachers and students experienced teaching as a lived experience subject to retrospection that provides insights for responsive decisions and action, a process that helps participants actively understand each other and build new knowledge. Also, students and teachers enhanced their learning, which resulted in new skills, strategies and communicative attitudes. As reported in teachers' diaries, "students' participation increased significantly"; "before the start of the project, students were asked questions; during the course students gradually increased the number of their questions to teachers"; and, finally, "collaborative learning and discussion in groups encouraged responsive and collaborative reflection". At the same time, teachers changed their perceptions of teaching and students' learning from delivery of content into response to different students' differentiated needs; teachers learned to respond to the readiness of students and students understood that teachers were ready to respect and give feedback to their own queries and needs regarding the fulfillment of gaps in previous learning.

However, teachers faced specific difficulties during the project. They referred to the limited time for coordination and situated learning at schools; the pressure for covering the content and the slow flow of the activities at the beginning of the project; the limited time of the project's implementation. They commented on the need to liberate themselves from the pressures of time and the achievement of results. In all the cases they stressed that the principal's and supervisor's participation in the groups' reflection and their encouragement to remain concentrated on the project's cyclical incidents and the responsiveness to students' needs helped change their attitudes towards teaching as covering content.

12.4 Conclusion

Today's educational policies are characterized by a deficit of personal introspection, reflection and development at the microlevel of education. Teaching consequently came to be perceived as a set of only measurable and pragmatic skills and techniques. It is strange that policy makers, stake holders and teachers always discuss what students should know and rarely, why students do not learn; it is even stranger that policy makers and academics investigate and document the teachers' theory–practice divide and rarely, what developmental procedures could change the situation. The results of the RELEASE study advocate the view that the practice–theory divide cannot be overcomed unless teachers experience their competencies and deficiencies in a dynamic school environment in which theory supports practice and practice reinforces theory.

Thus, teachers' empowerment through action research and situated learning at schools contributes to understanding of teaching as a cyclical endeavour through which teachers plan and act during teaching, aiming to respond to students' differentiated needs, evaluate their actions and re-plan new actions based on students' responses, reflection and participation. Pre-defined lesson plans and prescriptions of experts which are imposed on teachers have proved unable to respond to the real students' needs, since responsiveness demands the consideration of students' differentiated and changing reactions.

From this point of view, action research provides new theoretical insights into both teachers' responsive development at schools and teacher–student interaction. Action research promotes a differentiated teachers' development that counteracts the imposed pre- and in-service training systems and supports teachers' initiatives and responsiveness. In this participatory procedure, teachers exchange views, reservations and actions, and become more able to take responsible decisions. Responsiveness cannot be created through technical, closed systems of teaching, nor by teaching and learning prescriptions that ignore teacher–student reciprocal communication. It needs teachers' involvement in authentic contexts, real problems and a thorough understanding of students' needs. As a developmental procedure, action research can promote collegiality and the sharing of ideas and responsibilities with the people with whom teachers work, and thus effect a situation that changes the culture of the workplace. In the final analysis, responsiveness and responsive teaching presuppose cultural changes that value initiatives, self-understanding, collegiality and responsible decisions which meet identified needs. Development through action research revisits the Foucauldian ethic as a system of moral principles and rules of conduct in communities of persons and rejects routine, decontextualized procedures of imposed knowledge.

During the implementation of action research, schools and teachers need to be supported for participation in a cyclical, reflective process. In this context a partnership between schools and universities and/or pedagogical institutes for supporting mentoring and collaboration for changing school cultures and up-down training of teachers is recommended. Schools can be transformed into centres of pedagogy where situated learning could promote collaborative competences and attitudes for anticipating context-bound teaching and learning.

As a concluding remark, the results of this study advocate that action research—although a difficult undertaking—proved to be a transformative experience for all parties involved—participants, teachers, students and researchers. The most important result was teachers' consciousness and their gaining awareness of the fact that "the knowledge is inside us", as teachers wrote in their diaries in various different ways. Positive results from their actions enhanced their belief in their own narratives and educational practice. As one teacher put it: *"Better communication in my classroom gave me the confidence to share my ideas and practices with other teachers because I now knew that things work"*.

References

Brown, J., & Duguid, P. (1995). Organisational learning and communities of pratice. In M. D. Cohen & L. S. Sproul (Eds.), *Organisational learning*. Thousand Oaks: SAGE Publication, Inc.

Carr, W. (2004). Philosophy and education. *Journal of Philosophy of Education, 38*(1), 55–73.

Cochran-Smith, M. (2003). Learning and unlearning: The education of teacher educators. *Teachers and Teacher Education, 19,* 5–28.

Cochran-Smith, M., & Lytle, S. (1999). The teacher research movement: A decade later. *Educational Researcher, 28*(7), 15–25.

Doll, W. (1993). *A post—Modern perspective on curriculum*. New York: Teachers College Press.

Elliott, J. (1991). *Action research for educational change*. Milton Keynes: Open University Press.

Eraut, M. (2000). Non-formal learning and tacit knowledge in professional work. *British Journal of Educational Psychology, 70,* 113–136.

Freire, P. (1972). *Cultural action for freedom*. Harmodsworth: Penguin.

Gadamer, H. G. (1977). *Philosophical Hermeneutics*. Berkley: University of California Press.

Habermas, J. (1972). *Knowledge and human interests*. London: Heinemann.

Hargreaves, A. (1998). *The teacher in the post modern society*. Lund: Studentlitteratu.

Koutselini, M. (1997). Contemporary trends and perspectives of the curricula: Towards a meta-modern paradigm for curriculum. *Curriculum Studies, 5*(1), 87–101.

Koutselini, M. (2010). Participatory teacher development at schools: Processes and issues. In A. Campell & S. Groundwater-Smith (Eds.), *Action research in education—Fundamentals of applied research* (Vol. 2, pp. 243–263). Thousand Oaks: Sage Publications.

Koutselini, M. (2015). Empowering principals and teachers to develop participatory teacher leadership: Towards the meta-modern paradigm of teacher development. In C. Craig & L. Orland-Barak (Eds.), *International teacher education: Promising pedagogies*. Chennai: Emerald.

Pinar, W., & Reynolds, W. (1992). *Understanding curriculum as phenomenological and deconstructed text*. New York: Teachers' College Press.

Reason, P., & Bradbury, H. (Eds.). (2001a). *Handbook of action research*. London: Sage.

Reason, P., & Bradbury, H. (2001b). Preface. In P. Reason & H. Brandbury (Eds.), *Handbook of action research*. (pp. xxi–xxxii). London: Sage Publications.

Snoek, M., & Moens, S. (2011). The impact of teacher research on teacher learning in academic training schools in the Netherlands. *Professional Development in Education, 37*(5), 817–835.

Vygotsky, L. (1978). *Mind in society. The development of higher psychological processes*. Cambridge, MA: Harvard University Press.

Chapter 13
Teaching and Learning for Real-Life: The Application of Real-Life Moral Dilemma Discussion (Re-LiMDD) for Classroom Interaction

Vishalache Balakrishnan

Abstract One of the ultimate aims of education is ensuring that knowledge, skills and values learnt in school is applied in real-life by students. It is essential that teachers have knowledge of who they are educating rather than fill up the empty vessels that come to them every year (Freire in Pedagogy of the oppressed. Continuum, New York, 1986). The need to prepare a platform for students to be able to bring their real-life into the classroom and vice versa is the ultimate aim of global education. This chapter explores the use of real-life moral dilemma discussion (Re-LiMDD) in the teaching and learning process. It explores the process of resolving real-life moral dilemmas in social studies classroom and alternatives in non-social studies context. It critically analyses the Re-LiMDD process and the different components necessary to adapt such a teaching and learning strategy in the twenty-first century classroom for effective classroom interaction. The argument here is linking students real-life with content learnt in school encourages deep learning and equips students with higher order thinking skills (HOTS) in a natural and authentic process. It is suggested that teachers adapt Re-LiMDD in their daily teachings to resolve everyday issues occurring in the classroom; it can be directly linked with the content of the subject or with classroom relationship.

13.1 Introduction

Teaching and learning is a reciprocal activity which in traditional conventional understanding was teacher teaches and students learn. However, in recent years the notion of teaching and learning has taken a wider scope and it is no more a one-way track or teacher filling students with information as if they are hungry jugs waiting

---

V. Balakrishnan (✉)
Faculty of Education, University of Malaya, Kuala Lumpur, Malaysia
e-mail: visha@um.edu.my

to be filled. Rabindranath Tagore, the great Bengali Nobel Prize winner for literature and poetry told that true education can never be crammed and pumped from without; rather it must aid in bringing spontaneously to the surface the infinite amount of wisdom which is within oneself.

Knowledge, skills and values are three main components which most education system in almost all nations is striving towards to. It entails the need to develop holistically every child that starts an education journey first informally within the home environment then formally in the school and university environment. Within each stage, there are approaches and methods to provide knowledge, built skills and instil values in each and every child. The concept of 'No child left behind' is not just focussed on the paper chase for grades and excellent examination results but also to ensure that every child is allowed to develop and mature in their own capacity and attain knowledge, skills and values to a certain level suitable to their own cognitive, emotive and spiritual growth.

Technology boom has become the current talk in every phase of life. Teachers are mesmerised with the ample knowledge that students have based on their internet search and world view knowledge that they obtain in a touch of a finger, let it be from their computers, smart phones or tablets. Teachers are also challenged by the numerous questions asked by students during the teaching and learning process. If teachers are going to only focus on what they want to teach which is clearly prescribed in most top-down education system, then there starts an issue of ineffective classroom interaction.

Thus one alternative way to encourage effective classroom interaction is to link students experience with content taught in the syllabus and encourages deep learning in the use of real-life moral dilemma discussion (Re-LiMDD) in the classroom.

13.2 Classroom Interaction

Classroom interaction is the most essential space and time that involve effective communication between teacher and students and students and students during teaching and learning process. These interactions can exist in two forms. One is during the formal teaching and learning where activities such as brainstorming sessions, group discussions and pair work make up the formal aspects of teaching and learning. As for the other times, project work, service learning becomes part of the informal learning or outside the classroom setting. The focus here is on activities within the four wall of the classroom. It is a challenging task for the person called 'teacher' to ensure that every student in class is receiving knowledge, upgrading his or her skills and improving where values of egoism and utilitarianism is developing within and without.

In order to ensure that classroom interaction is effective, there are several characteristics that it should contain. This is also in line with characteristics for twenty-first century effective education. How to get students interacting in the classroom? Whatever is conducted should be meaningful, exciting, make sense to the students, provide some sort of connection with their own pool of knowledge, skills and experiences, create curiosity every time something new is being taught and is applicable to their own daily life either directly or indirectly. Such characteristics might lead to deep learning which is aimed by most curriculum and education system globally.

When students go through the learning and teaching process, they might get bored during the teaching and learning process. Factors leading to boredom include one-way process, top-down approaches without meaningful interaction and connections with students by teacher, and many more which makes the distance apart when students find it a tedious task to connect new knowledge, new skills and new values learnt which does not connect with their own real-lives.

13.3 Real-Life Moral Dilemma Discussion (Re-LiMDD)

Teachers bring cultural perspectives, values, hopes, and dreams to the classroom. They also bring their prejudices, stereotypes, and misconceptions to the classroom (Cochran-Smith 2004). Re-LiMDD is an alternative method of teaching and learning which encourages every single student to look forward towards the learning process as it involves them within the teaching–learning sphere. Students become the centre focus of teaching and learning and whatever is taught is linked to their own real-lives. It provides a connection and makes them excited and curious to know more.

13.3.1 Dimensions of Re-LiMDD

Re-LiMDD is made up of four components. All four components are interrelated and are the basic pillars to the foundation of Re-LiMDD. They include content, pedagogy, empowerment and participation (Fig. 13.1).

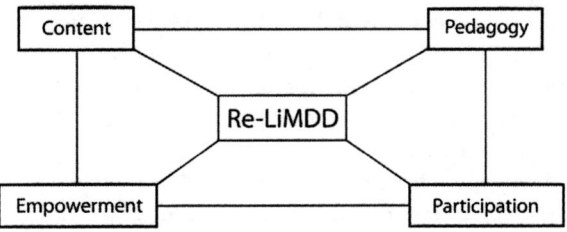

Fig. 13.1 The four dimensions of Re-LiMDD

13.3.2 Content

The content for this method of teaching and learning can be anything related to social science subjects that teachers present in the classroom. Content for Re-LiMDD is simply the real-life moral dilemmas provided by the students. For example: in a Geography lesson if teacher is teaching about environment, pollution and sustainability, students own examples of their local environmental issues can be part of the class discussion. In order to allow some system within the lessons, thematic forms of discussion should be arranged within the teaching and learning duration to ensure the bridge between the syllabus and the content. Currently most syllabus in schools spell out comprehensively the content areas to be learnt which leaves little or no space for students to express themselves or link the content matter to their real-lives.

13.3.3 Pedagogy

The pedagogy for Re-LiMDD is dialoguing, discussion, active interaction and engaging in critical thinking process. Re-LiMDD pedagogy is transformative in nature and encourages the development in students' knowledge, skills and values in an authentic and natural way. Decisions made need to be reflected upon. In other words the pedagogy for Re-LiMDD should allow reflective decision-making with either collaborative and/or personal moral action. This is essential for the twenty-first century as the whole world is becoming multicultural in nature where students are required to understand their social and moral responsibility as citizens in a local and global setting.

13.3.4 Empowerment

In order to implement Re-LiMDD effectively, power sharing is essential. It is a reciprocal process between students and students, and teacher and students. Each group should feel safe, comfortable and confident that they have equal power and privilege to voice their critics, opinion, arguments and suggestions. When students from different cultural backgrounds or even same cultural backgrounds come together, they have different ideologies about moral conflicts and how to resolve them; the need to engage in dialogue allows the voices of students to be heard. Students in current digital era have multiple resources for knowledge, skills and values which they pick along the way formally or informally. Thus, teachers are not merely knowledge transmitters but educators who prepare a platform for students to share their thoughts and be transparent to share power with students. Teachers also prepare the space and avenue for students to collaborate and cooperate among themselves to resolve issues and daily moral conflicts. The notion of power sharing is important and students tend to listen and dialogue better when there are fewer constraints from the teacher exercising an authoritative role.

13.3.5 Participation

In Re-LiMDD, students take on an active, critical participant role. There are moments when students become the capable peer (Vygotsky 1986) who leads the group discussion. It all depends on their life experiences and funds of knowledge. No student comes to school as an empty vessel and their learning becomes meaningful when their own knowledge, skills and values are tapped, challenged and questioned. Through a two-way process, it becomes natural for different students to take the lead. Teachers can take the lead if students lack the expertise. Active participation leads to divergent thinking and students benefit from various ideas which lead to creativity and higher order thinking skills (HOTS).

13.4 Process of Re-LiMDD

The Re-LiMDD takes place during the classroom interaction where there is bound to be the teacher and students. This process is developed based on a four-stage model adapted from Tharp and Gallimore (1988) who used a four-stage model of Zone of Proximal Development to show how children develop speech and language and their model was modified to fit in the Re-LiMDD within a collaborative group which is called Zone of Collaborative Development (ZCD). ZPD in social studies subject such as moral education can be seen as the gap between what students can morally decide and accomplish independently and what one student can achieve with the guidance of a more capable peer (Fig. 13.2).

Vygotsky (1986) introduced the notion of ZPD in relation to learning and development. It is based on his theory that learning is, at its core, a largely socially mediated activity, and that real learning takes place in students' ZPD. According to Vygotsky (1986, p. 188), "What the child can do in cooperation today he can do alone tomorrow. Therefore, the only good kind of instruction is that which marches ahead of development and leads it…".

Vygotsky (1978) conceptualised ZPD as a way of viewing what students are coming to know. The key to this approach is Vygotsky's claim that in order to match instructional strategies to a student's development capabilities accurately, what must be determined is not only his or her "actual developmental level" but also his or her "level of potential development" (p. 86). The actual developmental level reflects what the student knows and is able to perform at the moment. But Vygotsky argued that it "only captures mental functions that are fully formed, fully matured, fully completed —the end products of development" (Vygotsky 1978, p. 86).

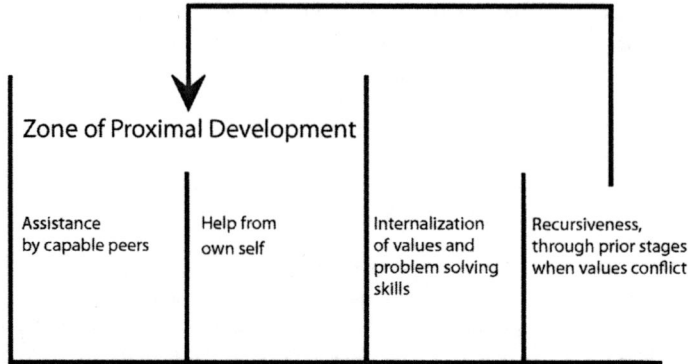

Fig. 13.2 Modified version of Tharp and Gallimore's Four-Stage Model of ZPD (1988) relevant to the teaching of social studies

Vygotsky's framework indicates that after a student receives instructional support from someone more capable in that particular situation, the student internalises the new idea, knowledge or skill and is more able to perform without help in the next similar conflict or problem-solving situation.

However, in current multicultural situations in many classrooms around the globe, Vygotsky's ZPD seems to be quite outdated and would be more relevant to use a ZCD approach (Balakrishnan and Claiborne 2012).

13.5 Zone of Collaborative (ZCD)

ZCD would fit well into the twenty-first century teaching and learning for several reasons. Firstly most social studies teaching and learning takes place in a collaborative environment within the four walls of the classroom. Most of the time, students would be collaborating with other students and teachers to acquire the learning outcome within each subject.

Second, the backgrounds of students are diversified. They come from different cultural and religious backgrounds. ZCD encourages the participants to use their cultural backgrounds and differences to express themselves during the Re-LiMDD. ZCD would therefore also provide the opportunity for students and teacher to learn from each other's cultures and experiences because of the equality in power sharing implicit in the process of collaboration.

Third, it is quite natural and intended that the real-life moral dilemmas would emerge from the students. The dilemmas might cover a vast area of issues that students would be looking into in a collaborative manner. ZCD has the potential to encourage students to be responsible for their own dilemmas and that of their friends. Rather than 'correct' solutions, students would develop a shared moral language as aspired in the Re-LiMDD philosophy.

Finally, ZCD fits neatly into the methodology of the avenue to listen to the voices of the students. They would be collaborating and hopefully identifying moral solutions based on their own capacity and with the help of their capable peers, i.e. in a ZCD.

13.6 Process Involved in Re-LiMDD Within the Zone of Collaborative Development (ZCD)

The model below is constructed to illustrate the process involved in ZCD. This model is generic in nature and can be utilised in any RE-LiMDD process. But what is unique about it is the notion of being sensitive to contextual complexities when students undergo the process of ZCD. The process becomes the method by which dilemmas are analysed in the context of a respectful, caring relationship. Throughout the process, there is a need to build a safe environment for the students to operate in and to be able to resolve dilemmas without being threatened (Fig. 13.3).

The strength of ZCD is that the characteristics of collaboration are applied at every stage. In ZCD, the cycles of discussion make it feasible for students to come back together as a group, collaborate and proceed with moral actions where applicable. Collaboration is the key point here and students share their experiences and knowledge and obtain help from the teacher or capable peers to resolve the real-life moral dilemmas. They might progress or regress depending on the support from them. However, the role of the teacher as a facilitator, a guide and a provoker settles the weaknesses of students not capable enough to lead the way in the teaching and learning process.

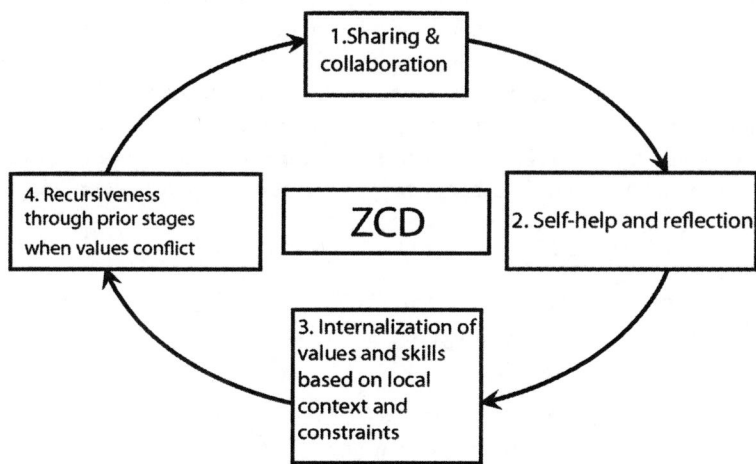

Fig. 13.3 Process in ZCD for Re-LiMDD

The whole Re-LiMDD process within the ZCD approach consists of sharing and collaboration, self-help and reflection, internalisation of values and skills based on local contacts and constraints, and recursiveness through prior stages when values conflict.

13.6.1 Sharing and Collaboration

The process of Re-LiMDD within the ZCD begins with building a safe environment for the students. Here the most practical solution is for teacher to construct a working agreement (WA) with the students to ensure the RE-LiMDD process progresses (Balakrishnan and Cornforth 2013). Then it proceeds to the sharing and collaboration phase. Students share their real-life moral dilemmas and collaborate with their groups to analyse the conflicts from different perspectives. Capable peers help in bringing the discussions to greater heights. Based on their experience and fund of knowledge, the capable peer—who may be an individual, a group or the teacher—would have skills to resolve any conflict that may arise.

13.6.2 Self-help and Reflection

The second phase of Re-LiMDD within the ZCD begins when individual students start their own reflections and provide self-help. This has the effect of incorporating into social studies the religious or cultural dimension based on the background of the students; until now strangely and sadly lacking in the literature. Students have their own capacity to reflect and this is given priority in Re-LiMDD. The reflection process enables students to use their reasoning to think through choices and actions within the subject learnt. The reflective phase also allows students to compare and contrast resolutions suggested, resolutions applied and future resolutions needed. It is an important phase because differences in values and orientations are likely to disturb thoughts and emotions, but because of the earlier collaboration and cooperation phase, students are in a better position to reflect upon the conflicts.

13.6.3 Internalisation of Values and Skills Based on Local Context and Constraints

The third phase of Re-LiMDD within the ZCD is the internalisation of values and skills based on local context and constraints. Without being sensitive to local context and constraints, knowledge, skills and values can be ambiguous because ideologies can be very subjective and differs according to different cultures and ethnic groups. When values are internalised and skills are absorbed during the process of Re-LiMDD, students become aware of such differences and able to apply skills based on these differences. Every dilemma faced would be different and unique in its own way.

13.6.4 Recursiveness Through Prior Stages When Values Conflict

The processes in this final phase in Re-LiMDD within the ZCD are applicable even when students are by themselves. It provides an opportunity for students to put into action what they have acquired and bring the social studies philosophy into perspective. The skills and knowledge acquired from capable peers may be applied directly or indirectly. At times these may not be applicable but the processes of collaboration, self-help, and internalisation of values can help the students face other moral dilemmas. They can ask for suggestions from groups of friends or other authorities. They can practice self-reflection and they can apply the Re-LiMDD within the ZCD in any other context. These cycles of ZCD repeat themselves every time a moral conflict is discussed. Vygotsky (1978) related that development of individuals contributes to the collective development of those around them. It is essential that developing collaborative relationships is considered in social studies as it makes students understand both local and global contexts.

13.7 Suggestions for Social Studies Curriculum for the Use of Re-LiMDD

Based on research and the research findings, I propose a social studies curriculum which is transformative in nature. It is almost inevitable when dealing with social systems and social processes such as education that there will be "inherent tensions between the centre and the periphery of the system" (Ling et al. 1998, p. 38). In order to implement Re-LiMDD in classrooms, the curriculum has to be transformative and be able to facilitate the voices of students. There are several factors which need to be considered in order to enable the practicability of Re-LiMDD in the classrooms. The diagram below which is designed based on research and research findings and analysis explains what the requirements are for a transformative curriculum based on Re-LiMDD.

13.8 Characteristics of a Transformative Social Studies Curriculum

The most important characteristic is to reflect students' voices and experiences. Without having the students involved, no curriculum can adequately reach out to the students. The first person and third person in morality in the any setting are to be taken seriously. Students of social studies need to understand realities and ideals in local and global ideology, both from the individual and from the third person perspective.

Based on longitude research, the notion of multicultural interactions is inevitable in the classroom setting. Without a notion of moral pluralism and allowing differences to be practised within the school community, social studies curriculum for Re-LiMDD might not work. This is because students need to understand differences and to live successfully within such differences. Notions of tolerance, reciprocity, and mutual respect are important in creating a multicultural classroom relationship where students learn about others, the world and themselves.

As demonstrated in research conducted using Re-LiMDD, collaboration and self/group reflections are two important elements in ZCD. These need to go together to allow students space for group and self-development. Research findings show that students presented their real-life dilemmas which were of current times (Balakrishnan 2012). The rapidly changing global and environmental context and how students will have to deal with new and very challenging moral discussions are beyond anything that have been experienced so far. As described in Fig. 13.4, issues in curriculum should always explore the current times. Re-LiMDD allows space for looking into current moral conflicts that students face and a more in-depth

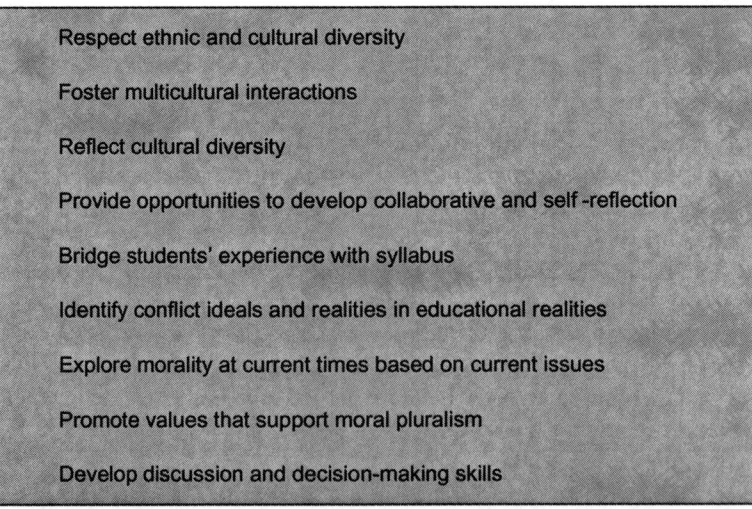

Fig. 13.4 Transformative social studies curriculum in relation to Re-LiMDD

reflection on how students' discursive construction of these issues might be changing would be useful. It is not practical to have a syllabus that focusses on issues of yesteryear if students of social studies talk about latest and current conflicts and challenges.

The use of Re-LiMDD fosters a culture of understanding which has been successful in encouraging students to understand and appreciate differences within and between themselves. This culture enables them to see themselves and others within a cultural kaleidoscope. In order for Re-LiMDD to work, the social studies curriculum would need to allow space for students to be reflective. Reflective students tend to resolve moral conflicts in a more holistic way, following through the process and thinking through the consequences of an action. They reflect upon their actions and moral choices that they make. The social studies curriculum can provide the opportunity to allow such processes to take place.

In many countries, subjects have a comprehensive curriculum which becomes the guide for teaching and assessing the respective subjects. However, for subjects to be able to use Re-LiMDD as an alternative pedagogy, requires some flexibility in the curriculum that would enable real-life dilemmas to be brought into the classroom and also the characteristics mentioned above.

Other than changes required in the social studies curriculum to enable the Re-LiMDD to work, the classroom is also equally important. Having a good curriculum does not guarantee quality in the classroom. Teacher preparation, awareness and practical training are necessary to ensure that Re-LiMDD works in the classroom. Most important of all, the notion of change must be accepted by all parties involved to make Re-LiMDD work within the classroom.

13.9 Social Studies Classroom

Logically, the social studies classroom should reflect the social studies curriculum as elaborated earlier (see Fig. 13.4). In order for the needs of different social groups to be met, negotiation and co-operation are necessary factors in everyday classroom relationships. In order for the students' voices to be heard, the classroom has also to be transformative in nature. For Re-LiMDD to become a reality in the classroom depends on four important factors as illustrated below (Fig. 13.5).

13.9.1 Students

Any student can be a student of Re-LiMDD as long as they are able to collaborate and cooperate with their peers in class and later self-help themselves. They would be able to increase their funds of knowledge trough their collaboration with their more capable peers. The Re-LiMDD within the ZCD process would encourage students to self-help and later internalise the skills and knowledge learnt. Later they

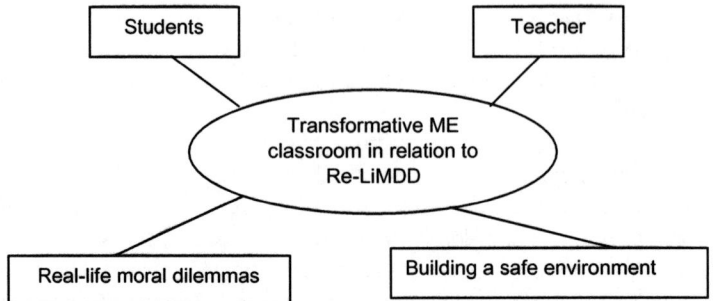

Fig. 13.5 Classroom factors supporting Re-LiMDD

are able to use skills and knowledge acquired in their own moral conflicts. The size of the class is also important in ensuring the feasibility of Re-LiMDD. An idea group for Re-LiMDD would be seven to nine students (Balakrishnan 2011). If classes are big in numbers, teacher can break down the class into several groups.

13.9.2 Teacher

The rapport between teacher and students is important in building a relationship of mutual trust and care for Re-LiMDD. To create rapport in a classroom, teachers need an honest personal relationship with students (Balakrishnan 2008). It makes it easier for students to relate and share their moral conflicts with others in the class. An effective transformative and empowerment curriculum must be implemented by "teachers who have the knowledge, skills, and attitudes needed to help students understand the ways in which knowledge is constructed and used to support power group relationships in society" (Banks 2006, p. 217). It has always been the ideal of education systems to encourage teachers to engage in dialogue, discourse, and activities that deepen their level of academic and intellectual maturity.

13.9.3 Real-Life Moral Dilemmas

Real-life moral dilemmas are the most important factor in Re-LiMDD. Ideally the real-life moral dilemmas are sourced from the students themselves to provide them with a sense of responsibility to their own conflicts. However, the students can relate their own dilemmas or source them from media, friends, or anywhere. This also provides some protection for the students who can present an issue concerning them, without identifying actual people concerned. The fact that students bring the dilemma to the classroom allows for open-speech situations free from constraints and power relations (Habermas 1984). Students are not in the situation where they have to adhere to issues presented by the teacher but those based on their own real-life scenarios.

The primary goal of any formal institution like schools should be to socialise individuals into the common culture and enable them to function successfully within it (Banks 2006). Using Re-LiMDD, the avenue to reach such a goal becomes practical and meaningful to the students.

13.9.4 Building a Safe Environment

Building a safe environment for the students in Re-LiMDD is indeed important. Students at the any stage are vulnerable to criticisms and it is imperative that during initial stages of the Re-LiMDD process, the teacher is able to build a safe environment for learning and development to take place and to ensure that as far as possible, students and their families' privacy/confidentiality are protected (Balakrishnan and Claiborne 2012). The notion of trust and honesty combined with the ethics of care and compassion should help a long way with this aspect. Students are unlikely to relate to or discuss issues with teachers who are authoritarian or who focus only on examination and syllabus content.

Guidelines for the Re-LiMDD process should be in place and agreed upon in the event of a difficult closure. For example in most countries, any issues dealing with drug abuse or child abuse are required by law to be instantly reported to the authority concerned. Students and teachers need to build a rapport long before Re-LiMDD can proceed.

13.10 Empowering Teachers and Professional Development in Applying Re-LiMDD

Pring (1984) emphasises the need for in-service training of teachers in the skills and strategies which shift the approach from instruction to the facilitating of active and experiential learning.

Ideally, in-service teachers and would-be teachers would undergo such a course involving Re-LiMDD as a module to allow them to have the experiential exposure and knowledge to handle such a method. In Re-LiMDD, teachers should be aware of their position and their role. Teacher education programmes should recognise and reflect the complex moral, ethnic and cultural identities and characteristics of the individual students in the classroom. "Professionalism includes being sensitive to individual pupils' needs and abilities" (Taylor 1996, p. 136). If Re-LiMDD is to function effectively in interactive, effective classrooms, teachers must be sensitive to students' needs where cultural and social aspects are concerned.

Re-LiMDD can be included as one of the approaches for teaching and learning in all teaching core courses.

13.11 Re-LiMDD in Non-social Studies Context

If understood and applied accordingly, Re-LiMDD can be applied in any subject as a generic teaching tool. Teacher needs to identify which part of a lesson can she or he insert the Re-LiMDD approach to provide that link of real-life and what is stated in the official curriculum document. As long as both teacher and students are comfortable bringing in a real-life situation to discuss and talk about solutions to the existing problem, Re-LiMDD can be applied in language, humanities, science and technology-based subjects.

13.12 Relevance of Re-LiMDD to Teacher Professional Development

In current times, when focus of education is on the holistic development of individual and collective groups of students, there is a need to ensure that teacher professional development includes Re-LiMDD in their formal and informal training. By understanding every student's real-life in the classroom or outside the classroom, teachers would be in a better position to educate them tactfully. Re-LiMDD encourages the need to be culturally sensitive and provide the support that is necessary in the holistic development of the students.

Teacher practice in the classroom becomes more meaningful as power sharing is an authentic practice in Re-LiMDD. The teaching and learning culture takes a new dimension as both parties work their way through daily real-life dilemma discussions which is relevant to the subject taught. Students who take responsibility of what is being taught become more aware of the world around them and are able to provide thoughts and ideas which links their own experience and wisdom. Teachers would find using Re-LiMDD useful as students become more empowered and have self-driven motivation to learn.

13.13 Implications for Using Re-LiMDD in the Twenty-first Century

Based on research conducted (Balakrishnan 2012), using Re-LiMDD as a teaching tool proved to be interesting, interactive and collaborative and meaningful. Interesting here refers to arousing curiosity, attracting or holding attention or provoking thought; enjoyable because of activities being varied, challenging, stimulating and exciting. The relevance of resolving the moral conflicts by sharing experiences and collaborating with their peers in spite of all the arguments, debates, laughter, giggles and jokes constituted an interactive, learning environment. Meaningful here means adding significance, meaning or purpose to somebody's life and in this case the lives of students in the classroom.

Re-LiMDD encourages HOTS as students take ownership of what is being discussed. It increases the effectiveness of teaching and learning within the classroom and also in project work.

13.14 Conclusion

Education not only involves the head but also the heart and action. A practical way of nurturing a sense of belonging is through involving students in the decision-making processes that shape the institutions and environments in which they spend their time (Thomson 2007). From a cultural studies perspective, culture is defined as everyday social practice (Kelly 2005). The cultures of students are interwoven with the family upbringing, their religion, their ethnicity and their local community as well as their understanding of the nation and the world. Through Re-LiMDD, such differences can be brought out to be discussed and understood with clear notions of unity within diversity.

Re-LiMDD encourages such a process to take place within the social studies classroom and promises a pedagogic space for twenty-first century schools.

References

Balakrishnan, V. (2008). Teachers using real-life dilemmas in moral education classroom. In C. L. Hoon, N. M. Salleh, W. H. W. Mamat, & B. Vishalache (Eds.), *Asia-Pacific moral, civic and citizenship education* (pp. 95–102). Kuala Lumpur: University of Malaya Press.
Balakrishnan, V. (2011). *Real-life dilemmas in moral education*. Kuala Lumpur: University Malaya Press.
Balakrishnan, V. (2012). *Using real-life dilemmas to teach moral education*. Kuala Lumpur: University of Malaya Press.
Balakrishnan, V., & Claiborne, L. B. (2012). Vygotsky from ZPD to ZCD in ME: Reshaping western theory and practices in local context. *Journal of Moral Education, 41*(2), 225–243.
Balakrishnan, V., & Cornforth, S. (2013). Using working agreements in participatory action research: Working through moral problems with Malaysian students. *Educational Action Research, 21*(4), 582–602.
Banks, J. A. (2006). *Cultural diversity and education* (5th ed.). Boston: Pearson Education.
Cochran-Smith, M. (2004). *Walking the road: Race, diversity, and social justice in education*. New York: Teachers College Press.
Freire, P. (1986). *Pedagogy of the oppressed*. New York: Continuum.
Habermas, J. (1984). *Theory of communicative action. Vol 1: Reason and the rationalization of society* (T. McCarthy, Trans.). Cambridge: Polity.

Kelly, P. J. (2005). Practical suggestions for community interventions using participatory action research. *Public Health Nursing, 22*(1), 65–73.

Ling, L., Burman, E., & Cooper, M. (1998). The Australian study. In J. Stephenson, L. Ling, E. Burman, & M. Cooper (Eds.), *Values in education* (pp. 35–60). London: Routledge.

Pring, R. (1984). *Personal and social education in the curriculum.* London: Hodder and Stoughton.

Taylor, M. J. (1996). Voicing their values: Pupils' moral and cultural experience. In J. M. Halstead & M. J. Taylors (Eds.), *Values in education and education in values* (pp. 121–142). London: The Falmer Press.

Tharp, R., & Gallimore, R. (1988). *Rousing minds to life.* Cambridge: Cambridge University Press.

Thomson, R. (2007). Belonging. In M. J. Kehily (Ed.), *Understanding youth: Perspectives, identities and practices* (pp. 215–231). London: Sage Publications.

Vygotsky, L. S. (1978). *Mind in society.* Cambridge: Harvard University Press.

Vygotsky, L. S. (1986). *Thought and language.* Cambridge, MA: MIT Press.

Chapter 14
Infusing Thinking-Based Learning in Twenty-First Century Classroom: The Role of Training Programme to Enhance Teachers' Skilful Thinking Skills

Muhammed Yusuf

Abstract The education stakeholders of the twenty-first century stress on the importance of thinking-based learning (TBL) where instructors are not only teaching students' critical and creative thinking (CCT) but also teaching them strategically and visually how to use the forms of skilful thinking techniques in the content of learning. TBL highly emphasizes on the types of thinking techniques that directly lead students to obtain higher order thinking skills. To meet the challenges of the twenty-first century, current classroom pedagogy should infuse TBL techniques into their content of learning. Academics should also conduct uncompromising TBL professional development trainings for teachers on how to apply TBL techniques in their teaching, since (a) the improvement of students occurs with the empowerment of teachers' abilities, (b) the majority of classroom instructors lack of adequate TBL skills, and (c) they find it difficult to identify where to apply the techniques in curriculum. This study aims to review TBL-related theories, applications, and practices in teaching and learning, emphasizing on the importance of TBL professional trainings to boost skilful thinking skills in school learning activities. Achieving these skills empowers teachers to infuse TBL into classroom activities and consequently enhance students' skilful thinking skills across the globe.

14.1 Cultivation of Thinking in Teaching and Learning

Historically, the cultivation of thinking in teaching and learning is ancient; particularly in the philosophy of the Greeks, the Islamic Philosophy, Islamic principles of jurisprudence, Logic, and its assets. According to the model of the behavioural

---

M. Yusuf (✉)
Faculty of Education and Human Development, Department of Educational Studies,
Sultan Idris Education University (UPSI), Tanjung Malim, Malaysia
e-mail: kuanademola@yahoo.com; kuanademola@gmail.com

perspective 1960s and 1970s, learning is a result of associations between stimuli and responses. Therefore, learners are fairly passive participants in the whole process of learning and they will be rewarded for correct responses and either punished or forgiven for their wrong responses. The instructional implications of this theory are (1) identification of some learning behaviours that the students will be able to master at the end of learning activities, (2) a given assignment or task should be divided into small parts and easy for learners to achieve, and (3) a given assignment must be in a logical sequence which leads to complete and expected learning behaviours.

In 1959, Alan Newell and Herbert Simon introduced General Problem Solving (GPS). The GPS model worked as a universal learning and cognitive thinking process. The GPS model talks about skeptical stances which contain three elements of classroom teaching and learning obstacles, back to basics, situated learning and IQ. It was found that teaching thinking worked in many approaches, but it appeared not to be successful during the first trials of the classroom application. In addition to this, when the teaching of thinking is too abstract in nature and disconnected, the teaching thinking is ineffective. Accordingly, effective thinking had less to do with a person's IQ, but more to do with what people are alert to and care about. Situated learning argues that effective thinking and learning take place in concrete physical settings and social structures while basic learning notices that teaching thinking technique will be useless if the learner does not have the necessary reading and writing skills.

In 1970s and 1980s, thinking as a cognitive process began where we started to structure learning activities effectively and guide the students' mind to deep thinking processes. Learners were not considered as passive participants in the whole process of learning. The instructional implications of cognitive, constructivist and memory theories include, but are not limited to the following, (1) mental and learning association; (2) students' learning responsibility; (3) previous and existing knowledge; (4) capacity, nature, and structure of memory; (5) information storage strategies such as analogy techniques, clear definition, and main points; and (6) the more the students were able to make a strong connection between previous and existing knowledge, the better the understanding.

In the early cognitive perspectives, students were moderately passive learners whilst teachers were dominant in the learning process. This vacuum leads us to another cognitive theory known as metacognition which is defined as thinking about thinking. In this perspective, students are actively involved in learning activities at all levels, and they are aware and the experience of learning moves from processing to progressing. Noticeably, the metacognitive approach leads to the establishment of a more specific—proactive approach of teaching and learning delivery, which is known as thinking-based learning.

In 1950s, TBL was developed to overcome the inadequate outcomes of conventional approaches used in teaching and learning in the classroom. TBL serves as an alternative teaching solution to one of many criticisms raised, namely that the traditional approach of teaching and learning was insufficient to prepare medical students to solve related problems in physics. Noticeably, TBL is being adopted in some learning organizations to teach learners in a range of different specializations.

14.2 Thinking-Based Learning Approach

In the thinking-based learning (TBL) approach, teachers not only teach students critical and creative thinking (CCT) skills, but they also teach them strategically and visually how to use different forms of skilful thinking skills in the context of learning. TBL emphasizes on different types of thinking skills such as reliable sources, compare and contrast, decision-making, parts–whole, the simple–complex thinking about problem solving, and others. Based on my observations, I would like to indicate a very unique distinction between the TBL approach and the traditional approach. In TBL, the instructor must teach students how to think skilfully since they teach learners how to use grammar correctly for a variety of languages such as Yoruba, Arabic, or English. They also teach them how to write a flawless essay, and how to speak politely and professionally in public.

In contrast, it is common practice in many traditional classrooms for teachers to develop a test or exam questions using Bloom's Taxonomy without teaching students how to use the eight techniques skilfully. For example in the knowledge recall category, the learners may be asked to list some information, whereas in the comprehension category of understanding, they may possibly be requested to prove that the knowledge has been internalized by the illustration and summarization of a main idea. At the application level, they may perhaps be ordered to dramatize or demonstrate how the internalized knowledge could be used in other situations. It is important to note that such teaching style is not an ideal in TBL.

In TBL classrooms, an instructor will no longer come into a classroom and just ask students to answer a few questions using Bloom's Taxonomy. He must make sure that the students possess the necessary skills to do the assignment, and if they do not, they have to be trained on how to skilfully apply the Bloom's Taxonomy analytical skills in their studies. On a whole, the TBL method mainly explores, provokes, and probes learning potential of the learners in order for them to become self-directed and intrinsically motivated learners; this then allows them to transfer the experiences they gained into future life.

In other words, through interactive experiences, thinking-based learning builds up students' understanding using thinking skills by ensuring the students work together or solve a problem individually or execute a given task. A successful TBL classroom leads students to the achievement of substantive skills of flexible knowledge, collaborative effort, critical thinking, and problem solving. Thus we can claim that TBL is the opposite of the traditional approach, as teachers are seen as learning facilitators who encourage students to seek self-knowledge rather than mere sources of information. Teachers in a TBL classroom are facilitating CCT skills among students to constantly think independently and creatively find a solution to learning problems in their own environment. Ultimately this means that the TBL ensures the focus of attention of the educators and students are on the material being taught. This is important as it allows learners to personally experience learning content or given activities beyond the factual information and knowledge being taught by the teachers.

As cited in a considerable amount of varying literature, the conventional approach results in students only gaining partial surface understanding of materials rather than recognizing the complex structure of learning materials and assigned problems. As learners, they are not in the position to transfer the obtained knowledge or skills in a new situation. This is because many students in the conventional approach concentrate on memorizing materials for exams rather than trying to understand the learning materials and use the obtained information successfully in another situation. This does not mean that memorization is bad in education, and it is an excellent and effective approach of learning when it is tailored to the deep understanding of learning materials. However, TBL aims to enhance students' knowledge, competency, deep motivation, and problem-solving abilities through noticeable class participation and active teamwork. By doing this, the learners can apply specific skills to gain practical and self-actualized knowledge allowing them to apply it in future-relevant situations.

It has been observed that students of the traditional lecture modules were less skilful to deal with problems that arose compared to their TBL lecture module counterparts. TBL students were reported to retain more acquired knowledge than those who learnt using the traditional approach. They were better able to recall the acquired knowledge and apply critical and creative skills in other studies. Studies on TBL indicated that while using TBL in the classroom, students demonstrated higher problem-solving skills compared to those who went through the traditional teaching approach despite both methods equally increasing students' knowledge.

The implementation of TBL technique is more complex compared to the traditional approach. Practically, the teachers or instructors in TBL are seen as teaching facilitators instead of mere tools to transfer a set of knowledge to students. In a TBL class, students should be allowed by themselves to determine the types of knowledge needed and choose suitable resources. Students are guided and provided with the necessary skills and techniques after considering factors such as the students' proficiency level, the difficulty of the learning task and time.

14.3 Thinking-Based Learning Challenges

It has been found that there are some challenges facing the application of TBL in the classroom. The TBL classroom requires substantial resources such as a TBL-trained teacher, learning materials, classroom equipment, and other facilities. Financially, not all schools can afford the needed resource in TBL classroom settings, especially when dealing with a large number of students. This, and the fact that it is also time consuming, poses challenges to the implementation of TBL which in turn could damage the effectiveness of TBL. It is also difficult to implement TBL in a new environment where teachers and students both do not have relevant skills and their teaching and learning are deep-rooted in the traditional approach of knowledge delivery. It might be hard for them to see the benefit of TBL and its educational implications since the exploration of knowledge from a new perspective using new practices can challenge educators. When TBL is being introduced in a new environment, students tend to rely mostly on their teachers to fully guide and provide complete information on given activities forgetting that the teachers are there as teaching facilitators. They might perceive the instructor to be non-helpful. But such sentiments may soon disappear once they get a better understanding TBL features and its benefits. Thus we may conclude that the TBL classroom success relies typically on the following factors; the teachers' commitment to play the role of a facilitator, the identification of relevant areas in the curriculum for TBL implementation, consideration of students' needs and their proficiency and proper structuring of the groups to accommodate all learners for better discussion and healthy interactions.

For an enhanced TBL classroom interaction, the instructor needs to carefully divide students into groups, since students show mixed responses towards TBL techniques. They are also more likely to have a positive influence of TBL on their learning performance as well as find this approach more enjoyable. Nevertheless, some students often demonstrate frustration surrounding the formats of TBL. This translates in them asking some alarming questions such as "what are we supposed to do?" "how do we do that" or "if you would only tell me what you want, I would do it" or "Dr, what does this chart tells? or "we are lost".

Further to this, the application of the TBL techniques in teaching and learning seems to be difficult for many countries because the majority of classroom instructors lack TBL skills and consequently, find it difficult to identify where to apply the techniques in the school curriculum and classroom instructions. Such a situation is not really surprising since many school authorities, especially in developing countries, do not seriously take into consideration that students' improvement in knowledge and learning occurs through the enrichment of the teachers' abilities. As a result, the teachers stick only to the traditional approach of teaching and learning. Thus, a dramatic attitude change must take place at both higher authority and instructors' level to move our educational system forward.

14.4 Infusing TBL in Twenty-First Century Teaching and Learning Classroom

In the model of education of the twenty-first century classroom teaching and learning, instructors are not only requested to teach students CCT and demonstrate to them strategically how to use different forms of skilful thinking skills in the content of learning, but they should also encourage the younger generation to make a paradigm shift by changing their ways of thinking. They have to think out of the box of inherent thinking ideas and be able to apply the creative thinking process in their daily life. Therefore, critical thinking can be defined as the mode of thinking about content or problems where individuals can professionally check, evaluate, and improve the quality of their thinking skills. In order to accomplish a given task or solve the problems, critical thinking is considered as a rational, reflective, and analytical skilful thinking that takes learning content apart radically and digs down to its root.

CCT skills are very important in today's education. The application of thinking skills in classroom teaching and learning provides learners the ability to analyse and solve problems wisely and reflectively. A TBL curriculum incorporates a real episode of thinking skills that involves a planned, proficient, purposeful application of appropriate thinking procedures and ways such as parts–whole, compare and contrast, the simple–complex thinking about problem solving, and others. This process is designed to habitualize skilful thinking into the minds of learners to become skilful thinkers who think about how they are going to do the thinking they want to do before engaging in it. In order to transform students to be skilful thinkers, the classroom instructor should be skilful at infusing the skillful thinking into the content of their teaching activities.

Having TBL infused in teaching and learning curriculums will accelerate the initiation of skillful thinking being practiced in academic settings. According to diminutive research done on TBL, the use of CCT in teaching and learning provided many positive effects on students compared to traditional methods, particularly in the development of students' thinking skills. However, it can be seen that teaching thinking skills critically and creatively is still not widely applied and practiced in schools and institutions of higher education since the traditional teaching techniques are still preferred by teachers and education stakeholders worldwide. This indicates the need for intensive academic writing and decision-making support to assist teachers to apply TBL skills and teaching thinking perspective into their classroom instructional contents.

The innovation and invention demands of the twenty-first century require new thinking skills and approaches in teaching and learning in the classroom. The previous conceptions of learning, skills, minds, and knowledge are no longer sufficient to efficiently deliver knowledge to students and enable them to apply the obtained knowledge in different situations skilfully. That means that new thinking skills and approaches in teaching and learning should be structured using twenty-first-century learning perspectives such as "learning by wholes" that allow students to experience learning activity "as it would exist outside" learning environments. Thinking-based learning covers a number of other teaching and learning perspectives such as metacognition, constructionism, design-based learning, project-based learning, and others.

14.5 TBL Professional Development Training as an Empowerment Tool for Teachers

Professional development has been described as a collaborative learning opportunity to develop human capacity. This can be done in many ways like coaching, technical assistance, and monitoring. Accordingly, there is a distinction between education and training. Education, defined widely, provides individuals with theories, concepts, issues, and arguments on certain areas of knowledge to stimulate attitude, belief, or behaviour of individuals in the long run while training provides knowledge and skills needed to stimulate certain tasks. Training programmes normally yield expected results in a short time.

From time to time, educators have observed that there are many important theories, skills, and issues that have arisen in teaching and learning environments. It is also almost impossible for an individual to deeply understand all the theories and completely master all related skills. Therefore, the need for professional development training is essential to improve teaches' knowledge and empower them with necessary and updated skills. Since the 1960s, the American educational system considered professional development training for school staff to be a national obligatory act. It was done to elevate the teaching standard of teachers and accordingly to improve the academic performance of learners. The latter is necessary since the underlying common purpose of professional development training programmes are to enhance the ability of the participants allowing them to perform well in their jobs and increase their lifelong learning skills. Thus providing TBL training programmes to enhance skillful thinking skills of teachers is important as it consequently improves students' learning outcomes.

As an implication of the study, this paper has explained the role that the skillful thinking skills training could play in infusing TBL in the classroom. The TBL training programmes could be used as one of the best practices to empower teachers' teaching ability and consequently enhance their students' thinking skill performance inside and outside the classroom. This is crucial since teachers becoming specialists in skilful thinking can be considered as teacher's best practice around the globe and "Pedagogy needs to be explored through the thinking and practice of those educators who look to accompany learners; care for and about them; and bring learning into life."

14.6 Summary

The twenty-first-century academic papers show that the traditional concept of classroom teaching and skills obtained is no longer adequate to enable many students to skillfully use the knowledge in different situations. In order to meet innovation and invention demands of this technological age, an urgent and radical reformation and transformation must be considered to penetrate the conventional methods of teaching and learning of mathematics, science, and other subjects in mainstream education. The present teaching practices should be injected with new thinking approaches that allow students to experience the classroom learning activity as it would be in real life.

Since the TBL contains several elements of other teaching and learning practices such as metacognition and constructionism, thinking-based learning techniques should be regarded as transformation tools to empower teachers to reform ongoing teaching and learning practices internationally. Developing countries should seriously take TBL and other related skilful thinking skills into consideration. Their educational systems should not miss the needed skilful thinking skills for teachers to survive in this technological age as they lost the golden opportunity to obtain the status of developed nations during the era of industrialisation revolution.

Further, educational research is encouraged to intensify its effort to produce a tested TBL instructional model for twenty-first-century teaching and learning of mathematics, science, and social science subjects. We are in need of preliminary first-hand information regarding the suitability of implementing the TBL in the mainstream school curriculum and in other learning higher institutions. In order to overcome the challenges faced by many teachers with TBL such as (a) a lack of adequate skills, (b) lack of preparation to foster thinking skills in students, and (c) difficulty of identification of where to apply the techniques of the TBL in the curriculum. Several workshops can be organized for teachers to learn how to build a better understanding of TBL techniques, how to identify suitable places to apply the techniques in the curriculum, and how to teach the techniques in the classrooms successfully. By doing these a strong recommendation can be made to academic decision-makers to empirically show the vacuum of skillful thinking in the curriculum which will allow them to take radical steps to improve it. This will serve as a way forward to override the TBL implementation challenges among teachers in schools.

References

Anuradha. A. G. (1995). Collaborative learning enhances critical thinking. *Journal of Technology Education, 7*(1), 1045–1064.
Aytan, T., Guney, N., & Gun, M. (2011). Creative thought in teaching Turkish language. *Educational Research and Reviews, 6*(50), 408–416.
Bahmani, S. (2016). Improved critical thinking in students using current events journaling. *International Journal of Sociology and Social Policy, 36*(3/4), 190–202.
Barrows, H. S. (1994). *Practice-based learning: Problem-based learning applied to medical education*. Springfield, Ill: Southern Illinois University.
Bigelow, J. D. (2004). Using problem-based learning to develop skills in solving unstructured problems. *Journal of Management Education, 28*(5), 603–613.
Bloom, B. S. (Ed.). (1956). *Taxonomy of educational objectives handbook I: Cognitive domain*. New York: McKay.
Brownell, J., & Jameson, D. (2004). Problem-based learning in graduate management education: An integrative model and interdisciplinary application. *Journal of Management Education, 28* (5), 558–577.
Daniel, T. W. (2010). Critical thinking why it so hard to teach? *Arts Education Policy Review*. http://dx.doi.org/10.3200/AEPR.109.4.21-32
Dewey, J. (1933). *How we think*. New York: DC Heath.
Guo, M. (2013). Developing critical thinking in English class: Culture-based knowledge and skills. *Theory and Practice in Language Studies, 3*(3), 503–508.

Hoidn, S., & Karkkainen, K. (2014). Promoting skills for innovation in higher education: A literature review on the effectiveness of problem based learning and of teaching behaviours. *OECD Education Working Papers.* http://dx.doi.org/10.1787/5k3tsj671226-en. ISSN 1993-9019.

Jump Up Speck, M., & Kipe, C. (2005). *Why can't we get it right? Designing high-quality professional development for standards-based schools* (2nd ed.). Thousand Oaks: Corwin Press.

Jump Up Speck, M., & Kipe, C. (2008). What do we mean by professional development in early childhood?. *National Professional Development Center on Inclusion.* The University of North Carolina.

Kampylis, P. G., Saariluoma, P., & Berki, E. (2011). Fostering creative thinking. *Hellenic Journal of Music and Culture, 2*(4), 46–64.

Lau, J. (2011). *An introduction to critical thinking and creativity: Think more, think better.* Canada: John Wiley & Sons, Inc.

McIlvenny, L. (2013). Critical and creative thinking in the new Australian curriculum part one. *Access, 27*(1), 18–22.

McMahon, G. (2009). Critical thinking and ICT intergration in a western Australian secondary school. *Educational Technology and Society, 12*(4), 269–281.

Neville, A. J. (1999). The problem-based learning tutor: Teacher? Facilitator? Evaluator? *Medical Teacher, 21*(4), 393–401.

Pascarela, E. T., & Terenzini, P. T. (2005). *How college affect students: A third decade of the research* (Vol. 2). San Francisco: Jossey-Bass.

Perkins, D. (2011). *40 years teaching thinking: Revolution, evolution and what next.* YouTube Video. http://www.youtube.com

Peterson, T. O. (2004). So you're thinking of trying problem-based learning?: Three critical success factors for implementation. *Journal of Management Education, 28*, 630–647.

Qamar, F. (2016). Effective of critical thinking skills for English literature study with reader response theory: A review of literarure. *Journal of Arts and Humanities, 5*(8), 37–50.

Sabine hoidn and kiira kärkkäinen. (2014). Promoting skills for innovation in higher education: A literature review on the effectiveness of problem-based learning and of teaching behaviours. *Education Working Paper, 100*, 64–74.

Schwartz, D. L., Lindgren, R., & Lewis, S. (2009). *Constructivism in an age of non-constructivist assessments.* New York: Routledge/Taylor & Francis Group.

Siswono, T. Y. E. (2014). leveling students'creative thinking in solving and posing mathematical problem. *Journal on Mathematics Education, 1*(01), 17–40.

Smith, M. K. (2000). *Local education, community, conversation, praxis.* Buckingham: Open

Swartz, R. J., Costa, A. L., Beyer, B. K., Reagan, R., & Kallick, B. (2010). *Thinking based learning: Promoting quality student achievement in the 21 st century.* Now York: Teachers College, Columbia University.

Swartz, R. J., Fischer, S. D., & Parks, S.. (1998). *Infusing the thinking of critical and creative thinking into secondary science: A lesion design handbook.* USA: Critical Thinking Books & Software.

Tishman, S., Jay, E., & Perkins, D. N. (1992). Teaching thinking dispositions: From transmission to enculturation. *Harvard Graduate School of Education.*

Wang, X., & Zheng, H. (2016). Reasoning critical thinking: Is it born or made? *Theory and Practice in Language Studies, 6*(6), 1323–1331.

Willen, W. W. (1994). A rationale for developing students' critical thinking through questioning. *Jurnal Pendidikan Guru, 10*, 33–44.

Yadav, A., Zhou, N., Mayfield, C., Hambrusch, S., & Korb, J. T. (2011). Introducing computational thinking in education courses. In *Proceedings of the 42nd ACM Technical Symposium on Computer science education—SIGCSE'11* (p. 465). New York, USA: ACM Press.

Yusuf, M. (2010). Memorization as a learning style: A balance approach to academic excellence. *OIDA International Journal of Sustainable Development, 1*(6), 49–58. http://www.ssrn.com/link/OIDA-Intl-Journal-Sustainable-Dev.html

Yusuf, M. (2015). Applied grandparenting modes in grandchildren cognitive and emotional development. *Australian Journal of Basic and Applied Sciences, 9*(25), 96–100.

Chapter 15
Theory into Practice: The Content of Pre-service Teachers' Reflections in North Cyprus

Anas Musa Ismail and Çise Çavuşoğlu

Abstract Although reflection is usually seen as a practice for in-service teachers, reflective practices are increasingly becoming popular in the field of teacher education as educational and transformative tools. Internship programmes require interns to reflect on their teaching practices with the aim of improving their performances. These reflections often pinpoint to a gap between what the interns expect based on the theories they have been introduced to during their training at the university/college and what they actually observe as 'best practice'. The following chapter explores what some pre-service English language teachers in North Cyprus have been reflecting on during their internship programme to understand how they approach the whole process and whether they use it as a way to empower themselves. It was found that these pre-service teachers focused mostly on their use of class activities, instructional materials, classroom management and teaching methods in their reflections on their practice teaching sessions. Students' reactions to the use of particular materials in class tended to influence the pre-service teachers' evaluation of their practices in their reflections.

15.1 Introduction

Teacher instruction could be described as adequately professional when it is not restricted to theoretical jargons, but rather accompanied by some practical works (Dewey 1904). The practical aspects do not only enrich understanding of the theoretical aspects that pre-service teachers are introduced to. They also prepare them to be 'skilled practitioners' as well as "reflective practitioners disposed to examine

---

A.M. Ismail
Department of English and Linguistics, Faculty of Arts and Social Sciences,
Federal University Dutse, Dutse, JigawaState, Nigeria

Ç. Çavuşoğlu (✉)
Department of English Language Teaching, Faculty of Education,
Near East University, Nicosia, via Mersin 10, Turkey
e-mail: cise.cavusoglu@neu.edu.tr

their teaching and their students learning critically" (Shulman 1998, p. 514). This means that internship programmes for pre-service English as a Foreign Language (EFL) teachers have a great deal of influence on developing the interns' professional practices when they are finally inducted into the teaching profession. According to Rauduvaite et al. (2015), teaching practice

> is such a period of studies when the initial professional steps are made, when the attitude towards teacher's activity, rights, obligations and responsibilities is shaped. It is the educational space where the quality of competencies acquired during the studies is revealed (p. 1049).

Thus, internship programmes that usually include several practice teaching sessions in real-life classrooms aim to bridge the gap between theory and practice in teacher education.

Despite the lack of clear-cut definition of reflection and reflective practices (Farrell 2012; Gelfuso 2016) and the best reflective practices that aid professional development (Farrell, as cited in Farrell 2012), pre-service EFL teachers are often asked to reflect on their professional practices during their internship programmes. They are required to reflect in different ways ranging from verbal interaction among themselves and/or between them and their instructors, to putting down their observations about their practices in a written form. It is often believed that such requirements will not only help them become aware of their approach to teaching and learning in general but also empower them by enabling them to become independent observers of their own teaching, and thus giving them the power to alter their practices where/if necessary. They consciously learn through personal observation and continuously improve on their professional practices via these reflections (Brookfield, as cited in Cunningham 2001). A good reflective practice indicates the practitioner's commitment to a 'transformative learning'—an indication of the practitioner's engagement in careful examination of his/her experience and professionally backing his/her practices and his/her approach to them (Moon 1999).

Such reflective practices are vital for pre-service and in-service EFL teachers because they are often perceived as motivational forces by their students and they contribute immensely in shaping their students' attitudes towards the target language, which is English in this case. Thus, the importance of the content of reflections by pre-service EFL teachers cannot be ignored as these reflections not only directly contribute to the learning outcomes of a given teacher training programme but also help pre-service teachers shape their eclectic approaches to teaching. In addition, we believe that analysing the ways that pre-service teachers reflect on their teaching practices is, in itself, a responsive practice that will enable teacher trainers to design better teacher education programmes. Hence, this chapter is dedicated to discussing the typical content of reflective essays written by pre-service EFL teachers during their internship programme by focusing on the results of a study which we carried out with such a group of interns at a higher education institution in North Cyprus. The term 'pre-service teachers' is used to refer to any student who is enrolled in a teacher training programme but has not yet finalized the requirements of the programme. In other words, they are not qualified as teachers yet. Before we move on to discussing the actual content of the reflections, we will need to set out some of the most recent theoretical models that exist in the literature related to reflection and teacher training.

15.2 Reflection Models

Several reflection models have been developed by teacher education scholars in the field of teacher education and training. These models attempt to provide guidelines and can be used as reflection templates for prospective reflective practitioners. Pappas (2010) proposes the following reflection model in a popular blog series of his (Fig. 15.1).

Pappas' taxonomy is reminiscent of Bloom's taxonomy of learning. Beginning from the remembering stage, a reflective practitioner begins by recalling what he/she did in the class, then tries to understand why is it so important that he/she remembers it. The person then asks him or herself whether, where and when it could be done again. At the evaluation stage, the reflective practitioner asks how well he/she did what he/she has done, which then leads the way to a consideration of what to improve on at the creating stage.

While Pappas' taxonomy appears to be abstract in nature, Gibbs (1988) proposes a more practical model and provides the reflective practitioners with a window to accessing their personal experiences (Fig. 15.2).

Gibbs' reflective cycle model provides, more clearly, reflection guidelines at various stages. Here is a brief description of the processes that are expected in each stage:

Stage I. Description. In the first stage the teacher describes what happened. Details of who is involved and the likely causes of the occurrence are often introduced at this stage. These include the role played by the teacher as well as the students. Information here needs to be relevant, clear and precise: no unnecessary details.

Stage II. Feelings. At this stage the teacher recalls his/her state of mind during the event. In other words, the reason why he/she paid attention to that particular event and his/her feelings concerning its outcome are revised.

Fig. 15.1 Pappas' taxonomy of reflection (adapted from Pappas 2010)

| Creating: What should I do next? |
| Evaluating: How well did I do? |
| Applying: Where could I use this again? |
| Understanding: What was important about it? |
| Remembering: What did I do? |

Fig. 15.2 Gibb's reflective cycle

Stage III. Evaluation. Here, the teacher judges what was good and what was bad about the incident. The teacher critically looks at how he/she dealt with the situation, evaluates whether he/she dealt with it appropriately or not by answering questions such as '*what was the effect of my decision?*'. He/she also discusses the theoretical basis of his/her decision, i.e. if he/she acted upon any.

Stage IV. Analysis. In the analysis stage, the teacher breaks the event into parts and makes sense of bits of information that made up the event. This is different from evaluation as teachers make more detailed exploration about the value of their judgment in the previous stage.

Stage V. Conclusion. By this stage, the teacher has a clear picture of his/her experience. At the conclusion stage, he/she discusses any possibility of repeating or avoiding what he/she has done, depending on whether the experience was negative or positive. Whether he/she could have done or changed something in the incident is also reflected upon.

Stage VI. Action Plan. This is where the teacher explains how he/she plans to deal with a similar situation in the future. This may include doing some more readings, consulting senior colleague in the profession, and anything that will help him manage the situation if it arises again.

The North Carolina reflection model is somewhat similar to Gibbs's model described earlier but different in the sense that the model introduces pre-description activity to the reflection exercise (see Fig. 15.3). Besides, the model is accompanied by rubrics to evaluate and classify teacher's use of the model.

In addition to the pre-description activity, a reflection rubric accompanies the model, where a detailed step-by-step guide is provided for the teachers to assess their reflective practices. Teachers are expected to use this rubric to assess themselves as well as their colleagues where peer assessment is used (Table 15.1).

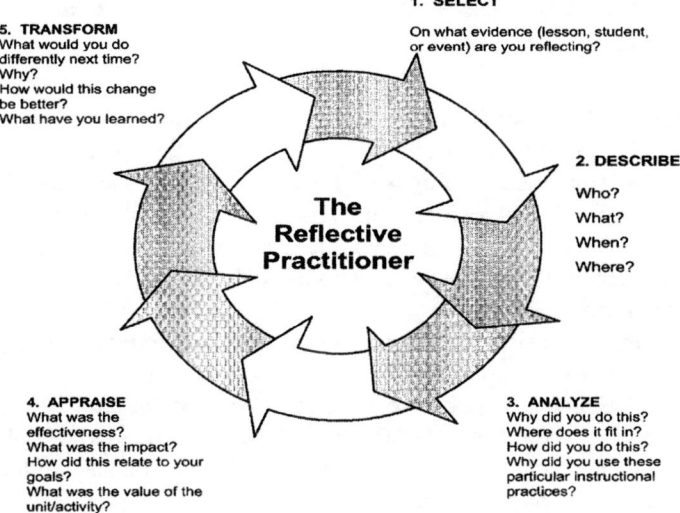

Fig. 15.3 North Carolina teacher reflection model (North Carolina Wesleyan College, 2012–2013)

Table 15.1 North Carolina teacher reflection rubrics (adapted from North Carolina Wesleyan College, 2012–2013)

Score	Pseudo-reflective (1)	Micro-reflective (3)	Macro-reflective (5)
	A reaction or retelling without thoughtful connection to other events	Self-awareness of the writer's own meaning-making process but limited to the immediate situation or event	Search for relationships, connections, justifications, consequences, evaluation, and critical processes
	Assertions are general and not supported with evidence from experience, theory or research	Assertions are specific and supported with evidence from experience	Assertions are specific, supported with evidence from experience and conceptually connected
	The perspective is undifferentiated and general regarding the needs of learners	The perspective is multidimensional, representing more than one learner or group of learners	The perspective is multidimensional in explaining how the event can be connected to a larger conceptual framework

15.3 Source of the Data: An Internship Programme in North Cyprus

The programme from which we collected our data to describe the content of pre-service EFL teachers' reflections was a compulsory internship programme offered by the Department of English Language Teaching, Near East University, North Cyprus, for all final year students. The general aim of the programme is to introduce the pre-service EFL teachers to the real-world teaching experience, beyond the theories they have been introduced to since the beginning of their studies at the department.

The programme consists of two parts which span over a period of one academic year. It comprises of two compulsory courses. Pre-service teachers are assigned by the Ministry of Education to observe professional practice of an in-service teacher, who also serves as their tutor, for 30 class hours at a particular school. They are required to complete a portfolio which is prepared by the course coordinator at the department. The portfolio contains three sections in which the pre-service teachers are required to complete specific tasks. In the first section, they are asked to observe and (a) report about the general structure of the school they are assigned to, the place of English language courses in the school and the responsibilities of their tutors and administrators, and (b) outline what they expect from the internship programme. The second part of the portfolio contains observation tasks and each task focuses on a different aspect of teaching, such as classroom management, lesson planning and so on. After the completion of each task, the pre-service teachers write a focused reflection in which they are expected to critically examine the practices of the teacher with regard to the focused/observed task. In the third and final part, the interns write a final report reflecting back on their expectations regarding this part of the programme and whether or to which extent their expectations have been met. The interns are expected to demonstrate their understanding of 'good practice' in English Language Teaching in their reflections throughout the portfolio. They are not expected to teach in this part of the programme.

The second part of the programme starts in the second semester. In this part, the pre-service teachers are expected to further observe 30 hours of classroom activities in their assigned schools while paying particular attention to the way English language teaching is being carried out. The interns are required to select five of the lessons they observed and prepare lesson plans for them. They also write a reflective essay for each of these observations, in which they reflect on the overall lesson they have observed and evaluate its effectiveness. During this period, the pre-service teachers meet with their programme coordinator at the university every other week and discuss their progress and the challenges they face. The coordinator uses the contact hour to further guide and advice the interns on these challenges and provide alternative solutions to the problems they report. It is believed that these practices will assist them in (a) recapping their theoretical knowledge which they have covered in the previous years, (b) improving their preparatory practices before the actual teaching sessions and (c) kick-starting their reflective practices by sharing their thoughts and experiences in class. They are also expected to teach twice during this part of the programme. One teaching session is observed by their respective tutors at the schools they are assigned to, and the other is observed by a supervisor assigned by their department at the university. They finally write two reflective essays, each focusing on each of the practice teaching they have done. It must be noted that the level of reflective practices among in-service teachers in North Cyprus is very low. In state schools, teachers are not required to reflect on their practices. Although some private schools do have their own peer evaluation systems in place, these can hardly be considered as critical reflection practice. Even if individual teachers carry out reflective practices before, during or after their teaching, such reflection is often disorganized, minimal and subconscious. Therefore, requiring pre-service teachers to integrate reflective practices into their practicum sessions has implications on many levels. First, as student teachers, they do not observe their mentors in state/private schools making time for reflection. Hence, they may develop a sense of reflection being an activity for pre-service teachers, i.e. students, only. Second, on a positive note, by reflecting on a daily basis, they may realize the benefits of the activity as they will also observe a change in their teaching sessions and their students' reactions. By reflecting on their previous as well as future performances, they will be able to engage in better responsive teaching. Third, eventually, it may encourage them to continue reflecting even after graduation, and therefore make a change in the status quo in this respect.

In the following section, we will be discussing the content of the interns' reflections and providing evidence from actual reflective essays of a group of interns in order to present the sort of arguments they presented in order to reflect on their practice teaching sessions.

15.4 The Content of Pre-service Teachers' Reflections

The importance of reflection for pre-service teachers has been stressed by instructors and tutors alike and pre-service teachers are often asked to write their reflections down in various formats. Yet, since these reflections, in most cases, form part of the assessment criteria, pre-service teachers are put under pressure to produce good essays, so they sometimes deflect from reaching the real aim of reflecting on the practices themselves and become focused on the essays more. As a result, pre-service teachers may not realize the real reason behind writing their reflections. Thus, it is important to explore the focus of the reflection of pre-service teachers as they produce reflective essays on their actual teaching experiences.

The aspects found to be frequently reflected upon by pre-service teachers were class activities, classroom management, instructional materials and teaching approaches and methods. In the following sections, reflective practices of the interns will be analysed and each of these content areas will be dwelled upon with references to excerpts from the actual reflective essays of some pre-service EFL teachers following their practice teaching sessions in their assigned schools.

Class Activities. Our analysis of several reflective essays by pre-service EFL teachers showed that class activities are of great importance to these interns. In their essays, they discussed the kind of activities they used, the rationale behind selecting a particular activity, and whether they achieved the objectives of selecting the activity. They also evaluated their use of those activities. The following excerpt illustrates how one intern concentrated on this aspect of his practice teaching and his reflection on it:

> During the preparation progress for the teaching session, I assumed that activities should include plenty of items so that three activities would be enough to fill the allocated time for teaching session. Although, the length of the activities was taken into account as an anticipated problem, the anticipation was not determined correctly (Imran, 1st Reflective Essay).

In this particular excerpt, the intern first discusses what he assumed the class activities should have contained; an assumption based on which he selected the activities for his first teaching session. Even though he took the duration that each activity would require into consideration while planning his lesson as he claimed in the essay, "the activities ended up being too long for the allocated time". Therefore, this created problems for his time management, and as a result he had to give one of the planned activities as homework. Imran also acknowledges and reflects on the deficiency of his activities by pointing out that although he felt the activities were suitable, they should have included a production activity and this, according to him, "should be taken into consideration for the next teaching". Imran seems to have used his assessment in his second teaching. In his second essay, he reflected on how he used warm-up activities as his production activities, which created an "opportunity for communication because warm-up activities usually are done to get interest or attention of the students to the topic" (Imran, 2nd Reflective Essay). This, according to him, seems to have worked as the students enjoyed it. Hence, his reflection activity seems to have been fruitful in this case, as he managed to select effective activities as well as have better timing for his activities in his second session.

While Imran seemed to have been independent in selecting the types of his class activities, Victoria, another intern, explains how she was guided and restricted by the curriculum in selecting her activities. She chose speaking activities that, as she stated, were "not difficult speaking activities for the sake of following the curriculum". Victoria also reported the problem of managing the duration of her activities but unlike Imran, whose activities were the source of the problem, Victoria attributes this problem to the students:

> The activities allowed all the students to show their potential *[sic]* and participate. However, the lesson was only 40 min and some students came 10 min late due to their lunch break...therefore when students came 10 min late, I had to repeat and lost time. As a result, I only managed to spend 5 min on the last activity instead of 10 min (Victoria, 1st Reflective Essay).

Hence, Victoria considered selecting shorter and fewer activities in her next teaching to overcome this problem. She wrote:

> A solution to this problem would be to choose shorter and fewer activities. This is what their actual teacher usually does because he knows that the students are always late for their afternoon classes (Victoria, 1st Reflective Essay).

Zuleiha, another intern enrolled in the teacher training programme of the university, reflected on the diversity of her activities and her rationale behind this diversification. She stated that:

> I used a variety of activities in order to provide richer options for the students to practice the new language. I was aware that the students have short attention spans and because of this I used different activities in order not to bore the students and to change the atmosphere in the classroom […] All the students in the class enjoyed doing the activities and all of them participated. I made the content of the activity relevant and meaningful to my students' world. I tried to test the same topic with different activities. After the lesson I realized that one of the activities was very easy. It was the second activity in which the students circled the appropriate adverb by looking at the picture. The students liked the activity but I thought that it was an easy one. I should have prepared an activity that is challenging and slightly beyond their existing proficiency level. I will take this into consideration and improve it in my second practice teaching (Zuleiha, 1st Reflective Essay).

Using varied activities, therefore, kept the class atmosphere dynamic and made it impossible for the students to get bored and distracted. Zuleiha, like Imran, reflected on the effectiveness of using those activities and observed that the students liked a particular activity she used because the activity was very simple and therefore expressed her determination to improve on that in her next teaching. However, in her second essay, Zuleiha did not discuss the difficulty level of her activities, neither did she mention how she improved her previous activities as she seemed determined in the first essay. Instead, she discussed the activities she used in the second teaching in which, again, she appraised the activities and identified her lapses:

> I could have involved more students in the speaking activity. I could have asked the same question to different students and got different ideas from the students. By this way, more students would have an opportunity to produce the new language that they have learned (Zuleiha, 2nd Reflective Essay).

Thus, unlike Imran and Victoria, she seemed to be concerned with the students' involvement in relation to classroom activities rather than time management.

Classroom Management. Classroom management is also a matter of concern for pre-service teachers. They often reflect on how some aspects of their lesson, due to their difficulty or 'enjoyability', make it difficult for them to control their students. As an example, Mariam briskly explained that she had to struggle for a conducive atmosphere for the students to learn what she had to teach:

> I found that I really try hard to provide a safe and comfort *[sic]* environment for my students to express themselves and their answers comfortably (Mariam, 1st Reflective Essay).

Despite this open explanation, Mariam did not mention why she had to 'try' so 'hard' to create that atmosphere for the students. She claimed to have succeeded in managing the situation as at the end "the students listened to me carefully and I could see that they respected me too" which she thought was because she made the students "feel that they were important and valued" (Mariam, 1st Reflective Essay). Zuleiha, on the other hand, explained measures she had taken when she discovered mid-way through the lesson that some of the students were busy "talking with each other" (Zuliha, 1st Reflective Essay). This is despite the fact that she warned them at the beginning of the lesson by stating the basic rules of her class, which seemed not to have worked, and necessitated her to devise another strategy to manage the class. She explained how she tactically asked one of the noise-makers a question "related to the topic of the lesson in order to get her attention" and thereafter dealt with all 'disruptions immediately' (Zuleiha, 1st Reflective Essay). Zuleiha reported in her essay how she praised her students in order to motivate and encourage their participation. She stated: "I praised the students and this encouraged them to participate more". This, according to Zuleiha, made her classroom 'smooth running' and seemed to have helped in successfully managing noise-making and distractions.

Often times, the pre-service teachers associate the timing of the lesson with their ability or inability to control and manage their classrooms. According to their reflections, morning hours make classroom easier to manage than afternoon hours when the pupils are tired, hungry and, therefore, exhausted. Using varieties of class activities help in easing the pupils' stress and gives the pre-service teachers an opportunity to effectively keep the students active and make the classrooms less boring even if the pupils are exhausted. Class activities and classroom management affect time management ability of pre-service teachers. They often report how they struggle to finish up what they have planned for in a particular lesson before the time of the lesson elapsed. This happens either due to miscalculation of the time an activity might take or certain students' behaviour, attitude or nature.

Instructional Materials. Pre-service teachers also reflect on the effect of instructional materials on their teachings. Using attractive and captivating materials like pictures makes lessons interesting to the students and is viewed by the pre-service teachers as one of the secrets behind a successful and enjoyable lesson. Imran, for example, described his use of pictures as materials for his lesson as one of the strongest aspects that contributed to the overall success of his teaching. He wrote:

> One of the strong aspects of this teaching session was the use of warm-up activity because it included pictures of the persons and item that they like and students got to chance to express their opinions about those item and the persons. These pictures really attracted student's attention and interest... Thus, warm-up activity created a lively environment in the classroom. It took a different direction from the lessons which students are used to (Imran, 1st Reflective Essay).

The attractiveness of the pictures as instructional materials, according to Imran, aroused students' interest and made them express their opinions, thus making the class lively because "nearly all of the students had something to say about the pictures" (Imran, 1st Reflective Essay). Amin, another intern, expressed a similar sentiment about the materials he used vis-à-vis the students:

> While preparing my materials, I wanted to pick interesting together with encouraging materials in order to motivate the students and also catch their attention to engage their

interest on the topic. By doing this, I maintained the students' interest without having any issues (Amin, 2nd Reflective Essay).

Even though he did not explain the sort of materials he used or how he used them, the essay suggested that the materials were central to his preparation for the teaching and the students' interest was aroused by them. Vusal explained how he created an imaginary environment as the material for his lesson, getting the students to engage and act in a fictitious environment. The imaginary setting was a restaurant and the students, while playing different roles, practiced restaurant conversation. Using the authentic materials like an apron and a wig for the role-play further made the situation resemble a real-world situation, and, therefore, looked more real to the students:

> The first thing that I had to do was getting the students used to ordering food at a restaurant. I came up with an idea of a role-play activity. I thought that they would learn better as well as they will enjoy [sic] the lesson by acting out a restaurant conversation. I brought some stuff like an apron and a wig to wear during the role-play activity (Vusal, 1st Reflective Essay).

These materials, Vusal explained, had paid off since the students enjoyed the activity and demonstrated their capabilities. He expressed that he was successful in using the materials because he carefully selected them, making sure that they would be suitable for the level of his students.

Mariam very briefly discussed the materials she used in her essay, saying that the use of authentic and varied materials made it easier to introduce the topic and to engage the students. A similar assertion was made by Zuleiha who reflected on how using interesting materials attracted the attention of the students and made them answer questions excitedly. The pictures used as the materials, according to her, "helped to bring outside world into the classroom and made the situation more real and in turn helped the students to use appropriate associated [sic] language" (Zuleiha, 2nd Reflective Essay). She felt that her use of authentic materials, "the real object and pictures brought a welcome change in [sic] the class and a break from typical class activities like reading and writing" (Zuleiha, 2nd Reflective Essay). Obviously, Zuleiha viewed her use of the authentic materials as a revolutionary move that challenged the status quo.

It is interesting to note here that pre-service teachers seem to refer to their proper utilization of their materials, therefore, suggesting the effectiveness of the materials. They appear to avoid mentioning any ineffective materials that needed to be changed or modified in their subsequent practices. The reason appears to be that the pre-service teachers use students' emotional reactions as a measure in gauging the effectiveness of the materials, and to some extent in assessing the overall success of their lessons. They seem to ignore how effective these materials are in facilitating the student's understanding of the content and the set objectives of their lessons. Similarly, noteworthy is the fact that pre-service teachers do not mention the role that the course book plays in their teaching sessions. They seem to rely on supplementary materials that they either invent or adapt from somewhere else, not from the course book.

Approaches and Methods. Another aspect of concern for the pre-service teachers when they reflect on their internship is how relevant the theories they have learnt are to the real classroom. They often reflect on the differences they felt there were between a particular method and approach to teaching and their experiences attempting to apply this approach to their teachings. Some of them were trying to test teaching methods and approaches they have learnt. In other instances, they were challenging the existing ones they found their tutors practicing at their respective schools. This is captured by Vusal in his first essay:

> While I was getting prepared for my teaching, I took into consideration that the classes they had with their teacher were very boring and everything was based on exercises so I tried to make the lesson enjoyable for them (Vusal, 1st Reflective Essay).

Although Vusal did not explicitly state the approach or method he intended to use, he seemed critical of the methods used by his school tutor, which he described as 'boring'. Hence he prepared his first lesson based on a method that would make the students enjoy the lesson. He was delighted that the students enjoyed his first teaching session. Reflecting on his second lesson, however, Vusal expressed his dissatisfaction of his approach. He noticed that he unintentionally bored the students with drills, a practice which, according to him, he always criticized previously. He wrote in his second essay:

> I was always criticizing the tutor that he was always giving too many drills to the students and he was boring the students. I think that I made the same mistake as well which I completely didn't intend to make the same mistake. I always criticize the teachers that give too many exercises for their students to do during one lesson. However, I can't understand how I did something that I always criticize and gave the students too many exercises (Vusal, 2nd Reflective Essay).

Like some other participants, Vusal seemed to have emphasized the students' enjoyment of the lesson as the primary criterion for evaluating the success of his teaching. This, obviously, seemed to be the criterion he used for evaluating and criticizing his tutor's method. However, as he regretted, he failed to change that in his second teaching (although he claimed to have succeeded in changing it in his first teaching) as he reported in the above excerpt from his first essay.

Moreover, it seemed from the interns' essays that most of their class activities were guided by those approaches they wished to practice. Reflecting on his second teaching, for example, Imran clearly stated what he set to achieve by selecting one of his activities. His post-reading activities, he explained, were meant to enhance the students' communicative ability. This was observed to be one of the things that were emphasized during their contact hours with their supervisors. The pre-service teachers were encouraged to use communicative approach to teaching English and this is what Imran and some others who reflected on this matter were found to have attempted, going by what they have reported in their essays. Imran's intent could be seen in the way he emphatically concluded his essay by stating how successful he was in designing the lesson in such a communicative-oriented approach when he wrote that: "In conclusion, the second lesson was more diverse, interesting and had more chances for communicative use of language" (Imran, 2nd Reflective Essay).

This highlights the relevance and influence of the class contact hours on the pre-service teachers' professional practices, which by extension suggests how they perceived and attempted to use the feedback they received from their coordinators during these hours. This influence is more obvious when we look at how they criticized their tutors' methods as exemplified by Vusal above.

Zuleiha also stated that she found after her first teaching that she would have to plan her next teaching session with activities that would aim at using communicative approach in the classroom:

> When the lesson ended I realized that I have to modify some of my activities in order to make them more challenging and communicative (Zuleiha, 1st Reflective Essay).

Hence, she intended to use more peer/collaborative work in her next class. However, Zuleiha did not reflect on whether she used any peer work in her second teaching and whether it was effective. Instead, she reflected on how the nature of her materials helped her in making the class communication oriented in the second teaching practice session. She claimed that "because the materials were interesting, they provided a good starting point of language work and communicative activities".

15.5 Understanding Reflective Practices of Pre-service EFL Teachers

Internship programmes have significant influences in starting and building up teachers' professional carriers. It is during the practicum that pre-service teachers begin to witness, first-hand, how schools and classrooms really operate. This sort of real-life experience gives them an opportunity to become familiar with the classroom atmosphere and understand further the challenges that they are likely to face in the future. It is also through internship programmes that these pre-service teachers first begin to understand in practical terms how the theoretical knowledge that they have learnt throughout their university/college years are put into practice. During the internship, pre-service teachers also receive feedback about their teaching practices when they are given the opportunity to teach in a real classroom with real students. This means that internship programmes have the potential of shaping the future professional careers of their participants.

Given this background, it is safe to say that internship programmes enable pre-service teachers to develop reflection abilities through their observations, analysis of context and their analysis of classroom events (Schön, as cited in Armutçu and Yaman 2010). As a result, an analysis of the reflective practices of interns during any internship programme would provide a glimpse of the sort of processes they are involved in while trying to put theory into practice.

In such an attempt, our discussion of the content of pre-service EFL teachers' reflective essays suggested that while reflecting on their use of materials in the class, pre-service teachers tend to evaluate the success of their use of a particular material in terms of the students' reactions to it, not with regard to the set objectives of the lessons. For some of the pre-service teachers, if not most, employing a particular material could be justified in as much as it arouses the students' interest. Little to no attention is given to whether the students 'understood' the lesson. Pre-service teachers feel their materials are good when the students 'like' or 'enjoy' them. They evaluate the success of their activities by the level of students' appreciation. Even when they feel adjustments are needed, they think so because the students did not enjoy the lessons or, as some of them put it, because the students 'got bored'. The implication of this perception could be seen and interpreted in two different ways.

First, it could be claimed that pre-service teachers who evaluated everything in their lessons based on such emotional concerns seemed to have misconstrued the idea of student-centred approach to language teaching. Although using such approach entails regarding students as the main concern of any professional practice, achieving the aims and objectives of one's lesson by facilitating their learning process and letting them learn what they ought to learn is the ultimate concern of such approach. Therefore, in a lesson where students 'enjoy' the lesson but do not improve themselves in terms of achieving the learning objectives set, the teaching approach cannot be called student-centred.

Second, they seemed to have prioritized the students' enjoyment over the aims and objectives of their lessons. Their perceptions are that if the students 'enjoyed' the activity, the lesson is successful. It is understandable that they try to put their students at the centre of the aims of the lesson as emphasized by most of the contemporary language teaching approaches. In this respect, the pre-service teachers' concerns (albeit subconscious or unknowing) about students' perceptions and emotions can be considered as a good development. This is partially what responsive teaching entails. According to Wallerstedt and Pramling (2016):

> 'responsive teaching' is a teaching practice where a teacher identifies and is responsive to the problems the students face and engage in, and, importantly, through introducing and scaffolding the appropriation of conceptual resources (scientific concepts in Vygotsky's terms) functional to taking on these problems. It denotes a practice not residing to either side of the dichotomy between conceiving teaching as, on the one hand, a matter of transmissive instruction or, on the other, only following and confirming the students' interests and concerns. Hence, responsive teaching, in this account, is not merely reactive but also proactive (i.e., forwards-directed). It recognises teaching at heart as a communicative practice, mutually established by participants rather than merely what can be ascribed to one of the actors (the teacher) (p. 395)

According to this definition, the fact that the participating pre-service teachers were concerned about students' enjoying their lessons shows that they were indeed responsive to the needs and interests of the students. However, it needs to be said that it is dangerous to entertain students to the detriment of the objectives of the lesson, which should ultimately be learning the content. By emphasizing the students' enjoyment, some of the essays appear to have failed to reflect on whether the lesson succeeded in achieving what it initially set to achieve.

The pre-service teachers' attempt to integrate their understanding of teaching into their reflection also gives us an insight into their perception of reflection. This suggests that the pre-service teachers perceive reflection, to some extent, as a means to test and demonstrate their understanding of various aspects of the teaching profession. Such an integration, if appropriately done, could lead to deep and critical reflection since being critical also entails measuring and evaluating one's understanding of any theoretical assumption in relation to its sociocultural implications. Suffice to say that pre-service teachers' concern for the learners' enjoyment of their lesson is not necessarily a bad thing. They only need to be supported in a kind of "structured cycles of planning, teaching and reflection" (Zambal-Saul et al., as cited in Davis 2006, p. 294), so that they understand better how to focus on learners without altering the content of the lesson. Hence, they not only need to be responsive but also be proactive following reflection. This support, if provided, would not only help the pre-service teachers acquire skills on how to achieve the aims and objectives of their lessons while at the same time meeting the learners' expectations, but it would also help them integrate their students and their ideas in their reflection (Davis 2006).

Similarly interesting is how the pre-service teachers avoid talking about the role of course books in their reflections. They mostly focus on the supplementary materials they have personally developed/invented or adapted from somewhere and ignore the course book in their reflection. This creates a gap for policy makers who need to evaluate the impact, relevance or otherwise of a particular course book they have recommended, and the extent to which these course books are considered helpful in achieving the aims of the curriculum.

Finally, understanding the perceptions of pre-service teachers about reflection as presented in this chapter would not only help teacher trainers develop their materials based on the anticipated challenges and needs of the pre-service teachers but also allow them to (re)modify the internship programmes based on these needs. It would help them further understand the psyche of their interns regarding reflection, therefore, giving them the opportunity to deal with the possible issues that may arise appropriately in advance of the internship program.

15.6 Implications for Educational Practices and Teacher Empowerment

From training to practice, reflection has so far proved to be an integral element of teaching and learning. In teacher training programmes, reflection is an invaluable tool to help pre-service teachers become independent evaluators of their own work and continue to improve themselves and their practices once they start the profession. In this respect, reflective practice of pre-service teachers is a tool for empowering teachers of the future in managing their day-to-day teaching and experiences. Carried out in the Northern Cypriot context, where reflective teaching is not a very common practice among in-service teachers, the present study suggests that there is a need to develop and incorporate reflective dialogue between the pre-service teachers and their supervisors and among the pre-service teachers themselves within internship programmes. This would help in providing the interns with a platform to share their experiences. Where these arrangements are already in place, they need to be enhanced and reviewed regularly in order to meet the needs of the pre-service teachers and to shape their conceptions regarding why reflection is such an important part of their future practice. This will also help deal with issues regarding misconceptions about reflective practices on the part of the pre-service teachers. Such (mis)perceptions may include, for example, the one found in this study of the participants' perception of reflection as a fragmented activity, not as a continuous one. As was also the case with Greek pre-service teachers in Galini and Kostas' (2014) study, having such limited understandings of what reflection itself is, "students/pre-service teachers remain at low levels of reflection" (p. 872) and cannot go into deep or critical reflection. Further examples of low levels of reflection among pre-service teachers were reported by Başkan et al. (2013) and Cengiz et al. (2014) in Turkey and by Rauduvaite et al. (2015) in Lithuania. These similar findings in different contexts can be attributed to the fact that in-service teachers in these countries are not required/encouraged to reflect on a regular basis. Therefore, pre-service teachers do not see this skill as an integral part of their training or as a skill that they will be needing once they graduate. They also show that reflective practices are impeded by partial understandings and/or applications of reflection and hence teacher training programmes in different social and cultural contexts may be lacking the element of 'training for reflection'. Overcoming these misconceptions and building a support system for the interns in the process will also further strengthen collaborative reflection and peer feedback among the pre-service teachers as they were found useful for the participants of the present study.

Before we conclude, it is important to point out that there is also a need for teacher trainers to help pre-service teachers by making them aware of other reflective strategies and the implications of adopting any other strategy than writing essays. This suggestion considers the limitations of written and observation strategies such as anxiety and the possibility that the presence of an observer may result in the behaviours that are not normal (Walsh et al., as cited in Susoy 2015). Video recording, for example, might be useful in overcoming these limitations. Another suggestion to improve the reflective practices of both pre- and in-service teachers comes from Burhan-Horasanlı and Ortaçtepe (2016) who suggest that online blogs and discussion groups "can serve as a platform where EFL teachers collaboratively reflect on their own and colleagues' beliefs and practices within an online community of practice" (p. 380). This will give the pre-service teachers a wide range of choices, therefore making reflective practices more intern-centred and less boring to them. This is especially needed in situations where reflective essays are the only reflection strategies that pre-service teachers are introduced to and expected to produce during the practicum program. This will not only enable them to reflect in a multi-modal manner but also empower them by equipping them with several possible means of reflection. Hence, they will be prepared to deal with possible problems as well as identify and follow good teaching practices in the future.

References

Armutçu, N., &Yaman, S. (2010). ELT pre-service teachers' teacher reflection through practicum. *Procedia – Social and Behavioral Sciences, 3,* 28–35.

Başkan, G. A., Yıldız, E. P., & Tok, G. (2013). Teacher training system in Finland and comparisons related to Turkey. *Procedia – Social and Behavioral Sciences, 83,* 1073–1076.

Burhan-Horasanlı, E., & Ortaçtepe, D. (2016). Reflective practice-oriented online discussions: A study on EFL teachers' reflection-on, in and for-action. *Teaching and Teacher Education, 59,* 372–382.

Cengiz, C., Karataş, F. Ö., & Yadigaroğlu, M. (2014). The investigation of pre-service science teachers' reflective journals. *Procedia – Social and Behavioral Sciences, 116,* 3297–3302.

Cunningham, F. M. A. (2001). *Reflective teaching practice in adult ESL.* Retrieved from ERIC database (ED451733).

Davis, E. A. (2006). Characterizing productive reflection among pre-service elementary teachers: Seeing what matters. *Teaching and Teacher Education, 22,* 281–301. doi:10.1016/j.tate.2005.11.005.

Dewey, J. (1904). The relation of theory to practice in education. In *Yearbook for the National Society for the Scientific Study of Education: Part I* (3rd ed., pp. 9–30). Chicago: University of Chicago Press.

Farrell, T. (2012). Reflecting on reflective practice: (Re)visiting Dewey and Schön. *TESOL Journal, 3*(1), 7–16.

Galini, R., & Kostas, K. (2014).Reflection of pre-service teachers in a tabletop exercise of lesson study during their practicum. *Procedia – Social and Behavioral Sciences, 154,* 868–873.

Gelfuso, A. (2016). A framework for facilitating video-mediated reflection: Supporting preservice teachers as they create 'warranted assert abilities' about literacy teaching and learning. *Teaching and Teacher Education, 58,* 68–79.

Gibbs, G. (1988). *Learning by doing: A guide to teaching and learning methods.* Oxford: Further Education Unit, Oxford Brookes University.

Moon, J. A. (1999). *Learning journals: A handbook for reflective practice and professional development.* London: Routledge.

NC Wesleyan College Department of Education. (2012). *The teacher education handbook: A handbook for all teacher education majors at North Carolina Wesleyan College.* Retrieved from http://ncwc.edu/wp-content/uploads/2016/12/The-Teacher-Ed-Handbk-RM-Fall-2016.docx

Pappas, P. (2010). A taxonomy of reflection: Critical thinking for students, teachers, and principals. *Copy/Paste.* Retrieved from http://www.peterpappas.com/2010/01/taxonomy-reflection-criticalthinkingstudents-teachers-principals-.html

Rauduvaite, A., Lasauskiene, J., & Barkauskaite, M. (2015). Experience in teaching practice of pre-service teachers: Analysis of written reflections. *Procedia – Social and Behavioral Sciences, 191,* 1048–1053.

Shulman, L. S. (1998). Theory, practice, and the education of professionals. *The Elementary School Journal, 98*(5), 511–526.

Susoy, Z. (2015). Watch your teaching: A reflection strategy for EFL pre-service teachers through video recordings. *Procedia – Social and Behavioral Sciences, 199,* 163–171.

Wallerstedt, C., & Pramling, N. (2016). Responsive teaching, informal learning and cultural tools in year nine ensemble practice: A lost opportunity. *Instructional Science, 44*(379), 397.

Part IV
Teacher Empowerment: Professional Learning Communities and Emerging Technologies

Chapter 16
Fostering Teachers' Professional Development Through Collaboration in Professional Learning Communities

G.M. Steyn

Abstract Emerging models for continuing professional development of teachers engage teachers in a collaborative learning through professional learning communities (PLC) as a way to spur their professional development and empowerment, and correspondingly, lead to positive changes in teaching practices and student learning. Learning communities are created in these collaborative models where teachers debate theoretical principles, share insights about their teaching and learning, design new instructional strategies, experiment new ideas in classrooms and reflect on results. Models such as Wenger's "community of practice", Hord's Professional Learning Community, Katz and Earl's collaboration model and Pedder and Opfer's professional learning model will be described. Schools can support teacher learning by promoting collaboration, team learning and collegial dialogue among staff, creating continuous learning opportunities, instituting systems to learn and to share learning. This study explored how a South African primary school succeeded in implementing and developing a PLC culture to empower its teachers to improve their learning and that of their students. Key factors in the success of the school's PLC were the leadership of the principal, who acknowledged the necessity for a collaborative learning culture, and the fact that the school had strong and experienced teaching staff who were committed to quality teaching and learning.

16.1 Introduction

Education authorities have recently focused on enhancing and unlocking the professional capacity of teachers by providing high-quality quality continuous professional development (CPD) activities (Brouwer 2011; Godbold 2013; Nehring and Fitzsimons 2011). Studies also confirm that teacher collaboration offers opportunities for empowering teachers and improving teachers' practice and student

---

G.M. Steyn (✉)
Department of Educational Leadership and Management, University of South Africa,
Pretoria, South Africa
e-mail: steyngm1@unisa.ac.za

© Springer Nature Singapore Pte Ltd. 2017
I.H. Amzat and N.P. Valdez (eds.), *Teacher Empowerment Toward Professional Development and Practices*, DOI 10.1007/978-981-10-4151-8_16

learning (Alrubail 2015; Christiansen and Robey 2015; DuFour 2014; DuFour and Reeves 2015; Forte and Flores 2014; Herbert and Rainford 2014; Poulos et al. 2014; UNESCO report 2014; Watson 2014).

The movement towards professional teacher communities within schools grew from the idea that individual teachers cannot be taken out of their school environment in order to train, empower and change them and then put back into the same school environment and be expected to change that environment. Instead, teachers require teacher communities within the school where they can learn together and apply that learning to their classroom practice. The emphasis in such learning communities should be on empowering teachers and developing their professional knowledge and skills and classroom practices for the sake of quality teaching and learning. It is therefore important that school administrators and teachers recognise and act on the increased significance of collaborative learning in professional learning communities (PLCs) in schools.

Various policy initiatives have attempted to improve the quality of teaching and learning in South Africa (Republic of South Africa 2007, 2011, 2012). The proposed professional learning model in the Integrated Strategic Planning Framework for Teacher Education and Development (2011–2025) that focuses on teacher collaboration in teams (Republic of South Africa 2011) was of particular interest for this study. Considering the numerous challenges South African teachers face, PLCs may empower teachers to improve their teaching methods, to share their beliefs and experiences and ultimately to promote their own learning and that of their students.

Studies show that there has been much development in understanding the phenomenon of a "professional learning community", but that there is not enough empirical research that can shed light on implementing and sustaining PLCs in schools. This study explored how a South African primary school succeeded in implementing and developing a PLC culture to empower its teachers to improve their learning and that of their students.

16.2 Conceptual Framework

The notion "professional learning community" has emerged from organisational theory and human relations and focuses on the (1) continual, intentional and collaborative learning that arises (2) among a cohesive teacher team (3) that emphasises shared knowledge and skills (4) within a caring and affectionate school culture that penetrates the professional lives of school administrators, teachers and their students (5) to eventually promote teacher empowerment as well as teacher and student learning (Huffman and Hipp 2003; Gaspar 2010).

Different lenses were used in the study to shed light on the phenomenon, PLC. Wenger's social learning theory primarily regards learning as the active, social participation of members within communities of practice (CoPs) and focuses on individuals and also social structures that enable these individuals to learn (Wenger 1999). Team members in CoPs have a shared vision, a clear learning focus and a shared skill and knowledge base, and they have developed procedures for review and reflection within their particular community. Leadership also plays a key role by providing appropriate infrastructures and the necessary resources for such CoPs to prosper (Wenger 2001) and for teachers to be empowered (Alrubail 2015). Moreover, Godbold (2013) states the teacher empowerment cannot be imposed by school leaders—they need to cultivate it.

Wenger's social learning theory (1998) identifies three main elements in a community of practice (CoP):

1. Mutual engagement delineates the way in which members in a CoP function (Li et al. 2009). Mutual commitment is deepened when such a community takes responsibility for its own learning and empowerment (Wenger 2000). It implies that team members should know each other well enough to interact productively and to identify the individuals who may be of assistance when required.
2. Shared repertoire is a common set of resources, language and understandings to facilitate and negotiate professional learning among team members (Li et al. 2009; Wenger 1998). Within their CoPs members develop customary ways of cooperating and forming personal relationships (Brouwer et al. 2012).
3. Joint enterprise is the joint processes within which team members work to understand and share goals (Li et al. 2009; Wenger 1998).

A second lens used in the study was that of the professional learning committee (PLC), as outlined in Hord's framework (1997). Hord (1997) defines a PLC as a team of teachers and school administrators who meet regularly and share their learning and then act on what they have learnt. Hord (1997) identifies five critical attributes of a PLC:

1. Supportive and shared leadership: Studies show a strong leadership presence in schools where PLCs function effectively (Christiansen and Robey 2015; Nkengbeza 2014; Outhouse 2012). To transform a school into a PLC therefore requires the endorsement of school leadership to actively initiate and nurture the whole school's professional development, to share leadership and ensure teachers' commitment and to remove obstacles that hinder teacher collaboration (Gaspar 2010; Terry 2013). School administrators need to model a vision of teacher collaboration, communicate confidence in teachers' competence and create time and structures to promote teacher collaboration (Piccardi 2005).
2. Shared values and vision: A shared vision and values guide all decisions and lead to required norms of behaviour for staff members (Nkengbeza 2014; Watson 2014). Collaborative models of professional development encourage pooled intelligence and collegial respect, commitment and trust among teachers that focus on student performance (Williams 2010).
3. Individual and collective learning: Interdependence among team members, where they learn individually and collectively, is considered a requirement for successful teacher communities. It implies that team members engage in a deep professional dialogue about subject knowledge and/or professional skills (Herbert and Rainford 2014; Watson 2014).

4. Shared personal practice: Hord (1997: 6) regards this attribute as a component of the "peers helping peers" process. When teachers share their practices, they address the needs of their students, identify solutions to professional challenges, stimulate professional dialogue and assist in building one another's expertise (Herbert and Rainford 2014). Moreover, sharing their practice is built on mutual trust and respect (Fulton and Britton 2011).
5. Supportive conditions: Hord (1997) distinguishes between two types of supportive condition: physical and human. The physical conditions comprise school policies and schedules, frequent team meetings and appropriate processes for professional dialogue and communication (Jaquith 2013; Terry 2013). The human conditions encompass the willingness of teachers to work collectively and to accept constructive feedback on their practice (Greer 2012).

When examining the development of PLCs, it is important to look at the stages of such development. DuFour, DuFour and Eaker in Reynolds (2008) identify four stages of PLC development: (1) the pre-initiation stage when teachers have not yet established a shared vision that is linked to student performance; (2) the initiation stage when teams are created and teachers address the idea of a PLC development; (3) the developing stage when most of the teachers accept and take ownership of the idea of a PLC development; and (4) the sustaining phase when teachers become willing and fully committed to use their professional community as a way to promote student performance.

16.3 Research Design and School Context

Based on a longitudinal study carried out since 2010 in the school, this school was purposively selected since it revealed promising data on the way in which PLCs developed in the school. The school in the study is a large, urban primary school within a middle-class community in South Africa with approximately 1850 students and 106 teachers at the time of the study. The school received the prestigious "Inviting School" award from the International Alliance of Invitational Education (IE) for manifesting the 5Ps (people, places, policies, programmes and processes) in the school (Purkey and Novak 2008). In essence, employing IE means developing and sustaining a welcoming school environment that is founded on respect, trust, optimism, intentionality and care for the sake of personal growth of all role players and increased learning outcomes (Shaw et al., n.d.).

During the tenure of the previous principal, the school showed among other things the school's focus on the professional development of individual teachers (Steyn 2009, 2010). However, with his appointment in 2010, the new principal refocused teachers' professional development on teacher collaboration by initiating a collaborative learning culture in the school (Steyn 2014a, b, c, 2015a, b). The principal started by instituting both vertical and horizontal teacher collaborative

Table 16.1 Annual national assessment results ANA (2014) for Mathematics in South Africa and the school (in percentages)

	South Africa	Case study school
Grade 4	37	68
Grade 5	37	68
Grade 6	43	80

Table 16.2 Annual national assessment results (2014) for Literacy (Home language) in South Africa and the school (in percentages)

	South Africa	Case study school
Grade 4	57	68
Grade 5	57	68
Grade 6	63	80

structures that included the whole school team, various departmental teaching teams and teaching teams within the various grades.

Tables 16.1 and 16.2 reveal the Numeracy and Literacy (Home language) results of the school in the study compared to those of South African schools (Republic of South Africa Republic of South Africa 2014), which show that the average performance of students in the school was significantly higher than that of averages in the rest of South Africa, particularly in Mathematics. Grade 3 Mathematics had the highest score in the ANA results in 2014. The high performance in Mathematics can be attributed to, among other things, the fact that the school reduced the number of students in this subject to 15 per class from Grades 4 to 7.

Although this study referred to a previous quantitative study in Steyn (2014a) which focused on the realisation of the five major attributes of a PLC, this study employed a qualitative approach. Qualitative data collection methods during 2015 included a focus group interview with selected teachers and various individual interviews with the principal and staff members. In the analysis of data, the five attributes of Hord's framework (1997) were used to explain the findings. Ethical approval for the study was obtained from the Gauteng Department of Education and the University of South Africa.

16.4 Findings

Based on Hord's framework, the findings describe the role of shared and supportive leadership; a common vision and values; collective learning and sharing the responsibility for student learning; shared personal practice; and continuous improvement and supportive conditions.

16.4.1 Shared and Supportive Leadership

The school principal played a key role when he instituted a PLC in the school. During his first year in office he realised that teachers worked in "very isolated" conditions and that the school had "little islands of excellence" (Steyn 2015a: 166). He had two major concerns: (1) to break the tradition of independence among and also in grades and (2) to improve the academic performance in the school by focusing on the learning of teachers and students (Steyn 2015a). He therefore took the initiative to initiate a PLC culture in the school. Changing the independent culture was a "huge challenge" for the principal and difficult for the teachers, but he considered it to be an "adapt or die" case (Steyn 2015a: 168).

The survey showed that 84.61% of teachers agreed that the principal consistently involved them in decision-making processes and that teachers valued the principal's shared and supportive leadership approach in creating a PLC (Steyn 2014a). Since 2011 many teachers have bought into the idea and taken "ownership" of collaboration (Steyn 2015c). The principal humbly viewed himself as "the cog in that big machine", but respected the crucial role of teachers in the successful teacher collaboration (Steyn 2015a: 165).

16.4.2 A Common Vision and Values

When the principal initially took office he realised that the school's vision was too elaborate. The school then collectively developed a vision to be "the best school" that revealed the ultimate ideal for the school: "The barefoot, fun, performance school with a Christian character that strives towards excellence and aims to develop each child in totality" (Steyn 2013: 6).

In particular, the principal placed a high premium on improved academic performance in the school (Steyn 2013) which was supported by 84.31% of the teachers (Steyn 2014a). In order to address this shared goal, the principal placed a strong focus on teacher collaboration. He succinctly explained his stance (Steyn 2015a: 168):

> Success in the classroom depends 100% on teacher collaboration … We are driving an idea … which is so fragile that if there is no continuity and collaboration you will not get to the final destination. … if we don't collaborate, we fail them [the students].

Apart from the focus on student learning, the principal made a firm commitment to the shared values of love, excellence, respect, integrity and faith that he had "inherited", but felt that it was also necessary to deliberately inculcate these values. Appropriate symbols in five pictures were then developed to illustrate these five values, which were displayed throughout the school. Moreover, every teacher in the school had to ensure that each of these values was inculcated for a 2-month period during the year in their classes.

16.4.3 Collective Learning and Sharing the Responsibility for Student Learning

Teachers' commitment to collective learning removed the isolation between teachers in and among grades which was confirmed by 86.54% of teachers in the survey (Steyn 2014a). The principal succinctly explained:

> Without professional collaboration, there can be no growth; no advancement; no development … The whole is more than the parts, and the system cannot function if all the parts do not work together … Everything is interconnected, and thrives and succeeds when in collaboration with other systems within the school.

The notion of interdependence in their PLC was echoed by many teachers during interviews. For them, collaboration was necessary to measure their own professionalism and also to ensure their own professional empowerment and development. Moreover, teachers stated that being part of a learning community meant that they had opportunities to collectively generate creative ways to solve problems and to share certain subject-related responsibilities, which was seen as a welcome relief for teachers, considering their challenging workload.

16.4.4 Shared Personal Practice and Continuous Improvement

The principal believed that it was human nature for people not to share their "intellectual property" and also wanted them to stop their "ridiculous" competitiveness (Steyn 2015a: 168). His strategy paid off when he instituted PLCs, where a lot of sharing, discussion and reflection took place. Sharing practices in the school occurred when teachers used the Integrated Quality Management System in classroom observations; 86.54% of teachers valued the feedback they received from peers after such observations (Steyn 2014a). With the introduction of the Curriculum and Assessment Policy Statement (Republic of South Africa 2011), teachers engaged in professional dialogue when they had to design new lesson plans and worksheets. The spirit among team members was usually of such a nature that teachers felt comfortable making contributions. Their often diverse perspectives were respected and these insights contributed to a more holistic view of any given issue under discussion.

16.4.5 Supportive Conditions

Structural conditions and conditions that fostered human relationships in the school created conducive conditions for individual and collective learning to occur.

Regarding the structural conditions in the school, well-structured avenues in the form of formal horizontal and vertical teams were arranged in the school's timetable. Team meetings occurred during assembly and test periods for the different grades and quarterly among the grades in the different departments. This arrangement not only allowed for continuity between different grades but also consistency within classes in particular grades. The school also provided the necessary teaching equipment such as computers, interactive whiteboards and data projectors to support teachers. Various training opportunities, depending on the needs of teachers, were constantly offered to empower teachers. A teacher commented that she could not think of "any other school that provided such support" in the form of collaborative learning and that she was "grateful" to belong to this school.

Although a high level of collaboration occurred in the school, both the principal and teachers expressed the need to have more frequent formal structured meetings. Although the school had been creative in scheduling team meetings, it remained a huge challenge to find ample time in the existing tight school programme for teacher collaboration.

Supportive conditions for PLCs also include the development of positive, caring and productive relationships in the school, which 92.16% of teachers confirmed in the survey (Steyn 2014a). Teachers valued a feeling of "togetherness" among colleagues that they regarded as of "inestimable" value. For the principal, the school had developed into a "brotherhood … where teachers cry together when it is difficult" since the introduction of PLCs (Steyn 2015a: 170).

As can be expected of individuals, differences sometimes occurred in the teams. In such cases, teachers preferred to address these problems as soon as possible and, if possible, in person. Nevertheless, the principal and teachers valued differences of opinion, but believed that they had to be properly managed so that set goals can be attained.

16.5 Discussion of Findings

In line with the study by Wells (2014), this study showed that by positioning teachers as professionals within PLCs, the school was able to empower teachers by improving their learning and that of their students. The transformation into a PLC required the principal's leadership to actively cultivate the whole staff's professional development (Evans 2014; Fulton and Britton 2011; Terry 2013). In essence, it was the principal's innovative and ongoing leadership that seemed to have had the most significant effect on changing the school culture (Evans 2014; Jaquith 2013; Outhouse 2012; Nkengbeza 2014; Terry 2013). Furthermore, it was important for the principal to capitalise on the expertise of teachers and build teacher leaderships to create and sustain effective PLCs in the school. By doing this, the principal showed that he adhered to the IE assumptions of respect and optimism (Purkey and Siegel 2003).

Teachers at the school bought into the idea of teacher collaboration. Teachers' collaborative activities in the school corresponded to the work of Pedder and Opfer (2011), where teachers regularly engaged in professional dialogue, observed each other and obtained valuable feedback on their teaching practice. The findings also support Wenger's joint enterprise, where team members worked in understanding and sharing goals (Wenger 1998). Teachers' commitment to a shared goal is regarded as a key characteristic of effective professional learning teams (Hord 1997; Nkengbeza 2014). Other studies also confirm the necessity of a shared goal, and that teachers should be inspired to attain this shared goal (Fulton and Britton 2011; Greer 2012; Jaquith 2013).

As far as Hord's (1997) third attribute—individual and collective learning—is concerned, the school succeeded in building a PLC. In their professional engagement, teachers enhanced both their individual and collective practices and ultimately the performance of students (DuFour 2014; Poulos et al. 2014; Forte and Flores 2014; Watson 2014). A recognised advantage of teacher collaboration in PLCs lies in the notion of "pooled intelligence" (Williams 2010: 4. Moreover, the findings reveal the presence of the mutual engagement and shared repertoire of Wenger's social learning theory, since team members employed various methods to actively interact and engage in their teams (Wenger 1998). In sharing their professional experiences, teachers extend their interpretations of classroom practices beyond those that were individually established. The focus on continuity and communication in this school also changed the previously isolated structures in the school. This study therefore supports Wenger's (2007: 1, 2) community of practice model, which emphasises the importance of teachers' joint enterprise.

The findings reveal the existence of supportive conditions and therefore confirm the existence of the two sets of factors of Hord's model (1997)—namely supportive structures and relationships in the school (Huffman and Hipp 2003: 12). The school structured various formal PLCs and the principal played a key role in creating the supportive structures for teacher collaboration. However, finding appropriate time for staff to collaborate in PLCs within a school's time-table, as shown in this study, is often cited as a barrier to an effective PLC (Terry 2013). Evans (2014) therefore states that principals need to understand the interventions required to ensure the most suitable strategies for professional development of staff.

The intentionally structured teams brought teachers together and assisted them to form close personal and professional relationships (Forte and Flores 2014). Their mutual engagement also connected them in ways that were deeper than mere "superficial similarities" (Brouwer 2011) and also broke down their previous isolation (Pedder and Opfer 2011). Furthermore, teachers' mutual engagement revealed a feeling of belongingness, cohesiveness and interdependence that was based on the presence of trust in and respect for each other (Fulton and Britton 2011). In the presence of trust and respect, teachers felt free to participate and share experiences (Katz and Earl 2010; Purkey and Novak 2008). The findings, however, showed that teachers sometimes experienced disagreements, which Wenger (1998) also acknowledges in communities of practice. The teachers nevertheless solved their differences in an amicable way for the sake of their shared goal (Greer 2012). Moreover, Brouwer (2011) believes that the joint enterprise in communities of practice may be more productive when diversity exists among team members.

When the developmental levels of a PLC in this school were considered, the findings showed that the school to a large extent operated on the developing stage of DuFour et al. (as cited in Reynolds 2008; Steyn 2015b). It had progressed from the pre-initiation and initiation stage in 2010 when the PLC was established to the developing stage, and when teachers bought into the idea of a PLC and collectively attempted to attain the shared vision of improved teaching and learning. Key factors in the success of the PLC in the school were the principal, who saw the necessity for introducing a collaborative learning culture in the school, and the fact that the school had strong and experienced teaching staff who were committed to quality teaching and learning. Being an Inviting School that continued to adhere to the assumptions of the IE approach was another promising factor in introducing a teacher learning community in the school.

16.6 Conclusion

The findings from this case study reveal how the school succeeded in introducing and developing a PLC to the level of the developmental stage of a PLC. The establishment of a collaborative school culture in the study manifested in a number of ways:

1. The school principal played a key role in initiating and developing a culture of teacher collaboration.
2. Formal collaborative structures in the form of PLCs and appropriate scheduled meetings were instituted in the school programme.
3. Instituting PLCs required teachers to take ownership of the idea, which also involved shared goals, trust, respect and continuous professional dialogue.
4. The development of the collaborative school culture required a willingness and commitment among teachers to sustain the PLCs.

Although this case study reveals the manifestation of PLCs within a particular school context, it is important to understand that schools that consider moving towards a more collaborative structure need to customise the implementation of a PLC to suit their particular needs and circumstances. The only requirement in making professional learning a reality is that the principal and teachers acknowledge that it is in their power to make a difference in the quality of their own professional learning and that of their students.

References

Alrubail, R. (2015). Administrators, empower your teachers. *Edutopiq*. Retrieved from http://www.edutopia.org/discussion/administrators-empower-your-teachers. Accessed August 23, 2016.

Brouwer, P. (2011). *Collaboration in teams*. Ph.D. thesis. The Netherlands: University of Utrecht.

Brouwer, P., Brekelmans, M., Nieuwenhuis, L., & Simons, R.-J. (2012). Community development in the school workplace. *International Journal of Educational Management, 26*(4), 403–418.

Christiansen, T., & Robey, P. A. (2015, Fall). Promoting systemic change through the integration of professional learning community practices with Glasser quality schools. *International Journal of Choice Theory and Reality Therapy, XXXV*(1), 7–13.

DuFour, R. (2014, May). Harnessing the power of PLCS. *Educational Leadership*, 30–35. Retrieved from http://www.educationalleadership-digital.com/educationalleadership/201405?folio=30#pg33. Accessed May 20, 2015.

DuFour, R., & Reeves, D. (2015, October 2). Professional learning communities still work (if done right). *Education Week Teacher*. Retrieved from http://www.edweek.org/tm/articles/2015/10/02/professional-learning-communities-still-work-if-done.html. Accessed July 19, 2016.

Evans, L. (2014). Leadership for professional development and learning. *Cambridge Journal of Education, 44*(2), 178–198.

Forte, A. M., & Flores, M. A. (2014). Teacher collaboration and professional development in the workplace: A study of Portuguese teachers. *European Journal of Teacher Education, 37*(1), 91–105.

Fulton, K., & Britton, T. (2011). *STEM teachers in professional learning communities: From good teachers to great teaching*. Retrieved from http://nctaf.org/wp-content/uploads/2012/01/1098-executive-summary.pdf. Accessed December 4, 2015.

Gaspar, S. (2010). *Leadership and the professional learning community*. Ph.D. thesis. Lincoln, NE: University of Nebraska.

Godbold, W. (2013). Empowered teachers will change the world. *SEEN SouthEast Education Network*. Retrieved from http://www.seenmagazine.us/Articles/Article-Detail/ArticleId/2899/Empowered-teachers-will-change-the-worldaccessed. August 23, 2016.

Greer, J. A. (2012). *Professional learning and collaboration* (Unpublished Ph.D. thesis). Blacksburg, VA: Virginia Polytechnic Institute and State University.

Herbert, S., & Rainford, M. (2014). Developing a model for continuous professional development by action research. *Professional Development in Education, 40*(2), 243–264.

Hord, S. M. (1997). Professional learning communities: What are they and why are they important? *Issues... About Change, 6*(1), 1–8.

Huffman, J. B., & Hipp, K. K. (2003). *Reculturing schools as professional learning communities*. Oxford: Scarecrow Education.

Jaquith, A. (2013). Instructional capacity: How to build it right. *Educational Leadership, 71*(2), 56–61.

Katz, S., & Earl, L. (2010). Learning about networked learning communities. *School Effectiveness and School Improvement, 21*(1), 27–51.

Li, L. C., Grimshaw, J. M., Nielsen, C., Judd, M., Coyte, P. C. & Graham, I. D. (2009). Evolution of Wenger's concept of community of practice. *Implementation Science, 4*(11), 1–8. Retrieved from http://www.ncbi.nlm.nih.gov/pmc/articles/PMC2654669/pdf/1748-5908-4-11.pdf. Accessed January 8, 2015.

Nehring, J., & Fitzsimons, G. (2011, September). The professional learning community as subversive activity: Countering the culture of conventional schooling. *Professional Development in Education, 37*(4), 513–535.

Nkengbeza, D. (2014). *Building a professional learning community in a conflict and post-conflict environment* (Academic dissertation). Jyväskylä, Finland: University of Jyväskylä.

Outhouse, C. M. (2012). *Evaluating the role of principals in teacher teams: A longitudinal analysis of principal involvement and impact in a district-wide initiative to increase teacher collaboration* (Unpublished Ph.D. thesis). Amherst, MA: University of Massachusetts.

Pedder, D., & Opfer, D. V. (2011). Are we realising the full potential of teachers' professional learning in schools in England? Policy issues and recommendations from a national study. *Professional Development in Education, 37*(5), 741–758.

Piccardi, J. M. (2005). *Principals' perceptions of factors affecting teacher collaboration in elementary schools* (Unpublished Ph.D. dissertation). Providence, RI: Johnson & Wales University.

Poulos, J., Culberston, N., Piazza, P., & D'entremont, C. (2014). Making space: The value of teacher collaboration. *Education Digest, 80*(2), 28–31.

Purkey, W. W., & Novak, J. M. (2008). *Fundamentals of invitational education*. Kennesaw, GA: The International Alliance for Invitational Education.

Purkey, W. W., & Siegel, B. (2003). *Becoming an invitational leader: A new approach to professional and personal success*. Atlanta, GA: Humanics Trade Group.

Republic of South Africa. (2007). *National Education Policy Act (27/1996): National policy framework for teacher education in South Africa*. Department of Education, Government Printer: Pretoria.

Republic of South Africa. (2011). *Integrated strategic planning framework for teacher education and development in South Africa (2011–2025)*. Pretoria: Department of Basic Education and Department of Higher Education and Training, Government Printer.

Republic of South Africa. (2012). *Action plan to 2014: Towards the realisation of schooling 2025*. http://www.education.gov.za/LinkClick.aspx?fileticket=XZGwrpV9gek%3D&tabid=418&mid=1211. Accessed May 4, 2014.

Republic of South Africa. (2014). *Report on the annual national assessment of 2014. Grades 1–6 and 9*. Pretoria: Department of Basic Education.

Reynolds, D. (2008). *How professional learning communities use student data for improving achievement* (Unpublished Ph.D. thesis). Los Angeles, CA: University of Southern California.

Shaw, D., Siegel, B., & Schoenline, A. (n.d.). Basic tenets of invitational theory and practice (ITP): An invitational glossary manuscript (Unpublished manuscript).

Steyn, G. M. (2009). Using reflexive photography to study a principal's perceptions of the impact of professional development on a school: A case study. *Koers: Bulletin for Christian Scholarship, 74*(3), 1–29.

Steyn, G. M. (2010, June). 'n Skoolhoof se perspektief op professionele ontwikkeling: 'n Enkele gevallestudie (A principal's perspective on professional development: A single case study). *Tydskrif vir Geesteswetenskappe, 50*(2), 244–261.

Steyn, T. (2013). Professional and organisational socialisation during leadership succession of a school principal: A narrative inquiry using visual ethnography. *South African Journal of Education, 33*(2), 1–17.

Steyn, G. M. (2014a). Exploring the status of a professional learning community in a South African primary school. *La Pensée Multidisciplinary Journal, 76*(5), 256–269.

Steyn, G. M. (2014b). Exploring successful principalship in South Africa: A case study. *Journal of Asian and African Studies, 49*(3), 347–361.

Steyn, G. M. (2014c). Teacher collaboration and invitational leadership in a South African primary school. *Education and Urban Society*. Available from http://eus.sagepub.com/cgi/reprint/0013124514536441v1.pdf?ijkey=EDDKppL1KsZpizJ&keytype=ref. Accessed December 9, 2015.

Steyn, G. M. (2015a). Creating a teacher collaborative practice in a South African primary school: The role of the principal. *The Journal of Asian and African Studies, 50*(2), 160–175.

Steyn, G. M. (2015b). The developmental level of a school-based professional learning community in a South African school. *Journal of New Generation Sciences, 13*(3), 197–213.

Steyn, G. M. (2015c). Creating a teacher collaborative practice in a South African primary school: The role of the principal. *The Journal of Asian and African Studies, 50*(2), 160–175.

Terry, W. (2013). Shared leadership. *Educational Leadership, 71*(2), 62–67.

UNESCO. (2014). *Teaching and learning: Achieving quality for all*. Paris: UNESCO. Retrieved from http://www.uis.unesco.org/Library/Documents/gmr-2013-14-teaching-and-learning-education-for-all-2014-en.pdf. Accessed December 5, 2015.

Watson, C. (2014, February). Effective professional learning communities? The possibilities for teachers as agents of change in schools. *British Educational Research Journal, 40*(1), 18–29.

Wells, M. (2014). Elements of effective and sustainable professional learning. *Professional Development in Education, 40*(3), 488–504.

Wenger, E. (1998). *Communities of practice. Learning, meaning and identity*. Cambridge: Cambridge University Press.

Wenger, E. (1999, January to February). Learning as social participation. *Knowledge Management Review, 6,* 30–33.

Wenger, E. (2000). Communities of practice and social learning systems. *Organization, SAGE Social Science Collection, 7*(2), 225–246.

Wenger, E. (2001). Organically grown. *T+D (Training and Development), 55*(6), 40–41.

Wenger, E. (2007). Communities of practice. Third annual National Qualifications Framework Colloqium. June 5, 2007. Velmore Conference Estate.

Williams, M. L. (2010). *Teacher collaboration as professional development in a large, suburban high school* (Unpublished Ph.D. thesis). Lincoln, NE: University of Nebraska.

Chapter 17
School-Based Professional Learning Community: Empowering Teachers as Assessment Leaders in the Change Context

Garima Bansal

Abstract India's Continuous and Comprehensive Evaluation scheme (CCE) seeks to introduce child-centered methods of students' assessment. Formative assessment is a major plank in this. The article draws upon Vygotsky's sociocultural theory to analyze and explain the processes of change that have underpinned the development of assessment reform. Case study is used as the research methodology to suggest that creation and regulation of school-based professional learning communities influence teachers' classroom-based formative assessment practices. It is argued that collaborative efforts of teachers supported by proactive leadership, keeping a consistent focus to change the practices at classroom level empower teachers to become formative assessment leaders.

17.1 Introduction

Change in the schooling systems in order to improve students' learning and their outcome is one of the common features across the world. For school improvement initiatives to succeed, "practitioners who are the foot-soldiers of every reform aimed at improving student outcomes" (Cuban 1998, p. 459) are required.

In line with this view, this chapter examines the ways in which educational change associated with formative assessment reform initiative can be situated in schools. Particularly, the role played by school-based professional learning community in empowering teachers to become assessment reform leaders is studied using case study of a school in India. I outline below research regarding school-based professional learning community before delineating the details of the context and the assessment reform initiative. It would be followed by identification of the critical factors required for establishing school-based professional learning community and how they relate to classroom-based formative assessment practices.

G. Bansal (✉)
Department of Education, Lady Irwin College, University of Delhi, New Delhi, India
e-mail: garima1agg@gmail.com

17.2 School-Based Professional Learning Community

School-based professional learning community is described as a professional learning community (PLC, henceforth) of professionals (teachers, supervisory heads, and the principal) working collaboratively "to reflect on their practice, examine evidence about the relationship between practice and student outcomes, and make changes that improve teaching and learning" (McLaughlin and Talbert 2006, p. 4). Theoretically, the model draws upon Vygotsky's (1978) work that regards individual learning "situated" in the social environment. Wenger's (2000), while drawing upon Vygotsky, characterized learning as interaction occurring in "communities of practice". These communities are characterized by "groups of people who share a concern, a set of problems, or a passion about a topic, and who deepen their knowledge and expertise by interacting on an ongoing basis" (Wenger et al. 2002, p. 4).

Inquiry into practice, similar to the action research (Fernandez 2002) concept, is central to the idea of a professional learning community. This idea finds echo is the work of Dewey (1929) when he pointed that educational data provides the subject matter for carrying out an inquiry. Stenhouse (1975), similarly, recommended teachers to be "classroom researchers" for the benefit of students' learning. Inquiry inherent to the PLC involves the following phases (i) planning: setting goals, actions, strategies (ii) evidence collection (iii) interpretation: interpreting the gap between achieved and intended outcomes (iv) utilization: implementing interventions to close the gap (v) evaluation: assessing the effectiveness of the intervention (Birenbaum et al. 2009).

School-based PLCs may vary along several dimensions: ideology (shared educational beliefs of the community and underlying instruction, learning and assessment conceptions), culture (ethos, values and norms), infrastructure (mechanisms supportive of professional development, collaboration and knowledge management), motivation (goal orientation, disposition, and expectations regarding professional learning and self efficacy regarding shared achievement of goals), and professional learning (nature of inquiry in which participants engage) (Birenbaum et al. 2011; Stoll et al. 2006; DuFour and Eaker 2002).

The article draws upon a case study of an Indian senior secondary school that has attempted to address changes in assessment policy by establishing school-based professional learning communities of teachers. First, I would begin with providing a brief description of the context in which this study was carried out followed by delineation of the research methodology. Finally, I conduct an analysis of the research data, examining the ways in which school-based professional learning communities work toward empowering teachers as assessment leaders in the change context.

17.3 The National Context

Schools in Indian educational system have adopted a traditional, high stake perspective to educational assessment, largely, borrowed from its British colonizers (Nawani 2015). She further pointed that traditional high stake assessment, "regards "sameness of treatment" and "remoteness of the examiner from the learner assessed" as being central to successful evaluation of learning" (p. 38).

Although formal system of board examination had been a dominant practice in the post-independence India yet a need to reform the practices had been reiterated by various educational commissions for long (GOI 1953, 1970, 1986, 1993). National Curriculum Framework of India (NCF 2005) observed, "Each school should evolve a flexible and implementable scheme of Continuous and Comprehensive Evaluation (CCE), primarily for diagnosis, remediation and enhancing of learning." (NCERT 2005, p. 115).

Consequently, Central Board of Secondary Education introduced Continuous and Comprehensive Evaluation scheme (CCE, henceforth) as an examination reform in the year 2009 in class IX in all its affiliated schools (CBSE 2014). The reform was instituted using a cascade model. It involved training of master trainers through workshops in the year 2009–2010 which was followed by them training principal and two teachers from another school located in the same district. The process followed till it reached the grassroot level of the teachers (CBSE 2014).

Through CCE scheme, formative assessment was emphasized whose details are delineated in the next section.

17.4 The Initiative: Formative Assessment

Formative assessment (FA) has been described as a social enterprise, a regular classroom affair, involving all (peers, teachers, students themselves) in the process of advancing students' learning with emphasis being laid on "interactive regulation" (Perrenoud 1998) of learning processes. Epistemological roots of formative assessment practices could be traced in the sociocultural learning theories propounded by Lev Vygotsky which suggest the importance of goal-oriented, tool-mediated learning occurring during the process of social interaction (Shephard 2000; James and Lewis 2012). William and Thompson (2007) have identified three processes of teaching and learning involved in a classrooms practicing formative assessment:

- Establishing where the learners are in their learning;
- Establishing where they are going; and,
- Establishing what needs to be done to get them there.

Heritage (2010) stressed upon the cyclic interaction between these strategies, thus, arguing that formative assessment is incomplete if formative feedback provided either by the teacher or peers or by learners to themselves is not utilized by the learners to improve their learning. This conceptualization of formative assessment is similar to the nature of inquiry cycle central to school-based professional learning community (Birenbaum et al. 2009).

The ways in which schools worked toward assimilation of change within their contexts are studied, in this paper, through a case study of a school. The school chosen for the study was extremely popular for its progressive educational practices in the country.

17.5 The School

Greenjingle School is a large senior secondary school, with over 1100 students and 50 teaching staff. The school building is located in the high-end suburbs of New Delhi, the capital city of India. Students usually belonged to high-income urban society. The school had high quality sports, music, and many other cocurricular activities.

School had been specifically popular in the country for its child-centered approaches. This school had a long tradition for opening its doors to educational researchers and other social scientists. It had actively participated in multiple national and international research-based projects with a particular focus on developing students as global citizens.

Hierarchically, principal was at the apex of the school administration. She was subordinated by two supervisory heads—academic and cultural—for the entire school. Supervisory heads were subordinated by discipline-based Heads of the Department (for instance, Science Head of Department, Sports Head of the Department). Academic heads were generally held responsible for the teaching–learning processes occurring in the classrooms, organization of remedial sessions, gifted programs, smooth implementation of school policies, etc., while cultural head ensured students' growth and development in cocurricular aspects. Discipline-based heads, called Heads of the Departments, tended to be the connecting link between the students, teachers, and school's academic head. All heads ensured monitoring of their staff's educational practices, students' activities and provided constructive feedback. Principal, Meena, held high repute among the school teachers. They often quoted that their principal was an innovative, creative, and a motivating leader. Teachers reported that she was always open for one-to-one interaction with her staff.

Many of the formative assessment strategies had already been in use in the Greenjingle School although they were not being explicitly practised under the aegis of formative assessment. Such practices provided a social context for ready acceptance of the reform initiative among the teachers. School's principal observed:

> CCE is not new for us, we have already been assessing students continuously and comprehensively since ages but yes now we have got an official sanction for our practices… certainly few changes are there, such as, nature of reporting to parents, format of making report cards etc. (Meena, Greenjingle School 2011).

The basic strategies already existing in the school were augmented and adapted, and comprised a variety of additional approaches to improve the levels of dialogue, discussion, and feedback essential to the reform initiative.

17.6 Methodology

Following Vygotsky (1978), it is believed that "official knowledge" (represented in this case, for instance, by Central Board of Secondary Education's guidelines, curriculum frameworks and the literature on formative assessment and CCE) is given concrete expression by the sociocultural activity of actors (in this case teachers and heads). Expression of human agency mediated through social interactions plays a major role in determining the shape taken by new approaches to teaching and learning in any school context (Priestley and Sime 2005).

Accordingly, this study places a greater emphasis on the meanings ascribed to the initiative by the school personnel (teachers, heads, principal), which in turn impacts the actions associated with the initiative, and the contexts within which they occur. Case study seemed to be the appropriate tool as it enables the researcher to "describe actions within a social setting and invites rather than tries to control the possibility of a rich array of variables" (Holliday 2007, p. 4).

17.6.1 Data Sources

Data collection took place in the academic year of 2011–2012. Five teachers, teaching secondary grade science, were chosen for this study (see Table 17.1). Pseudonyms and random assignment of gender have been used to prevent confidentiality and anonymity of the respondents and the school. This choice of teachers and grade level was deliberate as CCE was applicable only in the secondary grades. Science teachers and classrooms were chosen owing to researcher's academic background in sciences, thus, enabling her to better understand the epistemic, pedagogic, and assessment requirements of the discipline. Teachers were interviewed using semi-structured interview tool to understand their views on assessment reform, their epistemological stance, views about learners, assessment perception, assessment competency, etc. Semi-structured interviews with departmental heads and supervisory heads were conducted on the ways in which the changes in assessment procedures were being assimilated and accommodated in the school calendar, how they mediated between parents and school procedures between examination bodies and school teachers, etc., the ways in which they handled logistical and organizational issues while executing FA and so on. A total of eight hours of data from all the semi-structured interviews was collected.

Table 17.1 Details of teachers who participated in the study

Name of the teacher	Gender	Grade/s taught (number of students)	Professional experience	Educational qualifications	Topic of the lessons observed (hours)
Seema	Female	9 (32)	Joined in the current academic session	Bachelors in Science (B.Sc.) + Bachelor in Education (B.Ed.)	Force (5)
Neeta	Female	9 (30)	5 years in two different schools and 3 years in this school	B.Sc. + B.Ed.	Gravitation (4)
Raghav	Male	10 (29)	5 years in corporate sector and one year in this school	B.Sc. + Masters in Science (M.Sc.) (Chemistry) + B.Ed.	Light (5)
Gritha	Female	10 (33)	10 years in this school	B.Sc. + B. Ed. + Masters in Education(M.Ed.)	Sources of Energy (4)
Radha	Female	10 (27)	25 years in this school	B.Sc. + B.Ed.	States of Matter (3)

Non-participant field observation was used to construct a view of ways in which the school worked to assimilate assessment reform initiative. It included observation of the classroom practice of the teachers (for details see Table 17.1); and observation of staff meetings (among the teachers, between teachers and the head, and between the heads, discipline-based Heads of the Department and the Principal constituting total 7 h). Further, policy and school documents on assessment reform initiative were analyzed.

17.6.2 Data Analysis

Thematic analysis (Cohen et al. 2011) was used to identify broad areas of evaluation. The data so collected was transcribed and coded to identify themes. Some of the initial categories used in the beginning are as follows:

- Ways in which school management translated the vision of the initiative as described in the policy documents to its staff and students;
- The extent to which school management's efforts were taken up by the teachers and its concomitant impact on classroom practices;
- Types of classroom approaches adopted to embed formative assessment within the school.

These categories underwent a recursive cycle of analysis to reach the categories finally described in the next section.

17.7 Findings

The interview data and the supporting observations support the view that CCE initiative had been a success for the school. The school addressed the issue of change by establishing professional learning communities in the school. The upcoming discussion highlights the ways in which school established PLCs to enable successful assimilation of change in the educational processes.

17.7.1 Leadership's Role

School's principal was a source of inspiration for her staff. She provided requisite support and impetus for change in her school. This had a number of consequences.

First, the interview data suggested that school's principal had constantly been engaging herself in educational research. She conducted as well as participated in several professional development programs. Also, she was one of the master trainers trained by Central Board of Secondary Education in its training process. A teacher remarked,

> Our Principal is very knowledgeable about research in education and what is happening on the cutting edge (Rahav, Greenjingle School 2011).

She brought lots of research-based articles for teachers to read, encouraged systematic collection of students' data for making informed professional judgments, thereby, encouraging teachers to be "scholars". She encouraged every teacher to adopt one innovative formative assessment strategy for their respective classes. For instance, a teacher instituted a regular practice to paste the assessment criteria of all the upcoming assessment on one of the bulletin boards of the classroom to which students could refer invariably for a long period of time while preparing for extended projects. Another teacher developed individual student's portfolios.

Second, she seemed to be successful in creation of a whole school environment supportive of reform. School's corridors had several bulletin boards displaying innovative statements and procedures for pedagogic and academic enrichment of the teachers.[1] She empowered her academic and cultural heads to organize regular faculty meetings to hear the voices of teachers, make scrupulous investigations of their requirements, and eventually channelize schools' resources in the desired direction. During an interview she noted:

> I want to create a self-propelling system...a way of administration in which school runs the same way in my absence, i.e., all the mechanisms run smoothly without my supervision (Meena, Greenjingle School 2011).

---

[1]For instance, articles of educational relevance were regularly posted on school bulletin boards from daily newspapers, key statements from Assessment Reform Group were found to be posted, etc.

Following her vision, school heads engaged in joint enquiry with the teachers and encouraged them to become leaders. Such distributed leadership patterns invigorated the entire system.

Third, it was ensured that student achievement was continuously monitored. Grade-level teams of teachers examined students' data weekly to reflect on progress and determine where instruction needed adjustment. The teams studied students' standardized test scores, attendance records, classroom test scores, and formative assessments that were conducted periodically. This data collection was accompanied by an inquiry conducted to ascertain the gap between intended and observed outcomes. Teachers noted that in the spirit of assessment reform

> We have learnt to look at the test scores and other forms of students' data with an eye to understand what it actually means in the classroom and how we should use that information to change our teaching rather than adopting a judgmental attitude towards our students (Gritha, Greenjingle School 2012).

Another teacher suggested

> Once we got used to looking at data carefully and discussing it, we all became very sensitive to changes in student performance, and we wanted parents to stay abreast of their children's learning as well (Raghav, Greenjingle School 2012).

Following these views, teachers started communicating students' progress recurrently to their parents either through class reports or in meetings. An enhanced impetus of fostering parent–school ties was laid for improving students' outcomes.

Fourth, she installed mechanisms for continuous professional development of her teachers. Teachers attending professional development programs were made to present the key ideas to their colleagues in the staff meetings to carry them forward. This created a ripple effect fostering professional development of many teachers simultaneously.

17.7.2 Focus on Collective Learning

With the inception of CCE, school leadership laid a strong emphasis on collective learning of all professionals for assimilation of reform practices to attain improved students' learning and outcomes. This was achieved through invigorating "communities of practice" (Lave and Wenger 1991) to engage teachers in reflective dialogue regarding the *modus operandi* of change.

The process began by systematically creating avenues for collaboration among the staff. First, it entailed changes in teachers' and school's timetable. To begin with, school day for teachers was furthered by fifteen minutes to provide time for collaboration on academic issues. Teachers valued these sessions for planning and discussing about their practice and the reform program. One teacher spoke:

> In the initial meetings, I found it difficult to open up, I had this fear of being mocked at by others but now things have changed. Even though I am not certain but maybe it is the

frequency of meetings.....recurrent meetings in which people discuss ideas- from their experiences, research, documents- may have helped. I somehow feel safe. It's like... hmnn...ideas are being discussed and not people... (Seema, Greenjingle School 2012).

Maybe I will bring a unit to show others in my group what I did. They are going to look at it critically and maybe praise it or tell me how to polish it. The focus of the group is on kids' work so we can improve our teaching for the kids (Radha, Greenjingle School 2011).

Their views alluded to the founding of mutual respect, integrity and a relational trust among the community members. All the more, during observations it was found that communication in PLCs was geared by dialogic exchange of ideas where criticisms were being taken up constructively by the participants, thus, preventing the emergence of micro-politics fatal to the growth of PLCs.

Apart from this, systemic planning for collaboration occurred for the entire academic session. Teachers were encouraged to deliberate on issues through online Google groups, teleconferencing and were called periodically during vacations. Focus of the meeting was clearly chalked out and communicated to all the participants beforehand and they were encouraged to be "ready" with issues and concerns to be discussed.

It is clear from the interview data that PLCs encouraged collegiality on academic issues, lead to mutual interdependence for the common collective growth of the initiative.

Second, school worked to create "spaces" for informal collaboration among the staff. It entailed provision of workspaces having computer and Internet facility, a mini resource center and certain basic facilities of tea and coffee being made available to the teachers. Such spaces provided easier zones for engaging in professional exchanges rather than going to staffrooms located far away from classrooms which were likely to inhibit school-wide collegiality.

17.7.3 Focus on Classroom Practices

Formative assessment was understood as a "part of everyday practice by students, teachers and peers that seeks, reflects upon and responds to information from dialogue, demonstration and observation in ways that enhance learning" (AfL 2009). Principal, Meena, observed that for assessment reform initiative to be successful, it is essential to embed the changes in classroom practices. She along with school's cultural and academic heads enacted a system of classroom observation of teachers engaged in the reform process. This involved classroom observations being carried out by peers, academic and cultural heads, discipline-based Heads of the Department and the Principal periodically. Several teachers in the beginning considered it to be a "risky" stuff. Teachers remarked:

What do you mean you want to observe me teaching? ......Do they think over all the years I have not learnt how to teach them well.....? (Radha, Greenjingleschool 2011).

> I feel I am back to teacher education program where a supervisor is going to mark me …. it's threatening as I may get dropped down next year……. (Seema, Greenjingle school 2011).

Leadership listened to all these arguments and incisively worked to clear the air of skepticism hovering around the classroom observations. Principal while reminiscing about her initial sessions with resistant teachers noted,

> A great deal of time was initially spent in discussions with them. I used to address many of their concerns regarding the program and encouraged them to talk to teachers at other schools that had similar reform programs… (Meena, Greenjingle school 2011).

She further recollected,

> ……a lot of emotions were attached to it…..they began to look at me with skeptical eyes. But I was sure that formative assessment initiative requires changes at the classroom level and nothing but careful examination of pedagogic practices is essential….so I began to attend PLCs where they could interact with me continually, seek suggestions…….and I was always amenable to change if they could give me a valid argument (Meena, Greenjingleschool 2011).

School principal's participation on an equal pedestal in PLCs released the tension regarding classroom observations. PLCs generated norms for classroom observation which reflected a clear focus on unpicking the nuances associated with applicability of assessment reform, provision of constructive and qualitative feedback with clear suggestions on how the practice can be improved.

Gradually, teachers started taking classroom observations positively. One teacher remarked:

> I have learned to take her (referring to the Principal) criticisms as something supportive. She genuinely wants to help us improve our assessment practices and she is just as quick to praise as to give a suggestion for improvement (Neeta, Greenjingleschool 2011).

These practices seeded the reform at classroom level targeting the teaching–learning process directly.

17.8 Concluding Remarks: Implications for Practice

The scale of the challenge in establishing "learning-enriched" (Rosenholtz 1989) professional learning communities cannot be underestimated. Establishing PLCs is one of the ways to capture the "big picture" (Cizek 1995) of assessment reform, thus, situating the reform spirit in the school.

This study suggests that school-based PLCs can be successfully established by the means of:

- Proactive school leadership open to innovation and amenable to change;
- Provision of constant academic support through continuous professional development opportunities;

- Charting avenues of collaboration through changes in teachers' timetable and decrease in workload which can foster attention on academic issues;
- Creation of an enabling environment for mutual exchanges on academic issues by making arrangements for necessary infrastructure, such as, work stations having the basic computer and Internet facilities;
- Systematically planning the PLC meetings having clear agenda communicated to all the stakeholders beforehand;
- Providing flexibility and autonomy to teachers to adapt their practices according to their group of learners;
- Finding mechanisms for classroom observations and provision of constructive feedback to improve the classroom practices;
- Keeping the focus straight on academic issues and not on people preventing the emergence of micro-politics in PLCs.

PLCs create a cultural system which supports change both at conceptual, procedural, and policy level. PLCs empower teachers to become "assessment leaders" by:

- Providing exposure to innovative ideas, tools, and mechanisms required to incorporate the necessary changes at the classroom level;
- Building a strong collegial support among teachers;
- Creating strong relational ties between the teachers and school's administration;
- Encouraging classroom observations among the teachers with focus on provision of ways to improve the classroom practice.

School-based PLCs, thus, empower teachers to carry forward the reform intelligently supported with a deep conviction of its benefits to the student community. The ways of creating PLCs expounded in this study can serve as a springboard for global practitioners to forge newer and productive links between school's administration, teaching faculty, students, and parents for successful implementation of assessment reform.

The research reported in this paper, however, falls short in suggesting the ways in which school-based PLCs can be created across grades, schools, and between teachers teaching different subjects. Further, how the concept of school-based PLCs can be scaled up to the entire district or to the country is yet to be explored.

References

AfL. (2009). Position paper on assessment for learning. *Third international conference on assessment for learning*. Retrieved December 21, 2010 from http://www.fairtest.org/position-paper-assessment-learning

Birenbaum, M., Kimron, H., Shilton, H., & Shahaf- Brazilay, R. (2009). Cycles of inquiry: Formative assessment in service of learning in classrooms and in school-based professional learning communities. *Studies in Educational Evaluation, 35*, 130–149.

Birenbaum, M., Kimron, H., & Shilton, H. (2011). Nested contexts that shape assessment for learning: School-based professional learning community and classroom culture. *Studies in Educational Evaluation, 37*, 35–48.

Central Board of Secondary Education (CBSE). (2014). *CBSE CCE Report*. India: New-Delhi.
Cizek, G. J. (1995). The big picture in assessment and who ought to have It. *Phi Delta Kappa International, 77*(3), 246–249.
Cohen, L., Manion, L., & Morrison, K. (2011). *Research methods in education* (7th ed.). London: Routledge.
Cuban, L. (1998). How schools change reforms: Redefining reform success and failure. *Teachers College Record, 99*(3), 453–477.
Dewey, J. (1929). *The sources of a science of education*. New York: Horace Liveright.
DuFour, R., & Eaker, R. (2002). *Professional learning communities at work: Best practices for enhancing student achievement*. Bloomington, IN: National Educational Service.
Fernandez, C. (2002). Learning from Japanese approaches to professional development: The case of lesson study. *Journal of Teacher Education, 53*, 393–405.
Government of India (GOI). (1953). *Report of the secondary education commission: Mudaliar commission report*. India: Ministry of Education.
GOI. (1970). *CABE Committee on examination reforms*. Retrieved from http://www.teindia.nic.in/mhrd/50yrsedu/g/T/V/0T0V0E03.htm
GOI. (1986). *National policy on education*. Ministry of Human Resource Development. Department of Education: India. Retrieved from http://mhrd.gov.in/sites/upload_files/mhrd/files/NPE86-mod92.pdf
GOI. (1993). *Learning without burden*. India: Ministry of Human Resource Development. Department of Education.
Heritage, M. (2010). *Formative assessment: Making it happen in the classroom*. California, USA: Corwin.
Holliday, A. (2007). *Doing and writing qualitative research*. London, Thousand Oaks, New Delhi: Sage Publications.
James, M., & Lewis, J. (2012). Assessment in harmony with our understanding of learning: Problems and possibilities. In J. Gardner (Ed.) (2nd ed.), *Assessment and Learning* (206–229). London: Sage Publictions.
Lave, J., & Wenger, E. (1991). *Situated learning: Legitimate peripheral participation*. Cambridge: Cambridge University Press.
McLaughlin, M. W., & Talbert, J. E. (2006). *Building school-based teacher learning communities: Professional strategies to improve student achievement*. New York: Teachers College.
National Concil of Educational Research and Training (NCERT). (2005). *National curriculum framework*. India: New Delhi.
Nawani, D. (2015). Rethinking assessment in schools. *Economic and Political Weekly, L, 3*, 37–42.
Perrenoud, P. (1998). From formative evaluation to a controlled regulation of learning processes: Towards a wider conceptual field. *Assessment in Education, 5*(1), 85–102.
Priestley, M., & Sime, D. (2005). Formative assessment for all: A whole-school approach to pedagogic change. *The Curriculum Journal, 16*(4), 475–492.
Rosenholtz, S. J. (1989). *Teachers' workplace: The social organization of schools*. New York: Longman.
Shephard, L. (2000). The role of assessment in a learning culture. *Educational Researcher, 29*(7), 4–14.
Stenhouse, L. (1975). *An introduction to curriculum research and development*. London: Heinemann.
Stoll, L., Bolam, R., McMahon, A., Wallace, M., & Thomas, S. (2006). Professional learning communities: A review of the literature. *Journal of Educational Change, 7*, 221–258.
Vygotsky, L. (1978). *Mind in society*. Cambridge, MA: Harvard University Press.
Wenger, E. (2000). Communities of practice and social learning systems. *Organization, 7*(2), 225–246.

Wenger, E., McDermott, R., & Snyder, W. (2002). *Cultivating communities of practice*. USA: Harvard Business School Press.
Wiliam, D., & Thompson, M. (2007). Integrating assessment with instruction: What will it take to make it work? In C. A. Dwyer (Ed.), *The Future of Assessment: Shaping Teaching and Learning* (pp. 53–82). Mahwah: Lawrence Erlbaum Associates.

Chapter 18
Professional Learning Communities in a Web 2.0 World: Rethinking the Conditions for Professional Development

Yvonne Liljekvist, Jorryt van Bommel and Christina Olin-Scheller

Abstract The new technologies, in particular social media in Web 2.0, enable rapid change in people's behaviour, which needs to be considered in research on teacher empowerment and teacher professional development and growth. In this chapter we discuss how teachers in an informal, yet structured, way use social media to expand their professional learning communities beyond the local school context in Sweden. This is an example of how a new behaviour is emerging among teachers that changes the opportunities and the frames for professional development and growth. Through teachers' engagement in social media, such as Facebook, extended professional learning communities arise and teachers' professional development and growth become evident. Global levels influence local levels: teachers from different schools engage in structured discussions related to everyday practice, such as issues of learning goals in pre-school or topics related to a specific course in upper secondary school. The teachers' arena for professional development and growth has changed, which means that the context of teacher empowerment is rapidly changing too. Consequently, the chapter includes theoretical reflections on professional learning communities in a Web 2.0 world and how this phenomenon may affect our approach to enhancing teachers' professional development.

Y. Liljekvist (✉)
Department of Education, Uppsala University, Uppsala, Sweden
e-mail: yvonne.liljekvist@edu.uu.se

J. van Bommel
Department of Mathematics and Computer Science, Karlstad University, Karlstad, Sweden

C. Olin-Scheller
Department of Educational Studies, Karlstad University, Karlstad, Sweden

18.1 Introduction

In a review of research on teachers learning from teachers, White et al. (2013) have found that there is a complexity of settings in which teachers learn. The complexity is "influenced by both global and local forces, such as the recent pressure on teachers to meet different demands imposed on them [...] directly by politicians and national laws" (p. 421). The institutional context and the teachers themselves as learners are interdependent.

Moreover, the current evolution of social media and social network sites transforms the day-to-day practice, the lived experience, and with whom we share the experience. There are no distinct borders between "the life on social media" and "the real life" (Ellison and Boyd [sic] 2013). In recent years teachers have started to use different online forums, such as web sites, personal blogs, Twitter or Facebook, as resources in terms of networking, sharing knowledge, giving and taking advice, sharing and discussing curricular material, etc. (e.g. Bissessar 2014; Hew and Hara 2007; Manca and Ranieri 2014; Liljekvist 2016; Rutherford 2010; Ruthven 2016; van Bommel and Liljekvist 2015). The teachers' arena for professional development and growth has changed, and hence the context of teacher empowerment is rapidly changing too. Teachers initiate activities on social network sites, or activities can be initiated within formal professional development. This is an example of how teachers' practice changes and develops, thereby affecting conditions and professional development opportunities.

The development of professional learning communities (PLC) seems to have a positive impact on school improvement. Vescio et al. (2008) have described the following five essential characteristics of a PLC: in a PLC, teachers (1) share values; (2) develop norms; (3) have a focus on students' learning; (4) discuss curriculum, instruction and student development in an ongoing dialogic process; (5) focus on cooperation in such a way that teaching practice is de-privatised and knowledge is shared.

In this chapter we examine the theory-building potential when rethinking the new conditions for professional development in order to understand how PLCs work in a Web 2.0 world. We argue that teachers' online communication, as one part of their everyday practice in the local school, can be looked upon as a new extended learning community that challenges and advances teachers' practice. This means that teachers (regardless of whether or not they have the opportunity to work in a local PLC at their school) may combine their professional knowledge, based on local practice and the curriculum, with knowledge acquired and developed at a global level, that is, with colleagues on social media and social network sites. In this chapter we show how teacher movement into social media is connected with professional development at a local level. We start by outlining the everyday practice of teachers in an age where the use of Web 2.0 tools is a common occurrence. We describe the role social media and social network sites play in teachers' day-to-day experiences, and provide insight into Swedish teachers' day-to-day practice. The Swedish example lays the ground for a discussion regarding the theoretical assumptions and opportunities of PLCs, as well as the methodological issues regarding research within PLCs that includes teachers' knowledge-building on social media and social network sites.

18.2 Day-to-Day Experiences of Today's Teachers

The epistemological assumptions in learning communities are that knowledge is situated in day-to-day lived experiences, and that a professional [teacher] best understands his or her everyday practice through critical reflection with others who share the same experience (Buysse et al. 2003). Avalos (2011) has explained that this is a consequence of the situated nature of teachers' professional development: teachers' professional learning and growth are embedded in the school environment and its culture. It is also, she continues, intimately related to how the present educational system and policies affect teachers' work life. However, teachers' day-to-day experiences are changing.

Facebook, as one type of social network site, offers opportunities to comment and to share, like Twitter and other websites, but it also provides opportunities for the "members" to ask questions and to get responses from others. Thus, the teachers themselves can activate pedagogical discussions of teaching and learning. This differs from how more monologic Internet resources work, such as blogs or websites (cf. Liljekvist 2016; Ruthven 2016). Rutherford (2010) concluded that a social network site "provides teachers with an opportunity to engage in informal professional development that is participant driven, practical, collaborative" (p. 60). This opportunity changes the way day-to-day experience of teachers is shared and discussed, as excerpts in the next section will show. These discussions are separate from the local, surface-level, work-related issues, and hence give opportunity to focus the conversation on an issue and critically discuss pedagogical subject matter. Admittedly, the quality of the knowledge-sharing on social media varies, but our point is that the activities on social media constitute a new and vibrant dimension in teachers' day-to-day lived experiences (cf., Bissessar 2014; Borba and Gadanidis 2008; Ellison and Boyd 2013).

Nevertheless, the opportunity for teachers to extend their lived experience to a social network site is, of course, not enough to develop a sustainable PLC. It takes reflection and mentoring, as well as shared norms, focus on students' learning, and de-privatised practice as shared knowledge (Avalos 2011; Buysse et al. 2003; Stoll et al. 2006; Vescio et al. 2008). In the following section we present some empirical findings from our ongoing studies to outline how PLCs seem to operate in the social media context. The purpose of these excerpts from the Swedish context is to illustrate the need to develop theory, rather than to make empirical claims per se.

18.3 The Swedish Example

Social network sites are widely used in Sweden. For example, 50% of the inhabitants actively use Facebook every day (Findahl and Davidsson 2015), and many teachers create and become members of specialised Facebook groups. The group members are spread throughout Sweden and unified by being practicing teachers. Social network sites can thus be viewed as emerging communities of practice (Goodyear et al. 2014).

Narrow thematic themes can have relatively few members, such as "Mathematics for course 2b in upper secondary school" with about 200 members. Not surprisingly, more generic themes appeal to more teachers. Hence the group "Mathematics for lower primary school" has 12,000 members and the group "Reading with older students" has 2500 members. Generic themes that are of interest to all Swedish teachers can attract groups of up to 35,000 members (In all, there are approximately 130,000 teachers in compulsory school and upper secondary school in Sweden).

However, the question is whether or not this social network phenomenon is likely to function as extended professional learning communities (ePLC). In terms of our findings, we can see examples of shared day-to-day practice in the social network sites where situated knowledge is established and reflected upon. In the excerpt below from a focus group interview, we can note such PLC characteristics as well as the limits of social media regarding PLC features.

Teacher 1   Facebook is my colleague, sort of. When I prepare my lessons […] that is, when I'm at home [laughs] I frequently use my Facebook group to discuss [pedagogical] things to make my instructions better and so on.
Teacher 2   Yes, for me it is valuable since the working days are so intense […] it is in the evening I have time to think
[…]
and to discuss […] things […] or kinds of problem […] I mean teaching dilemmas […] of course not some students' [social] behaviour.

Both teachers express that Facebook gives them the opportunity to reflect, at home (teacher 1) and in the evening (teacher 2). Teacher 1 claims to use Facebook to establish situated knowledge—making instructions better. The same teacher also states that students' social behaviour is something that is not discussed in the Facebook groups. This implies that the teachers in the Facebook group act as in a local PLC, but, evidently, without the shared responsibility for one specific student group.

The members of the different Facebook groups have chosen a specific domain in which to engage, for instance, teaching mathematics or Swedish. The community in a Facebook group is solely determined by the engagement of its members, who are all registered as practitioners. Any member can initiate a discussion by posting a "status"; others can continue and reply with a "comment". Shared values and norms develop in the group.

Status 1	I would like to know your thoughts on how to plan lessons on how to tell the time in grades 1–3. Thanks!
Two of the comments in the succeeding thread	(A) Start indicating the weekly schedule times on the board with small clock faces so the clock becomes an everyday experience. Tell the students to wear a wristwatch and use it daily. Let the students work two-by-two with different teaching materials. (B) As there is only one goal which addresses weight, length, time and volume, I use about 2 lessons in the course of two weeks each term. Maybe some homework also. Then you can always challenge (the students) to practice it, for instance, through games, apps and so on during the term. I also think it is more interesting [for the students] to work with this topic when they are a bit older, 7–8 years, because their parents expect them to be on time more.

These teachers give advice to the question posted in status 1, based on their own experience. They do not merely answer the question described in the status, but also put the question in relation to the syllabus as a whole.

There are also members (C) in the group who read the thread without actually taking part in the discussion:

Comment	(C) Thanks for wise thoughts and advice! Good idea showing the big clock in the morning. A new task for the classroom host tomorrow ☺.

Borko (2004) has claimed that critical discussion on teaching does not come about by itself, and that teachers need to "collectively explore ways of improving their teaching and supporting one another" (p. 7) in order to develop their teaching. This is shown in the communication between teachers A and B, and the teacher posting status 1. Another kind of in-depth discussion evolves from status 2 below, leading to a discussion on national test results compared to student grades.

Status 2	What is your opinion on the difference between the results in the national tests and students' grades? It seems (nationally) that results on the national tests are lower than the individual grades on tests throughout the year …

It is also clear, as van Bommel (2014) has shown, that teachers need substantial pedagogical content knowledge in order to be able to communicate the planning of lessons, the use of textbooks, etc. Status 3 below illustrates the need for such knowledge. When a teacher asks for (and further evaluates and discusses) a digital tool fulfilling specific subject-matter requirements, substantial pedagogical content knowledge is needed.

Status 3   I need some help with an app or a programme for "Smartboard" (interactive board), which can demonstrate an exercise like:
$7 + 5 = 10 + 2 = 12$
I want to be able to change and be able to show 'filling up the tens'.

In the social network sites, we can see how teacher practice becomes quite de-privatised, and, hence, shared knowledge can develop. The focus in the communication is fairly often on student learning, and different types of media are used. In status 4 below, a teacher shares a film on classwork outdoors in geometry, showing how the lesson was orchestrated and the learning outcome to be assessed.

Status 4   I want to share with you a film of our work outdoors today in geometry, for age 7. Circles, squares and triangles (then a link to a film showing parts of the outdoor lesson, and the outcome of the students' work).

In the Swedish example we have now seen how teachers discuss, for instance, curriculum, instruction and student development, an activity that is one of the five essential characteristics of a PLC (Vescio et al. 2008). The teachers' everyday experience also takes place in social media, which means that the practice becomes de-privatised and shared knowledge seems to develop. How can we understand the interdependence between teachers' professional development in their school context and the phenomenon of digitally ePLC?

We know that PLCs are mainly constructs to describe important features in the processes of professional development to promote student learning in the local school (cf. Horn and Little 2010). However, our point is that social media change the frames of communicative behaviour. Social network sites and social media are vibrant parts of the everyday lived experience of teachers and nowadays they have a more or less global colloquium in addition to fellow teachers in the local school or school district. Further, our results indicate that teachers communicate on social network sites as if they address their status updates and comments to "some colleagues". It does not appear to be a deliberate communication with all (thousands) the individual members.

We argue that this extended professional context may have implications for research conducted with PLCs as a theoretical stance. It is an example of an emerging teacher behaviour that changes the opportunities and the frames of professional development and growth. In the following sections we outline some implications regarding inquiries into PLCs and social media in the form of theoretical and methodological reflections.

18.4   PLCs and Social Network Sites: Some Theoretical Reflections

In a PLC, teachers share values and develop norms and they have a focus on student learning. As mentioned, the dialogue in a PLC is an ongoing process where teachers discuss the curriculum, instruction and student development. Further, the focus on collaboration leads to a de-privatised practice, and the teaching hence becomes shared knowledge (cf. Avalos 2011; Stoll et al. 2006; Vescio et al. 2008).

In a social network site, the de-privatising practice takes form in several ways. Some teachers post pictures or documents of material they have created and examples of student efforts, but short descriptions of the work situation can also be found. As other teachers do not know the specifics of the classroom or school concerned in the posted status, some background is given. However, since it is possible to give a much more colourful description of the background, the absence of more detail implies that there are values, norms and practices that are considered to be shared knowledge, thus indicating a developing ePLC practice.

Findings from various educational settings reveal how social network sites used as professional resources are not an isolated phenomenon and that the impact they have on professional development varies (see, e.g. Bissessar 2014; Liljekvist 2016; Manca and Ranieri 2014; Rutherford 2010; Ruthven 2016). Communication in social network sites makes the ongoing dialogue asynchronous; that is, a status posted on one day may yield replies several days (or weeks) later. This aspect may contribute to the focused dialogues regarding, for instance, curriculum, instruction and student development on social network sites. New ideas or questions not directly related are posted as a new status and therefore do not interfere with the actual discussion thread of each status. The communication hence supports the development of shared pedagogical subject knowledge on more than a surface level. Individual members can, of course, go into a synchronous session such as a chat or video conference outside the group, but this lies beyond the scope of the studies underpinning the theoretical discussion in this chapter.

If we consider the term "professional" in PLC, we know that it is not merely a question of teachers' knowledge-sharing, but a matter of the foundation of the local school culture that expects collaboration and involves an ongoing inquiry into the practice of improving student outcomes (Stoll et al. 2006). The assumption is that what teachers do together in out-of-class meetings is important and affects their professional development as well as student learning (Leder 2008; Stoll et al. 2006). If, then, the lived experience of teachers is branching out to social network sites, this should affect the notion of "togetherness" and "out-of-class meetings".

There are, however, key characteristics (cf. Stoll et al. 2006) that are not possible to develop in a social network site more or less "open to all": first, as there is no "local school" within the Facebook groups, there is no collective responsibility for student learning in the respective local school, and, second, the communication in the Facebook groups is not a form of in-school collaboration. Kling and Courtright (2003) have pointed to the fact that groups on social media have a different role from the local group of people working together. For instance, colleagues on Facebook could be reached regardless of time and place. They put forward the role of social network sites and social media as enhancing, extending and supporting wider group processes and objectives.

Nevertheless, our results show that a local PLC in Sweden is very likely to be influenced by the teachers' professional communication on social network sites, and hence, a need for theoretical development of a digitally extended professional learning community (ePLC) arises. The teachers' empowerment and opportunities to develop shared knowledge and a sustainable, reflective, professional inquiry at the local school level may thus be enhanced—partly because of the professional communication on social network sites. Research on professional learning also stands to benefit generally from the recent opportunity to study digital communication (see, e.g. Bissessar 2014; Borba and Gadanidis 2008; Dalgarno and Colgan 2007; Goodyear et al. 2014; Hew and Hara 2007).

18.5 Opportunities When Studying Teachers' Professional Learning in an Online Context

It is well known that a key factor in the progress of educational reform is teachers' capacity on both the individual and collective level, and how strongly it is linked to the "school-wide capacity" for promoting learning (Horn and Little 2010; Stoll et al. 2006). Capacity can be seen as a combination of skills, motivation and positive learning, in addition to organisational, infrastructural and supportive structures that can promote sustainable learning over time for all levels in the school system (Avalos 2011; Stoll et al. 2006). Thus, even if practicing teachers need to change their teaching because of external reforms, it can be difficult to integrate reform practices due to institutional and social expectations.

When it comes to supportive structures, it is not merely a question of digital resources. White et al. (2013) have shown that the relationships between the support given (e.g. by experienced teachers) and the supportee (e.g. the individual teacher, a group of teachers) can be of different kinds, such as teacher educators as guides, teachers and researchers working together, or teachers working together to design their own developmental activities. White and colleagues have pointed out the similarities and differences between the knowledge that teachers and teacher educators/researchers, respectively, bring to the learning interface. They stated: "neither group had all the knowledge that was needed for the development of teaching, but working together they could become a unified, powerful developmental force" (p. 422). This is also in line with studies emerging from in-service training of language teachers in Sweden (Sundqvist and Olin-Scheller 2013) as well as the review of teacher education by Leder (2008), where she has put forward the core factors of "community building" and "networking" as means for in-service teachers' out-of-class meetings.

Teachers' empowerment is an important aspect when the learning arena is extended to social media. White et al. (2013) have stressed that teachers' knowledge is pre-eminent in in-school situations, and researchers and teacher educators have "much to learn about issues that influence what can happen in schools, and what is needed to put research-based knowledge into practice" (p. 422). As social network sites can be seen as out-of-class meetings, they afford researchers the opportunity to conduct systematic studies of important factors and issues.

It is a matter of studying "the learning of practicing teachers: how they learn, what they bring to their learning efforts and how these efforts are reflected in changes in cognition, beliefs, and practices" (Avalos 2011, p. 4).

Webster-Wright (2009) has stated in her review of research informing professional development practice that it is necessary for us to learn from teachers' authentic learning situations: "To gain further insights to enhance support for professionals as they learn, there is a need to understand more about how professionals continue learning through their working lives" (p.704). She has called for research aimed at understanding more about the experience of professional learning in order to support it more effectively, rather than merely developing professional development programmes. Studying how teachers use social media and social network sites will yield empirical findings to problematise, thus enabling researchers to move beyond the idea that formal and informal learning are different types of learning (e.g. Borba and Gadanidis 2008; Dalgarno and Colgan 2007). In this respect, such studies can identify and theoretically develop some aspects of professional development, teachers' empowerment, and how to understand professional learning in a multitude of communities.

18.6 Methodological Implications

Conducting research on the Internet is challenging because of "Internet time" (Karpf 2012); that is, the rapidly changing context and content, and the code-based modifications: "Standard practices within the social sciences are not well suited to such a rapidly changing medium. Traditionally, major research endeavours move at a glacial pace" (p. 640). Karpf has concluded that it is important to take "Internet time" seriously when designing studies and he has thus recommended a question-driven methodological pluralism.

In studies on social media and social network sites, we need to analyse specific activities on the site, for example, asynchronous or synchronous communication, the different representations and the digital resources used. Ellison and Boyd (2013) have pinpointed the need to contextualise the activity-centric analyses because the way members position themselves within the social network site shapes their experience of it (e.g. due to innovations and technical changes implemented). Hence, a mixed method approach may be the natural choice.

Moreover, the ethical considerations are perhaps far more delicate when making inquiries into social network sites. What kind of data are we dealing with? Can the communication displayed be considered public record like debates in newspapers, or is it a private conversation? On the one hand, everything is most certainly already on record at the companies supplying the technical solutions, but, on the other, people using social media and social networking sites may well think of it as a personal and private sphere. When the studied groups are large, it is more likely that the members regard the communication as public, and hence the topic discussed may not be delicate, for example, psychological health or socio-economic personal issues (Ellison and Boyd 2013; Robert 2015). However, the members of different social network groups have chosen a specific domain in which to engage and the theme in the group may well have a focus on delicate issues (cf. Roberts 2015). In education research this may be slightly less of a problem. However, the research community needs to take these questions very seriously. This is not only a question of the respondents' feelings and stances, or personal situation, it is also a matter of how the intervention (i.e. to explore the group activity) per se disturbs the communication pattern, the trust and the evolving norms, the participation pattern, and so on, in the group studied (Ellison and Boyd 2013; van Bommel and Liljekvist 2015). It is a matter of maintaining public trust in researchers as well as the possibility to conduct research in online environments in the future.

18.7 Conclusion

The teachers' arena for professional development and growth has changed in communities where Web 2.0 tools are commonly used. Social media and social networks are used for teachers' learning and knowledge-sharing, both in formal professional development programmes (e.g. Dalgarno and Colgan 2007) and in informal settings created by teachers themselves (e.g. Bissessar 2014; van Bommel and Liljekvist 2015). Hence, the frames of teacher empowerment are rapidly changing too since social media and social network sites support and enhance teachers' professional development.

In this chapter we argue for the need to rethink and develop theories that take the conditions for professional learning into account if we are to understand PLCs in a Web 2.0 world better. In other words, knowledge of how informal professional development in social media and social network occurs and develops may change researchers' and stakeholders' approach to how teachers' professional development is best served.

The literature shows fairly consistent views of the conditions under which an efficient (local school) PLC operates and the kind of activities and pedagogical considerations that a PLC should involve and aim for. On the one hand, collaboration in a PLC has to be close to the day-to-day practice, but on the other, social media and social network sites change the way teachers work together, and with whom and when they have in-depth pedagogical discussions. Teachers' professional discussions in social network sites tend to be related to reviewing lessons, teaching problems and pedagogical subject matter, and tend to generate new ideas for practice collectively. Hence, the teacher behaviour that is important for a PLC to emerge is already evident outside Web 2.0 in local school contexts, and thus this enables a digitally extended professional learning community (ePLC) to develop.

Acknowledgements The research was funded by the Swedish Research Council (Dnr. 2015-01979).

References

Avalos, B. (2011). Teacher professional development in teaching and teacher education over ten years. *Teaching and Teacher Education, 27*(1), 10–20. doi:10.1016/j.tate.2010.08.007

Bissessar, C. S. (2014). Facebook as an informal teacher professional development tool. *Australian Journal of Teacher Education, 39*(2), 121–135. doi:10.14221/ajte.2014v39n2.9

Borba, M. C., & Gadanidis, G. (2008). Virtual communities and networks of practicing mathematics teachers: The role of technology in collaboration. In K. Krainer & T. Wood (Eds.), *The international handbook of mathematics teacher education: Participants in mathematics teacher education* (Vol. 3, pp. 181–209). Rotterdam, The Netherlands: Sense Publishers.

Borko, H. (2004). Professional development and teacher learning: Mapping the terrain. *Educational Researcher, 33*(8), 3–15. doi:10.3102/0013189X033008003

Buysse, V., Sparkman, K. L., & Wesley, P. W. (2003). Communities of practice: Connecting what we know with what we do. *Exceptional Children, 69*(3), 263–277. doi:10.1177/001440290306900301

Dalgarno, N., & Colgan, L. (2007). Supporting novice elementary mathematics teachers' induction in professional communities and providing innovative forms of pedagogical content knowledge development through information and communication technology. *Teaching and Teacher Education, 23*(7), 1051–1065. doi:10.1016/j.tate.2006.04.037

Ellison, N. B., & Boyd, D. (2013). Sociality through social network sites. In W. H. Dutton (Ed.), *The Oxford handbook of Internet studies* (pp. 151–172). Oxford, England: Oxford University Press.

Findahl, O., & Davidsson, P. (2015). Svenskarna och internet. *The Swedes and the Internet*. https://www.iis.se/docs/Svenskarna_och_internet_2015.pdf

Goodyear, V. A., Casey, A., & Kirk, D. (2014). Tweet me, message me, like me: Using social media to facilitate pedagogical change within an emerging community of practice. *Sport, Education and Society, 19*(7), 927–943. doi:10.1080/13573322.2013.858624

Hew, K. F., & Hara, N. (2007). Knowledge sharing in online environments: A qualitative case study. *Journal of the American Society for Information Science and Technology, 58*(14), 2310–2324. doi:10.1002/asi.20698

Horn, I. S., & Little, J. W. (2010). Attending to problems of practice: Routines and resources for professional learning in teachers' workplace interactions. *American Educational Research Journal, 47*(1), 181–217. doi:10.3102/0002831209345158

Karpf, D. (2012). Social science research methods in Internet time. *Information, Communication & Society, 15*(5), 639–661. doi:10.1080/1369118X.2012.665468

Kling, R., & Courtright, C. (2003). Group behavior and learning in electronic forums: A sociotechnical approach. *The Information Society, 19*(3), 221–235. doi:10.1080/01972240309465

Leder, G. C. (2008). Pathways in mathematics: Individual teacher and beyond. In K. Krainer & T. Wood (Eds.), *The international handbook of mathematics teacher education: Participants in mathematics teacher education* (Vol. 3, pp. 309–330). Rotterdam, The Netherlands: Sense Publisher.

Liljekvist, Y. (2016). Mathematics teachers' knowledge-sharing on the Internet: Pedagogical message in instruction materials. *Nordic Studies in Mathematics Education, 21*(3), 3–27.

Manca, S., & Ranieri, M. (2014). Teachers' professional development in online social networking sites. In J. Viteli & M. Leikomaa (Eds.), *Proceedings of EdMedia: World Conference on Educational Media and Technology 2014* (pp. 2229–2234). Association for the Advancement of Computing in Education (AACE).

Roberts, L. D. (2015). Ethical issues in conducting qualitative research in online communities. *Qualitative Research in Psychology, 12*(3), 314–325. doi:10.1080/14780887.2015.1008909

Rutherford, C. (2010). Facebook as a source of informal teacher professional development. *Education, 16*(1), 60–74. doi:10.14221/ajte.2014v39n2.9

Ruthven, K. (2016). The re-sourcing movement in mathematics teaching: Some European initiatives. In M. Bates & Z. Usiskin (Eds.), *Digital curricula in school mathematics* (pp. 75–86). Charlotte, NC: Information Age Publishing.

Stoll, L., Bolam, R., McMahon, A., Wallace, M., & Thomas, S. (2006). Professional learning communities: A review of the literature. *Journal of Educational Change, 7*(4), 221–258. doi:10.1007/s10833-006-0001-8

Sundqvist, P., & Olin-Scheller, C. (2013). Classroom vs. extramural English: Teachers dealing with demotivation. *Language and Linguistics Compass, 7*(6), 329–338. doi:10.1111/lnc3.12031

van Bommel, J. (2014). The teaching of mathematical knowledge for teaching: A learning study of primary school teacher education. *Nordic Studies in Mathematics Education, 19*(3), 185–201.

van Bommel, J., & Liljekvist, Y. (2015, February). Facebook and mathematics teachers' professional development: Informing our community. In K. Krainer & N. Vondrová (Eds.), *Proceedings of the Ninth Congress of the European Society for Research in Mathematics Education* (pp. 2930–2936), Prague: Czech Republic. https://hal.archives-ouvertes.fr/hal-01289653

Vescio, V., Ross, D., & Adams, A. (2008). A review of research on the impact of professional learning communities on teaching practice and student learning. *Teaching and Teacher Education, 24*(1), 80–91. doi:10.1016/j.tate.2007.01.004

Webster-Wright, A. (2009). Reframing professional development through understanding authentic professional learning. *Review of Educational Research, 79*(2), 702–739. doi:10.3102/0034654308330970

White, A. L., Jaworski, B., Agudelo-Valderrama, C., & Gooya, Z. (2013). Teachers learning from teachers. In M. A. Clements, A. J. Bishop, C. Keitel, J. Kilpatrick, & F. K. S. Leung (Eds.), *Third international handbook of mathematics education* (Vol. 27, pp. 393–430). New York, NY: Springer.

Chapter 19
Emerging Technologies as Tools for Enhancing Mathematics Professional Learning Communities in Botswana

M.J. Motswiri, E. Zimudzi, K.G. Garegae and A.A. Nkhwalume

Abstract This chapter explains policy initiatives and the potential for the use of information and communication technologies (ICTs) in professional learning communities (PLCs) in in-service mathematics teacher education in Botswana. The Botswana context, and how ICTs could support teacher empowerment through PLCs, was explored. The key arguments are based on literature review and documentary analysis of relevant government policy documents pertaining to continuing professional development (CPD) and comparison with the global trends in PLCs. We found that the current top-down policy initiatives pose challenges in implementing and sustaining PLCs, and that there is need to involve the mathematics classroom practitioners. The study recommends the use of ICTs in PLCs to address teacher empowerment issues of access, autonomy, competency and learning standards for the country to remain competitive in the global economy. The availability of this information will assist in formulating policy on mathematics teacher empowerment, enhancing professional development and effective classroom practice.

19.1 Introduction

In an effort to remain competitive in the global economy, the Government of Botswana endeavours to reform its education system (Government of Botswana 2015). With sustained levels of economic growth over the years to move to an

M.J. Motswiri (✉) · E. Zimudzi · K.G. Garegae · A.A. Nkhwalume
Department of Mathematics and Science Education, University of Botswana, Gaborone, Botswana
e-mail: motswimj@mopipi.ub.bw

E. Zimudzi
e-mail: Zimudzi@mopipi.ub.bw

K.G. Garegae
e-mail: garegaek@mopipi.ub.bw

A.A. Nkhwalume
e-mail: nkhwalumeaa@mopipi.ub.bw

upper middle income country over a 40-year period, the education system is failing to equip students with skills to contribute productively to industry and to society (World Bank Group 2015; Government of Botswana 2015). Hence, the aim is to place great emphasis on the development of human resource for a knowledge-based and globally competitive economy. Through its Education and Training Sector Strategic Plan (ETSSP), it seeks to provide CPD for teachers, and mathematics as a subject is one of the priority areas (Government of Botswana 2015, p. 63). Among the critical concerns identified are lack of a comprehensive CPD system, weak CPD strategies, and generally lack of policy on CPD (Government of Botswana 2015, p. 77). PLCs are a promising way to achieve continuing teacher development, more so that the digital world brings with it platforms that encourage their implementation and growth.

The potential of ICTs in supporting CPDs for teachers is well-documented (Albion et al. 2015; Brooks and Gibson 2012; Farooq et al. 2007; Hairon and Dimmock 2012). The UNESCO (2002) report, for example, has stated that ICTs were becoming powerful tools to improve teacher training. Their introduction in mathematics began in school classrooms before encroaching into teacher training and development. Notwithstanding, the integration of ICT in teacher education institutions has become ubiquitous as shown by plethora of literature (Albion et al. 2015; Kler 2014). The structure of teacher development programmes needs to be aligned to the current situation. In the past, transmission models, such as the training model, the award-bearing model, deficit model and cascade model, were used to upgrade teachers' skills (Sywelem and Witte 2013). As years passed, transitional models, including standard-based model, coaching or mentoring model, and community of practice model were employed followed by transformative models where there was a paradigm shift from teacher control to teacher autonomy (Sywelem and Witte 2013; Kennedy 2005). Teacher autonomy models were found necessary as views on knowledge and knowing shifted from fixation or objectivity to be socially constructed hence the emergence of social constructivism. PLCs are based on the notion that teachers are transformative agents and thus should be allowed to continually develop, learn and test ideas in their practice through reflection and action research (Giroux 1995).

This chapter highlights the policy initiatives of PLCs in Botswana, its top-down influence and a set of practices. It considers the ideas and insights into pertinent literature and educational policy to better understand the pedagogies of ICTs as tools for CPD in mathematics. It raises arguments for the accelerated use of ICTs in the implementation of PLCs with mathematics teachers in Botswana. The chapter commences through a discussion of the country's ICT infrastructure, the PLCs in continuing teacher education as implemented in the Botswana context and internationally, and their potential as tools for enhancing CPD. The key question is how well the ideas and practices are associated with schools as PLCs are implemented in a top-down management system.

19.2 The Botswana Context

Botswana is a Southern African, sparsely populated country with a population of about 2 million people (2015). The education system comprises 7 years of primary school, 3 years of junior secondary and 2 years of senior secondary school. The government has invested heavily in education, building schools and providing the necessary infrastructure including ICTs.

The country compares favourably with the best on the African continent in terms of access and use of ICTs. With a network readiness index of 3.4/7 (refer to Table 19.1), knowledge intensive jobs at 17.9% and mobile network subscription/100 population at 160.6% (World Economic Forum 2015, p. 132), Botswana is poised for widespread adoption and use of ICTs in teaching. The Government of Botswana is committed to "position Botswana for sustained growth in the digital age by serving as a key catalyst in achieving social, economic, political and cultural transformation within the country" (Government of Botswana 2004, p. 3).

19.3 Professional Learning Communities (PLCs) in Botswana

A PLC is a group of people sharing and critically interrogating their practice in an ongoing, reflective, collaborative, inclusive, learning-oriented, growth-promoting way (Mitchell and Sackney 2000; Toole and Louis 2002). In schools, the community is formed by teachers coalescing into subject-based groups with the aim of bettering their practice by sharing knowledge and experiences. The purpose of learning communities is to facilitate opportunities for teachers to share stories of their challenges and successes (Wenger 2009). They act on feedback to develop insights into making their practice more effective and practical. The ideal operationalization of such being informed by a process aimed at engaging school teachers

Table 19.1 Summary, Botswana network readiness index (Global Information Technology Report 2014, 2015)

Indicator	2014	2015
Secondary school enrolment %	81.7	81.7
Adult literacy %	85.1	88.5
Mobile telephone subscriptions/100	153.8	160.6
Internet users %	11.5	15
Tertiary education enrolment %	7.4	7.4
Mobile network coverage %	–	96.0
Knowledge intensive jobs %	96.0	17.9
Households with internet %	9.1	10.6
Mobile broadband internet subscriptions %	74.9	74.1
Use of virtual social networks/7	5.4	5.4
Internet access in schools/7	3.5	3.5
Quality of maths/science education/7	3.4	3.6

and administrators to continuously seek and share learning, and act on their developed insights to improve students' learning outcomes (Astuto et al. 1993; Hord 1997).

However, the operations of such a community can be extended beyond the confines of an institution and bring together teachers in various schools. Where the learning community extends beyond the boundaries of individual school, a cluster of schools is established thus forming a critical mass of organisation of subject teachers.

A cluster system of In-Service Training for Secondary School Teachers for Science and Mathematics which is under the Department of Mathematics and Science Education (DMSE-INSET) at the University of Botswana was employed to support similar purposes, specifically as a follow-up strategy for enhancing chances of school and classroom implementation of workshop outcomes. At least three schools in close geographical proximity were considered to describe a collaborative critical mass for sharing experiences and reflective exercises. The minimum of three schools was forced by logical circumstances that included distance between the schools. Such a learning community would be expected to collaborate and reflect on their practice, develop insights into their practice and establish practical and effective practice in the context of the conditions of their geographical, economical and social cluster. Finally, the cluster would be expected to produce a detailed report of their meetings and share with the DMSE-INSET staff for further guidance and support. Such feedback was critical for future plans and action on teachers' professional development support. Invariably, various activities that the membership of a cluster undertook required technological facilitation that included communication, hosting and running of meetings. DMSE-INSET has designated functions to promote network professional development and school improvement activities across the schools.

The cluster was therefore used as a strategy for workshop training follow-up activities to bridge communication and isolation challenges that teachers find themselves in without the most needed peer support and/or that from workshop facilitators. The gap between training and implementation has often been seen as the weakness of in-service training and implementation of educational change, and ICTs could close this gap by enhancing communication across distances.

The current arrangement involves organising workshops to address selected issues with heads of departments from schools. The heads of departments would then workshop the teachers at their respective schools. It is a top-down management system whereby information is passed from the top to the lower echelons of the system. It is time-consuming and costly to run workshops in one place since this involves a movement of people, accommodation and feeding during the workshops. This traditional view that those who attend workshops increase their content and self-efficacy (Moodley 2015) works to the detriment of PLCs. Trust et al. (2016) suggest that the cultural activity be embedded in a specific social activity that form the backbone of society. This view is consistent with Wesely (2013) and Hou (2015) who see professional development as a continuous process. They argue that education reform is an ongoing process built around the personal growth of the teacher; that voluntary participation and empowerment are the key factors in the success of PLCs and that the teachers are more accessible online because of reduced spatial and temporal constraints.

The Government's strategy to endorse CPD (Government of Botswana 2015) as a vehicle for curricular and pedagogical change to achieve desired student learning outcomes is generally consistent with international expectations (Farnsworth et al. 2016; Hairon and Dimmock 2012; Weshah 2012). PLCs are credited with broader developments in the field of teacher professional development including lifelong and continuous learning (Boitshwarelo 2007; Shehu 2009), community learning, reflective practice and inquiry-based and evidence-informed practice (Ayling et al. 2012; Boylan and Woolsey 2015). PLCs have also been credited as vehicles for establishing collegial relationships and for capacity building in various school subjects (Boitshwarelo 2007; Hord 2004). They are focused on the learning of the teacher, and pointed towards the result of teaching. Teachers share their collective intelligence on the knowledge, experience and divergent viewpoint.

Notwithstanding the international claims for the positive effects of PLCs on CPD (Brooks and Gibson 2012; Lee and Brett 2015; Popp and Goldman 2016), there is lack of research on ICTs' role in enabling PLCs to function successfully on instructional practices and student learning outcomes in Botswana. There is a strong case for strengthening the present knowledge base with regard to establishing and sustaining PLCs in this context. Investigating PLC processes and their impact on instructional practices and learning outcomes across different contexts will inform the knowledge base on their successful implementation and sustainability in the Botswana context.

19.4 Methodology

The key arguments discussed in this paper are based on literature review and documentary analysis of relevant government policy documents pertaining to CPD in Botswana. Other secondary sources of information used to support the discussions in this paper included informal conversations between the authors and DMSE-INSET staff. International literature was used for comparison with the current trends in continuing teacher education in Botswana. The primary reliance on document analysis was apparent as the research on the implementation of PLCs in Botswana is in its infancy. Only three papers (Batane 2004; Boitshwarelo 2007; Shehu 2009) were available when we searched Google Scholar for literature on PLCs and CPD in Botswana. The analysis specifically focused on policy documents since they were considered fundamental to understanding the policy justifications that underpin the PLC policy initiative. Our interest in the policy documents was mainly on current CPD initiatives and the processes and structures expected to be put in place by schools in Botswana.

The researchers focussed on the rationale for the PLC policy initiative and possible impact and implications for mathematics teachers. The process involved seeking explanations of the phenomenon by eliciting pertinent data, then testing the data against tentative themes, modifying them, and then repeating the process until the data were consistent with the thematic framework. Data analysis involved reading appropriate sections of each of the documents to get a holistic impression. This was followed by the structuring of section content into units of analysis, the elicitation of codes to capture the meanings of the sentences, and finally, the generation of themes based on these codes. These categories provided explanations to the rationale of the PLC policy initiative which included teacher competency; characteristics of PLCs, leadership support for PLCs; and the possible implications for teachers which included workload and top-down work structure. These themes formed the conceptual framework for the reporting of findings and the discussion. Internal coherence during the data analysis was also sought in order to strengthen the findings. The authors were cognisant of the lack of interview data to support the explanations generated from the documentary analysis, with potential for further in-depth study.

19.5 The Botswana Policy Context Shaping the Introduction of PLCs

Botswana's Ministry of Education and Skills Development (MoESD) considers PLCs as conducive to promoting "professional development so that it contributes and impacts positively on the quality of the education system" (Government of Botswana 2015, p. 76). The idea is to establish the Teaching Council to develop a CPD system that will oversee the setting of standards and frameworks envisaged to produce a quality teaching workforce. The initiative is top-down in nature, being run by the school heads, to deliver INSET as part of decentralised teaching support system.

> The value of teacher-initiated professional development through sharing, collaboration, reflection and inquiry is not embodied. There is no acknowledgment that self-directed teachers are engaged in action research to solve problems identified in relation to the curriculum and classroom pedagogy. In summary, the strategy in teacher professional development has focused on raising teacher competency by bringing in more workshops and training, i.e. the policy direction has been placing responsibility on the management, rather than on the teachers. In contrast, the trend emerging on the international scale is for the use of reflection and inquiry (Albion et al. 2015; Hargreaves et al. 2013; Hou 2015; Postholm 2012), and action research in order to interrogate and develop subject content and pedagogical knowledge (Hairon and Dimmock 2012). This can only be possible with the involvement of the classroom practitioner's initiative (Hairon and Dimmock 2012; Postholm 2012). The commitment to making all Botswana schools PLCs rests on the idea of "thinking schools" (Hairon and Dimmock 2012, p. 413).

19.6 Stakeholder Preparedness for the Implementation of PLCs

Key findings from (Bleiler 2015; Hairon and Dimmock 2012) indicate that the degree to which the PLC initiative is successful in practice is likely to hinge on, first, teacher preparedness and second, the school leadership and support for their implementation (Hairon and Dimmock 2012). Studies indicate that pedagogic practices in Botswana schools still remain strongly teacher-centred, reliant on formal didactic teaching, rote learning, and summative testing (Schweisfurth 2015; Tabulawa 1997) though the policy platforms encourage more learner-centred approaches.

One constraint on teachers' commitment to PLCs is teaching workloads the teachers already have, and the pace of educational change (Batane 2004; Tabulawa 1997). The top-down managed PLC may be seen by teachers, who already have teaching and administrative duties, as yet another burden.

Concerned with issues of implementation over PLC processes, stakeholders need to ask: "How much flexibility actually exists for schools to shape their PLCs within government framework and policy guidelines?", "To what extent do the characteristics of effective PLCs captured in generic literature apply to Botswana?", "How do teachers learn in such communities?" And "How do PLCs bring about improvement in classroom practices and student learning outcomes?" The link from PLC activities to student learning outcomes is mediated by many factors, including school culture, teaching effectiveness, time, engagement, and learning practices and materials.

The other challenge is the centralised (top-down control) system deeply entrenched in the education system, from the MoESD to the district, school heads, department heads and teachers. Policy initiatives by the MoESD are cascaded down to the teachers, a mirror of the public administration established in all public sectors in Botswana. It permeates both school heads and teachers' relationships.

The ETSSP policy document emphasises training and no social interaction initiatives. A number of scenarios from literature are possible with such a policy direction. Hairon and Dimmock (2012) speculates that school heads may command teachers to carry out PLC activities rather than winning their commitment, thereby resulting in resistance. Others may not provide enough resources for PLC activities, and teachers may just present themselves without collaboration or reflection. School leaders may alternatively delegate responsibilities to subordinates who may not cope with the workload. Although others may be pro-active and committed to the implementation and sustainability of PLCs, ultimately, leader competences will play a large part if the PLCs are implemented and sustained across the mathematics curriculum.

19.7 ICTs and Professional Development for Mathematics Teachers in Botswana

In Botswana, mathematics is a high priority compulsory subject up to senior secondary level, making it difficult for teachers to collaborate during teaching time. Mathematics instruction in schools, therefore, places teachers in isolation from their peers. While the opportunity for mathematics teachers exists through the Botswana clusters as learning communities, the efficiency and effectiveness can greatly be enhanced by employment of innovative interventions mediated by emerging ICTs readily available for use in the context of their practice.

ICTs have made it possible, for example, to communicate, simulate processes, illustrate concepts, and draw graphics; offering teachers the possibility of renewing and familiarising with the development in current trends in mathematics education (Weshah 2012). There is a wide variety of emerging ICTs available for use, including open-source software, mobile learning technologies, massive online open courses (MOOCs), SMS messaging and video conferencing applications. Subject team meetings, classroom visitations and collaboration meetings can now be replaced by ICT facilities available at affordable cost.

Weshah (2012) points out that web 2.0 tools and services are useful for reflection, sharing and construction of knowledge. Studies by Hou (2015) with online learning experiences indicated that they contributed positively to professional development of teachers. Participants recognised the significant presence of their peers in supporting and transforming their learning, and that the web-encouraged voluntary participation and vibrancy within the community. Albion et al. (2015) suggested linking research to practice as a way of facilitating evidence-based policies. Flagg and Ayling (2011) indicated that teachers were interested in professional development communities that embedded construction of knowledge and professional identity as they engage. They all emphasised the importance of learning and participating identities. These views were elaborated by Bleiler (2015) and Boylan and Woolsey (2015) on using ICTs in professional development. Trust et al. (2016) although acknowledging that there is a dearth of research on professional learning networks, suggests that the anytime, anywhere availability of learning networks and their capacity to respond to diverse interests and needs offer possibilities for professional growth. These and other more recent studies (Dogan et al. 2016; Koh et al. 2016; Popp and Goldman 2016) indicate a shift to practice-based professional development in CPD.

Cloud computing services, for "ubiquitous, on-demand network access to a shared pool of configurable computing resources, e.g. storage and applications, that can be rapidly provisioned and released with minimal management effort or service provider interaction" (Mell and Grance 2011, p. 2) is of critical importance today. PLCs data and activities can be accessed through a cloud on a pay-per-use pricing, for example, Dropbox and Google Drive, for storage data services and applications; and Apple I Cloud for online storage and backup.

The proliferation of web 2.0 services has led to increased interactivity and collaboration in PLCs users of the Internet. Web 2.0 has brought with it forums, microblogging sites, social networking, social bookmarking and wikis (Weshah 2012). Researchers predict that these technological advances will very quickly change the educational and cultural landscapes entirely (Wesely 2013), increasing access and sharing in communities. Botswana is well poised for the adoption of these ICTs in mathematics professional development communities with immense benefits. Such promise is highly likely in supporting to strengthen Botswana mathematics professional communities, their development and operationalization as communities of learners to revolutionise teacher practice through reflective practice leading to improved student academic outcomes.

The widespread adoption and use of mobile devices with associated services to the larger community has offered opportunities for teachers to use ICTs in CPD. These technologies have come at much reduced cost; and are therefore affordable to many, notwithstanding their usability.

The Botswana Government's intent on becoming an informed nation through technology use has not made a great impact on the actual use of technologies in mathematics classrooms (Garegae and Moalosi 2011). Despite the constructivist approach to teaching and learning that the curriculum demands, a number of problems encountered such as large classes and issues relating to resistance to change have not helped teachers to smoothly harness ICTs in PLCs practice.

19.8 Implications and Conclusions

This discussion has foregrounded the influence of Botswana policy initiatives in shaping the implementation and sustainability of PLCs in mathematics teaching. Botswana has forged a unique centrally driven culture in Africa, which addresses issues of access, equity and the improvement of the quality of education, economic prosperity and equitable distribution of wealth being the main drivers of its social, cultural, political and educational evolution. PLCs are seen by the Botswana government as an appropriate twenty-first-century professional development platform to enhance teacher competency and student outcomes. Issues like access, autonomy, competency and standards speak to teacher empowerment.

However, as this paper has argued, the top-down dependency in Botswana poses particular challenges for teachers and school heads charged with implementation at school level. For example, the current notion of PLCs and their influence is likely to be confined to pedagogical practices, subject expertise and student learning, a clear outcome of a centrally driven culture. Hence, a paradigm shift is required in the pattern of influence relations for mathematics continuing teacher professional development (Boylan and Woolsey 2015). It is therefore imperative that the various ICTs should be availed to the schools in one way or the other.

New mathematics software is 'put' into the hands of teachers through cloud computing and web 2.0 services every day, and the developers monitor their effectiveness and improve them. Accessing the software will benefit the teachers through digital participation and global reach. They will, in turn, use the digital technologies as research tools, leading to validate the credibility of sources and draw conclusions by analysing data. Accessing ICTs could also be used as teaching aids in the mathematics classroom in forms of simulations of mathematical formula and equations; for example, enabling them to vary teaching approaches. This will empower the teachers to create a visual and interactive experience (Albion et al. 2015) with the students, possible only through access to a variety of ICTs. The teacher will have the liberty to choose the software most appropriate for the task at hand.

ICTs scaffold the processes of articulation, critical thinking and reflection, which are the foundations of knowledge construction (Hargreaves et al. 2013; Koh et al. 2016). The Internet communication tools allow the teachers to share experiences and reflections not bound by place and time. The 24/7 asynchronous communication and ubiquitous tools allow the teachers to take control of their work day and external collaboration in ways that significantly enhance effectiveness and efficiently. Teachers can also configure various softwares for students' personalised to specific learning styles, level and pace in mixed-ability classrooms. These can only be provided by ICTs in PLCs, providing interventions that are tailored to local needs. In PLCs, teachers have control over the software itself, and are able to adapt the software to their own needs.

Investing in ICTs through PLCs would empower the mathematics teachers to participate in the determination of PLC goals and policies and to exercise professional judgment about what and how to conduct them. They will be able to develop and adopt learning standards for their students easily. They will have the power of choosing instructional strategies, designing lessons and providing academic support. This will, in turn, move decision-making to mathematics teachers about the software they want to use in the classroom (Kler 2014); and these can only be provided through a decentralised system with active participation of classroom practitioners.

ICTs have greater opportunities to support reduction of teachers' isolation in the teaching of mathematics in Botswana. That, their challenges would be shared and experiences exchanged will go a long way to support mathematics teacher classroom practice, leading to enhanced application. In other words, ICTs provide mathematics teachers with possibilities to engage, access resources, share resources and experiences, demonstrate concepts, communicating ideas among others without leaving the work place. This will reduce the professional development meetings costs, including feeding, travel and accommodation costs. Improved teacher interaction would enhance effective classroom practice leading to improved students learning outcomes.

References

Albion, P. R., Tondeur, J., Forkosh-Baruch, A., & Peeraer, J. (2015). Teachers' professional development for ICT integration: Towards a reciprocal relationship between research and practice. *Education and Information Technologies, 20*, 655–673.

Astuto, T. A., Clark, D. L., Read, A.-M., McGree, K., & Fernandez, L.deK.P. (1993). *Challenges to dominant assumptions controlling educational reform*. Andover, MA: Regional Laboratory for the Educational Improvement of the Northeast and Islands.

Ayling, D., Owen, H., & Flagg, E. (2012). Thinking, researching and living in virtual professional development community of practice. In M. Brown, M. Hartnett & T. Stewart (Eds.), *Future challenges, sustainable futures. In Proceedings ascilite Wellington 2012* (pp. 67–74).

Batane, T. (2004). Inservice Teacher Training and Technology: A case of Botswana. *Journal of Technology and Teacher Education, 12*(3), 387–410. Norfolk, VA: Society for Information Technology & Teacher Education. Retrieved August 22, 2016 from https://www.learntechlib.org/p/11428

Bleiler, S. K. (2015). Increasing awareness of practice through interaction across communities: The lived experiences of a mathematician and mathematics teacher educator. *Journal of Mathematics Teacher Education*, 231–252.

Boitshwarelo, B. (2007). Are Secondary Schools in Botswana Conducive Environments for ICT-supported Teacher Professional Development. In C. Montgomerie & J. Seale (Eds.), *Proceedings of EdMedia: World conference on educational media and technology 2007* (pp. 1326–1330). Association for the Advancement of Computing in Education (AACE).

Boylan, M., & Woolsey, I. (2015). Teacher education for social justice: Mapping identity spaces. *Teaching and Teacher Education, 46*, 62–71.

Brooks, C., & Gibson, S. (2012). Professional learning in a digital age. *Canadian Journal of Learning and Technology, 38*(2), 1–16.

Dogan, S., Pringle, R., & Mesa, J. (2016). The impacts of professional learning communities on science teachers' knowledge, practice and student learning: A review. *Professional Development in Education, 42*(4), 569–588.

Farnsworth, V., Kleanthous, I., & Wenger-trayner, E. (2016). Communities of practice as a social theory of learning: A conversation with Etienne Wenger. *British Journal of Educational Studies ISSN, 62*(2), 139–160.

Farooq, U., Schank, P., Harris, A., Fusco, J., & Schlager, M. (2007). Sustaining a community computing infrastructure for online teacher professional development: A Case study of designing tapped In. *Computer Supported Cooperative Work, 16*, 397–429.

Flagg, E., & Ayling, D. (2011). Teacher engagement in a Web 2.0 world: Developing your online teaching and learning community of practice. In G. Williams, P. Statham, N. Brown & B. Cleland (Eds.), Changing Demands, Changing Directions. *Proceedings Ascilite Hobart 2011*. (pp. 386–391).

Garegae, K. G., & Moalosi, S. S. (2011). Botswana ICT policy and curriculum concerns: Does school connectivity guarantee technology integration into mathematics classroom? In E. E. Adomi (Ed.) *Handbook of research on information communication technology policy: Trends, issues and advancements* 9th ed., (pp. 15–32). Hershey

Giroux, H. (1995). Teachers as Transformative Intellectuals. *Social Education, 49*(5). ERIC

Government of Botswana (2004). *Maitlamo Botswana's national ICT policy*. Gaborone: Government Print.

Government of Botswana (2015). Republic of Botswana Education & Training Sector Strategic Plan (ETSSP 2015–2020).

Hairon, S., & Dimmock, C. (2012). Singapore schools and professional learning communities: Teacher professional development and school leadership in an Asian hierarchical system. *Educational Review, 64*(4), 405–424.

Hargreaves, E., Berry, R., Lai, Y. C., Leung, P., Scott, D., & Stobart, G. (2013). Teachers' experiences of autonomy in Continuing Professional Development: Teacher learning communities in London and Hong Kong. *Teacher Development, 4530*(August 2016), 19–34.

Hord, S. M. (1997). *Professional learning communities: Communities of continuous inquiry and improvement.* Austin: SEDL.

Hou, H. (2015). What makes an online community of practice work? A situated study of Chinese student teachers' perceptions of online professional learning. *Teaching and Teacher Education, 46,* 6–16.

Hord, S. M. (Ed.). (2004). *Learning together, leading together: Changing schools through professional learning communities.* New York: Teachers College Press.

Kennedy, A. (2005). Models of continuing professional development: A framework for analysis. *Journal of In-service Education, 31*(2), 235–249.

Kler, S. (2014). ICT integration in teaching and learning: Empowerment of education with technology. *Issues and Ideas in Education, 2*(2), 255–271.

Koh, L. H. J., Chai, C. S., & Lim, W. Y. (2016). Teacher professional development for TPACK-21CL: Effects on teacher ICT integration and student outcomes. *Journal of Educational Computing,* 1–25.

Lee, K., & Brett, C. (2015). Dialogic understanding of teachers' online transformative learning: A qualitative case study of teacher discussions in a graduate-level online course. *Teaching and Teacher Education, 46,* 72–83.

Mell, P., & Grance, T. (2011). The NIST definition of cloud computing recommendations of the national institute of standards and technology. *NIST Special Publication,* 800–145.

Mitchell, C., & Sackney, L. (2000). *Profound improvement: Building capacity for a learning community.* Lisse, NL: Swets & Zeitlinger.

Moodley, M. (2015). *Science teachers' attendance of professional development programmes and their use of computer software in teaching.*

Popp, J. S., & Goldman, S. R. (2016). Knowledge building in teacher professional learning communities: Focus of meeting matters. *Teaching and Teacher Education, 59,* 347–359.

Postholm, M. B. (2012). Teachers' professional development: A theoretical review teachers' professional development: A theoretical review. *Educational Research, 54*(4), 405–429. http://doi.org/10.1080/00131881.2012.734725

Schweisfurth, M. (2015). International journal of educational development learner-centred pedagogy: Towards a post-2015 agenda for teaching and learning. *International Journal of Educational Development, 40,* 259–266.

Shehu, J. (2009). Professional development experiences of physical education teachers in Botswana: Epistemological implications. *Teacher Development, 13*(3), 267–283.

Sywelem, M. M., & Witte, J. E. (2013). Continuing professional development: Perceptions of elementary school teachers in Saudi Arabia. *Journal of Modern Education Review, 3*(12), 881–898.

Tabulawa, R. (1997). Pedagogical classroom practice and the social context: The case of Botswana. *International Journal of Educational Development, 17*(2), 189–204.

Toole, J. C., & Louis, K. S. (2002). The role of professional learning communities in international education. In K. Leithwood & P. Hallinger (Eds.), *Second international handbook of educational leadership and administration.* Dordrecht: Kluwer.

Trust, T., Krutka, D. G., & Paul, J. (2016). Computers & education "Together we are better": Professional learning networks for teachers. *Computers & Education, 102,* 15–34.

UNESCO. (2002). *Information and communication technologies in teacher education: A planning guide.* Division of Higher Education: UNESCO.

Wenger, E. (2009) *Communities of practice: A brief introduction,* http://www.ewenger.com/theory/accessed August 2016.

Wesely, P. M. (2013). Investigating the community of practice of world language educators on Twitter.
Weshah, H. A. (2012). Understanding the pedagogies of blogs, wikis and discussion boards. *International Journal of Instructional Technology and Distance Learning, 9*(6), 59–77.
World Bank Group. (2015). *Botswana: Systematic country diagnostic.* Washington DC: World Bank.
World Economic Forum. (2015). *The global information technology report 2015.* Geneva. Available at http://www3.weforum.org/docs/WEF_Global_IT_Report_2015.pdf

Chapter 20
Using an E-Portfolio for Teaching and Teacher Continuous Learning: A Process for Professional Development Enhancement

Byabazaire Yusuf

Abstract Generally, studies on e-portfolios are related to supporting professional development of pre-service teachers in their initial training programs. This chapter focuses on a pilot study in which postgraduate in-service teachers implemented a teaching e-portfolio for 4 months. The focus was on teaching the English language and writing reflections during the teaching and learning process. It shares the experiences of in-service teachers in using e-portfolios for teaching and continuous learning. A qualitative research approach based on a focus group strategy was employed. Because in-service teachers were busy and worked in distant rural schools, asynchronous virtual focus group discussions were employed to mitigate time and distance constraints. Implementing a teaching e-portfolio can be a source of new technology proficiency demands for a teacher. However, if one is able to meet learners' technological expectations each time an instructional challenge comes up, it means that one is ready to learn new ICT skills all the time. A teaching e-portfolio has the potential to facilitate the sharing of content knowledge and pedagogical skills, as well as to promote collaborative activities. This way a teacher who uses a teaching e-portfolio can experience continuous learning leading to professional development enhancement.

20.1 Background and Literature Review

Education researchers have discussed different types of e-portfolios in teacher education. However, most of them are related to supporting pre-service teachers in their initial training process. Meyer et al. (2010) highlighted the main functions of an e-portfolio including: (1) showcasing accomplishments and reflections, (2) assessing professional development endeavours and (3) supporting the actual professional development process. On the basis of the three main functions outlined

---

B. Yusuf (✉)
School of Education and Modern Languages, Universiti Utara Malaysia, Sintok, Malaysia
e-mail: byabazaire@uum.edu.my

above, pre-service teachers are known to have used e-portfolios based on specific goals to accomplish their training and professional needs in one of the following ways.

Pre-service teachers use learning e-portfolios to produce a documentary on their path to becoming trained teachers. The process includes highlighting, sharing and, most importantly, reflecting on important documents such as classroom management plans, behaviour modification plans, plans to meet inclusive teaching needs and video recordings of practice teaching sessions (Strudler and Wetzel 2011, p. 162).

Pre-service teachers use assessment e-portfolios to provide access to documentary evidence of their academic accomplishments. This way they are able to convince their professors that they qualify to meet the set assessment criteria of their professional training program (Strudler and Wetzel 2011).

Pre-service teachers use digital archives to set up personal collections of artefacts related to their teacher training activities without adding any relevant annotations to the content.

Similarly, pre-service teachers provide e-portfolio-based documentary evidence suitable for securing a job offer. The evidence is used to justify that they qualify and meet the school's set criteria for employment purposes (Barrett and Knezek 2003).

Moreover, pre-service teachers also use multipurpose e-portfolios to meet multiple objectives. They include: storage of archival documents, engaging in reflections on them, sharing them, using them for assessing initial training programs or for securing a teaching post (Strudler and Wetzel 2011, p. 163).

Generally, the desire to meet a specific objective by pre-service teachers is always the driving factor for the choice of the type of e-portfolio employed. Therefore, the composition of the e-portfolio is normally influenced by the objectives of the initial teacher training program (Barrett 2007).

20.2 Electronic Portfolio Platforms

Presently, several different types of e-portfolio platforms exist. Sometimes the electronic support system determines the type of e-portfolio to be set up. Generally, pre-service teachers prefer setting up e-portfolios on website hosts like Google Sites (Zheng et al. 2009) as well blogs (Hughes and Purnell 2008). On the other hand, schools and higher education institutions also provide online learning platforms for e-portfolios such as Mahara and Blackboard (Clark and Neumann 2009). Other options include: in-house platforms such as Eduportfolio (Karsenti and Collin 2010) as well as EPEARL (Meyer et al. 2010).

When choosing an e-portfolio platform, a user should look beyond the initial teacher training objectives and think of how this technology will be useful for continuous professional learning over an entire teaching career. Pre-service teachers may be unable to envision this purpose when they are in their early training program. Therefore, educators, mentors or their professors should counsel them at the earliest time possible so that they are able to make informed decisions.

20.2.1 Functions of the E-Portfolio in Initial Teacher Training

Here are some of the common uses of e-portfolios for the majority of teachers in their initial training program. As may be noticed, the purpose of an e-portfolio may depend on the needs of the program or the teacher trainees as the situation may require.

20.2.1.1 For Reflection

This is regarded as one of the core functions of the e-portfolio in an initial teacher training program. Primarily, teachers are expected to master reflection as an essential skill. For instance, some bodies like the National Council for the Accreditation of Teacher Education in the United States consider this skill component very seriously (Ostorga 2006). When applied properly, reflection can nurture and sharpen a critical attitude and objective assessments of their competency and professional skills by pre-service teachers (Gresso and Lomicka 1999). On one hand, an e-portfolio can generate adequate information with regard to the learner's progress while at the same time providing ample opportunities "...to transform previous learning into active and authentic knowledge" (Lin 2008, p. 199).

20.2.1.2 For Assessment

Educators responsible for the training and nurturing of pre-service teachers benefit from e-portfolios. They use them innovatively to evaluate both the outcomes and the process of professional development (Goupil et al. 1998). This makes an e-portfolio a useful tool as it provides a reliable means of assessment for individualized student professional development processes.

20.2.1.3 For Exposure

Both during and after a pre-service training program, an e-portfolio can be beneficial as a tool for professional exposure in different ways. For instance, after completing their pre-service program, students can use an e-portfolio in the process of finding a teaching post (Whitworth et al. 2011). In this regard, Kitchenham (2008) indicated that many pre-service teachers in Canada reported using their e-portfolios as an important tool for securing employment. Although some principals were sceptical with regard to the validity of e-portfolio content, others generally found that content beneficial in terms of an initial assessment of the candidates' teaching efficacy and organizational abilities (Strawhecker et al. 2007–2008).

20.2.1.4 For a Social Function

Generally, an e-portfolio makes it easy for teachers to distribute and share information with others (Godwin-Jones 2008). By using the comments feature, pre-service teachers are able to communicate extensively with their peers on an issue of particular interest in the learning process. Other interested parties such as teachers, parents, and other students may join the discourse. Viewing the portfolios of peers and posting comments as feedback could lead to the social construction of knowledge. As this cycle continues, potential exists for the establishment of particular learning communities (Albion 2008).

20.2.1.5 An E-Portfolio for Teaching and Teacher Continuous Learning

The teaching profession requires its members to continuously update their knowledge and skills if they are to remain relevant in today's ever-changing environment. Therefore, a teacher's ability to utilize ICT-based resources for professional development enhancement is crucial. ICT integration has become one of the essential skills in teacher professional practices and training and has been emphasized by experts and educational organizations around the world (Mann 2014; Weller 2013; Wells 2014). In this context, various web-based technologies have become important and dominant in this environment. Hence, people have dramatically increased their engagement with computers, the Internet and the World Wide Web (Castells 2004).

One of the web-based technologies that can contribute to a better teaching and learning process is the teaching e-portfolio. A teaching e-portfolio can be used for the documentation of teaching evidence from a diversity of sources. By engaging in the selection and organization of material for an e-portfolio, a teacher can both reflect on and improve on the teaching process. Teaching e-portfolios are, therefore, beneficial when used for critical reflection and learning purposes. They can enable the public to access individual teaching practices and facilitate collective learning and knowledge sharing (Lorenzo and Ittelson 2005). Because teachers need to seek continuously new ideas to improve their teaching and learning process, an e-portfolio can serve as an ideal technology for enhancing their professional development.

This section of the chapter shares the experience of in-service teachers in using e-portfolios for teaching and teacher continuous learning. The participants in this study were enrolled in the Master of Education program (MEd) on a part-time basis at a public university in Malaysia. After taking a course in Information and Communication Technology (ICT) in Education and having developed an e-portfolio as a required course project, they became interested in taking the process one step further with encouragement and support from the course instructor. They participated in a pilot study on the use of an e-portfolio for teaching and learning for four months starting in June 2014/2015. In this regard, two main questions were addressed during the pilot study:

1. What innovative ideas did teachers learn to improve their knowledge of teaching and learning?
2. What challenges did teachers face in implementing an e-portfolio in teaching?

The participants were all English language teachers in secondary schools. In total, sixteen (16) teachers participated in the study. The researcher had a three-hour brainstorming session and briefing with the participants at the onset of the study. Apart from the e-portfolio project the participants had undertaken during their course, this was the first time that they implemented an e-portfolio in the actual teaching process in the school. Hence, making the process simple in order to sustain their motivation was important. During the session, the agreed upon criteria for a teaching e-portfolio in this study were that:

1. Each teacher would develop a teaching e-portfolio for teaching the English language;
2. A teaching e-portfolio would provide documented evidence for teaching English from a variety of sources and would provide context for the evidence; and
3. The selection and organization of the teaching materials for the e-portfolio would help each teacher to reflect on and improve the teaching of English.

For data collection in focus group interview discussions, participants agreed that, because some teachers would be unable to participate in face-to-face focus group sessions (due to time and distance constraints), asynchronous virtual focus groups would be set up using the Google Groups platform.

20.3 Methodology

A qualitative research methodology, which employed a focus group strategy, was chosen for this study. The participants were initially contacted via phone calls. This was followed up upon by an email message seeking their confirmation and commitment to participate in the study. Those who replied and affirmed their commitment formed part of the focus group discussions. As Stewart and Shamdasani (2015) advised, special care and consideration of the influences of environmental factors, individual differences and interpersonal factors were addressed.

According to Kruger's (1988) guidelines, focus groups were conceived in three phases, namely, (1) conceptualization, (2) interview session, (3) analysis and reporting. In the conceptualization phase, the purpose of the study was established, a sample of study was determined and a plan of study developed. The interview phase involved the process of developing appropriate questions (with a good mixture of why, what and how mainly for probing participants for more ideas and input). Asynchronous virtual focus group discussions (text-based communication postings that do not occur in real time using Google Groups Platform) were employed in the study. The moderator's main role was to start a discussion thread, and to share new questions with the participants at intervals previously agreed upon. He would also engage participants by probing for comments from the participants to obtain a consensus of ideas for every issue or topic. The participants responded at their own convenience but within a set deadline. All focus group interview discussions were downloaded for the analysis phase. Finally, in the analysis and reporting phase, the researcher was engaged in the verification and analysis process, which resulted in a descriptive report for the evolving issues and themes from the study.

Prior to conducting the focus group interviews, the interview guide questions were tested with a pilot group to ensure their reliability for the study process. Lastly, the scissor-and-sort technique was applied to the data analysis process. The report summary from the data analysis was shared in the virtual focus groups for review by the participants for the purpose of validation.

20.4 Results and Discussion

Overall, four asynchronous virtual focus group discussions (comprising 4–6 in-service teachers per group) were conducted. A total of sixteen (16) in-service teachers participated in the study. All were secondary school English language teachers. Of the sixteen (16) participants, four (4) were males and twelve (12) were females. The study participants had varied teaching experiences ranging from less than 5 years (four participants), 5–10 years (six participants) and 10–15 years (six participants).

20.5 Innovative Ideas for Teaching English Language

The participants agreed that the e-portfolio experience helped to enrich their knowledge of and skills for teaching the English language. The ideas shared by some colleagues in their e-portfolios, and their reflections on the various activities helped to illuminate their teaching practices in their classrooms. Certain ideas encouraged some participants to acquire technology proficiency in order to be able to facilitate their students' learning process. The innovative ideas for teaching

English language as shared among the participants indicated a continuous learning process.

(a) **Writing for authentic audiences with a clear purpose**

The idea of teaching writing with an authentic audience in mind was considered extremely valuable. Students often lacked motivation to write as there was not much importance attached to the writing activities. The moment they knew that their work was going to be read by someone (other than their teacher and classmates), their perception and motivation for writing tasks changed.

Said one participant:

> When students heard that their best piece of writing would appear in the school's monthly newsletter, they became motivated to write. They were more careful about what they were writing .... Their choice of words and phrases were more articulate.

Another one added:

> Suddenly, their grammar, spelling, and punctuations were improving. I didn't have to remind them over and over again like before.... There are some children who understand that their parents are really keen to know how they are doing in school.

In reference to this parental involvement, one of the participants observed:

> Previously two of the boys in my English class never used to care about their work. Now they are working hard and have improved their writing skills tremendously.... They want to impress their parents when their articles are included in next month's class newsletter.

(b) **Forming writing groups using wikis**

Assigning individual writing tasks for students can be boring at times. However, when students were given writing tasks in groups they were rejuvenated. They liked working together and collaborating to produce something as a group. They complemented each other's weaknesses.

Said one participant:

> Some of my students come from backgrounds where they use English to communicate even at home. When they work in groups, they help those who are relatively weak.... The weak students eventually gain confidence and their writing gets better.

Another one added:

> Since they are doing their group work on a wiki, they can do it anytime and anywhere they want. They are responsible for their learning.... They know their work must be ready before the deadline.

Another participant interjected:

> They need feedback though to keep motivated and engaged in their work. Otherwise some will lose their sense of direction.... When they get regular feedback on their work they know someone is monitoring their activities.

The discussion also revolved around the question of assessing individual contributions in these wiki groups, and group sizes that were ideal in order to allow members to maximize their potential. Small groups with manageable numbers were suggested. Also group members were assigned with tasks for which they were accountable.

Said one participant:

> It is amazing how they can produce some very impressive essays in these writing groups. There is no doubt even those who are weak eventually get to improve their writing skills. When it is a graded activity, I just give the same grade to all group members….

One participant clarified:

> For me, I always assign each member of the group with a specific task. I also rotate the tasks. That's why you need to keep the number small and manageable for each group.

(c) Forming writing clubs and providing publishing opportunities

Students have different interests through which they feel motivated to learn. For instance, some like sports, music, technology, pets, etc. Writing clubs could be formed based on some of their hobbies and interests. Students can produce both printed and digital stories based on their interests. This means that teacher professional skills have to include technology proficiency in order to facilitate successful student digital projects.

Said one participant:

> My students are very excited when they are assigned roles as editor, illustrator, proof reader, researcher and group leader for the monthly short story series projects. Through these roles, they have expanded their knowledge in terms of vocabulary, grammar, punctuation and overall communication skills.

Another participant explained her classroom situation saying that:

> Sometimes I have parallel publishing projects running side by side. Sports, pets, technology, music, and nature are some of the popular themes for the short story series. I like the competition it brings to the classroom. Team members for each project compete against each other. Everyone works hard, and they are improving by the day.

In one school, some students got very motivated when their teacher initiated a project to exchange their published work with a neighbouring school. They wanted to be the first to produce a digital story for this project.

The participant said:

> I have no choice. I have to learn to guide my students when they get involved with technology. I'm learning with my students how to use Windows Movie Maker, VideoPad and Audacity. It is an exciting new experience… Everyone wants to be a narrator for the digital story…. They want their images in….

Another participant added in agreement, "Yes, teaching is getting more exciting now. Technology integration is the way to go. Teenagers love technology. It is their playing field. Let us learn something from them".

In addition to learning the English language, students learned to plan, collaborate, identify and apply appropriate technology skills that were required to accomplish their projects.

(d) **Dramatizing characters, situations, and events**

The use of drama to engage and inspire students can bring a lot of benefits and fun to the young English language learners. Students have to learn to put their ideas, thoughts, feelings, imaginations and expressions in the English language. On introducing the strategy for the first time, one participant noted that, "Initially, all students were shy and afraid of making mistakes. Now they have become more bold, confident and creative. They are expanding their English vocabulary".

After introducing the drama approach for more than a month, one participant observed that, "This is the time when students have real fun with the English language. I can see that they have acquired more vocabularies, improved grammar and word pronunciations are getting better".

Using drama in teaching can bring out the students' best talents and innate feelings about life and what they admire as one participant observed:

> They read and rehearse a lot before the drama sessions. I can see the personalities they admire brought alive on stage. I can see their choice of characters implying their interests in movie acting, politics… Most important are their word pronunciations, choice of vocabularies and phrases.

Another participant added, "My students are getting motivated to learn English. It is not boring anymore. They are learning new vocabularies, phrases, and synonyms to enrich their expressions".

While referring to the video clips uploaded by some participants in their e-portfolios, one participant observed that, "The video clips were extremely helpful when introducing the drama approach for my English lessons. My students were excited to see what others were doing in their schools".

20.6 Challenges of Implementing an E-Portfolio Project

The participants expressed the existence of various challenges during the 4-month period in which they piloted the implementation of e-portfolios in the teaching of the English language in their schools. Some of the challenges included: information overload, lack of proper training to use technology, copyright and privacy issues, lack of collegial support, time constraints and network/Internet connection issues.

(a) **Internet connection issues**

It was evident through this study that network infrastructure or Internet connection were essential elements for the successful implementation of the e-portfolio project among the participants. For instance, one participant who did not have access to Internet at home commented:

> I have to do everything during the day at school as I don't have access to Internet at home…. I'm either teaching or reading and updating my e-portfolio at school…. The time is not enough.

Another participant facing the same problem added,

> I have to apologize to everyone. I'm taking too long to update my e-portfolio and also post my comments. Lately, I have a poor Internet connection at school as well as my house.

(b) **Access to and reliability of technology**

Some of the participants admitted that, although they were excited about the prospect of implementing e-portfolios in their teaching, they faced problems of access to and reliability of technology.

Said one participant:

> Initially, I shared a computer with my daughter who had just graduated and was living with me. When she eventually got a job and went to live with a relative near her workplace I resorted to doing my work at the village cybercafé. Sometimes the connection speed is too slow or it is closed for maintenance.

Another participant added:

> There are computers in school. Only two or three are useable, and others need repair and that has not happened for quite long. I go very early and leave very late in order to have access to a computer.

(c) **Amount of time and effort needed for implementation**

All the participants pointed out that a huge amount of time and effort were required to implement a teaching e-portfolio. Although all participants had previously taken a core educational technology course in which the course project involved developing an e-portfolio, they still found it challenging. Said one participant, "It required a lot of time and effort to set up the e-portfolio. I would have taken longer if I had not gone through the experience before." Another participant affirmed, "Getting the e-portfolio ready with all the teaching materials took a lot of time. Moreover, you need patience and commitment to keep writing reflections".

20.7 Conclusion

The novelty of this chapter lies in the fact that implementing a teaching e-portfolio can be the beginning for further demands of technological proficiency in order to meet the needs of twenty-first century learners. A good example shared in this study is that, when the students wanted to produce a digital story, the teacher had to learn some movie editing skills (using Windows Movie Maker, VideoPad, and Audacity) in order to facilitate the completion of the project. This can happen regularly. However, if a teacher is able to meet the technological expectations of learners each time an instructional challenge comes up, this means that he or she is ready to learn new ICT skills all the time. This way an e-portfolio can lead to teacher empowerment to integrate ICT in the teaching process.

Generally, this study suggests that some in-service teachers are ready to take technology integration issues seriously. They would like ICT-driven resources and digital media literacy issues to be part of their professional development programs as well as lifelong learning, provided they are given the necessary technical support in order to succeed. There may be some challenges in implementing e-portfolios for teaching; nonetheless there are indications that e-portfolios have emerged as an essential facet of teaching, learning and assessment practices in the twenty-first century education field.

20.7.1 Limitation of the Study

As is normally the case with the use of a focus group strategy, the findings of this study cannot be generalized; however, it should provide a baseline to future researcher and teacher education providers.

20.7.2 Implications and Way Forward

The study encouraged participants to reflect on their teaching materials and pedagogical strategies in addition to engage in knowledge sharing, and collaborative activities. This method was a good way of igniting and sustaining some essential professional development practices required for the continuous learning of teachers in the profession. School leaders could encourage, support and reward e-portfolio implementation as it provides lifelong learning opportunities (Tosun and Baris 2011)

A well-planned e-portfolio implementation strategy can enable teachers to achieve technological proficiency and other twenty-first century professional development goals relating to information literacy, media literacy and information and communications technology (ICT) literacy. This would make them more technologically savvy and ready to handle digital native learning needs. Hence, institutional support can go a long way towards making these professional development goals achievable.

The implementation of an e-portfolio system for teaching without adequate training can lead to adverse consequences for the school. Therefore, school leaders should be at the forefront of initiative efforts for intensive awareness campaigns on academic honesty and copyright and privacy issues. Alternatively, they could draw up professional development practice guidelines governing the implementation of e-portfolios in the schools.

On the other hand, e-portfolio implementation enabled students to develop a range of skills particularly as they worked on group activities. The skills include:

planning and management, communication and leadership, technology proficiency and English language practice. Finally, e-portfolio implementation promoted engagement and enthusiasm among students. School leaders could encourage and support teaching e-portfolios as a means of augmenting active learning, creativity and student-centred pedagogical approaches.

References

Albion, P. (2008). Web 2.0 in teacher education: Two imperatives for action. *Computers in the Schools, 25*(3), 181–198. doi:10.1080/07380560802368173

Barrett, H. C. (2007). Researching electronic portfolios and learner engagement: The REFLECT Initiative. *Journal of Adolescent & Adult Literacy, 50*(6), 436–449. doi:10.1598/JAAL.50.6.2

Barrett, H. C., & Knezek, D. (2003, April). *e-Portfolios: Issues in assessment, accountability and preservice teacher preparation*. Paper Presented at the Annual Meeting of the American Educational Research Association, Chicago, IL.

Castells, M. (2004). The impact of the Internet on society: A global perspective, *MIT Technology Review*. Retrieved 14 September 2016 from https://www.technologyreview.com/s/530566/the-impact-of-the-internet-on-society-a-global-perspective/

Clark, W., & Neumann, T. (2009). *ePortfolios: Models and implementation. WLE Centre Occasional paper in work-based learning, 5*. Retrieved 14 September from http://www.wlecentre.ac.uk/cms/files/occasionalpapers/op5_ eportfolios_models_and_implementation.pdf

Godwin-Jones, R. (2008). Emerging technologies. Web-writing 2.0: Enabling, documenting, and assessing writing online. *Language Learning & Technology, 12*(2), 7–13. Retrieved on 14 September 2016 from http://llt.msu.edu/vol12num2/emerging.pdf

Goupil, G., Petit, E.-L., & Pallascio, M.-C. (1998). Le portfolio: Un pas vers une évaluation plus "authentique" orientée vers l'acquisition de compétences. *Revue québécoise de psychologie, 19*(2), 167–181.

Gresso, H., & Lomicka, L. (1999). Le portfolio: Une méthode active, constructive, réflective. *Tracer, 15,* 23–30.

Hughes, J., & Purnell, E. (2008). Blogging for beginners? Using blogs and eportfolios in teacher education. In *Proceedings of the 6th International Conference on Networked Learning* (pp. 144–153). Retrieved on 14 September 2016 from http://www.networkedlearningconference.org.uk/past/nlc2008/abstracts/Hughes.htm

Karsenti, T., & Collin, S. (2010). The Eportfolio: How can it be used in French as a second language teaching and learning? *International Journal of Technologies in Higher Education, 7*(1), 68–75. Retrieved on 14 September 2016 from http://www.ritpu.org/spip.php?article177

Kitchenham, A. (2008). E-Portfolios in teacher education: The UNBC experience. *Collected Essays on Learning and Teaching, 1,* 138–144. Retrieved on 14 September 2016 from http://ojs.uwindsor.ca/ojs/leddy/index.php/CELT/article/view/3194

Krueger, R. A. (1988). *Focus groups: A practical guide for applied research*. Newbury Park, CA: Sage Publications.

Lin, Q. (2008). Preservice teachers' learning experiences of constructing e-portfolios online. *The Internet and Higher Education, 11*(3–4), 194–200. doi:10.1016/j.iheduc.2008.07.002

Lorenzo, G. & Ittelson, J. (2005). *An overview of e-Portfolios. EDUCAUSE learning initiative: Advancing learning through IT innovation*. Retrieved on 14 September 2016 from https://net.educause.edu/ir/library/pdf/ELI3001.pdf

Mann, A. (2014). Science teachers' experiences in integrating information and communication technology (ICT) into their teaching practices. *Master of Teaching*, Department of Curriculum, Teaching and Learning. Ontario Institute for Studies in Education of the University of Toronto.

Retrieved on 14 September 2016from https://tspace.library.utoronto.ca/bitstream/1807/67042/1/Mann_Amandeep_S_201406_MT_MTRP.pdf

Meyer, E., Abrami, P. C., Wade, C. A., Aslan, O., & Deault, L. (2010). Improving literacy and metacognition with electronic portfolios: Teaching and learning with ePEARL. *Computers & Education, 55*(1), 84–91. doi:10.1016/j.compedu.2009.12.005

Ostorga, A. N. (2006). Developing teachers who are reflective practitioners: A complex process. *Issues in Teacher Education, 15*(2), 5–20. Retrieved on 14 September 2016 from http://eric.ed.gov/?id=EJ796265

Stewart, D. W., & Shamdasani, P. N. (2015). *Focus groups—Theory and practice. Applied Social science research series* (3rd ed.). Thousand Oaks, CA: Sage Publications Inc.

Strawhecker, J., Messersmith, K., & Balcom, A. (2007–2008). The role of electronic portfolios in the hiring of K-12 teachers. *Journal of Computing in Teacher Education, 24*(2), 65-71. Retrieved on 14 September 2016 from http://eric.ed.gov/?id=EJ834060

Strudler, N., & Wetzel, K. (2011). Electronic portfolios in teacher education: Forging a middle ground. *Journal of Research on Technology in Education, 44*(2), 161–173. Retrieved on 14 September 2016 from http://tl.unlv.edu/~strudler/StrudlerWetzel11.pdf

Tosun, N., & Baris, M. F. (2011). Using information and communication technologies in school improvement. *Turkish Online Journal of Educational Technology., 10*(1), 223–231.

Weller, A. (2013). The use of Web 2.0 technology for pre-service teacher learning in science education. *Research in Teacher Education, 3*(2), 40–46. Retrieved on 14 September 2016 from http://www.uel.ac.uk/wwwmedia/microsites/riste/Article-6.pdf

Wells, D. (2014). Embedding information and communication technology across the curriculum—Where are we at? *Research in Teacher Education, 4*(2), 11–16. Retrieved on 14 September 2016 from http://www.uel.ac.uk/wwwmedia/microsites/riste/Article-2-David-Wells.pdf

Whitworth, J., Deeing, T., Hardy, S., & Jones, S. (2011). Perceptions regarding the efficacy and use of professional portfolios in the employment of teachers. *International Journal of ePortfolio, 1*(1), 95–106. Retrieved on 14 September 2016 from http://www.theijep.com/pdf/IJEP36.pdf

Zheng, W., Wang, F., Liu, Z., & Zhao, C. (2009). Construction and application of instructional E-Portfolio system with Web 2.0 and Google services. In *Proceedings of the 1st International Conference on Information Science and Engineering* (pp. 3265–3268). doi:10.1109/ICISE.2009.423

CPSIA information can be obtained
at www.ICGtesting.com
Printed in the USA
LVOW07*1622090517
533888LV00009B/167/P